APOLOGIES TO THUCYDIDES

* * *

*   *   *

Apologies to Thucydides

Understanding History as Culture and Vice Versa

*   *   *

MARSHALL SAHLINS

THE UNIVERSITY OF CHICAGO PRESS • *Chicago & London*

*   *   *

MARSHALL SAHLINS is the Charles F. Grey Distinguished Service Professor Emeritus of Anthropology at the University of Chicago. The author of numerous books, Sahlins is a fellow of the American Academy of Arts and Sciences and a member of the National Academy of Sciences.

The University of Chicago Press, Chicago 60637
The University of Chicago Press, Ltd., London

Printed in the United States of America
13 12 11 10 09 08 07 06 05 04   5 4 3 2 1

ISBN (cloth): 0-226-73400-5

Library of Congress Cataloging-in-Publication Data

Sahlins, Marshall David, 1930–
Apologies to Thucydides : understanding history as culture and vice versa / Marshall Sahlins.
p.   cm.
Includes bibliographical references and index.
ISBN 0-226-73400-5 (alk. paper)
1. Thucydides. History of the Peloponnesian War. 2. Greece—History—Peloponnesian War, 431–404 B.C.—Historiography. 3. Fiji—History—19th century. 4. Historiography. I. Title.
DF229.T6S24 2004
996.11—dc22

2004008115

∞ The paper used in this publication meets the minimum requirements of the American National Standard for Information Sciences—Permanence of Paper for Printed Library Materials, ANSI Z39.48-1992.

CONTENTS

* * *

ILLUSTRATIONS

* * *

FIGURES

PLATES

ACKNOWLEDGMENTS

* * *

It would not be possible to acknowledge all the students, colleagues, archivists, and audiences at lectures and seminars who have contributed to this book—on certain of its subjects, notably the great Polynesian War, I have been teaching and doing research for more than 25 years. But I must single out the classicists who read the long first chapter and helped with Greek concepts, Greek spellings, and, without exactly telling me to chuck it, warned me about the errors I was making: Paul Cartledge, James Redfield, Nicholas Rudall, and Richard Saller. Of course, they are not responsible for the historical or theoretical shortcomings still remaining in that part of the work. For research assistance in Fiji and in the archives, not to neglect his heroic work in saving the data on computer files, I am especially indebted to Mark Francillon. My gratitude also to Elizabeth Branch Dyson, David Brent, and Claudia Rex for various good offices at the University of Chicago Press. Finally, it is a pleasure as profound as it is a duty to acknowledge the invaluable assistance of Fergus Clunie on matters of Fijian ethnography and history. Fergus gave unstintingly of his own time and research results (much of it as yet unpublished) to make this book much better than it would have been otherwise.

AUTHOR'S NOTE

* * *

The following names and terms are printed elsewhere in this volume on a detachable bookmark for readers' convenience. If the bookmark is missing, you may want to mark this page.

SOME FIJIAN TERMS AND TITLES

i taukei: native, original occupant, owner
matanitū: kingdom, government
mataqali: clan, kind
Papalagi: Whiteman, Whitemen
Roko Tui Bau: sacred king of Bau
Roko Tui Dreketi: sacred king of Rewa
turaga: chief
vanua: land, country
vasu: sacred uterine nephew
Vunivalu: war king in Bau, Rewa, and other lands

PRINCIPAL FIJIAN PERSONS

Adi Qereitoga: favorite wife of Ratu Tānoa, mother of Ratu Raivalita
Adi Talātoka: principal wife of Ratu Tānoa
Komainaua: high Bauan chief, sometimes henchman of Ratu Cakobau
Ratu Banuve: Vunivalu of Bau in late eighteenth century, father of Ratu Tānoa
Ratu Cakobau (Ratu Seru): Vunivalu of Bau, 1853–83, son of Ratu Tānoa
Ratu Gavidi: a chief of the fisher-warriors (Lasakau people) of Bau
Ratu Mara: a leader of the Bau Rebellion, 1832–37
Ratu Namosimalua: ruling chief of Viwa Island
Ratu Naulivou: Vunivalu of Bau, 1804–29, older brother of Ratu Tānoa
Ratu Qaraniqio: Rewan king (Roko Tui Dreketi), 1843–55, younger brother of Ro Kania
Ratu Tānoa: Vunivalu of Bau, 1829–43, father of Ratu Cakobau and Ratu Raivalita
Ratu Varani: a high chief of Viwa, henchman of Ratu Cakobau
Ro Cokānauto: paternal half-brother of Ro Kania and Ratu Qaraniqio
Ro Kania (Banuve): Rewan king (Roko Tui Dreketi), 1831–43
Selemi: boon companion of Ratu Raivalita
Seru Tānoa: a leader of the Bau rebellion, 1832–37
Tui Kilakila: ruling chief (Vunivalu) of Cakaudrove, c. 1834–54

PRINCIPAL FIJIAN KINGDOMS

Bau: southeast Viti Levu, Koro Sea islands
Cakaudrove: Taveuni Island and adjacent Vanua Levu
Lau: eastern islands
Macuata: northern Vanua Levu
Nadrogā: southwestern Viti Levu coast
Rewa: Rewa Delta, and Beqa and Kadavu Islands

See figure 3.3 (below on p. 218) for a diagram showing the relations of the rulers of Bau and Rewa.

INTRODUCTION

* * *

This book is about the value of anthropological concepts of culture for the study of history—and vice versa, as along the way it shows certain values of history for the study of culture. Each of its three long chapters consists of ethnographic discussions of one or another problem of understanding history posed by Thucydides' great text on the Peloponnesian War. The book thus does homage to Thucydides as the ancestor of a historiography that is still with us. The "apologies" of the title come from the critique offered by modern anthropology to the venerable teachings of Thucydides—for which we are forever in debt.

The book effectively originated in a conversation I had some years ago, it was perhaps 1987, with a colleague and friend, James Redfield of the classics department at the University of Chicago. He was remarkably interested when I said I was working on a war in the Fiji Islands in the mid-nineteenth century that much resembled the Peloponnesian War. From 1843 to 1855 the kingdoms of Bau and Rewa, the first a great sea power and the second a great land power, each the leader of some lesser Fijian lands, engaged in a conflict of unprecedented severity that eventually put the domination of the entire archipelago at stake. The similarities to the famous struggle between Athens and Sparta were enough that Mr. Redfield and I agreed to explore them in a joint course on "The Peloponnesian and Polynesian Wars." The comparison proved revelatory for both Greece and Fiji. I was even inspired to write a long paper on the Spartan dual kingship, marking its differences from the complementary diarchies of Fiji and many other such divided sovereignties. Instead of a sacred king and a war king, each with his own functions and spaces of rule, the Spartan kings were twinned and inseparable, duplicates in all respects except that one was senior to the other. To compress a complex argument—that passed by way of Castor and Polydeuces as well as other royal twins of Greek mythology, one of whom was usually sired by a god—I concluded that Spartan kings represented something like an empirical version of the king's two bodies. One was relatively divine, the other relatively human, but otherwise they mirrored each other: here was lasting confirmation of the divinity of monarchy. When I showed this paper to Mr. Redfield, he allowed that with some revisions I ought to publish it—under a pseudonym.

It might have been the better part of wisdom to do the same with this book. It is likewise marked by reckless trespass on the disciplinary territory of classical studies. To judge from Max Weber's remarks (as conveyed by Paul Veyne) on the legitimacy of comparing the Athenians to (so-called) barbarians such as the Fijians, the exercise may be as offensive to the sensibilities of classical scholars as it is patently naïve: "The idea of a sort of politico-social equality in history which would want—at last! at last!—to give Bantu and Indian peoples, so outrageously despised up to now, a place at least as important as the Athenians, is quite simply naïve" (Veyne 1984: 52).[1]

But I do not lobby for cultural relativism here so much as for cultural relevance. If the past is a foreign country, then it is another culture. *Autre temps, autre moeurs.* And if it is another culture, then discovering it takes some anthropology—which is always to say, some cultural comparison. The more so if the issue is the Athenians as Thucydides described them. In the text that follows, I cite Simon Hornblower's pertinent question, "Did Thucydides ever envision a time when civilized human beings would not speak what we call classical Greek?" The problem is not simply Thucydides' taken-for-granted attitude toward the culture whose history he

1. Worse yet, I am comparing the Athenians to famously cannibal Fijians without even knowing ancient Greek. Lacking the language, one has little hope of being taken seriously by classicists. But if they don't want anthropologists and others of such ilk to comment on the Greek texts, why do they bother doing so many translations?

was writing; it is rather his presumption that the culture didn't matter. Culture was not of interest to him by comparison to an underlying human nature which customs and laws cannot resist, and which, in any case, ensures that under similar conditions people will always act pretty much the same way. They will be driven by the same desires of power and gain, the same hopes thereof, and the same fears of losing them. As the Athenians said to the hapless people of Melos they were about to destroy, "Of the gods we believe, and of men we know, that by a necessary law of nature, they rule wherever they can" (Thuc. 5.105.2). One may conclude that Thucydides is still very much with us, not only because he raised the important questions about society and history, but because he begged them in the same fashion as we do: by resorting to the universal practical rationality of human beings, born of their innate self-interest.

It is not coincidental that the interest in Thucydides was revived in Western Europe during the seventeenth century, thus with the development of modern capitalism, and by such writers as Thomas Hobbes. (Plutarch, Xenophon, and Livy seem to have been more popular in Renaissance Italy, along with Plato and Aristotle, but Thucydides was celebrated by Hobbes, Hume, and many since.) Even apart from the particular passages of Thucydides echoed in Hobbes's conception of the state of nature, how could we fail to recognize in ourselves that agonistic cum creative spirit of the Greeks at work, as Vernant says (1968: 10), not only in the struggles between cities but "in all human relations and even in nature herself." And today, at the beginning of a new millennium, Thucydides seems more relevant than ever. In an era marked by the global triumph of neoliberal ideology, not to mention the unashamed talk of American imperialism, it is comforting to know our acquisitiveness is an inevitable human disposition. Nothing to be ashamed of. Although it was the original sin, self-pleasing in its several modern scientific versions—from sociobiology and evolutionary psychology to rational choice economics and international relations realism—turns out to be the fortunate fault indeed. Hence Thucydides' current popularity. "While Thucydides' persistent focus on self-interest may be offensive to some, his notion that self-interest gives birth to effort, effort to options, makes his 2,400-year-old history of the Peloponnesian War a corrective to the extreme fatalism basic to Marxism and medieval Christianity" (Kaplan 2002: 45–46).

It would have been interesting to directly confront the Spartans—as contrasted to the Athenians—with the same "corrective." To believe Thucydides' descriptions of the Spartans' habitual character, either they were deficient in human avarice and the will to power, or else we would have to suppose that what is of interest and value to a people is culturally rather than naturally constructed—and whatever is (supposedly) inherent in human nature may be variously and meaningfully sublimated. Given the differences between the austere and conservative Spartans and the enterprising Athenians, the interest of Thucydides' *History* may be its demonstration of the cultural relativity of practical reason rather than its universal validity. It could well be that the notion of a competitive, self-interested human nature as the mainspring of history is itself a particular cultural self-consciousness, a particularly Greek and specifically Athenian ideology, to which Thucydides gave eloquent voice. In that case, however, in advocating some anthropology of Thucydides' *History,* I am not saying we can just take the celebrated "native's point of view"—at least not that celebrated native's.

Like ethnography itself, an anthropology of history requires that one get outside the culture at issue, the better to know it. There is a certain paradox in the notion that Herodotus, who never lost his identity while describing the customs and myths of the Persians or the Egyptians, should be reckoned more of an anthropologist than Thucydides, whose *History of the Peloponnesian War* was written from the vantage of a native participant (a cashiered Athenian general). The implication is that it takes another culture to know another culture. Of course, there is no single native viewpoint in any case, only so many different "subject positions," each with their interested take on a phenomenon that is itself intersubjective and greater than any one of them. Hence one reason for an external intelligence. Besides, to recall Ruth Benedict's remark that the last thing an intelligent fish would be likely to name is the water in which it swims, how much can the participants know of the culture by which they know? I am taking the rather heretical position that we have to recall the prematurely censured "ethnographic authority" from the epistemological Siberia to which she was banished (cf. Clifford 1983). Surely it is important to grasp the native's (or natives') viewpoint(s). But to do so requires what Mikhail Bakhtin commended as "the creative understanding" of the anthropologically savvy outsider. It requires what Bakhtin called "exotopy," an external vantage on the culture.

As collated and commented by Tzvetan Todorov (1984: 107–12), Bakhtin's notion of exotopy referred initially to the independent relation of the reader of the literary text to its author. Maintaining his or her interpretive integrity, the reader creatively enhances the authorial meanings and intentions. The experience of the text is enriched by the experience of the reader. At a certain moment, however, Bakhtin shifts the register of the dialogue.

He moves beyond the relation of subject to subject, to the level of intercultural understanding. At issue now is the externality of the ethnographer, and what thus is brought to bear on the culture under observation is the experience of other cultures—notably including the observer's own. A given form of life becomes comprehensible by its calibration in the array of other cultural schemes. Bakhtin, as Todorov remarks, offers a better grounding for the integrity of anthropology than its practitioners have come up with. Here is Bakhtin's golden passage, reproduced in full, beginning with his critique of an ethnography from the natives' viewpoint:

> There is an enduring image, that is partial, and therefore false, according to which to better understand a foreign culture one should live in it, and, forgetting one's own, look at the world through the eyes of this culture. As I have said, such an image is partial. To be sure, to enter in some measure into an alien culture and look at the world through its eyes, is a necessary moment in the process of its understanding; but if understanding were exhausted at this moment, it would have been no more than a single duplication, and would have brought nothing new or enriching. *Creative understanding* does not renounce its self, its place in time, its culture; it does not forget anything. The chief matter of understanding is the *exotopy* of the one who does the understanding—in time, space, and culture—in relation to that which he wants to understand creatively. Even his own external aspect is not really accessible to man, and he cannot interpret it as a whole; mirrors and photographs prove of no help; a man's real external aspect can be seen and understood only by other persons, thanks to their spatial exotopy, and thanks to the fact that they are *other.*
>
> In the realm of culture, exotopy is the most powerful lever of understanding. It is only to the eyes of an *other* culture that the alien culture reveals itself more completely and more deeply (but never exhaustively, because there will come other cultures, that will see and understand even more). (Bakhtin in Todorov 1984: 109–10)

It takes another culture to know another culture. I offer a small ethnographic (or ethnohistorical) demonstration that also has the advantage of showing that the dialogue is reciprocal, as it concerns the revelatory comments of a high chief of the Tongan Islands in the early nineteenth century on this stuff Europeans call "money." The example has a certain further interest in the present context, since a good part of this book is analogously concerned with the commentary offered by Fijian culture on the practices of the European ancestors, including the pecuniary penchants of the ancient Athenians. (Tonga was a few days' sail by canoe from Fiji.) In his case, Finau, the Tongan chief, responds to a description of money offered by William Mariner, a young Englishman who had been many months in the Islands, seconded by another Tongan who knew something of the habits of *Papalagi* ('Whitemen') by hearsay. The conversation must have been entirely in the Tongan language.[2] But what he had thus heard did not satisfy Finau. He "still thought it a foolish thing that people should place a value on money, when they either could not or would not apply it to any useful (physical) purpose" (Martin 1827, 1:213). The account continues as reported speech:

> "If," said he, "it [money] were made of iron, and could be converted into knives, axes and chisels, there would be some sense in placing a value on it; but as it is, I see none. If a man," he added, "has more yams than he wants, let him exchange some of them away for pork or *gnatoo* [bark cloth]. Certainly money is much handier, and more convenient, but then, as it will not spoil by being kept, people will store it up, instead of sharing it out, as a chief ought to do, and thus become selfish; whereas, if provisions were the principal property of a man, and it ought to be, as being the most useful and the most necessary, he could not store it up, for it would spoil, and so he would be obliged either to exchange it away for something else useful, or share it to his neighbours, and inferior chiefs and dependents, for nothing." He concluded by saying, "I understand now very well what it is that makes the Papalangis [Europeans] so selfish—it is this money." (Martin 1827, 1:213–14)

Finau's "discovery of the economy" is a lot like the more famous one of Aristotle's: "surely it is absurd that a thing should be counted as wealth, which a man may possess in abundance, and yet nonetheless die of starvation" (*Pol.* 1257b; cf. Polanyi 1957). And in the course of the chief's acute disquisition on European economic habits, one also learns a lot about the Tongans' own. (The pronominal "one" of the last sentence is not incidental: the epistemological relations are now triadic at least, involving also the anthropologist.) Finau gives voice to the Tongan system of production for

2. The communicative success nonetheless should give one pause about the supposed impossibilities of translation, although in any case, the anthropological project is rather one of exegesis than translation, quite different in its epistemological economy and transcriptive objectives.

use and to a political economy of chiefly power based on the redistribution of wealth rather than its gainful accumulation (as productive capital). As in Aristotle's lament for a passing Athenian economy, Finau speaks of a material life embedded in a specific social order, hence of a system of production with qualitative and finite ends. "The amount of household property which suffices for a good life is not unlimited," wrote Aristotle, "nor of the nature described by Solon in the verse, 'There is no bound to wealth stands fixed for man'" (*Pol.* 1256a).

Allow me to anticipate some results of the similar comparisons ventured here—at last! at last!—between the Peloponnesian War as described by Thucydides and the Polynesian War of the nineteenth century between the Fijian kingdoms of Bau and Rewa.

One finding concerns the distinctive character of the empires of Athens and Bau, both as political formations and in their modes of domination. Beyond their similarities as maritime powers, Athens and Bau exercised an imperial hegemony without actual sovereignty. Their subject peoples were tributary economically and subservient politically, but they remained largely or wholly independent administratively. Athens and Bau interfered abroad to create subject regimes like or at least compliant with their own. But unlike conquest empires, such as the Roman or the European colonial regimes of modern times—although resembling in significant respects the current American imperium—they would control other polities without governing them. By what means, then, absent the institutions of direct rule?

Bau and Athens were hardly the only hegemonic powers to rule by intimidation, but they were unusual in their reliance on a politics of demonstration in place of administration. They were empires of signs: of positive displays of grandeur and culture, and draconian examples of violence and terror, excessive in both cases, as these shows of force were designed to bring other peoples more or less voluntarily into submission. If in the pages of Thucydides Athens appears on one hand as "the school of Hellas," on the other she is "the tyrant city." If her monuments, her theater, and her festivals were by far grander than those of any competing city, most notably the austere Sparta, so was her cruelty more than proportionate to any that resisted her—since it was meant to serve the additional purpose of terrifying "the others." "Punish them as they deserve," Cleon urges the Athenians, in response to a rebellion at Mytilene, "and teach your other allies that the penalty of rebellion is death." Confronted with a similar defiance of his authority, the great warlord of Bau, Ratu Cakobau, told a passing European visitor that if he did not kill and eat the rebellious chief, all of Fiji would laugh at him. In these empires, the demonstration of superiority became an obsession, something of an end in itself—that also brought them to their end.

Fiji shows the way to another point of historiographic interest: a critique of the overreliance on what may be called "tradition-history" at the expense of "dialectic-history." The systematic contrasts of cultural order between Bau and Rewa call attention to the process of complementary opposition—what Gregory Bateson called complementary schismogenesis—as a mode of historical production. The two kingdoms are structural antitypes, transformations of one another. Indeed, the great aristocratic genealogies of Fiji, which figure the ruling dynasty of Bau as the sister's son and usurper of the ancient royal lineage that includes the Rewa kings, rather literally make the point that their differences are akin to one another. Here is differentiation by competition, of the kind recently recognized as "cultural identity politics," with the result that the major institutions and values in each society appear as inverted forms of the other.

And were not the well-known oppositions between cosmopolitan Athens and xenophobic Sparta likewise interdependent? Many of the striking cultural differences between Athens and Sparta of the classical period were relatively recent formations, developing in the century or so of their intense rivalry. So, against the grain of finding the reasons of a people's current existence in their unique past, I argue that these competing societies are usefully considered in counterposition to one another, as a system of their differences. Recent theoretical talk has pinned the blame for treating societies in isolation, as if they were bounded and closed entities, on the rise of nationalism. But nationalist ideologies were not the first to endow societies with a unique cultural heritage and thus perceive them as historically *sui generis.* If modern anthropologists and historians are likewise inclined to self-sufficient narratives of independent cultures, they have had many models of the same in the stories peoples almost everywhere tell of their adherence to ancestral traditions of ancient memory. Tracing the resemblance of existing cultural practices to earlier ones, the logic of such tradition-history is a simple one of diachronic succession. Like Aristotle finding precedents for the Spartan constitution in Crete, history in this mode is understood by the similarities of the present to the past. In that respect, tradition-histories are often stories of time immemorial. By a famous "invention of tradition," the Spartans claimed a hoary antiquity for their unique constitution, bequeathed virtually all at once by the culture hero Lycurgus. Yet such traditions of ancient origin and self-determination aside, the evidence accumulates that many of the salient differences between the Spartans and the Athenians at the time of the Peloponnesian War had emerged during the past century, or even the preceding fifty years, and in relation to one another. Each people thus proved they were equal to and better than, the same as and different from, the other. Attention should be paid to such relatively synchronic processes of complementary opposition. Dialectic-history: the past is more than just one other country.

The middle section of this book responds to another problem posed by Thucydides' text, but the ethnography used to address it is even more adventuresome than comparisons of ancient Greeks and classical Fijians. Here I muster a famous incident from American baseball history, the structure of scientific revolutions (à la Thomas Kuhn), Napoleon Bonaparte, and the shipwrecked Cuban boy Elián Gonzalez, among other unlikely examples, in an attempt to respond to a critical question about the nature of historical agency. Is it individual or collective? Why is it that Thucydides relates the Peloponnesian War sometimes in terms of difference-making persons, such as Pericles or Alcibiades, and sometimes as the action of collective entities, such as the Spartans or the Athenians? If Themistocles' creation of a formidable navy set Athens on the way to imperial expansion, still (and consequently) it was "the growing power of the Athenians and the fear this inspired in the Spartans" that was the "truest cause" of the war between them. Of course, Thucydides is hardly the only historian to thus switch registers without apparent motivation between history-making individuals—"commander narratives," as W. R. Connor calls them—and accounts in which whole peoples or states appear as the acting historical subjects. For that matter, it is a common, average folkloric inclination, a cultural habitus, to speak sometimes of George Bush or Bill Clinton creating this or that problem, sometimes of "the economy" going into the tank or "America" feeling insecure in the face of a terrorist threat. Is there wisdom in this alternation, or just confusion?

Wisdom, I believe, following an astute observation by J. H. Hexter on the rhetoric of American baseball history. It all depends on the kind of historical change at issue, whether it is a developmental trend or a revolutionary event of the kind that changes the order of things. Notice that when Thomas Kuhn talked about scientific paradigm shifts, he gave them proper names like "the Newtonian revolution" or "the Einsteinian revolution." But when he talked about the normal course of scientific advance, within the paradigm, the acting subject was "the profession," the physicists in general, or even "science" itself. Questions about "the individual and the society," apparently left for dead since the nineteenth century, thus come back on the historiographic agenda. I try to deal with them: first in the abstract, with a high-flying theoretical discussion of "subjectivity" and "cultural determinism," and then with an anthropological attempt to integrate the main oppositions at stake by specifying the structural conditions involved in the empowerment of certain individuals as significant historical agents. Some, like Napoleon or the sacred kings of the Fiji Islands, are systematically authorized to make history by their command position in a structural order designed to realize their will; others, like Elián Gonzalez and his relatives, have greatness thrust upon them by their position in a certain situation, a structure of the conjuncture that makes what they do fateful for the larger society. I thus write of systemic and conjunctural agency or the cultural production of likely and unlikely celebrities.

Jean-Paul Sartre is an important theoretical presence on and off stage through the last half of the book, notably in the form of his notion that societies have to live out historically the idiosyncrasies of the individuals in whom they personify themselves. Building on Sartrean insight, the long last chapter, "The Culture of an Assassination," goes on to address the often debated issues of order and event and structure and contingency. It also returns to Fiji and to something like "Shakespeare in the bush": a dramatic tale of political intrigue and royal fratricide in the ruling house of the kingdom of Bau that in the telling would be more worthy of the talents of the Bard than my own. The long story of contention for the rule of Bau among the sons and heirs of the aging war king Ratu Tānoa culminated in 1845 with the death of one of the fraternal enemies, Ratu Raivalita, by the order of the other, Ratu Cakobau. The latter name, one to conjure with still in the Fiji Islands, helps make the point that this event was a defining moment in Fijian history. Ratu Raivalita's death cleared the way for Ratu Cakobau's ascendancy to the kingship of Bau, and under his aegis Bau achieved a supremacy throughout Fiji that continued through the British colonial period and well into the twentieth century. But it does not require much counterhistorical speculation to argue that matters would have turned out differently, much differently, had Ratu Raivalita's own plot to kill Ratu Cakobau not been thus unmasked and undone, making him the victim instead. For among other consequences was the fate of the great Polynesian War then in progress between Bau and Rewa.

If Ratu Raivalita's conspiracy, which included the Rewa king, had succeeded in eliminating Ratu Cakobau, the war would have ended then and there, and without serious consequences for either party. The most probable outcome would have been a return to the *status quo ante.* As it actually turned out, however, Ratu Raivalita's death left Rewa vulnerable to a devastating attack that included the king among the fallen, and set the conditions for ten more years of bloody battle. To understand how these different outcomes were at stake in the enmity of the brothers will require investigation of the Fijian privileges of the *vasu,* the sacred uterine nephew. Suffice it to say here that Ratu Raivalita, whose mother was sister to the king of Rewa, was thus, as a sacred nephew, the party of Rewa within Bau; whereas Ratu Cakobau was a native *vasu* (sister's son) to Bau, as his mother came of ancient Bauan royalty, making him a chief of the highest local status and of undivided loyalties. By virtue of these kinship relations, the great collective struggle between Bau and Rewa devolved upon the interpersonal rivalry of the brothers, multiplying the animus of the latter conflict by the struggle for domination of the Fiji Islands, which is what was at issue in the former. The larger social forces would now work themselves out in the personal ambitions and contentions of the young Bauan chiefs. But then, the fate of states being thus personified, structure submits itself to contingency.

For nothing in the larger conjuncture, the organization and situation of Bau and Rewa, specified that Ratu Cakobau would survive Ratu Raivalita rather than the reverse. The "system" may have intensified their contention to the point of murderous hatred, but it could not script who would kill whom. Certainly not in this period, when rivals could be easily potted off by pistol or musket shot. Contemporary accounts of Ratu Raivalita's death indicate that either of the chiefs could well have been killed were it not for the misfiring of the guns, or else of the wills, of certain bystanders. Structure and contingency are thus mutually determining without being reducible the one to the other. The relations between the two kingdoms constituted the conditions of the events that in turn fatefully affected their respective historic fortunes. It is only because either outcome would have been structurally coherent—the end of the war had Ratu Raivalita succeeded, or its brutal continuation by Ratu Cakobau—that history, in retrospect, seems totally ordered by the cultural scheme. But cultural coherence and cultural continuity do not mean that historical outcomes are culturally prescribed. The dialogue of the collective and the individual, structure and event, category and practice indicates that the continuity of the cultural order is an altered state brought about by contingencies of human action. The claim is not that culture determines history, only that it organizes it.

CHAPTER I

* * *

THE POLYNESIAN WAR

WITH APOLOGIES TO THUCYDIDES

Viti, or Fiji, is an archipelago in the South Pacific Ocean, midway between the Tongan islands and the French colony of New Caledonia, having, according to Dr. Petermann's recent calculations, a superficial area equal to that of Wales, or eight times that of the Ionian Islands.
BERTHOLD SEEMAN, 1862 (1973: 274)

Our stay had been instructive; for however well versed a person may regard himself in the knowledge of mankind, a visit to the Feejee Islands will bring new ideas.
CHARLES PICKERING (1849: 169)

Thucydides says he started to write about the war between the Peloponnesians and the Athenians from the time it began, convinced "that it would be a great war, and more worthy of relation than any that preceded it. . . . Indeed this was the greatest upheaval yet known in history, not only of the Hellenes, but of a large part of the barbarian world—I might almost say, the whole of mankind" (1.1.1–2).[1] Being similarly situated at the center of the world, Fijians of the nineteenth century must have thought their own war between the kingdoms of Bau and Rewa was as extensive in compass and portentous in significance (figs. 1.1, 1.2).[2] Bau, a great sea power like

1. As a rule, I follow the Crawley (1876) translation of Thucydides (Crawley 1934; cf. Strassler 1996). Sometimes I take a consensus among major translations, consulting also the Warner (1972), S. Lattimore (1998), Jowett (1998), Bloomfield (1829), and Hobbes (1989 [1629]) versions. Occasionally I use the original translations of specific passages by classical scholars commenting on them—philology being a foreign country, somewhere in the Balkans.

2. Standard Fijian spelling is used here. The major peculiarities relative to English are the following: b = mb (as in "ember"); d = nd (as in "endow"); g = ng (as in "singer"); q = ng (as in "England"); c = th (as in "the").

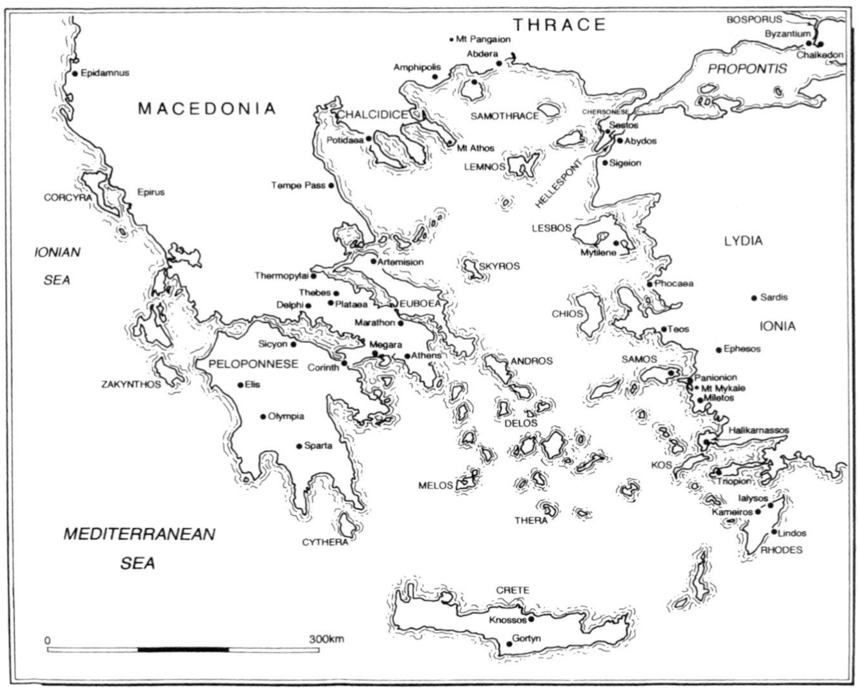

1.1 Ancient Greece

Athens, and Rewa, a great land power like Sparta, each at the head of a league of allied lands (*vanua*), battled from 1843 to 1855 in a war that raised the possibility of unifying all of Fiji under the hegemony of the victor—and in the end foreclosed it.[3] As foreign missionaries, merchants, and mercenaries increasingly became involved, Fijians learned for themselves the truth in the sage Aetolian Greek's admonition to his countrymen: that if

3. I do not wish to make a terminological/typological issue over the use of *king* and *kingdom* with reference to nineteenth-century Fijian polities. I follow the contemporary English and French sources in using them here—and also in alternating between *king* and *chief* on occasion. The terms *land* and *country* I use to translate the Fijian *vanua:* a political entity, usually of several towns, united under its own paramount, and claiming independent origin and distinctive identity. Such lands may be autonomous or they may be subject traditionally in some capacity and degree to a 'chiefly land' (*vanua turaga*) such as Bau, in which case they are included in the Bau kingdom (*matanitū*). In these "galactic polities," to adopt Tambiah's term, there are all shades of integration of particular lands in greater kingdoms, and (like Greece) any such land is always in some sense or aspiration independent: a 'land of itself' (*vanua vakai koya*).

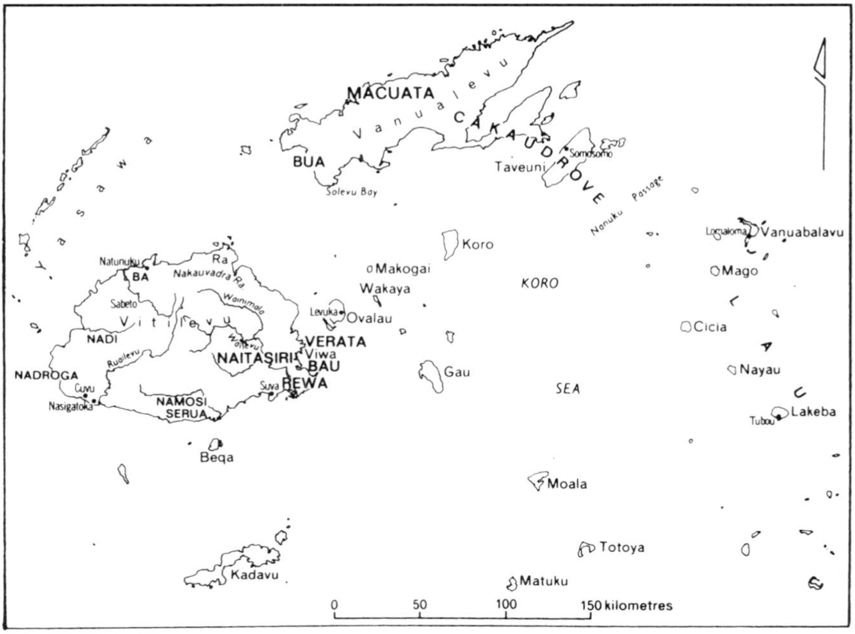

1.2 The Fiji Islands, principal kingdoms

they didn't stop fighting with each other, they would soon be unable to call even their quarrels their own (Gomme 1937: 123). The Bau-Rewa war was finally terminated by the intervention of a South Seas "Great King," King George Tupou of Tonga, eastward of Fiji, whose large fleet of ocean-going canoes carrying two thousand fighting men played a role something like that of the Persians in giving the victory to Bau. It was the greatest war ever fought in the Pacific Ocean before World War II. With apologies to Thucydides, then, and despite the fact that in Fiji the sea power won, I am calling it the "Polynesian War."[4]

"Comparing great things with small ones," you could justly say: a phrase Thucydides himself sometimes used, and put to good effect as a historiographic device. Here I not only adopt the conceit, I redouble the hubris by claiming that the Polynesian War also has something to teach us about the writing of history. By comparison to Thucydides' great text, I try to show

4. In other places I have indicated the role of Europeans in Fijian wars of the nineteenth century, as well as the integration of muskets, whale-tooth valuables, and other trade goods in Fijian politics (M. Sahlins 1991, 1994, both reprinted in M. Sahlins 2000).

what difference anthropology might make, and more particularly what difference a concept of culture could make, to our inherited historiography. For Thucydides had been too much influenced by the sophists' opposition of custom (*nomos*) and nature (*physis*). The Greek historian believed that if he was to achieve his ambition of writing a history that would be instructive to all peoples at all times, he would have to discount their conventional differences in culture in favor of their essential similarities in nature—human nature.

The practical rationality that Thucydides found only natural to humanity was destined to make him the ancestor of international relations realists as well as historians. A staple in military academies and Harvard's Kennedy School of Government, his *History*, in the late twentieth century, was "probably more influential . . . than ever before" (Kagan 1988: 43). Indeed, as Robert Kaplan recently put it (2002: 45): "The *Peloponnesian War* may be the seminal work of international relations theory of all time. It is the first work to introduce a comprehensive pragmatism into political discourse. Its lessons have been elaborated on by such writers as Hobbes, Hamilton, Clausewitz, and, in our own era, Hans Morgenthau, George F. Kennan, and Henry Kissinger." It is true that anthropologists rather honored Herodotus as the real "father of history"—which was frivolous enough on their part, since for a long time they claimed to be studying "historyless peoples." Relating all the tales, tall and short, that the "barbarians" told him, Herodotus had the kind of ethnographic sensibility that appealed to anthropologists. For the same reason, however, the less credulous historians of the "what actually happened" school could only consider him "the father of lies." Put into the comparison Thucydides' project of motivating history by underlying human desires of power and profit, and you can see why he became the parent of Western historiography—one might almost say, of Western social thought. Apparent cultural differences apart—these being so many superficial expressions of the one basic, self-regarding human nature (Latour 2002)—everybody turns out to be much the same. Received narrative strategies, moreover, have not been designed to give other impressions, since their usual (if implicit) principle of causation is likewise (Western) common sense. The classicist Richard Meier speaks about the misleading seductiveness of "political historiography"—a category in which Thucydides could easily be included—referring to the way it makes each development seem to follow inevitably from the last and give rise necessarily to the next. It is, he says, adopting the words of Robert Musil, "the most time-honoured perspective for curtailing understanding" (1998: 89). So one might conclude that if anthropology was for a long time "historyless," history has been for even longer "cultureless."

COMPARING WARS

Such is Thucydides' influence that hardly any modern war involving Europeans escapes comparison with the Peloponnesian War. Not even the Cold War, which Gen. George C. Marshall once described as the Russians playing the Spartans to our Athenians: an ominous analogy, since the Spartans won. During World War I a reading of the Melian dialogue, in which the people of Melos fecklessly put their trust in the gods and their Spartan allies to save them from destruction by the Athenians, was held at the University of Toronto with the Germans as the Athenians, the British as the Spartans, and the Belgians as the poor Melians (Crane 1998: 1–2). But easily the best of the genre was Basil Gildersleeve's "A Southerner in the Peloponnesian War" (1915), a sustained reflection on the similarities of that conflict to the American Civil War. Gildersleeve was a celebrated classical scholar who spent his summers campaigning with Robert E. Lee and his winters teaching at the University of Virginia, a pattern rather like the seasonality of ancient Greek warfare. Yet he was properly skeptical of the comparison in which he was indulging. "Historical parallel bars," he wrote, "are usually set up for exhibiting feats of mental agility. . . . The attempt to express one war in terms of another is apt to lead to a wresting of facts" (Gildersleeve 1915: 55–56). In the end, what Gildersleeve found to be similar in the two wars was common to all wars: the killing, maiming, and frightening, the hunger and the fatigue—the suffering was common.

Still, I am not even the first to set up historical parallel bars between Greece of the fifth century B.C. and Fiji of the nineteenth century A.D. Horatio Hale, who was in a better position to know both, remarked on the resemblances on the eve of the Polynesian War. An ethnologist and philologist with a classical education, Hale was in Fiji in 1840 as a member of the United States Exploring Expedition. There he discovered a politics of intrigue, subversion, and periodic battle among small independent states that bore "a striking similarity to that which prevailed among the Grecian republics. Mbau, Rewa, and Naitasiri are the Sparta, Athens and Thebes of Viti [Fiji]" (1846: 58). The analogy ignored the fact that Bau, as the aggressive sea power, was the true Athens of Fiji, while Rewa, like Sparta, was the more conservative land power, living off the agricultural labor of subjugated peoples. In likening Bau to Sparta, Hale was probably thinking of certain parallels in their warrior ethos. Still, when it came to characterizing the "constant intrigues and machinations" of Fijian *poleis,* "carried on with a degree of shrewdness and craft that frequently excited our admiration," Hale was dead on so far as Fiji was concerned, and without twisting the facts too much, he was describing practices that did resemble the politics of fifth-century Greek city-states. If ancient Greek history, as Simon Hornblower remarked, is largely summed up in an old text fragment that reads "the small states fear the secret diplomacy of the great" (1987: 184), the history of nineteenth-century Fiji is encapsulated in the (still current) proverbial expression, "conspiracy à la Bau" (*vere vakaBau*). Here is Hale's summary of the Fijian attainments in politics that he found surprisingly like those of the Greeks: "To weaken a rival state by secretly exciting its dependencies to revolt,—to stir up one class of society against another, in order to take advantage of their dissensions,—to make an advantageous treaty with a powerful foe, by sacrificing a weak ally,—to corrupt the fidelity of adherents, by bribing them with the anticipated spoil of their own master,—to gain a battle before it is fought, by tampering with the leaders of the opposing force,—all these, and many other tricks of the Machiavellian school, are perfectly familiar to the subtle chieftains of Viti" (1846: 51; also 58).

If one had to choose a single analogy to events of the Polynesian War from the many possible examples in the Peloponnesian War, it would probably be the Corcyraean uprising of 427—itself, according to Thucydides, the model of civil strife (*stasis*) throughout Greece for years to come. A sedition of the democratic "many" gotten up by the oligarchic "few," which thus threatened the allegiance of Corcyra to Athens, the event then gained historical intensity and momentum by the intervention of the Athenians on the side of the people as against the Spartans' support of the city's elite (Thuc. 3.70–85). Transforming internal strife into pan-Hellenic war, such structural relays of larger enmities into local ones help account for the violence of these conflicts. No longer parochial in scope, neither are they limited to the means and ends of civic power. Instead, by the respective links of the few and the many to Sparta and Athens, the local opposition took on the greater scope and temporality of the Spartan resistance to Athenian expansion, and a ferocity to match (Romilly 1968: 216).[5] So Marc Cogan (1981: 268–69) observes that the development of the conflict between Athens and Sparta as an ideological battle of democracy

5. For other examples of the intensification of lesser, internal oppositions by their integration in larger outside oppositions, see P. Sahlins (1989); M. Sahlins (1991: 81) and (1992).

and oligarchy, or alternatively of Atticism and liberation therefrom, when transmitted to civic disorder in Corcyra and elsewhere, added the animus of high-mindedness to local party ambitions. In the same ideological vein, and with similar effects of magnifying the stakes of internal dispute, was the Spartan pose as liberators whose armies could offer the cities of the Athenian empire "freedom" from their "enslavement" (e.g., Thuc 4.84–88). Absorbed thus into the larger Hellenic war, parochial struggles for power took on values as irreconcilable as they were abstract.[6]

Again with all respect, I speak to this cultural ordering of violence by way of critique—which given the scholars involved could well be classified in the historiographic category of "chutzpah" (*hybris*). For Thucydides, the Corcyraean atrocities were famously anti-structural. They represented the emergence of a natural human disposition of ruthless self-interest, against which all convention and morality were powerless. Historians have remarked that Thucydides' depiction of the stasis at Corcyra—and also the plague at Athens—served as a primary source of Thomas Hobbes's idea of the state of nature.[7] (Hobbes, it should be noted, was the first translator of Thucydides directly into English.) For when the sedition of the elite was foiled at Corcyra by the intervention of an Athenian fleet, the city turned upon itself in something like a war of every man against every man, coupling crimes against kinsmen with sacrilege against the gods, and sowing "death in every shape":

> During the seven days that Eurymedon [the Athenian commander] stayed with his sixty ships, the Corcyraeans were engaged in butchering those of their fellow-citizens whom they regarded as their enemies; and although the crime imputed was that of attempting to put down the democracy, some were slain also for private hatred, others by their debtors because of the monies that they owed. Death thus raged in every shape;

6. Fijian war could involve the same kinds of relays between local and larger quarrels: for some years the Bau-Rewa war was largely a proxy fight between the lesser lands of Tokatoka and Nakelo in the Rewa Delta. But it was not until the end, with the conversion of Bau's ruling war king Ratu Cakobau to Christianity in 1854 (thus adding another and transcendental level to the conflict) that it became markedly ideological as well.

7. See, for example, Brown (1987); Connor (1984: 99); Crane (1998: 258–59); Manicas (1982); Orwin (1988); Sainte-Croix (1972: 26–28). For reservations, see Grene (1989: xi). Not so often remarked is the similarity between Thucydides' depiction of early Greece (1.2–3), rendered culturally underdeveloped, nomadic, and disunited by fears of predation, and Hobbes's analogous passage on "the incommodities" of the state of nature—the famous "nasty, brutish and short" passage (1962: 100).

and, as usually happens at such times, there was no length to which violence did not go; sons were killed by their fathers, and suppliants dragged from the altar or slain upon it; while some were even walled up in the temple of Dionysus and died there. (3.81.4)

By comparison, consider the notices from the pen of the Methodist missionary, Mr. John Hunt, chronicling the destruction of Rewa by Bauan forces in December 1845. Rewa had been betrayed from within by secret negotiations with the Bau ruler and military commander Ratu Cakobau. At a prearranged signal, when the Bauans had the town surrounded, the conspirators set it ablaze:

> The town was in flames before some of the people were awake, and before any could make their escape the awful massacre commenced. The disaffected party in Rewa who had joined the traitorous messenger [the one who had conspired with the Bauans], were foremost to kill their fellow townsmen. This made the case peculiarly dreadful, as it was quite uncertain who was friend or foe. Others influenced by love of gain would murder those who were fleeing with them for their common safety, merely to possess the little property they were taking with them. (Hunt, *J:* following 19 October 1845)

> Three hundred were massacred in a very short time, and it is said one hundred of them were killed by the Rewa people themselves. Even some who had not previously joined the enemy now became the murderers of their neighbours, through the hope of gaining their property, though they themselves would perhaps be plundered of their dishonest gains and murdered by some other neighbour the next minute. . . . Of course, there is no prospect of Rewa being again the residence of a Missionary for a length of time. (Hunt *WMMS/L:* n.d. [30 March 1846])

The destruction of Rewa in 1845 was the culmination of a sustained campaign masterminded by Ratu Cakobau, the effective war king, or Vunivalu, of Bau—though his aging father Ratu Tānoa still officially held that title.[8] The tactics of this campaign represented Fijian warfare at its

8. *Ratu* is a chiefly title used in Bau and Bauan areas. *Ro* is the Rewan equivalent. Although Europeans—together with Fijian enemies of Bau—often style Ratu Cakobau without title, just "Cakobau," Bauans and many other Fijians would not be so disrespectful. (The same goes for "Rev." or "Mr." applied to the Protestant missionaries, "Father" to

height, which is also to say classic "conspiracy à la Bau." Deftly combining force, intimidation, bribery, and intrigue, Ratu Cakobau alternated invasions by allied armies with secret negotiations involving gifts of maritime wealth and noble women to chieftains of inland towns, inducing them to defect to the Bauan side. The "traitorous messenger" who conspired to deliver up the town to the besieging Bauans was the traditional envoy or "Face to Bau" (*Mata ki Bau*) in Rewa, an office corresponding closely to the Greek *proxenus* (Hocart 1913: 115). Like the *proxenus,* the Fijian envoy acted as an intermediary in dealings with a particular foreign land and as the protector of its interests in his own. That this mediation could lead the Fijian envoy to betrayal of his own people was also like the Greek *proxenus* (Thuc. 3.2.3).[9] Although not exactly class-based, as might be said of the revolt in Corcyra, the dissension in Rewa in an analogous way allowed the forces and ambitions of Bau to exploit a fundamental division between the Rewan powers-that-be and the underlying population. The envoy came from a clan (Navolau) that led the 'real people of Rewa' (*kai Rewa dina*), in categorical and sometimes practical opposition to the chiefly clans. The "real people" were clans of indigenous stock and inferior status who nonetheless claimed the dignity of original 'owners' of the land (*i taukei*), by contrast to the ruling chiefs who, as elsewhere in Fiji, were descended from powerful immigrants. Report has it that the envoy who conspired with Bauans was indeed acting on behalf of "his party and the real people of Rewa" (Lyth *TFR,* 1:205). The Rewa king was one of the three hundred victims of their successful intrigue. We do not know if three hundred is an accurate figure, but it is said that more people were killed than could be eaten by the Bauans, and they had to call in reinforcements for that purpose (Wallis 1851: 168).

Such numbers and textual references suggest the need of a brief parenthesis on historiographical issues before we enter into more systematic comparisons. First, the numerical scale of things in Fiji—the size of armies, towns, and so forth—was generally between one-tenth and one-twentieth the corresponding numbers for Greece, perhaps even less in relation to outsized Attica, whose population in the fifth century is usually

the Catholic.) Ratu Cakobau also had other names; to many, he was always "Ratu Seru," the name of his youth and young manhood.

9. In Fiji the office is hereditary and based on some ancient connection, usually of kinship, between the envoy's clan and the land in question: in this particular case, according to modern informants, the "traitorous messenger" was descended from a Bauan woman married into Rewa.

estimated at two hundred thousand to three hundred thousand people. The ruling towns of Bau and Rewa around the beginning of the war numbered about three thousand people each, while the kingdom (*matanitū*) of Bau has been estimated at fifteen thousand (Derrick 1950: 61). The latter number is a bit problematic, mostly because the degrees of subjugation of other lands to Bau varied at the peripheries of its power. The estimate of fifteen thousand probably includes islands of the Koro Sea, where Bau clans often held land rights, as well as countries (*vanua*) in and around the Rewa Delta in the traditional status of 'tribute-payers' (*qali*) or 'warrior allies' (*bati*) to Bau.[10] Armies mustered by Bau have been estimated as high as five thousand men, sometimes even more, although I believe that two thousand or three thousand is more typical of the largest forces. It is rather in naval statistics that Bau could most closely match Athens (cf. Casson 1991; Gomme 1937: 190–203). Bau's ocean-going double canoes ranged upwards of one hundred feet or more in length and carried fifty to two hundred fighting men, though many of the available vessels were smaller.[11] Contemporary notices of Bauan fleets of forty or fifty canoes sailing to an attack are not uncommon. Unlike the ship's company of Greek triremes, virtually all the men in these canoes were warriors, who manned the fleet that transported them to the field of battle; actual naval engagements were relatively rare in Fiji. The Bauan fleets were like those of the Athenians, however, in not carrying substantial food supplies, and this imposed similar difficulties in sustaining military campaigns. The logistical difficulties were probably greater for Fijians, who could sometimes provision themselves at subordinate towns while en route and could raid enemy gardens in the field, but who did not have the versatility of using local food markets as the Greeks did. In all these naval respects, Rewa was not half the match for Bau, and usually much less—like land-based Sparta relative to Athens (for most of the Peloponnesian War). As for historical sources, the primary texts on the Bau-Rewa war are surprisingly rich. They include the letters and daily journals of a number of missionaries, logs and jour-

10. There is a standard opposition between subject lands or *qali* presumably subordinated by conquest, and the relatively independent warrior-allies or border lands (*bati*), whose affiliation with a major kingdom such as Bau or Rewa is founded on contract and exchange (of women, bodies taken in war and wealth). The *qali* lands pay tribute in goods, perhaps also food and services. Labor as well as warriors may be requisitioned from the *bati* lands, but it should be solicited with valuables and rewarded with feasts.

11. The maximum estimated length of the Greek trireme, about 36 meters, corresponds pretty well to the length of the largest Fijian canoes of the nineteenth century (Taillardat 1968: 186).

nals of *bêche-de-mer* (trepang) traders and of the occasional beachcomber, journals and published works of visiting naval ships, and Fijian oral traditions as recorded in local publications or by ethnographers. Some evaluations of these sources have been offered elsewhere (M. Sahlins 1991, 1994). Suffice it to note here that during the twelve years of the Polynesian war, there were one or two missionaries stationed near or in Bau and for much of that time also in Rewa. These were all from the Methodist Missionary Society of London, except the French Marist fathers stationed at Rewa during the last few years of the war. Some of the Methodists—Revs. William Cross, John Hunt, Richard Burdsall Lyth, Thomas Jaggar, and Thomas Williams in particular—had serious ethnographic interests; many kept separate notebooks on Fijian customs. Their daily journals or diaries were much concerned with war and politics, for in the hierarchical Fijian system, where the chief's will was usually the general will, the road to heaven as well as to hell was paved with chiefly intentions. End of parenthesis.

"SUPPOSE WE WERE ISLANDERS"

There are deeper and more interesting resemblances between the Peloponnesian and Polynesian Wars, notably the similar ecology of Athenian and Bauan power. Most striking is the desire of their rulers to make islands of their respective cities, the corollary in turn of their distinctive commitment to sea power. The strategies of warfare and expansion pursued by Athens and Bau have to be understood as practices of a certain thalassic culture: "If they march against our country, we will sail against theirs," the Pericles of Thucydides says in advocating war with the Spartans. Even if the Spartans laid waste to all of Attica, he argued, it would mean less than the loss of a fraction of the Peloponnesus, since they could only make up their loss by battle, while the Athenians could always draw supplies from the islands and mainland cities they controlled. "The command of the sea is indeed a great thing. Consider for a moment. Suppose we were islanders—could you conceive of a more impregnable position? In our present circumstances we should develop a strategy that approximates that situation, by letting our land and our [rural] houses go, while guarding our city and our sea" (1.143.4–5).

To make the city an island was the logical end of the radical strategy promoted by Themistocles to meet the Persian invasion of 480 B.C. Actually, Themistocles' critical move had come in 483, when he persuaded the Athenians to use a rich strike of silver for the construction of 200 triremes, instead of giving a handout of 10 drachmas to every citizen as had been proposed.[12] Ostensibly the ships were for an ongoing war with Aegina, which itself had a powerful fleet. But given their eventual deployment instead against the Persians at Salamis, Herodotus credits this pretext of the Aeginetan war with having saved Greece, "for it compelled the Athenians to become men of the sea" (7.144). Or again Plutarch, echoing Herodotus by way of Plato, says Themistocles turned the Athenians "from steadfast hoplites into sea-tossed mariners"—a fateful turn to movement and risk (Plut., *Them.* 4).[13]

In 480 the Athenian men literally abandoned the land for the sea. The Athenian fleet became the "wall of wood" that the Delphic oracle had foretold could save the city (Hdt. 7.141). Xerxes' troops could have the satisfaction of sacking an empty Athens, "things that have no life and soul," as Plutarch has Themistocles say; "but what we still possess is the greatest city in Greece, our 200 ships of war" (Plut., *Them.* 11). After the Persians had withdrawn from Greece, and while the task still remained to clear them and pirates from the eastern seas, Themistocles persuaded the Athenians to continue adding twenty triremes a year to their fleet, a policy that committed them to a certain economic as well as a maritime destiny. As part of the same strategy, Themistocles had a wall built around Athens—deceiving the Spartans, who opposed the project, by a famous diplomatic ruse—and fortified the Piraeus as a port. In 460 the long walls between the city and the Piraeus were begun, and about 445, when a second south wall was built parallel to and about 180 yards from the north wall, Athens was connected to the sea by a protective corridor, even as she was insulated from the land by the city walls. "Insulated"—etymologically, the word means something like "made an island" (fig. 1.3).

By the time of the Peloponnesian War (431), Themistocles' project of putting Athens on a maritime basis had been fully achieved (Momigliano 1944). It only remained for Pericles to manage the withdrawal of the coun-

12. On the disparity of the number of triremes proposed by Themistocles—between 100 (Aristotle, Plutarch) and 200 (Herodotus)—see Picard (2000: 28). The Aristotelian *Constitution of Athens* indicates that Themistocles did not say what he wanted to do with the money from the silver strike, but simply used it in a novel arrangement with rich Athenians to sponsor the building of the triremes later deployed at Salamis (*Ath. Const.* 22.7).

13. So Gregory Crane: "The Athenians as a people were a qualitatively new entity. Independence from the agricultural produce of their own land was almost as novel as if they had suddenly acquired the ability to fly and separate themselves from the surface of the earth. [Seems to me Aristophanes had something to say about that.] The Athenian state was indeed something new and, if it did not terrify its neighbors in the Peloponnese, it should have" (Crane 1992a: 253).

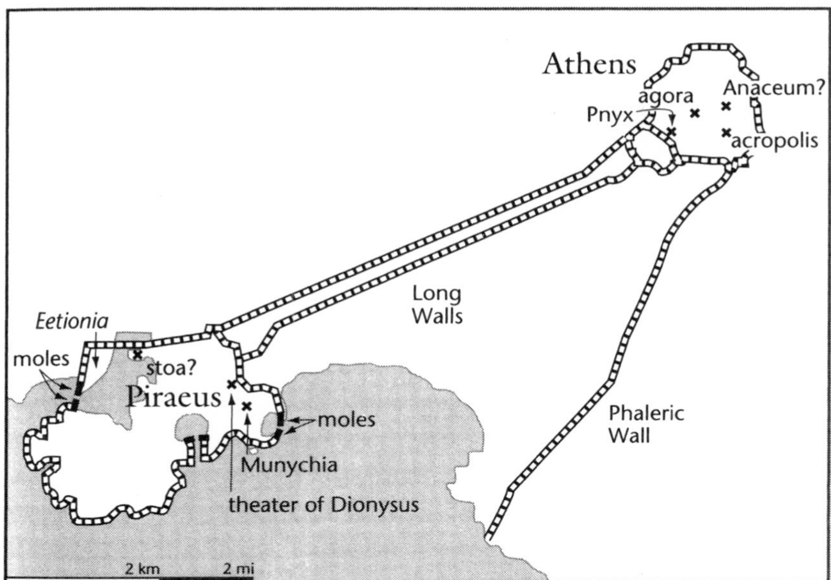

1.3 The long walls of Athens

try population within the city walls to effectively make Athens an island, totally impregnable so long as she controlled the seas—but also totally dependent on that control for her existence. What we learn from Thucydides on this score, says Jacqueline de Romilly, is that "Athens is a maritime power, that her constant aim is control over the sea, that her field of action is the islands and that the means she is using to achieve these aims is her fleet. She needs money to maintain this fleet and her empire provides her with this. Thalassocracy is avowed as an already conscious and coherent system. The idea is present from one end of the work to the other" (Romilly 1963: 66).

Mutatis mutandis, so too for Bau. Bau is a maritime power; its field of action is the islands. Or as it was put by Ratu Deve Toganivalu, a Fijian intellectual writing around the beginning of the twentieth century:

> The principal work in Bau was sailing in their sacred canoes [large overseas canoes]; they were in the habit of sailing away to the islands of Lomaiviti [central Fiji, the Koro Sea] to collect tribute; they levied their cargo, that is yams, taro, *madrai* [preserved breadfruit] and valuable goods [*i yau*]. They did not plant much food but ate from the levies made upon their tributary lands in Lomaiviti, and certain other lands

> [principally on mainland Viti Levu]. There was no property made in Bau; they obtained their wealth from Lomaiviti and other lands (Toganivalu 1911: n.p.; 1912a: 15).[14]

"Suppose we were islanders—could you conceive of a more impregnable position?" A small, crowded island of about 23 acres lying less than a mile off the southeast coast of Viti Levu, also man-made in important respects, Bau was clearly the realization of the same strategic thinking as Periclean Athens. According to the Bauan tradition, the occupation of the island by the ruling chiefs of Kubuna from their homeland on the adjacent mainland coincided with their domination over much of eastern Fiji.[15] The Koro Sea was the Bauans' Aegean. I am unsure whether archaeological good sense is as convincing as a quotation of Pericles for making the argument that a parallel project of insularization had marked the history of Bau. But since Thucydides allowed himself the liberty of giving his speakers the words that, in his opinion, the occasion demanded (1.22.1), I am emboldened to make the case for Bau from the sometimes eloquent testimony of maps and photographs, with some ethnography thrown in. From these sources it appears that the project of ruling a large polity from a small offshore island represented the convergence of two historical precedents: the one foreign, the ancient royal settlement in the nearby Tongan archipelago; the other, the traditional Fijian palisaded and moated village.

For some centuries before European contact, the eastern Fijian kingdoms had been importing Tongan cultural forms, including many of the rites and trappings of chieftainship (Clunie 1986). Indeed, the establishment of the Bau kings on the island not only replicated the strategy of certain fifteenth-century Tongan rulers, but rehearsed the same political reasons for the move. It was the assassination of two sacred rulers (*Tu'i Tonga*) that induced the first secular king (*Hau*) of Tonga to place his residence on a small island in the lagoon off Mua (in Tongatapu), constructing a causeway to connect it to the mainland. "This step was almost certainly a means to ensure his defense from enemies within Tonga" (Campbell 1992: 17). Just so, popular Bauan tradition has it that the first of the current dynasty

14. I have slightly amended the translation, using the 1912 Fijian version.

15. Modern Fijian traditions usually date the occupation of Bau by its ruling clans to 1760, based on generational reckoning back to the king supposedly responsible for the move. No credibility can be given this method, however, since Fijian genealogies are generally foreshortened to six to eight generations before the time of the speaker. There is abundant evidence of other kinds, notably in the land records of Bauan dependencies, that the occupation and expansion of Bau began much earlier than the mid-eighteenth century (cf. M. Sahlins 1994).

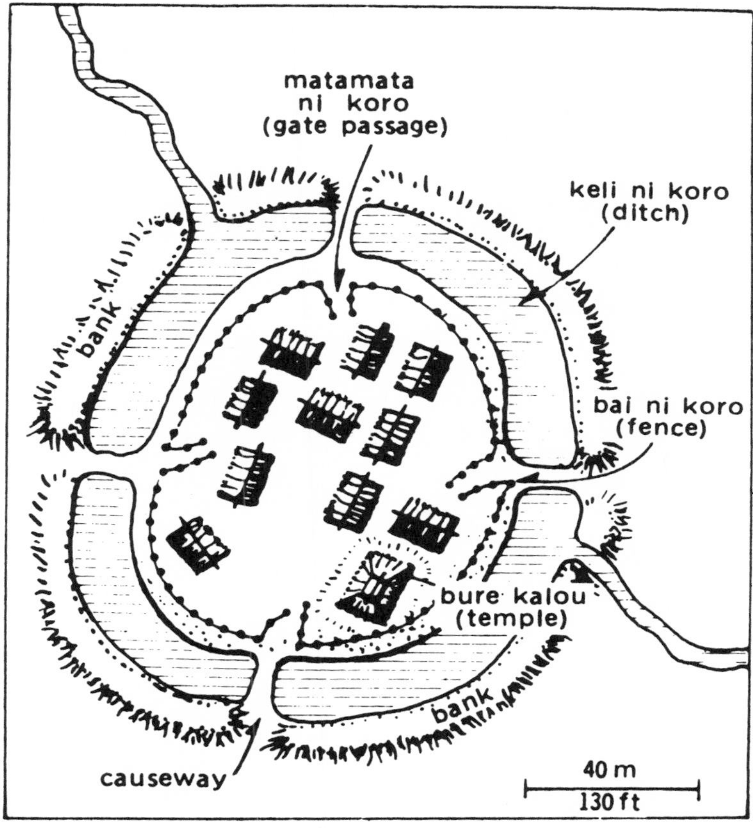

1.4 Sketch plan of a traditional Fijian moated village

of war kings, one Ratu Nailatikau—the equivalent of the second, secular king in the Tongan diarchy—initiated the move of the ruling clans to the island, an event preceded by the assassination of at least one sacred king (Roko Tui Bau).[16] If, as seems likely, this too was a defensive measure, still the Fijians also had their own conventions of fortification, to which Bau island felicitously conformed. Consider the accompanying illustrations of the traditional Fijian palisaded and moated village (figs. 1.4, 1.5, 1.6). In the

16. The major Fijian kingdoms were typically ruled by a diarchy of the war king (Vunivalu) and so-called sacred king (Roko Tui). Uniquely in Bau, the Vunivalu was the supreme king, although the Roko Tui Bau took precedence in ritual. Besides the popular tradition that Bau was settled under the aegis of the first Vunivalu, there is another, effectively removed from general circulation, that gives the credit for the move to the first Roko Tui Bau (Ratu Vuetiverata).

1.5 Moated village in the Rewa Delta (1948). (White's Aviation Library, GeoSmart Ltd.)

1.6 Siege of a moated village in Vanua Levu, 1856

1.7 Bau c. 1950

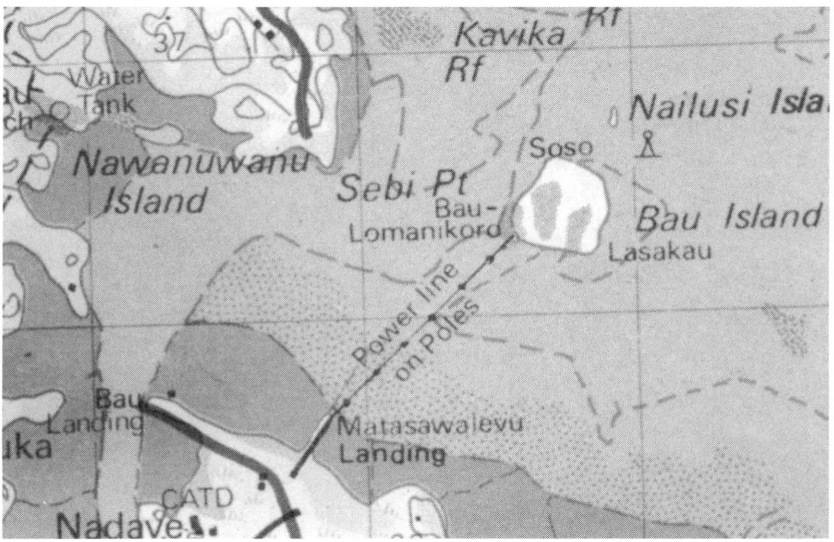

1.8 Bau (23 acres) off Viti Levu

nineteenth century and for some centuries before, this was the dominant settlement form in the river valleys and lowland regions of Fiji's main island (Parry 1977). It was called *koro waiwai,* which roughly translates as "water fort" (or moated village), but it is noteworthy that the term *waiwai,* referring to the surrounding moat, may designate either an inland water pool or a deep area in an offshore reef. Now, look at Bau (figs. 1.7 and 1.8).

1.9 Bau canoe slip, c. 1920

Set in and protected by offshore waters, yet less than a mile from the mainland, Bau is essentially a saltwater translation of the old fortified village. It has the same structural features as the classic moated settlement, except that here they are geographical rather than man-made. The main human modifications of Bau are those that made it virtually an offshore naval base: the twenty-six jetties for ocean-going canoes that surround the island and that, in their megalithic construction and protective function, have something of the palisade about them (fig. 1.9; Hornell 1926).[17]

THALASSOCRACY AND ECONOMY

Densely packed with houses and temples, Bau afforded its three thousand inhabitants no room for gardening, even were its chiefly denizens so inclined (figs. 1.10 and 1.11). There was no food production on the island,

17. The jetties and much of the shoreland were lined with large sandstone slabs as high as 11 feet, 8 inches, as wide as 4 feet, 8 inches, and as thick as 8 inches. They had been conveyed from as far as 30 miles away on the Viti Levu coast. Hornell found a precedent in the stone-faced docks of Mua, in Tonga (1926:31). Bauan tradition attributes the docks to the original inhabitants of the islands (Levuka people), thus earlier than the chiefly settlement (ibid., 31).

1.10 Bau in the 1890s

apart from fishing by certain clans of 'sea people' (*kai wai*). Neither did the Bauans themselves produce any exchangeable wealth (*i yau*) except for certain highly decorated bridal skirts. The skirts adorned what Bauans sometimes say was their greatest exchange valuable, the chiefly women whose marriages to rulers of other lands were important political moves. Apart from some local Tongan craftsmen making ivory and pearl-shell valuables—metic craftsmen, one could say—the whole material existence of the island was imported from places near and far, largely through relations of domination.

Like the Athenian empire, Bau's maritime power brought it wealth, and wealth in turn sustained its power.[18] Its daily subsistence came primarily from villages of 'household men' (*kai vale*) on the nearby mainland, cultivating lands directly or indirectly under the control of Bauan chiefly

18. I use the impersonal third-person *it* in anaphoric reference to Bau and other Fijian lands. The traditional English feminine *her* and *she,* although justifiable on many grounds for Athens, not least because of the eponymous goddess, would not sit well for Fijian countries.

1.11 Bau Island, 1856

clans.[19] The food was cooked for these Bauan gentlefolk by serving women, who also fetched the wood and water. Rev. Joseph Waterhouse, stationed at Bau in the mid-1850s, gives a glimpse of these arrangements, as viewed from the small hill on the island:

> Occupying an elevated post of observation, you note the wood and water carriers, poor women who have to propel their canoes for a distance

19. I am using English *clan* as a somewhat rough translation of the Fijian *mataqali.* Apart from technical problems with the definition of *clan,* the roughness comes from the Fijian possibilities of using the term *mataqali* relatively, to refer to groups of various degrees of segmentation, since it more broadly means "kind" or "species" and in that sense can also be applied to animals or categories of other sorts: one can speak of a *mataqali* of work, activity, and so on. Fijians generally refer to these clanic groups by proper name with the prefix *Kai,* 'people,' thus the "So-and-so People."

> of more than a mile, fill their pitchers, gather wood, collect leaves for cooking purposes, return to the city, and carry their loads to their several homes. The vegetable dealers [*sic*]—crowds of serfs [*sic*]—heavily burdened with yams, dalo [taro], bananas, sugar-cane, native bread [preserved breadfruit], etc., coming to deposit their cargo with those who rarely pay, and scarcely thank them. It was thus that the royal families were supplied with daily food. (1866: 44)

All the principal clans of Bau had such provisioning arrangements. They also held lands in islands of the Koro Sea, usually worked by local people with the harvests coming to Bau. First-fruit tributes of yam gardens and bearing trees were annually brought to Bau from countries (*vanua*) standing in various degrees and kinds of subjugation, mostly from nearby islands and the Viti Levu mainland. These places were in addition levied for feast foods, for raw material used in construction, and for men to build the houses and temples of Bau. Many of the dependent lands, and some semi-independent ones even farther away, sent quantities of wealth goods (*i yau*) to Bau yearly or twice yearly, these being the special products of their locales, everything from tapa cloth to canoes. Such tributes to Bauan power were rendered from as far as Macuata in the extreme north of Fiji, Lau in the extreme east, and Moala and Gau to the south. Bau even had colonies of a sort, a development unique in Fiji. These were communities of Bau 'sea people' (*kai wai*), renowned canoe men and warriors, who were the original inhabitants of Bau island and in a residual sense still its 'owners' (*i taukei*). They had been sent off some generations since by the Bau chiefs—for some fault, according to most traditions—and settled in several parts of Eastern Fiji.[20] Although they thus found a place in other kingdoms, it was always as 'foreigners' (*kai tani*), for they retained their identity as Bauans and their allegiance (in principle) to the Bau kings. Indeed, the Levuka people of Lau, as originals of Bau, installed the Vunivalu and his wife in their truly Bauan titles (Tui Levuka and Radini Le-

20. The peoples in question are the Butoni and Levuka original 'owners' (*i taukei*) of Bau. They were established in Lau, Cakaudrove, Batiki, Nairai, and possibly other places. Published notices of them appear in Hale (1846: 62), Williams (1931, 1:138), Waterhouse (1866: 158–64), and Erskine (1853: 180–84), the last with an extensive description of a Butoni visit to Bau with "tribute" for "their own sovereign" (also cited by Waterhouse). The missionary journals of Messrs. John Hunt and Richard Lyth at Cakaudrove have numerous references to the doings of the Butoni and their mixed responses to demands on their fleets by the Bau war king, Ratu Tānoa (e.g, Lyth *J:* 9 December 1840, May–July 1852; Hunt *J:* 29 October 1840).

vuka).[21] Every once in a while the various Bauan colonials returned to the homeland with the spoils of their marauding or wealth they had otherwise accumulated, for which they were liberally rewarded by the Bau chiefs. On other occasions, their canoes could be put at the disposal of the Bau chiefs for war or ceremonial expeditions. Given the resources flowing into this small island of 23 acres, one can appreciate that the Bauans, more than any other Fijians, realized the proverbial description of royalty: "The chiefs just sit, and everything comes to them." The very disproportion between their inactivity and their wealth was the sign of their superhuman, invisible power (*mana*).

Still, the Bau rulers' this-worldly, active, and pragmatic deployment of their wealth turned their power into relations of domination. Mobilizing the gods and men for war, making alliances and arranging conspiracies, rewarding friends and undermining enemies, the wealth that flowed into Bau was the stuff of its hegemony. Some of this was strategic matériel: ocean-going canoes and expertly fashioned war clubs and spears. Much was goods in the special forms and exorbitant quantities of ceremonial prestations: huge bales of tapa cloth, towers of sinnet, and rolls of mats. Some again was treasure: whale teeth and ornaments of ivory and pearl shell. Coming from the islands and the east, many of these things were specially valued on that score, as 'chiefly goods' (*i yau vakaturaga*), by inland peoples of Viti Levu.[22] Mediating this flow from sea to land, which was also in Fijian terms from "above" to "below," the Bauans used the imported riches to dazzle the local warrior chiefs. Most useful in such political respects were the teeth of the sperm whale (*tabua*), the most valuable of all valuables.

Presented as binding proposals of marriage and assassination, as offerings to gods and chiefs, or in return for providing cannibal victims, the whale tooth, as Lt. Charles Wilkes commented, "is about the price of a human life" (1845, 3:90). The great Fijian ethnographer A. M. Hocart believed there was something of the god in such precious items as whale teeth, from which he derived his own theory of their value, "a few ounces of divinity are worth pounds of gross matter" (1970b: 101). Like the silver thesaurized in Athenian sanctuaries that Pericles believed could assure victory over the financially deprived Spartans, the accumulation and disbursement of treasure, especially whale tooth treasure, was a privileged instrument of Fijian warfare. In the nineteenth century whale teeth proved

21. In 1833 or 1834, when the Vunivalu Ratu Tānoa was waiting out a coup d'état in Bau, he was installed as Tui Levuka in Lau by the Levuka people (Twyning 1996: 54–55).

22. See Rokowaqa (1926) on sea-land, or chiefly-*bati* (warrior), exchange.

more powerful than European muskets. Never very effective in Fijian battle, muskets were less desirable than war clubs for Fijian killing, and in any case by about 1840 they were widely distributed among the major kingdoms (Clunie 1977; M. Sahlins 1994). The increasing supplies of whale teeth from European trade in the same period, however, simply gave the ruling chiefs, into whose hands they mostly came, more means of political maneuver. This was especially true since, for such purposes as assassination or alliance, there seems not to have been much inflation: one or a few good whale teeth could still kill or marry. But what did increase was available power: the influx of whale teeth meant there was now more political clout in circulation in the Fiji Islands—which the rulers of Bau knew well how to use.

Bau was able to differentially draw power from European trade, both goods and personnel, because it already had the power to control it. The *bêche-de-mer* commerce of the 1830s and 1840s is indicative, since the main fishing grounds were situated off the northern coasts of Viti Levu and Vanua Levu, far beyond the limits of Bau proper—but not beyond its reach or grasp.[23] The shipping often stopped at Bau beforehand, to shower the ruling chiefs with presents and make arrangements for setting up distant trading stations. Bau's influence in the *bêche-de-mer* areas usually depended on chiefs of allied lands who in turn had some authority there, and these chiefs were often sent out with the *bêche-de-mer* vessels to organize the traffic. Alternatively, the middlemen came from the small settlement of Whites at Levuka on Ovalau Island whose leader, the American David Whippy, was the acknowledged Bauan proxenus, the *Mata ki Bau* (Envoy to Bau) of the European community.[24] If necessary, the Bauan chiefs could dispatch armed parties to intervene in the trade, either to maintain the peace or to secure their own share. The objective of these uses of Bauan power was the means thereof: not only muskets, but the riches in whale teeth and other goods the traders brought.

"Fijian warfare is very expensive," remarked the missionary Mr. Thomas

23. The remarks on the *bêche-de-mer* trade in this paragraph are adapted from M. Sahlins (1994: 50); an extensive documentation from contemporary sources may be found in the footnotes to that passage (ibid., 83–84).

24. It was such arrangements, among others, that led the historian R. A. Derrick to sum up the pre-1874 influence of Whites in Fijian warfare as rather less than decisive: "The acts of a handful of traders and settlers make up so much of the recorded history of the years before Cession that it is easy to attach too much importance to them; they were often little more than eddies on the surface of a flood of native life conditioned by the native wars and all that went with them" (Derrick 1950: 52).

Williams, "especially when foreign aid [i.e., the aid of allied Fijian lands] is called in" (Williams and Calvert 1859, 1:42; cf. Williams 1931, 2:346–47). Reverend Williams was referring in particular to the devastation, not to mention the humiliation, suffered by the Cakaudrove people in 1846, when they enlisted the Bauans to help them chasten their rebellious warrior allies (*bati*), the powerful Natewa people of southeastern Vanua Levu (see fig. 1.2). The Bauans left off fighting Rewa for a while to assist the Cakaudrove people—to their own economic and political advantage. By the time the Bau fleet arrived at Somosomo, the seat of the Cakaudrove chiefs, the latter already had been wooing their help for five years—at a cost, Mr. Williams observed, "not easily calculated, including two or three first-rate canoes, several smaller ones, 50 rolls of cynet [sinnet], 150 bales of [bark] cloth, many hundreds of *masis* [white bark cloth] averaging 30 yards long, fishing nets and hundreds of whale teeth, besides mosquito curtains [of colored tapa cloth], fancy articles and women" (Williams 1931, 2:347).

The Bau army of over three thousand, including a contingent of Tongans, arrived in a squadron of eighty-four canoes, and proceeded to eat the Cakaudrove people out of home and garden.[25] They remained for nearly six weeks of continuous hospitality and periodic festivity. By the time of the climactic ceremony involving the review of the Bauan force and the pledge of their support, the Cakaudrove people had presented them with many thousand fathoms of tapa cloth and at least 170 whale teeth, among other goods. Huge piles of cooked yams and taro, topped by special festive dishes and large sea turtles, were offered to the Bauans on this occasion, as well as a wall of kava plants some 35 feet long and a pile of uncooked yams "amounting to about 38,000" (Williams 1931, 2:347; the Methodist missionaries loved to count and measure such things). In return for all this, the

25. According to Williams, there were sixty-six double canoes and sixteen single canoes; several hundred Bauan warriors also arrived overland from Vuna. In his journal, Williams speaks of a host of three thousand Bauans; in a letter to London he speaks of himself as surrounded by fourteen to fifteen thousand fighting men, most of them strangers to himself (1931, 2:355n). What to make of this larger estimate? To judge from a Fijian account of the expedition, the larger number would not be out of line, as it speaks of 160 canoes making three trips to ferry the Bauan army (Anon. of *Na Mata* 1891 [6]). The list of Bauan lands contributing to the force—Namara, Namata, Buretū, Levuka, Dravo, and Yatu Mabua (Maumi, Ovea, Mokani)—certainly suggests a considerable army; but Reverend Williams's estimate of fourteen to fifteen thousand men is three or four times larger than other recorded expeditions.

Bau leader Ratu Cakobau approached his royal counterpart of Cakaudrove "with a single whale tooth in his hand, [and] presented it with an assurance of help" (ibid., 2:350).

The ensuing battles with the Natewa rebels were desultory and indecisive, apparently by prearrangement between them and the Bau war king. Some empty towns were burnt, five or six men were killed on either side, and the Natewans then surrendered—to the Bauans! Ratu Cakobau had undermined his Cakaudrove allies, and after having eaten them out as well, he now made off with their canoes and canoe builders. Reverend Williams assessed the damage: "They [the Bau people] have nearly stripped the land. Scarce a canoe has escaped them. They have not left one carpenter. . . . The land is in a pitiable state, the lowest class of visitors having scoured the country round in search of food. . . . The folly of Tuilaila [the Cakaudrove war king] is evident to everyone but himself. He has suffered infinitely more than his enemies of Natewa, and they have altogether removed his yoke and gone over to Bau" (Williams 1931, 2:355–56). The Cakaudrove king, concluded Mr. Williams, "may look upon himself as *done.*"

Some months earlier, Mr. Williams's colleague, Rev. John Hunt, commented that in a remarkably short time Ratu Cakobau had "raised Bau to a degree of prosperity to which perhaps, no Fijian state ever attained before," and if he continued on this course, he would be "in every sense the Emperor of Feejee" (in Lyth *L:* n.d., c. 4 January 1845). Clearly, it would be an oversimplification to say that Bau became a dominant and domineering maritime power from economic motives. In origin, it was more the other way around. Bau's unique commitment to the sea entailed a politics of wealth: the constitution of material gain as a historical force. Mr. Hunt reports a conversation with a Bauan notable just a few days before the outbreak of the great war with Rewa: "A Bau chief told me the people of Bau do not wish to fight [Rewa] as they shall gain nothing by it. If they fight at Somosomo or Lakemba [Lau] they obtain riches, but Rewa being another kingdom [i.e., like Bau] they have nothing to expect from them. So covetousness has a great deal to do with Fijian wars" (Hunt *J:* 13 November 1843).

All the same, Bau did go to war with Rewa—which did not really disprove Mr. Hunt's conclusion about covetousness so much as it confirmed his earlier observation about Ratu Cakobau's imperial aspirations.[26] Or,

26. In fact, Mr. Hunt did not attribute Bauan war solely to "covetousness," or at least not solely to material covetousness. He goes on in the same passage to faithfully reproduce

taken all in all, the great Polynesian War was the culmination of a reciprocal dialectic of political and economic expansion set off by Bau's distinctive maritime orientation. Imperial domination and economic exploitation became each other's means and end. I consider the political dimension further on, as certain structural elements of the system of domination will have to be examined first. Here the question is one of economism as a telos: not simply its articulation among the relevant history makers as individuals, but its constitution as an objective of social action, thus its enfranchisement as a main historical force. We should not take material acquisitiveness for granted. As Marcel Mauss put it, it is not something behind us, a natural condition, so much as it is before us, a moral value. Hence it is not so much an inevitability as it is an invention. The argument applies to Athens as well as to Bau, or even more so. Making itself an island, dependent on control of the seas, Athens likewise created the conditions of the possibility of its singular politics of wealth: "To reign, for the Athenians, means living off foreign countries, taking their corn, hindering their trade in every possible manner and taxing the product of whatever wealth they deigned to leave them" (Romilly 1963: 74).

For Athens the economism was the more radical because it was chrematistic, articulated to the development of money and markets. In this regard fifth-century Athens differed greatly from other Hellenic cities, where it was not altogether unique (cf. Polanyi 1957; Kallet 2001; Picard 2000). A large proportion of the (large) Athenian population was dependent on monetary earnings for livelihood, many of them through public employ, thus adding popular voice to the state's quest for revenues. The so-called Old Oligarch complained of the numerous common people who "think themselves worthy of taking money for singing, running, dancing and sailing ships, so that they become wealthy and the wealthy poorer" (Ps.-Xen., *Const. Ath.* 1.13). All this came to a critical pass during the Peloponnesian War, as the culmination of the turn to thalassocracy that began in the Persian War. In effect, trade followed the flag rather than vice versa: "Athens became the center of Aegean commerce only after it established itself militarily and politically as a dominant power" (Meier 1998: 37). The Athenians claimed as much themselves when defending creation of their empire

---

the Augustinian triple libido—lust of wealth, power, and carnal pleasure—as the source of all Fijian strife. "'Whence come wars and fightings among you. Come they not hence, among your lusts that war in your members?' Desire of power, women or property is the grand cause of all their wars" (Hunt *J:* 13 November 1843).

before the Spartans in 432. "We were compelled . . . to advance our empire to its present state," they said, "first of all by fear, although later by honor too and lastly also by profit" (Thuc. 1.75.3).[27] The continuing war with Persia was the "fear"; the assumption of leadership of the Hellenes was the "honor"; the "profit" developed from a strategy of overcommitment to naval power relative to Athens' initial resources and techniques. A political overreach led to an economic takeoff. So observes Olivier Picard in connection with Themistocles' ship-building projects, beginning with the 200 triremes of 483/482: "The armaments decided upon are of a magnitude, it must be underlined, that are beyond the city's capacities of mobilizing, and the techniques to be put in place are fraught with long-term consequences. Doubtless a calculating mind such as tradition attributes to Themistocles would be conscious that he was not simply proposing a circumstantial measure, and that he was engaging the city in a policy of *longue durée*" (2000: 28, cf. 37).[28] Maneuvering the Athenian assembly into a state policy of maritime expansion, Themistocles thus destined Athens to a brilliant economic career: "Themistocles persuaded the people each year to construct and add twenty triremes to the fleet they already possessed, and also to remove the tax upon metics [foreigners] and artisans, in order that great crowds of people might stream into the city from every quarter and that the Athenians might easily procure labour for a greater number of crafts. Both of these policies he considered to be most useful in building up the city's naval forces" (Diod. Sic. XI.43).

By the mid-fifth century, manufacture, immigration, and population were all flourishing (Meiggs 1972: 262ff.). So was the commerce by which the city imported basic means of subsistence, manufacture, and luxury consumption, including the timber, pitch, sails, rope, copper, tin, and iron that built the ships that cleared the seas of all competition, piratical and Persian (Casson 1991). Likewise for all sorts of deluxe goods: "Whatever the delicacy in Sicily, Italy, Cyprus, Egypt, Lydia, Pontus [the Black Sea], the

27. Translation by Orwin (1994: 46); see Orwin's discussion of the Athenians' argument, including the reversal of honor and fear in 1.76.2. The Crawley translation reads: "The nature of the case compelled us to advance our empire to its present height; fear being our principal motive, though honor and interest afterwards came in" (cf. Hornblower 1991b: 120). Thucydides' general evolutionary theory in the "Archaeology" is discussed later in the text.

28. Meiggs had earlier said as much: "If Themistocles, especially in his naval bill, was thinking of the danger from Persia, he seems to have thought in terms of an expanding trade to accommodate an expanding fleet" (1972: 262).

Peloponnesus or anywhere else—all these have been brought together in one place by virtue of naval power" (Ps.-Xen., *Const. Ath.* II.7).[29] Critically, the staple grain on which the city survived came from the farthest reaches of Athenian power: Sicily, Egypt, and, the greatest source, the Crimea. As it was not situated in the most fertile grain-growing area, Athens was far from able to feed her burgeoning population from her own countryside—even less so during those phases of the Peloponnesian War when the Attic peasantry withdrew into the city. In some years, grain imports may have reached 1 million *medimnoi,* about 1.5 million bushels, enough to feed 250,000 people (Cohen 2000: 16n).[30] It is not necessary to suppose from this—as Cornford did in a well-known argument (1971)—that the need for Crimean and Sicilian grain was the *raison d'être* of the Athenian empire. More the other way round: the empire was the reason of the need. And with such dependence on trade, all those living by it, as well as the state, grew increasingly attentive to the main chance, especially in the decades of the Peloponnesian War. "In the days of Perikles, and more intensely during the great war, a change began to take place which gave economic factors an ever-increasing importance in the life of the polis" (Ehrenberg 1951: 49).

In a "notorious passage" of the *Constitution of Athens* (24.3), as Moses Finley deemed it, involving a "preposterous arithmetic," Aristotle wrote that the empire had "provided the common people with an abundance of income. . . . More than 20,000 men were maintained out of the tribute and the taxes and the allies." The arithmetic is preposterous, according to Finley, because the state payroll summarized by Aristotle left out the navy among other considerable expenses, but this only underscores that "Aristotle had the key to the unique Athenian system, the principle of payment to citizens for public service, for performing their duties as citizens" (Fin-

29. The Old Oligarch's statement is closely paralleled in Pericles' funeral oration (Thuc. 2.38.2). Meiggs (1972: 264) cites a catalogue of imports mentioned in a comedy produced in the 420s: "From Cyrene silphium and oxhides, from the Hellespont mackerel and all kinds of salted fish, from Italy salt and ribs of beef . . . from Egypt sails and rope, from Syria frankincense, from Crete cypress for the gods; Libya produces abundant ivory to buy, Rhodes raisins and sweet figs, but from Euboea pears and fat apples. Slaves from Phrygia, . . . Pagasae provides tatooed slaves, Paphlagonia dates and oily almonds, Phoenicia dates and fine wheat flour, Carthage rugs and many-coloured cushions."

30. Supposing an Attic population of 300,000, Casson writes that it would be supplied for a year by something less than 100,000 tons of grain, or 800 average boatloads (not including naval convoys)—very little of which would be grown in its own fields (1991: 101–2; see also Sainte-Croix 1972: 46–48).

ley 1999: 172). Aristophanes' *Wasps, Knights,* and other comedies, Finley points out, were all about a decadent economic system in which the milking of the state by the general populace was complemented by arriviste politicians with dubious origins in trade who made the venal interests of the citizenry the means of their own advancement: "You know the 'I-will-never-betray-The-Athenian-rabble-and-I'll-always-fight-for-the-plebs-people'" (*Wasps* 666–67). These are "the new politicians of fifth-century Athens," as Robert Connor (1992) designated them. Some of them too young and many of them nouveaux riches, these were the people who from the 420s or earlier were replacing the old-time pols of aristocratic lineage, such as Pericles, whose own authority had been backed by landed wealth and networks of powerful friends (Ehrenberg 1951). Here were the likes of Cleon "the tanner," Hyperbolus "the lamp-maker," Cleophon "the lyre-maker," and other such men of the agora, who as demagogues or 'leaders of the people'—a term apparently without prejudice, but indeed implying the rhetorical skills that could carry the democratic assembly—were thus transmitting the force of popular venality, as well as their own, into the policies of the state.

A caveat: not to think that the "ancient simplicity" was finished by the late fifth century. Consider the put-down of the pandering Cleon (Paphlagon) by his rival Sausage-Monger in Aristophanes' *Knights,* when the former promises Demos (The People) he will rule over Greece and make big money judging law cases in Arcadia. Telling how Cleon is only in it for his own corrupt profit, Sausage-Monger warns that if Demos, lately forced into the city by the war, "ever goes back to the country again and lives in peace, and takes fresh courage from eating grits and makes the acquaintance of pressed olive, then he will realize what benefits you have cheated him out of with your state pay; then you'll find him coming back, a fine rustic, hunting for a vote-token to use against you" (*Knights* 801–9).

There would be other famous versions of this nostalgia for the receding virtues of production for use, limited to what was needed for the good life of the household and the city, by contrast to an "unnatural" pecuniary trade whose appetite for gain knew no bounds (Arist., *Pol.* 1256b–1258b). Referring to Aristotle's *Politics,* Karl Polanyi asked:

> To what purpose did he develop a theorem comprising the origins of family and state, solely designed to demonstrate that human wants and needs are not boundless and that useful things are not intrinsically scarce? The explanation is obvious. Two policy problems—trade and price—were pressing for an answer. Unless the question of commercial

> trade and the setting of prices could be linked to the requirements of communal existence and its self-sufficiency, there was no rational way of judging of either. . . . [C]ommercial trade, or, in our terms, market trade, arose as a burning issue of the time. It was a disturbing novelty. (1957: 83–84)

Marx spoke of the sublimity of the ancient conception that made man the aim of production, in comparison with a modern world in which production is the aim of man and wealth the aim of production (1973: 487–88). The formulation is perhaps too binary to accommodate a classical Greece where the good old days had not yet given way to an interest in accumulation as such—Marx's M-C-M′—as the hegemonic principle of the economy.[31] But Athens' dependence on seaborne trade and tributes, and her citizens' dependence on the city for incomes, all intensified by the military expenses of securing and defending the empire, had made economic calculation a main principle of the city's historical action.[32] One hesitates to say "*rational* calculation" in connection with the Sicilian expedition, but Thucydides does note how eager the populace was for it, how they saw in it a fine opportunity "to earn wages at the moment, and conquests that would supply a never-ending fund of pay for the future" (6.24.3). Through a largely textual analysis of Thucydides, Lisa Kallet sees there a progressive transformation of the Athenian empire to pecuniary purposes. "Power increasingly becomes a means to an economic end: the Athenians' transformation of their system of control into an economic *archē* [empire]" (2001:

31. Thus Victor Ehrenberg, speaking of late fifth-century Athens: "Not even then, however, did economics overrule the moral aspects of life. It was, in fact, the other way round. In the very plight of everyday life, and even among the lower classes, the ideal was not so much to become rich as to lead a good life, and it seemed the duty of the State to provide for this. That is why the number of those who were living on the State steadily increased" (1951: 335–36). Consider also the Socratic rebuttals of Alcestus in Plato's *Gorgias* and Theopompus in *The Republic.* The *Gorgias* also resonates with Ehrenberg's point that the sophists' "essentially practical and opportunistic outlook" weakened traditional values relative to the growing economic rationalism (ibid., 273).

32. In this connection, Ehrenberg again: "It is possible, though only with certain reservations, to speak of a 'military party,' and among those who stood for war, the war-profiteers, especially manufacturers of arms, are not lacking, nor are those who had embezzled public funds intended for prosecution of the war; money was in circulation, and many benefited by this" (1951: 307). So in the end: "This desire for gain was no longer confined to a group that had become more or less proletarian and was therefore compelled to earn a living. The whole people was included, and in their desire to make money took active part in economic life" (ibid., 323).

291; cf. Ehrenberg 1951: 323 and passim). This emergence of materialism as a culturally specific formation is what I am talking about: not the economic determination of history, but the historical determination of economism.

Complementing Polanyi's discovery of Aristotle's "discovery of the economy," one may speak of "the invention of economic determinism." Thucydides' grand narrative of cultural evolution in the so-called "Archaeology" (1.2–19), stressing the transformative role of the wealth acquired through sea power in bringing the Hellenic world out of barbarism, may be the earliest example of such economistic theorizing. Destined to have a great intellectual career, economic determinism begins as a certain self-consciousness of the emergent Athenian empire, which itself was powered by the emergence of an independent chrematistic sphere. Unlike later anthropological schemes of evolution that featured the material consequences of the agricultural revolution, for Thucydides the maritime revolution, the technical mastery of the sea, was the basis of further cultural development. In other respects, however, the course of that development through Thucydides' "Archaeology" was much as it is still in the theoretical systems of modern archaeological science, where nomadic hunting and gathering gives way to the settled life of the neolithic age, followed by increased surplus production and the formation of cities, civilizations, and, finally, empires. Just so, in Thucydides' treatment, the gains from commerce, conquest, and the suppression of piracy, all made possible by sea power, allowed certain peoples to escape the unsettled and uncultivated conditions of the earliest times and set the course for (Athenian) empire. Tradition had it that Minos of Crete was the first ruler to build a navy. Neither in this case nor in others was Thucydides concerned with the reasons or means of the preliminary "primitive accumulation"—with the exception of Corinth's introduction of a trireme fleet, which he attributed to the favorable location on the isthmus that had already made her a commercial emporium. But Thucydides was specially concerned to show how accumulated wealth allowed the first maritime peoples to transcend the incessant hostilities and consequent insecurities of their original condition. Otherwise, like some barbarians still, they would have to suffer "the incommodities of the state of nature" (as Hobbes later rephrased it): a fear-driven, migratory existence that precluded even the cultivation of the ground beyond the barest minimum, let alone trade, cities, or "any other form of greatness" (Thuc. 1.3.2).

The accumulation of stores of wealth by maritime powers changed all that. It led to large, walled cities in coastal locations (where before only the interior had been occupied, for fear of pirates, and only peripatetically so in the beginning), to ethnic confederations (like the Hellenes at Troy, although they still did not have that common name), and to the power of one city to subjugate and dominate others (thus empire). Thucydides figures the economic stimulus as developing in a double sense, objectively as increasing accumulations of wealth [*chrēmatōn*] and subjectively as increasing desires of gain [*kerdōn*], the latter marching in tandem with the former, such that together, "as the power of Hellas grew, and the acquisition of wealth became more of an object, the revenues of the states increasing, tyrannies were established almost everywhere" (1.13.1).

Or so Crawley translates it. The shifting translations of this and like passages over the centuries, incidentally, are revelatory in many ways, not least by the developing tendency to endow the ancient text with up-to-date capitalist categories. Consider the statement in the "Archaeology" (1.8.3) so often quoted in evidence of Thucydides' economism, here on display as the motivation of submission as well as imperial domination. At one extreme, Hobbes [1629], with a lingering aura of feudalism, speaks of "the meaner sort" and "servitude," even as the pertinent material interest is a generic "desire of gain": "For out of desire of gain the meaner sort underwent servitude with the mighty, and the mighty with their wealth brought the lesser cities into subjection." At the other, capitalist extreme of "profits" and "capital," here is Rex Warner's translation [1954]: "The weaker, because of the general desire to make profits, were content to put up with being governed by the stronger, and those who won superior power by acquiring capital resources brought the smaller cities under their control."[33]

There is something more than ethnocentrism in these variations, however: there is the common substrate of Thucydides' economism. That was the great originality of his system, as de Romilly claims, and what made it thoroughly modern: "not only a critical and reasoned history, but also positive and realist in the modern sense of the term, one that places economic factors in the first rank" (Romilly 1967: 266). Still "modern," "positive," and "realist" do not make the primacy of economic factors universal or even true. This economism was in origin the reflexive consciousness of a

33. Besides indicating a similar transformation of the economic categories, other, parallel passages indicate that the operative objective-economic factor at issue in Thucydides is the accumulation of stores of wealth, something like the category of "surplus" in the analogous anthropological and archaeological treatises on cultural evolution. So "plenty of riches" (1.7), as Hobbes (1989) translated *plōimōterōn,* became "a greater superabundance of wealth" in Bloomfield (1829), "a greater supply of capital" in Crawley (1876), and "general capital reserves" in Warner (1972).

certain cultural-historical formation—appropriately enough lost from favor and view in Europe until its renewed popularity in the seventeenth century.

The economic ideology had echoes in similar formations elsewhere, and not only in Fiji. Thalassocratic Venice was given to the same acquisitiveness, as Gary Wills notes in a recent work that draws repeated parallels between the Lion City of the Renaissance and Periclean Athens. The same acquisitiveness and the same imperial ecology. Built on a chain of man-made, walled-off islands rising out of the marsh, Venice too was formed on a vision of insular impregnability and maritime domination. Without important resources of its own, Venice became spectacularly rich by the economic exploitation of her naval power. Wills remarks of the resemblances:

> Periclean Athens, a sea empire, used its land enclave as a staging area for ventures into a watery world of restive subordinates or hostile rivals. Athenians, as much as Venetians, felt that they were different from the rest of mankind, separate, autochthonous, sprung out of their own turf. . . . The naval skill of the Athenians secured the Delian League, from which they extracted tribute to adorn their polychrome Athens—just as Venetian seamen brought back the plunder of Byzantium to be incorporated in the iridescence of their martial shrine, the basilica of St. Mark. Athenian tribute money was brought in formal procession to the theater of Dionysus for the religious contests of that god. In Venice, the rich reliquaries captured in the East were carried about on feast days of tutelary patron saints. (Wills 2001: 13–14)

Venice resembled Athens, as Wills said, not because of conscious imitation, "but because the structure of the two sea empires made them reach for similar solutions to the problems they faced" (13). To persuade oneself that the economism of these sea empires was indeed historically distinct and structurally grounded, it is only necessary to follow Thucydides' various comparisons of the kinetic Athenians with the relatively immobile Spartans. These were the Spartans who in the fifth century were making a virtue of the material self-denial allegedly established hundreds of years before by their renowned lawgiver Lycurgus—the hero who invented a form of iron money so large in bulk and small in value that it could not be readily transported or accumulated. Considering also the Lycurgan laws of consumption that would create a universal condition of self-sufficient poverty, why then, asked Xenophon, "should money-making be a preoccupation in a state where the pains of its possession are more than the pleasure of its enjoyment?" (*Const. Laced.* VII.2). Here was another relation to acquisition—Spartan.

NATIONAL CHARACTER, CULTURAL ORDER

Comparison with Fiji will suggest that the contrast of Spartan autarchy with Athenian enterprise is not merely structurally grounded but historically connected. From the late sixth century, especially, Sparta and Athens evolve against one another, as cultural antitypes.[34]

For Thucydides, however, the differences between the Spartans and the Athenians were a matter of character, not structure. (He was the forerunner not only of our rationalist historiography but also of the current revival of collective subjectivities, the "national characters" of sacred memory, with the same faults of essentialism as historical description and indeterminacy as cultural explanation.) To believe Thucydides, so did the Greeks of the time make much of ethnic temperaments, since the most sustained exposition of such differences between the Spartans and the Athenians is attributed to the Corinthians, in a speech urging the Spartans to get off their butts for once and respond appropriately to the Athenians' breach of the Thirty Years Peace. Compared with the Athenians, the Corinthians remonstrate, you Spartans are slow of action, blunt of perception, given to procrastination, innocent of innovation, prisoners of convention, and besides overcautious and defensive, with a fear of leaving home that is only matched by an ignorance of what is happening abroad. Of course, the Athenians came out with all the opposed qualities of energy, enterprise, and derring-do. "To describe their character in a word, we might truly say they were born into the world to take no rest themselves and to give none to others," the Corinthians concluded, whereas "your [Spartan] habits are old-fashioned compared to theirs" (1.70.9–1.71.2).

Ceaseless motion or "the search of power after power"—to adopt the singularly appropriate Hobbesian expression (or derivation)—was certainly the way the Athenians appeared in Thucydides' description of the fifty-year run-up to the war, the Pentecontaetia (as it is now called). This was the period in which the empire was established, at first as an alliance under Athenian leadership, the Delian League, then turning into a tribu-

34. I take the useful term *antitype* from Jonathan Hall's discussion of the development of a categorical opposition between "Hellenes" and "barbarians" (2002: 179).

tary system under Athenian domination and exploitation. Clearing the Aegean of pirates, driving the Persians back to Asia, putting down rebellions, and expanding their imperium, the Athenians, in the Pentecontaetia, are "in action in every quarter of the eastern Mediterranean, sailing around the Peloponnese ([Thuc.] 108.5), establishing control of the narrows of the Corinthian Gulf (103.3), and engaged in northern Greece (100.2), Asia Minor (100.1), Cyprus (112.4), and Egypt" (Connor 1984: 44).[35] The Spartans, having yielded the leadership of the Hellenes to the Athenians after 478, now withdrew into the Peloponnesian shell that so exasperated the Corinthians. Even after the war with Athens began, the Spartans persisted in fighting old-fashioned land campaigns, marked by their brevity and, considering the enemy, their futility. Summer after summer in the first years of the war, the Spartans invaded, ravaged, and then withdrew from the Attic countryside, an operation that lasted forty days or less. The strategy was based on a condition to which Athens was a great exception: that Greek cities depended largely on their own domestic grain supply.[36]

Even so, the Spartans had this thing about going beyond their own boundaries. Often enough their campaigns were aborted there for failure of the necessary sacrifices. Under the aegis of the king (one of the two) who led the army, the sacrifices were initiated inside Sparta, and, if successful, the fire from the altar was carried to the border. "There the king offers sacrifice again to Zeus and Athena. Only when the sacrifice proves acceptable to both these deities does he cross the borders of the land" (Xen., *Const. Laced.* XIII.2–3). Thucydides tells of the Spartans calling off three different campaigns because the omens for crossing their frontiers were unfavorable, two in 419 and one in 416 (5.54.2; 5.55.3; 5.116). "On these occasions," observe Goodman and Holladay, "Sparta's enemies benefited greatly from her scrupulousness" (1986: 156). Thucydides also notes two times the Spartans quit the field because of earthquakes (a bad sign), one in 426 when they were on their way to the annual invasion of Attica (Thuc.

35. Five fragments of a monument set up by the Athenians in 465 to commemorate the year's casualties show them fighting in five different theaters in the northern Aegean, from the eastern border of Macedonia to the Asian side of the Hellespont (Dardenelles) (McGregor 1987: 45; cf. Palmer 1992: 59). Moses Finley observed that Athens "was at war on average more than two years out of every three between the Persian wars and the defeat by Philip of Macedon at Chacronea in 338 B.C., and that it never enjoyed ten consecutive years of peace in all that period" (1986: 67).

36. It appears that the Spartans did little serious damage to Athenian agriculture, especially during the Archidamian war (Hanson 1998: 131ff.).

3.89.1; 6.95.1). These famous warriors had a reputation for arriving too late for the battle, as at Marathon, having been delayed by obligatory religious tabus or performances. They were known, too, for suspending military operations in mid-course so they could return to Sparta for their great annual festival, the Hyacinthia (Hdt. 9.7–11; Paus. 3.10.1, 4.19.4; Xen., *Hellen.* 4.5.11).[37] Although the Athenians could likewise subordinate military strategy to ritual scruple, as in the disastrous instance of Nicias at Syracuse, they were much less given to do so than the notoriously pious Spartans. Sparta was "the one Greek state which held the reputation of being willing on occasion to sacrifice her own and, often, her allies' interests in fulfilling her duty to the gods" (Goodman and Holladay 1986: 154; cf. Hodkinson 1983: 273–74). The Athenians were thus lucky in their enemies. Commenting on the Spartans' inability as late as 411 to capitalize on some spectacular successes by descending on the Piraeus, Thucydides wrote that "here as on so many occasions the Spartans proved the most convenient people in all the world to be at war with. The difference between the two characters, the slowness and want of energy of the Spartans as contrasted with the dash and enterprise of their opponents, proved of the greatest service, especially to a maritime empire like Athens" (8.96.5).

The Spartans' boundary phobias, like the other conservative dispositions with which the Corinthians taxed them, are aspects of a supposedly venerable and distinctive cultural system, which classical scholars have come to call "the Spartan mirage" (Ollier 1933–43). Skepticism now attends the tradition of a unique Spartan culture, marked for centuries by its austerity, autarky, and xenophobia, its disdain of commerce and the arts, the "barracks life" of Spartiate men and boys, and a production system based on state serfs. Considered to be of ancient origin and longstanding, these institutions were attributed in the main to the legendary lawgiver Lycurgus—of whom Plutarch said it is impossible to determine anything that is beyond dispute (*Lyc.* 1). Plutarch was not the first to recount the traditions of Spartan uniqueness, however, as these have been retailed from the fifth century onward and by the likes of Herodotus, Xenophon, Plato, and Aristotle. Also Thucydides, who found it relevant to his *History* to note that Sparta "at a very early time enjoyed good laws," adding the unusually speculative assertion that "it has possessed the same constitution for more

37. In one span of thirty-eight years, the Spartans left off battle ten times because of earthquakes, according to Goodman and Holladay (1986: 155). They do not give the dates, but the period extends into the fourth century. Goodman and Holladay do provide a detailed and documented discussion of the influence of religion in Spartan campaigns.

than four hundred years" (1.18.1). Characteristic of modern reservations about this argument are A. W. Gomme's remarks in his exegetical commentary on Thucydides' text. The reference in Thucydides' passage would not be to Sparta's political constitution, says Gomme, as this was, apart from the dual kingship, not exceptional among aristocratic Greek polities. The reference rather was to "the way of life peculiar to her"—but that "we know from archaeological evidence . . . hardly existed before about 600 B.C. . . . The contempt for the arts and for trade, the dislike of the foreigner, the refusal of what almost all other peoples have regarded as essential amenities of life—all of which the Greeks of the fifth century and later especially associated with the Spartan *eunomia* and with the Lycurgan constitution—were not prevalent before the first half of the sixth century" (1945: 129).

Research since Gomme's day would date the development of a "different Sparta" even later. Many of its distinctive features do not appear until the fifth century, some only after the Persian War.[38] Hence this sense of a "mirage" now widely accepted among classical historians, or what the anthropologists know as "the invention of tradition." All the same, much like the archaic Greek invention of its Mycenaean tradition, or for that matter the Renaissance invention of its Greco-Roman tradition, this one was successful. The so-called mirage was by all accounts alive and well in Thucydides' time, both the idea of it and in large measure the reality. In this light such debunking terms as *mirage* and *invention* become less than useful. Giving the phenomenon an air of inauthenticity, not to say a bad name, they reflect the scholarly genealogy we have determined for it at the expense of its historical value and significance for its own time and for the peoples concerned. Consider that the very lateness of the distinctive Spartan system, sanctioned by the tradition of its great antiquity, would make it in all such respects the contemporary antithesis of "revolutionary Athens." Our historiographic conversation with Thucydides, then, might run something like this: the celebrated differences of collective temperament between the Athenians and the Spartans are motivated by differences between their cultural orders, while the differences between their cultural orders are motivated by each other.

The comparison with Fiji again, perhaps by its very cultural distance, brings the historiographic point home. We can then return again to the so-called mirage.

38. On the "mirage," see, among others, Huxley (1962), Cartledge (2001, 2002), Hodkinson (1983), and Rawson (1969).

STRUCTURES OF FIJIAN HISTORY

If one were to write a Pentecontaetia of the Polynesian War of 1843–55, thus going back to the end of the eighteenth century, it would describe Bau (like Athens) as ever moving and expanding by comparison to a relatively immobile Rewa (like Sparta). Rewa was not altogether confined to its own borders, but it was much more constrained in its external ventures. Consider their respective arenas of marauding and battle, as illustrated in the accompanying map (fig. 1.12).[39] Bau was operating on a different scale than Rewa. Most of Rewa's forays were within a radius of 10 to 15 kilometers of the capital: fights with its own rebellious subjects (*qali,* e.g., Noco), with contentious allies (*bati,* e.g., Nakelo) or with nearby enemies (Tamavua or Suva, the latter a Bauan town). Rewa's farther reach consisted of descents on the southern islands of Beqa and Kadavu, again for the most part to secure the authority it had already established there.[40] In the same period Bau fleets were operating all over the Fiji Islands, from one end to the other. In the late eighteenth or early nineteenth century Bauan forces fought in the

39. The data presented here are no doubt incomplete (fig. 1.12). The distribution of Bauan and Rewan battles is plotted from the main missionary and voyaging sources and from traditions referring to Bau under the reigns of the war kings Ratu Naulivou and Ratu Banuve, and referring to Rewa back to Ro Tabaiwalu. Apart from missing information, the Bauan battles are underestimated because many of the targets were attacked more than once, even during a single campaign, when an unsuccessful army returned to Bau, regrouped, and attacked again. The Rewan data are also underestimated, in smaller part due to the same pattern, but I suspect in larger part for the absence of indications of operations along the south and southwestern coast of Viti Levu, where Rewa was influential.

40. In the kind of exception that proves the rule, a joint Bau-Rewa expedition of 1809, under Bauan leadership, is reported to have attacked a town on the Teidamu River in northern Viti Levu and another town eastward, near Viti Levu Bay (both unnamed). The curiously detailed account of this campaign comes to us thirdhand, from the pen of one Edwin Turpin, who had it from Samuel Whippy (son of the well-known David Whippy), who had it from a Norfolk sailor who, with three other Whites, is said to have been a participant. The reason for the expedition was a famine in southeastern Viti Levu, which induced Bau and Rewa chiefs to arrange a truce and combine to search other parts of Viti Levu for food. Over two thousand fighting men were said to have taken part, sailing in a fleet of 166 canoes, more than three-quarters of which were Bauan. The leader of the army was Ratu Tānoa, brother of the Bau war king Ratu Naulivou. The expedition reached Nadi, where it was royally treated and provisioned: "we lived like conquerors"—and indeed feasted on large numbers of cannibal victims contributed by the Nadi people. The Nadi chief also recalled a visit, when he was very young, by the predecessor and father of Ratu Naulivou, Ratu Banuve. The Nadi people acted like subjects of Bau; had they not, according to the text, they would have been attacked (Turpin *DN*).

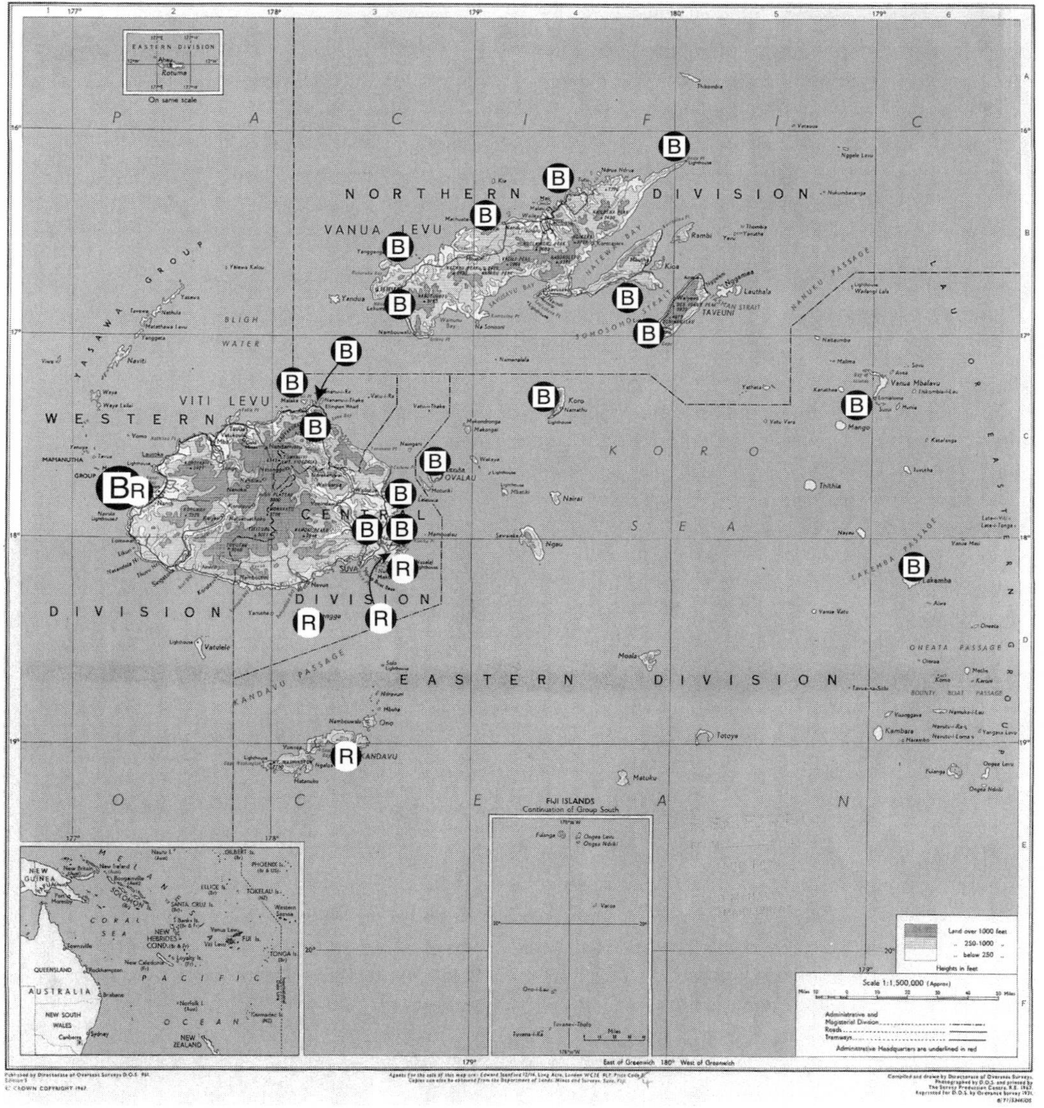

1.12 Fiji: Areas of Bau and Rewa marauding and battle from the late eighteenth century to 1843

easternmost Fijian islands of Lakeba (Lau) and Vanuabalavu. A large Bau army, including allies from northeastern Viti Levu (Nakorotubu), successfully attacked the fortified town of Kedekede in the interior of Lakeba, causing its abandonment and toppling the Lau king, in favor of a chief from the resident Bau sea people (Reid 1990; Koto Ms). In a renowned battle off Vanuabalavu, a Bauan fleet caught up with and killed their sacred king (Roko Tui Bau) who had been driven out of the island by the party of the war king (Anon. of *Na Mata* 1891 [1]: 13–14). In the 1840s Bau was warring on the north coast of Vanua Levu, hitting towns all the way from Macuata to Udu Point at the eastern end of the island. Bau also fought on the northern (Ba) coast of Viti Levu, in Malake, Ovalau, Verata (several times), Bua, Naigani, Koro, and several times in the Rewa Delta, as far upriver as Kasavu. But an interesting text of a French visit to Fiji during this period affords another way of judging Bau's singular political motion.

On 25 May 1827 Capt. Dumont D'Urville took on board the *Astrolabe* at Lakeba, Lau, a high Bauan chief, Ratu Tubuanakoro, together with a brother of the Lau king, one or two Tongans, and a local notable whose father was Tongan and mother a sister of the Lau ruler (D'Urville 1832: 409).[41] D'Urville was searching for the ill-fated La Pérouse, Ratu Tubuanakoro for tributes, a function he exercised "in a great number of islands of the Fijian archipelago" on behalf of his father's brother, Ratu Naulivou, the Vunivalu of Bau (Gaimard 1832: 698). (The naturalist M. Gaimard also refers to Ratu Naulivou as "the king of the Fiji Islands," an exaggeration—not without significance in the present context—to which European visitors were often disposed.) During the week that Ratu Tubuanakoro sailed on the *Astrolabe,* he won the unqualified admiration of the French for his dignity and intelligence. His gentle manners, agreeable appearance, and accommodating character, D'Urville said, "showed him to be much superior, in my eyes, to all the savages I had observed up to then," while "his intelligence ceded nothing to that of men not long ago celebrated in the arts and sciences" (1832: 426–27: an apparent reference to the *philosophes* of the Enlightenment; perhaps those offended by this comparison of Fijians to classical Greeks can find some consolation in that). The Bauan showed his dignity in part by a noble indifference to where the French chose to put him ashore; for the winds had made it impossible for D'Urville to disembark his passengers at Lakeba, and he now proposed to leave them at So-

41. Dumont D'Urville speaks of six Tongans and Fijians aboard the ship; Gaimard, his naturalist, of five. The Lau royal was Soroqali; the Tongan, a uterine nephew to Lau (*vasu ki* Lau), was Lualala.

mosomo, the Cakaudrove capital on Taveuni Island. The prospect drove the Tongans to tears of despair. But Ratu Tubuanakoro was able to reassure his colleagues he would protect them at Cakaudrove. When the *Astrolabe* then failed to make Taveuni, all the passengers except Ratu Tubuanokoro again fell into a panic, thinking that they were being taken off to Europe. However, they were well pleased when D'Urville decided to make for Moala Island, where a brother of Ratu Tubuanakoro was likewise acting as a "tribute collector" for Bau.[42] This was in all probability Ratu Cakobau, the chief destined to become Fiji's greatest conqueror, who according to a well-known tradition was circumcised as a youth in Moala—an occasion for a large-scale prestation of property (Toganivalu *TkB*). Meanwhile, even as Ratu Tubuanakoro was maintaining his chiefly serenity through all the disquiet of his companions, he gained the respect of the French for the lessons he gave them in the geography of Fiji, "nearly all the islands of which he had visited himself" (Gaimard 1832: 698). He was, M. Gaimard remarked, "the don Luis de Torrès of this archipelago."

In the course of the week, Ratu Tubuanakoro furnished Gaimard with a remarkable list of sixty-three inhabited islands, together with estimates of their populations. He also indicated their respective positions on the Krusenstern 1813 map of Fiji that the French were using. Ratu Tubuanakoro's list is remarkable both for its extent—from the Yasawa Islands in the northwest to Lau in the southeast—and for the accuracy of his population figures. With the exception of the largest islands, whose interior settlements would be unknown to him, Ratu Tubuanakoro's estimates are quite in line with later censuses. On such matters the Bauan was deferred to by the Lau royal on board, who allowed that he was not qualified himself, while acknowledging that Ratu Tubuanakoro "was the Fijian most appropriate to furnish information of this nature" (Gaimard 1832: 708). The French were to have further proof of that, although they did not quite realize it. For later, a great chief of Nadrogā in southwest Viti Levu (perhaps the king, Na Kā Levu) also provided the French with the names of sixty-five inhabited and fifty-seven uninhabited Fijian islands—or so they thought. Since this list hardly corresponded with Ratu Tubuanakoro's, Dumont D'Urville suspected it was somewhat bogus, perhaps including names of districts as well as islands. As it turned out, a great many of the

42. The tributes, as noted by M. Gaimard (1832: 700), were "whale teeth, which are the money of the country, canoes, young girls of 10 to 12 years old, bark cloth, mats, sinnet, shell, bananas, coconuts, chickens, pigs, yams, and in general all the useful products of the earth." On the significance of the young girls, see Tcherkézoff (in press).

places on the Nadrogā list are neither islands nor districts, but merely villages of Viti Levu. The Nadrogā chief could hardly match Ratu Tubuanakoro's knowledge or experience of all of Fiji, and probably no other Fijian could either—unless it were another Bauan.[43] So far as the Rewans are concerned, the direct comparative evidence of their reach is limited to a slight anecdote, though it does involve a personage of status analogous to Ratu Tubuanakoro, namely Ro Cokānauto (also known as "Phillips"), a paternal half-brother of the Rewa king. In answer to an inquiry made in 1840 by a member of the U.S. Exploring Expedition concerning the location of rivers other than the Wailevu on which Rewa was situated, Ro Cokānauto spoke only of "another large river . . . on this island, but he did not know the precise locality" (Pickering *J:* 17 May 1840). The apparent ignorance of Ro Cokānauto is all the more remarkable because the second largest river of Viti Levu, the Sigatoka, reaches the sea on the southwest coast, an area were Rewa had some political influence. But evidently not the kind of authority and familiarity enjoyed by Bau over a considerable part of the Fijian archipelago.[44]

43. In another testimony to Ratu Tubuanakoro's getting around, the *bêche-de-mer* trader John Eagleston encountered him at Macuata on the north coast of Vanua Levu in November 1831 (*UD:* 343). And by way of analogy to D'Urville's experience with the Nadrogā chief, one of the U.S. Exploring Expedition officers, George Foster Emmons, told of taking a voyage to the Yasawa Islands in northwest Fiji with the Tui Bua, paramount of Bua in western Vanua Levu, as pilot. The chief repeatedly warned Emmons he was off course, pointing out the correct one. Fortunately, Emmons ignored him, for "if I had followed the directions of King Tuibor [Tui Bua]—who was sent with me as knowing all about these islands—I should finally have found myself a long way to leeward of the Asawa [Yasawa] group and there is no telling where I should have brought up" (Emmons *J:* 8 and 9 June 1840).

44. Rev. John Hunt, on two different trips to various parts of Viti Levu in the 1840s, offers somewhat discrepant accounts of the comprehension of the Bau and Rewa dialects by other Fijians. In the first, a circumnavigation of the island in 1843, he found the Rewa dialect understood by chiefs on the west coast, which emboldened him to preach to them "in the Rewa and Bau dialects and we found that in every place one or two of the chiefs had, by means of intercourse with Rewa and Bau people, acquired so much knowledge of their dialects as not only to understand it, but to speak it well" (*WMMS/L* Hunt et al., n.d. [in the hand of Hunt]). In a trip to the northern, Ba coast in 1847, however, Reverend Hunt mentions only the Bau dialect as understood by "most of the chiefs and their attendants," which he found remarkable, as he could scarcely understand a tenth of the local Fijian (*J:* 4 June 1847). A couple of days later, he writes: "Though their language is very different, yet they understand a great deal that is said in the Bau dialect. Bau has rendered great service to Christianity in its extensive influence, just as Rome did of old to the world [*sic*]. Perhaps when this great project is accomplished, Bau like Rome will be brought down" (*J:* 6 June 1847). Mr. Hunt got his wish.

1.13 View of Rewa, 1840

Just so, from 1843, when Bau and Rewa came into protracted conflict, they showed the same sort of differences in character and strategy. Rewa was on the defensive almost the whole of the war. Until about 1852 Rewa was no match for Bau's combination of mobility, force, and wealth—not to mention the conspiratorial cunning of its ruling chiefs. Benefiting then from a rebellion in Bau, the defection of many Bauan towns, and a falling-out of the Bauans with European traders, Rewa for a while gained the upper hand. But in 1855, with victory in its grasp, Rewa suddenly collapsed when its charismatic king Ratu Qaraniqio died unexpectedly—about which event more will be said in the next chapter. Otherwise, Rewa's landed, agricultural situation in the rich delta of the Wailevu River made it as vulnerable as it left the resources of Bauan power inaccessible. A specialized ecological zone featuring the intensive cultivation of swamp taro (*Cyrtosperma chamissonis*), the Rewa Delta hosted a population upwards of twenty thousand in just 96 square miles, "probably the largest concentration in the Pacific at this time" (Parry 1977: 19; figs. 1.13 and 1.14). The great part of this area was occupied by Rewa and its dependent lands—until the damage Bau inflicted on local food supplies and its attacks on Rewan towns shifted the correlation of forces. Rewa had canoes, perhaps one-third as many ocean-going canoes as Bau, but here again it could not contend with the latter's superiority. In the two major sea battles that took place in the

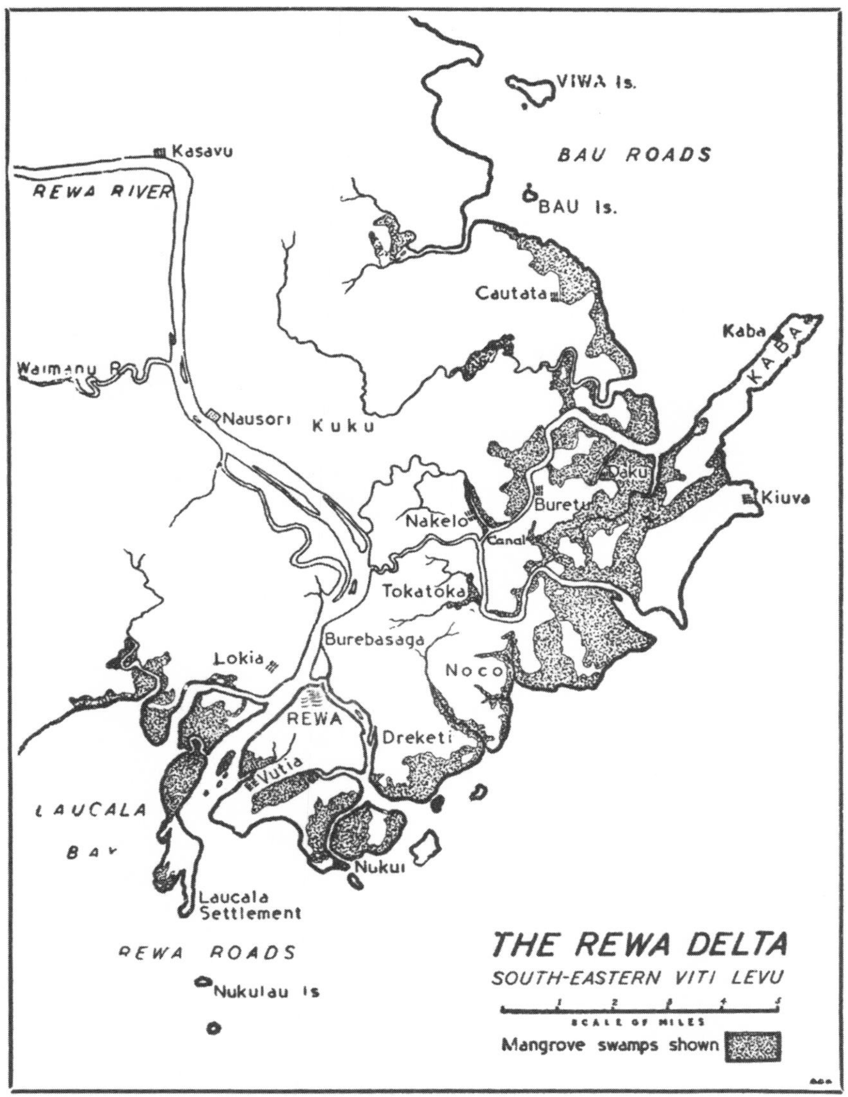

1.14 The Rewa Delta

first year of the war, the great Bauan double canoes inflicted serious losses on Rewan vessels returning to the capital from Kadavu Island. (Toganivalu 1912b: 170; Hunt *J:* 5 February 1844; Jaggar *J:* 1 June 1844). "These battles," comments Fergus Clunie, "clearly show the naval supremacy of Bau, a vital factor in her rise to a dominant position in Fiji" (Clunie 1977: 23). Combined with the defection to the Bau side of a town (Nukui) commanding the entrance to the Wailevu River, the early naval defeats seem to have cut Rewa off from its Kadavu subjects and their wealth for much of the war.

Deprived of support in the Delta as well, Rewa was destroyed not once but twice: in 1845 and again in 1847. When the king was killed in the first battle, the leadership fell to his younger brother Ratu Qaraniqio, who organized the resistance and the reoccupation of the Rewan capital on both occasions from a refuge in the mountains. Reverend Hunt tells how Bau wore down Rewa's defenses in the Delta during the first campaigns of 1843–45. He describes the desertion of the Rewa cause by Tokatoka, an important country of six towns situated along the strategic river channel connecting Rewa and Bau waters. A longstanding warrior ally of Rewa, Tokatoka, said Mr. Hunt, "put up a noble resistance and [was] not taken after all, but being wearied out with watching and hunger they joined the Bau party. This was the case with many Rewa towns. The riches of Bau were too much for them" (*J:* following 19 October 1845).

As it was in fifth-century Greece, so in nineteenth-century Fiji: the differences in the way the contending powers waged war involved something more than "national character," or whatever one might chose to call the contrasting dispositions that Thucydides invoked to account for differences of historical praxis between Spartans and Athenians. Bau's aggressiveness expressed the singularity of its structure in the Fijian scheme of things. The Bau polity was a distinctive transformation, by way of inversion, of the normal Fijian system—of which Rewa, for its part, was a classical version. Basil Thomson, who knew Fijian constitutions well from his stint as a native lands commissioner in the 1890s, considered Rewa "the most perfect example of a Fijian state known to us" (1908: 366). Bau would then have to be the most unusual example, consistently differing in many cultural dimensions, from the mode of production to mythology, passing by way of a radical contrast in the system of descent groups and an inverted form of dual kingship that subordinated the sacred ruler to the war lord.

Rewa's classic constitution was constructed on the basic Fijian dualism of indigenous 'land people' (*kai vanua*), who were the original 'owners' (*i taukei*) of the country, and immigrant ruling chiefs whose overseas origins made them "sea" in contrast to the underlying "land" (Hocart 1952: 27ff., 1970a: 268ff.). The land people notably included the 'true Rewans' (*kai Rewa dina*), who are credited with reclaiming the Rewa Delta from swampland, constructing an elaborate system of ditched and raised fields for the cultivation of the giant swamp taro and other crops. Tradition finds these originals yielding the rule to successive waves of chiefly lineages, culminating in the advent of sacred kings from Verata on the east coast of Viti Levu,

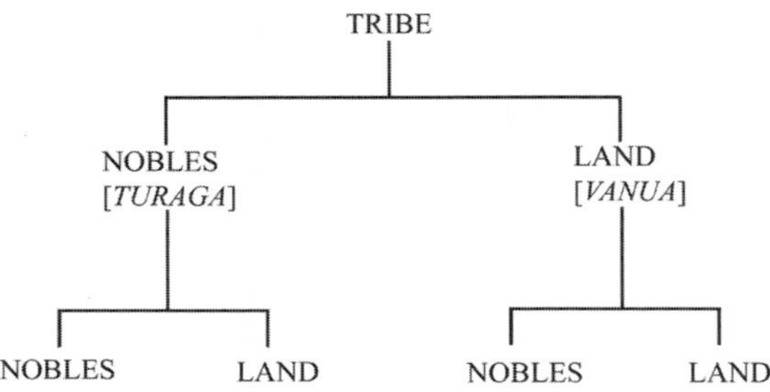

1.15 Basic structure of the Fijian "tribe," after Hocart

the traditional hearth of the aristocracy that ruled the major Fijian kingdoms. Basil Thomson's admiration of the Rewan polity was perhaps due to the way the dualism of indigenous land people and immigrant chiefs was carried through the entire system: from the kingship itself, a characteristic Fijian diarchy, through the relations between different lands (*vanua*) in the kingdom, different villages (*koro*) in each land, and different clans (*mataqali*) in each village.[45] One is reminded of the Lauan expression purveyed by A. M. Hocart and often quoted by Fijianists: "In Fiji all things go in pairs, or the sharks will bite" (1952: 57).[46] A diagram from Hocart's study of Lau can serve as a model of how this dualism works out at various levels of the typical Fijian land, or what Hocart called the "Tribe" (fig. 1.15).

In actuality, the Rewa system is somewhat more complex, a scheme of two intersecting forms of dualism, the one as it were vertical, the other horizontal. The first, the kind depicted by Hocart, divides the society into two more or less equivalent parts, with each moiety headed by one of the two kings, the sacred king (Roko Tui Dreketi) and the war king (Vunivalu). Technically, this is a *diametric* dualism, as distinct from the *asymmetric* form that stratigraphically opposes the ruling chiefs to the underlying people. The one reciprocal and the other hierarchical, the two are

45. Hocart cites a Rewan in his fieldnotes: "In Rewa 2 chiefs Roko Tui Ndreketi [the sacred king] & Vunivalu [the war king]: they divide Rewa & all subject towns & mataisau [royal carpenters] between them. There is not a town in Rewa where they have not both authority" (*FN* 2515).

46. Hocart, on Fijian recursive dualism: "It is a feature of Fijian society that, take any community you like, it will divide into two, and each half will exhibit the same structure as the whole—that is, it will subdivide into two parts, each of which is to the other as the major divisions are to one another. And so you can go on dichotomizing down to the clan, which is divided into subclans, senior and junior, inner and outer" (1968: 113).

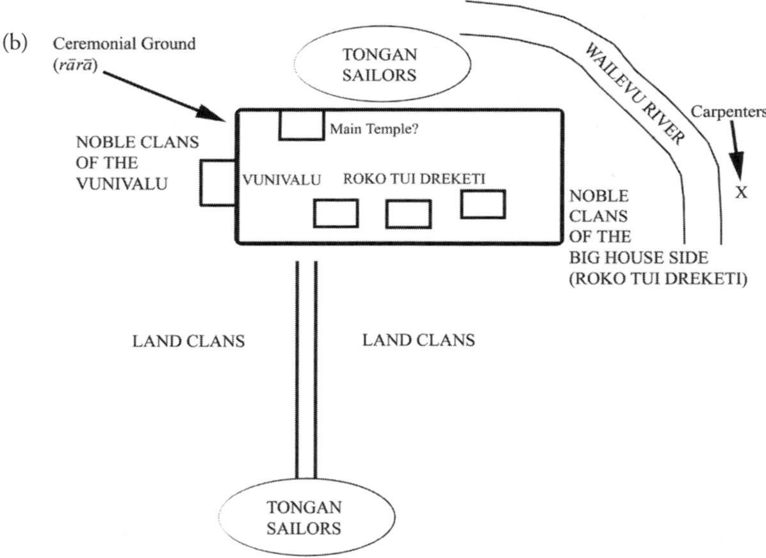

1.16 Rewa dualisms: (a) Cross-cutting moities; (b) Spatial relations

alternate structures of historical action, appropriately salient in different situations.

The diametric system (fig. 1.16a) is primarily an organization of internal affairs. Each moiety is in principle composed of the same kinds of groups—each has its chiefs, its priests, its sailor clans, and so forth—although the side of the Roko Tui Dreketi takes ritual precedence over that of the Vunivalu. Consistent with this difference of 'chiefly' and 'land' sides (*turaga* and *vanua*) is the traditional history of the royal titles. The supreme king, Roko Tui Dreketi, is the scion of the late-coming, sea-borne immigrants who usurped the rule of the earlier established war kings. This dynasty of sacred kings is descended from Fiji's ranking aristocrats: a royal lineage whose senior branch rules over the old kingdom of Verata on the east coast of Viti Levu and whose cadet branches hold the sacred kingships (the "Roko Tui" titles) in several Fijian countries.[47] But the Vunivalu hails from inland kings of rather dubious origins and antisocial dispositions, not given to the proprieties observed by true chiefs, yet by the same heritage suited to activities likewise beyond the social bounds—bloodshed and war. Originating in the uplands of Viti Levu, whence they were forced to flee for betraying the creator god (Degei) in Fiji's first war, the ancestors of the Vunivalu became the rulers of the indigenous people of the land. Their royal title, Vunivalu, translates as "God of war" or "Root of war," an office and function as military leader they assumed when they in turn surrendered the country to the parvenu Roko Tui Dreketi people. "War is their work," as Rewans say.[48]

In principle, the Vunivalu is the active king of the diarchy, while the paramount Roko Tui Dreketi "only sits"—a diacritic exaggeration, of course—receiving the offerings of the kingdom in his capacity as the human form of the gods, thus ensuring its continuity and prosperity. The Vunivalu, by contrast, acts: he leads not only in war but in many collective works by virtue of his status as the original ruler of Rewa's people.[49] Yet, as ethnographers of Fiji have argued, it is somewhat misleading to contrast the Roko Tui Dreketi to the Vunivalu as the sacred king to the war king or the stable to the active ruler (Hocart 1970a: 163). For, on the one hand, the Vunivalu also had aspects of divinity; indeed, as the procurer of human sacrifices by acts of transcendent violence, this "God of war" was in some respects the more terrible of the two kings. And, on the other hand, the

47. A tradition recounted by the pseudonymous Ko Veivuke (1897: 79) tells that the first Roko Tui Dreketi to rule Rewa was a sacred nephew (*vasu*) to that kingdom—thus implying the hierogamic union of a daughter of the indigenous people with the stranger-kings (of Verata descent) that marks other Fijian dynastic origins (see M. Sahlins 1985: chap. 3).

48. Early Sparta has been said to have had a similar system, its four villages divided into two pairs. One pair was close to the acropolis and under the senior of two royal homes, the Agiadai; the other pair, lower, in the marshes, settled later, was the home of the junior royal line, the Eurypontidae.

49. Thus European visitors of the early and mid-nineteenth century regularly designated the Vunivalu as "the governor." In practice, however, his military functions seem to have been upstaged at this time by younger brothers of the Roko Tui Dreketi, who were trying to make names for themselves, in rivalry with the king and each other, by establishing reputations for belligerence. However, it remained the case that the Vunivalu was "a man of great influence among these people [of Rewa], so much so that it is said they never go to war without his Consent, or Consulting him" (Stuart *J:* 18 May 1840).

Roko Tui Dreketi, for all his sacred power as the people's 'human god' (*kalou tamata*), was on that account the author of the practical policies and collective actions of the kingdom as well as the ritual fount of its well-being.[50]

The second form of dualism, the asymmetric dualism, was centered on the paramount Roko Tui Dreketi. The people revolved around the king "like planets around the sun," as Hocart put it in an analogous context, arguing that this centralized system was on its way to replacing dualism of the classic symmetrical or diametrical sort. Diametric dualism had become cheap in Fiji, Hocart thought, worked to death by the people's fondness for it. It was decadent: "A new and more solemn interest seems to have already been encroaching upon the old dualism weakened by excess. That newer enthusiasm was the service of the chief. He and his family were so far exalted above the rest as to upset the old balance of paired groups. . . . The two sides that used to face each other, equal except in precedence, have begun to break up into units which all face the chief, like planets around the sun" (1952: 58).

The centralization observed by Hocart may owe something to colonization. As usual, the British colonial administration was content to "find *the* chief"; it was never able to recognize Fijian dual kingship. My own reading, however, is that the asymmetric system has long coexisted with the bilateral one. Or rather it is the same system perceived and activated another way, by emphasizing—and repeating—the hierarchical distinction between chiefs and subjects. The effect is a scheme that is centralized in structure and at the same time concentrically laid out in space, focusing in both dimensions on the divine core of the polity, in Rewa the Roko Tui Dreketi. This hierarchical order is salient in events that concern the sacred king's person and, what is often the same, in relations between Rewa and outside powers, whether human or divine.

In such contexts, the kingdom operates as the worship of its "human god," the Roko Tui Dreketi (Hocart 1970a). The forms of obeisance owed the sacred king are the same as those accorded the invisible deities. "If reverence and devotion are required, as well as a belief in the supernatural, to make up religion, then the true religion of the Fijians is the service of the chief" (Hocart 1952: 26). Such "reverence" includes the practical obligations of the people to the chief. While collectively identified with regard to

50. For other examples of the traditional Fijian diarchy, see Hocart's descriptions thereof in the lands of Noco, Toga, Suva, Tokatoka, and Nakelo, all in the Rewa Delta (*HF:* passim); or again, his discussion of Bua, Cakaudrove, and various Vanua Levu lands (1952: passim; cf. Hale 1846: 61).

the ruling chiefs as the underlying "land," the several clans (*mataqali*) of the people are also differentiated by descent and identity as fishers, sailors, cultivators, carpenters, priests, or heralds of various kinds. Rarely are these full-time, specialized occupations. They are rather the distinctive functions the groups perform for the king and kingdom, services that they render to the Roko Tui Dreketi in ways tantamount to worship—the same term being applicable to serving the king and worshiping the god (*qaravi koya*). To invoke another (Ho-)Cartesian meditation, "there is no religion in Fiji, only a system which in Europe has split up into religion and business" (Hocart 1952: 256).

The centralized system is also a spatial order, appearing on the ground as a series of concentric zones, at the core of which are the establishments of the ruling personages and presences of the kingdom. The circles are built outward by the repeated use of the opposition between core and periphery, which is also a distinction of more and less divine power (*mana*)—hence Hocart's characterization of the system as the "inner and upper" versus the "outer and lower" (1968: 113). The absolute center is the ceremonial ground (*rārā*) of the kingdom, the site of major rituals and festivities (fig. 1.16b). Around the ceremonial ground are the domestic establishments of the two kings, the temples of great gods, and the tombs of departed rulers—all the spiritual cum political powers. The underlying land clans are domiciled beyond the ceremonial center, in Rewa along two rows running parallel to the Wailevu River.[51] Together, these land and chiefly people constitute Rewa proper or Lomanikoro ('Center of the village'). Beyond them, in settlements of close proximity but distinct name, are villages of 'foreigners' or 'outsiders' (*kai tani;* literally, 'different people'): two communities of Tongan sailors and another of the king's carpenters. The Tongans, Rewa's principal canoe men, are said to have come in the nineteenth century. Assimilated to Fijians in language and custom, they remain distinct in ethnicity, a minority population both in status and numbers—which, as will be seen momentarily, makes a nice contrast to the large presence of sea people in Bau.[52]

Again taken together, this central population of chiefs, land people, and

51. This may very well be a spatial realization of the diametric or moiety system, insofar as the two rows stretch outward from the houses of the Roko Tui Dreketi's people and the Vunivalu's. (In a brief period of fieldwork in Rewa, I was not able to check this out.) In some other Fijian places, such as Tubou in Lakeba, there were indeed chiefly and land sides of the village, separated by a shallow ditch (cf. Hocart 1970a: 255–56).

52. Something of an endogamous, outcast group, the carpenters may be classified with the Tongan sailors as sea people (*kai wai*), being water-borne also: they came down the Wailevu River, arriving by inland waterway. They are the land side of the sea people (see Rokowaqa 1926).

outsiders constitutes the *koro sau,* the 'ruling town' of Rewa, and as such it is the core of another series of concentric zones of the same nature. Beyond and around the ruling town are villages and lands of the indigenous Rewans, many of them related to land clans of the capital. Farther out are the countries of subject peoples (*qali*) and border allies (*bati*)—thus completing at the level of the kingdom as a whole the same concentric series of chiefs, land people, and outsiders that is found within the capital itself. The allied and subject lands have their own paramounts and their own gods, and accordingly a sense of their own independence, at the same time that they recognize their longstanding subordination to Rewa. The warrior allies or 'borders' (*bati*) are situated mainly to the north of the capital, in the Rewa Delta. As their contribution to the kingdom takes the form of fighting men rather than food, the latter being retained by them to supply the former, these border lands form a populous network of towns quite across the delta, where they faced the outlying communities of the Bau kingdom. The subject lands (*qali*) of Rewa lay primarily in the southern part of the delta and in the islands of Beqa and Kandavu. More servile than the border warriors, they could be levied for food as well as wealth and men—although Rewa's control in this area was not always secure, and had to be reaffirmed from time to time by force. To judge from missionary journals, in the nineteenth century, Rewa was fighting its own subjects as much as it was fighting Bau.

We shall see further on that in some respects, the Rewan spatial scheme resembled the Spartan landscape, with its true Spartiates in the center and the *perioecoi,* the slaves (helots), and the allies in successively peripheral regions.[53] But structurally as well as spatially, this "most perfect example" of a Fijian polity was significantly different from Bau.

It is true that Bau retained the essential features of the classical Fijian kingdom. It had the characteristic diarchy of sacred king and war lord, Roko Tui Bau and Vunivalu, each at the head of a moiety of clans, towns, and other lands (diametric dualism). At the same time, power radiated outward from the ceremonial center of Bau Island, on which were situated the residence of the Roko Tui Bau and the principal temple of the kingdom (concentric dualism). But in two significant ways, the Bauans overturned the typical Fijian order: structural transformations that tradition associates with the ruling chiefs' move to the island from the Viti Levu mainland. Fundamental to Bau's maritime orientation, here 'sea people' (*kai wai*)—

53. The land peoples surrounding the chiefly town are counted within the kingdom of Rewa proper, in which respect, as well as by their original possession of the country, they are indeed similar to the *perioecoi* of Sparta—particularly if it is true, as sometimes said, that the latter were descended from bronze age Achaeans (e.g., Huxley 1962: 25).

fishers, sailors, and sea warriors—became the mainstay of the kingdom, as opposed to indigenous cultivators or 'land people' (*kai vanua*); while fundamental to its militarism, in Bau the diarchy was inverted, making the Vunivalu war king the effective head of state and relegating the sacred king, the Roko Tui Bau, to a merely ceremonial precedence.

The indigenous people or 'owners' (*i taukei*) of Bau island were canoe men, by contrast to Rewa and other polities where the natives were land people and the sea people were foreigners. According to the tradition, Bau was originally home to four groups of sea people who served the chiefs of the adjacent mainland—the area called Kubuna, which is still the ceremonial name of the kingdom. Some generations (or centuries) back, the Kubuna chiefs drove the two leading sea groups off the island and then took up residence themselves. The exiled peoples, the Butoni and Levuka, settled in several other islands in and around the Koro Sea. These are the communities referred to earlier as quasi-colonies of Bau, since they were still known as Bauans and considered the Bau rulers to be their own "true chiefs." Back on Bau, two of the early sea peoples, the Lasakau and Soso groups, remained in place when the immigrant kings settled, and continued to function as royal fishers. They were also notable sea warriors. The Lasakau People (Kai Lasakau) especially: they were widely known as the 'dangerous men' (*tamata rerevaki*), not only because of their prowess, but for their office as procurers of the cannibal victims required in important ceremonials—in which pursuit they did not scruple about finding their prey in lands subject to Bau or even among their own kin in other kingdoms. "Very bloodthirsty and cruel," said Reverend Jaggar of the Lasakau, "much feared on that account; the circumstance of their having plenty of canoes at their command enables them the more effectively to carry their schemes into practice" (*WMMS/L:* 3 March 1845). A main source of Bauan power, which depended not a little on a reputation for terror, these sea peoples, unlike their (Tongan) counterparts in Rewa, were not marginal to the ruling town spatially, nor were they the lesser part of it numerically. Their own ceremonial grounds were near or adjacent to the principal ground at the center of the island. Taken together, the two sea clans clearly outnumbered the chiefly clans and their land people adherents on the island. The kings of Bau based their rule not on native cultivators but on native sailors and fishers—which is to say in Fijian categories, as in political strategies, not on the land but on the sea.[54]

54. The most complete version of the population of the island by sea people is found in the Lasakau, Soso, and Kubuna testimonies before the Native Lands Commission in NLC/TR (Bau), Tailevu North.

The second great transformation of the Bau polity was the inversion of the diarchy, the overthrow of the sacred kings (Roko Tui Bau) by the war kings (Vunivalu), who thus became in all but ritual respects the supreme power. Just how and when this happened is uncertain. It was certainly made definitive, however, in the early nineteenth or late eighteenth century when the reigning Roko Tui Bau was driven from the island and eventually killed by the Vunivalu's party. The overthrow was then politically sealed, even as it was also ritually undone, by installing one of the Vunivalu's people in the Roko Tui Bau title. For the existence of the sacred chief was a structural necessity, a condition of the possibility of the Bauan social order. Far from being able to eliminate the Roko Tui Bau kingship, the usurpers could not even deny its preeminent dignity. One reason was that in the traditional dual system of Bauan clans and lands, a moiety of the population of the kingdom were inherited subjects of the Roko Tui Bau. They had no relations or obligations to the Vunivalu except such as were transmitted through their "own chief," as the sacred king was known to them. The Roko Tui Bau was also ritually indispensable. As the human god, recipient of sacrifices in the principal temple—which, incidentally, gave him the reputation as the greatest cannibal in Fiji—the Roko Tui Bau's sacramental functions were the guarantee of the kingdom's welfare. Among these functions was his right to install the Vunivalu, thus giving legitimacy to the latter's greater authority on the condition of retaining his own chiefly superiority.[55] Still, the war lords governed Bau. The mayhem they customarily wreaked beyond the borders of the kingdom was now inscribed at its center, as its ruling principle. For these people were warriors by origin, by descent and therefore by nature. "We will fight till we die," Ratu Cakobau told the missionary. "We will teach our children to fight; and our children's children shall fight" (Waterhouse 1866: 86).

Here is the big historiographic point: such transformations of the Fijian cultural order should not be considered in isolation, as independent developments. The differences between Bau and Rewa are systemically and historically related. They are interdependent differences. This indeed is the sense of history encoded in the High Fijian Genealogy that encompasses the founding dynasties of the major kingdoms (fig. 1.17).[56] I call this the

55. Derived apparently from the Vunivalu people (Tui Kaba) and become the de facto second king of the diarchy, the Roko Tui Bau of the 1830s at least was not as inactive as traditional norms prescribed. Like the Vunivalu in Rewa, he could be designated by visiting Europeans as "the Old Governor" (Osborn *J:* 12, 28 July 1834).

56. I am making a distinction between the High Fijian Genealogy connecting the ancestors of different kingdoms and the local genealogies serving as charters for each of them. Such local genealogies are sometimes connected to the High Fijian Genealogy or sometimes

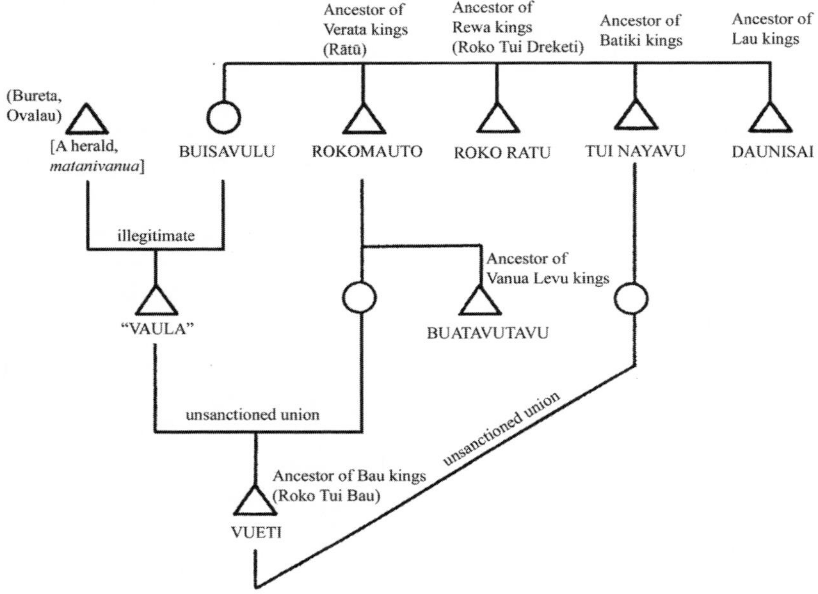

1.17 High Fijian Genealogy

High Fijian Genealogy because it amounts to an ancestral charter of the ruling aristocracies in much of windward Fiji: the littoral kingdoms of eastern Viti Levu, southern Vanua Levu, Lau, and certain Koro Sea islands. Like Greece, whose old nobility was significantly pan-Hellenic (Gernet 1981: 279–80), so were the Fijian polities interconnected by chiefly descent. The journeys of the royal ancestors constituted the natural order of their countries—the landscape, as named from parts of their bodies and incidents of their voyages—in the course of constituting the social order. First published in the 1890s (Denicagilaba 1892–94 [5]: 9–11), the genealogy is of unknown antiquity, although it clearly codifies political relations that have been in place since the beginning of the nineteenth century and in some cases much earlier. Key elements of the affiliations between the ancestors of Bau, Verata, and Batiki Island as set forth here are duplicated in more mythical terms in texts collected by Rev. William Cross in the 1830s

they replicate its relations in terms of specific, historical persons (e.g., Vuetiverata in Bau, as analogous to the mythical Vueti, founder of the Roko Tui Bau line). For the comparable distinction in classical studies between the Hellenic and polis genealogies, see J. Hall (1997: chap. 3).

and in more humanized terms in lineage genealogies collected recently in and around Bau (Cross in Lyth *TFR:* 97–98; Rosenthal *FN:* 3/18/88).[57]

The central figures of the High Fijian Genealogy are the ancestors of the Verata and Bau kingdoms, the divine Rokomoutu and the upstart Ratu Vueti, respectively. As it unfolds through the generations, the genealogy amounts to a narrative of the superiority achieved by the Bau ancestor Ratu Vueti, a figure of undistinguished paternity, over the first-born son of the ancient Fijian nobility, the godly Rokomoutu. In its own way, the genealogy thus rehearses the well-known historical tradition that in the not too distant past the parvenu Bau kingdom displaced aristocratic Verata as the leading *matanitū* in the Fiji Islands. Verata, Fijians say, is a 'kingdom of [the] blood' (*matanitū ni dra*), by invidious contrast to Bau, the notorious 'kingdom of force' (*matanitū ni kaukauwa*). Bau issued from a misalliance between the older sister of the great Rokomoutu and a lesser chieftain from a land of no particular account. Unnamed, this progenitor of Bauan kings is identified by a lesser title, as a herald (*matanivanua*) from Rakiraki in Viti Levu, a country associated with the creator god Degei and the indigenous first people. The ancestor of Bauan royalty would thus be a chieftain of the underlying land people, not even a chief (*turaga*) as such, and the capture of the high-ranking sister of the great Rokomoutu by the low-born herald of the native people is the reverse of the hypergamous union of the indigenous woman with the immigrant prince at the foundation of other Fijian ruling lines. The appropriation of the divine woman, moreover, was repeated in the following generations in the form of unsanctioned alliances between Bau ancestors and daughters of the Rokomoutu/Verata aristocracy. The significance of the High Fijian Genealogy for the differences between Bau and Rewa is that in this patrilineally oriented society, a younger brother such as the Rewan ancestor (Roko Ratu) is of the same nature as the older (Rokomoutu) and is entitled to succeed him, while a uterine nephew such as the Bauan ancestor (Ratu Vueti) is the plunderer of his maternal kinsmen. Indeed, as the earthly successor of their god, the uterine nephew is their divine usurper.

57. Because the High Fijian Genealogy was published in connection with an origin story (the Kaunitoni myth) involving a European-influenced cosmography, the genealogy risks being dismissed by the same sort of (cultural-genealogical) thinking that has deemed the myth inauthentic, despite its own clearly Fijian structural relationships (cf. France 1966). As for the genealogy, key elements such as the sister's son relations of Bau to other major kingdoms are found in the Cross and Rosenthal texts—from Viwa and Nakorotubu—and the Bau and Batiki land records. The *veitabani* or reciprocal oppositions of party subsisting between Bau and Verata likewise imply their descent from a brother and sister.

Here we need to know more about this special kinsman, the Fijian *vasu* or 'sister's son.' Highly obligatory and attended by various tabus, the rights accorded the *vasu* have earned this personage the anthropological description of the "sacred uterine nephew." In the prototypical ritual expression of *vasu* custom—often enough documented historically in the practical relations of high chiefs—an outrageous youth defiantly seizes the sacrifice destined for the gods of his mother's brother's people (Hocart 1915, 1923, 1926). The sons of the maternal uncle, the cross-cousins of the *vasu,* may show their resentment by pummeling him, but he keeps the offering (Hocart 1952: 142, 255). Consuming the sacrifice, appropriating the consecrated things, the uterine nephew thus replaces the god of his mother's people. What began in transgression is now sublimated in the divine honors and privileges accorded the *vasu* by his maternal relations. Hence the aforementioned charters of the origins of Fijian dynasties in the union of a powerful stranger-prince with a daughter of the indigenous people of the land, whence issues the child, *vasu* to the people, whom they will nurture (and domesticate) as their king. In the same way as he assumes the god's role ritually, the offspring of the daughter of the land gains the rule of it politically—the rule (*lewā*) but not the soil (*qele*), which remains with the native owners (*i taukei*). The foundation myth of the kingship has all the virtues of a Frazerian sacred marriage: the synthesis of heavenly procreative powers with the bearing earth, which is more saliently in Fiji a civilizing process that brings the cultural benefits of sea-borne kings to a relatively uncultured land people.

We can now appreciate what the High Fijian Genealogy is saying about arriviste Bau. The Bau kingship is the inverted image of Fijian royal legitimacy, a lineage of dubious and inferior descent that usurps the daughters of the ancient Fijian nobility. Bau is out of line: out of the royal patrilineal line by its lowly native origin, and doubly out of line for its ancestors' high-handed seizures of noble women. The "kingdom of force," Bau stands against the established chiefly order like the eternal uterine nephew, with an inherent disposition to overturn it—a kingdom defiant and divine.

It may be noted parenthetically that a charter myth of the same general form as the Fijian, involving a stranger-prince of godly descent who takes a daughter of the indigenous king and founds a new regime of political and natural order, is told of many a Greek city, as a perusal of Pausanias and Apollodorus would show. In the context of the analogous feat pulled off by Pelops—the fatal trick he played on the king of Pisa and Elis that garnered him the latter's daughter and kingdom—Préaux notes the extensive Indo-European distribution of this topos: "Every foundation of the city, every conquest of royal power becomes effective from the moment that the stranger charged with a sacredness by the gods or by the fates, endowed moreover with the force of the warrior, symbolically gains possession of a new land either by receiving peacefully, or by conquering valorously or through a ruse, the daughter of the King of the Land" (1962: 117; cf. M. Sahlins 1985: 73ff.).

But such analogies apart, the interesting historiographic issue is whether there obtain relationships of difference between Athens and Sparta similar to those the Fijians envisioned between Bau and Rewa. Precisely by coding the oppositions among the major Fijian kingdoms in genealogical terms, Fijians make a historical kinship out of their structural antitheses. The contrasts between polities are kindred differences. Bau's transgressions develop in systematic counterpoint to Rewa's conventions—which in turn are affirmed in the process. The process is coevolutionary. It is what Gregory Bateson called "complementary schismogenesis": a competition by contradiction, in which each side organizes itself as the inverse of the other. And since Bau's dynamism and Rewa's conservatism are in this way interdependent, one cannot write the history of one without the other. To adapt a phrase of Carlo Ginzburg's, "no island is an island."

ATHENS AND SPARTA AS HISTORICAL ANTITYPES

Behind the characterological contrasts between Athens and Sparta as perceived by Thucydides (and ventriloquated through the Corinthians) were large differences in cultural order that not only had their own histories but also had an interdependent history of complementary opposition. Athens and Sparta, I will argue, developed their fifth-century forms through the complex dialectic that engaged their internal conditions to their mutual relations. Dynamically interconnected, they were then reciprocally constituted. "Athens and Sparta," observed Victor Davis Hanson, "are states in a real war, but they are also metaphysical expressions of opposite ways of looking at the universe" (1996: xi). Athens was to Sparta as sea to land, cosmopolitan to xenophobic, commercial to autarkic, luxurious to frugal, democratic to oligarchic, urban to villageois, autochthonous to immigrant, logomanic to laconic: "one cannot finish enumerating the dichotomies," as Raymond Aron says (1961: 108). Athens and Sparta were cultural antitypes.

Consider, for an example, the cosmopolitan inclusiveness of the Athenians as against the xenophobic exclusiveness of the Spartans—an antithesis that itself extends from the ritual register through the political and the practical. One could say that the Athenian empire made an annual spectacle of itself in the great procession of the Panathenaia—famously represented in the Parthenon frieze—engaging foreigners as well as citizens in carrying the yearly sacrifices to the city goddess (Parke 1977). First opened to the participation of the Hellenic world in the late sixth century, the Panathenaia was elaborated in the fifth century, especially under Pericles. In the form of the Great Panathenaia (with athletic contests) held every fifth year, it became in effect a celebration of the Athenian domination that helped create it. Virtually all sectors of the heterogeneous Attic population, including the foreign residents, as well as people from the colonial cities and the tributary subjects, participated in the pageant of obeisance to Athena. A similar ritual submission marked the annual City Dionysia, which was indeed "the time when more Athenians and foreigners were gathered together in Athens than on any other occasion" (ibid., 133). A festival for opening the sailing season, the Dionysia was also the main theater season and the time the tributes of the allies were due—for display on the dancing floor of the theater.

Paul Cartledge (2001: 18–20) makes an interesting comparison between this politico-ritual encompassment and the exclusiveness of the Spartans' great national ceremony, the Hyacinthia, designed rather to differentiate the pure Spartiate core of the state. Spartan citizens alone were represented in the processions, thus distinguished from the helots, who were in attendance, and the peripheral Laconians (*perioecoi*) and foreigners, who were altogether excluded. Cartledge comments:

> The Hyakinthia's military-style processions and musical and athletic contests . . . were open only to Spartan citizens. Indeed the only non-Spartans present at the Hyakinthia—in contrast especially to the Gymnopaidai festival, at which distinguished foreign guests were made welcome, or the Promakheia, at which the Perioikoi were given a significant role—were Helots. . . . The Hyakinthia in short, like the Spartan system of urbanization as a whole, was consciously designed to emphasize and reinforce the centre's separation from and hierarchical domination of the periphery. Whereas the normal and normative Greek *polis* united town and country in a harmonious political symbiosis, Sparta was in this respect, as in so many others, atypical, if not unique. (20)

Distinguished guests perhaps excepted, foreigners as a rule were not warmly welcomed in Sparta of the fifth century—any more than Spartans were wandering much abroad. Whether or not the prohibitions to such effect were laid down by Lycurgus, as was generally believed at the time, the periodic 'driving out of foreigners' (*xenēlasia*) was still in force when the Peloponnesian War began (Thuc. 1.144.3; Xen., *Const. Laced.* XIV.4; Powell 1988: 214). Referring to the Spartans' alien act by invidious contrast to the Athenians' openness to all comers, Pericles offered the kind of functional explanation that still appeals to many moderns: namely, that Sparta's exclusion of foreigners was motivated by the concern to guard her secrets from her enemies (Thuc. 2.23.1). The explanation ignores the complementary disadvantage of preventing Spartans from living abroad, thus keeping them ignorant of their enemies—as the Corinthians said they were. Taken together, these measures are more reminiscent of the antiforeign edicts that the Chinese have been issuing periodically since the T'ang dynasty to protect themselves against spiritual pollution. Witnessing something similar to such pollution in the decadence that followed Sparta's victory in the Peloponnesian War, Xenophon came to just such a conclusion about the virtues of the old exclusion laws: "There were alien acts in former days, and to live abroad was illegal; and I have no doubt that the purpose of these regulations was to keep the citizens from being demoralized by contact with foreigners" (*Const. Laced.* XIV.4).[58] The Great Wall of China functioned at least as much to keep the Chinese in as it did to keep the barbarians out, marking the ecological cum cultural limit beyond which the specifically Chinese order could not be sustained (O. Lattimore 1940). The comparison is perhaps apt, inasmuch as Lycurgus, when asked whether Sparta should not be enclosed by a wall, is supposed to have replied that "the city is well fortified that hath a wall of men" (Plut., *Lyc.* 19). The Spartans were enjoined to fortify themselves against the outside in their customs and dispositions. They could best resist invasion, Lycurgus said, "by continuing poor, and not coveting each man to be greater than his fellow" (ibid.). Lycurgus, observed Plutarch, "was as careful to save his city from the infection of foreign habits as men usually are to prevent the introduction of a pestilence" (ibid., 10).

As Moses Finley put it, no Greek state was a match for Sparta in exclusiveness and xenophobia: "The whole system was closed against outside influence, against outsiders in person and against imported goods" (1964: 65). As the (invention of) tradition goes, Lycurgus prohibited the private

58. Likewise Plutarch, who says Lycurgus forbade Spartans to travel about lest they acquaint themselves with "foreign rules of morality, the habits of ill-educated people, and different rules of government." Plutarch also disagrees with Thucydides on the reasons Lycurgus banished strangers from Laconia. It was not, he says, because they would learn something in Sparta, but that they might "introduce something contrary to good manners" (*Lyc.* 27).

possession of silver and gold, and banned all imports and luxury goods. Sparta was to be self-sufficient materially, as it was closed socially and politically. The Spartans did not mint their own coins until the third century, even though their iron spit money was not acceptable abroad. The lawgiver thus "took away from wealth, as Theophrastus observes, not merely the property of being coveted, but its very nature of being wealth" (Plut., *Lyc.* 10). Nor were Spartan citizens permitted to engage in commerce or mechanical trades.[59] The state-allotted lands of Spartiate men were worked by helot labor, while they lived their famous barracks culture of rigorous military training, age-grade organization, public discipline, communal eating groups, and institutionalized pederasty (cf. Hodkinson 1983; Plut., *Mor.* V.3). The system effectively devalued the household (*oikos*). In fact, it was "a reaction against the tradition of the *oikos,*" say Austin and Vidal-Naquet, "reducing family life to a minimum" (1977: 82–83). As such it would deprive the economy of energy—as by the limitation or suppression of desire. Simplicity, austerity, and equality were to rule consumption. And in this society of 'peers' (*homoioi*), an essential uniformity was enjoined in the objects of personal and familial existence: houses and furnishings, dress and diet. "Luxury," says Plutarch, "deprived little by little of that which fed and fomented it, wasted to nothing and died away of itself" (*Lyc.* 9). Athenaeus tells of a certain visiting Sybarite who, upon dining in Sparta, remarked it was "no wonder that the Spartans are the bravest men in the world; for anyone in his right mind would prefer to die ten thousand deaths than to share in such poor living" (*Deip.* 4.138.2).[60]

59. "And indeed one of the greatest blessings Lycurgus procured his people was the abundance of leisure which proceeded from his forbidding them the exercise of any mean and mechanical trade. Of the money-making that depends on troublesome going about and seeing people and doing business, they had no need at all in a state where wealth obtained no honor or respect" (Plut., *Lyc.* 24).

60. Although Agesilaus was presiding over the decline of Sparta, the sayings attributed to him by Plutarch (in "Sayings of the Spartans") distinctively include several references to Lycurgan material restraint and the unusual Spartan economy. Unlike many of the other bons mots recorded by Plutarch that seem to be freely exchangeable among Spartan rulers (he gives the same anecdotes to different kings at different times), those of King Agesilaus referring to the Spartans' disdain of money, commerce, and the like are often uniquely so attributed (Plut., *Apoth. Lac.* 72; see Plutarch [1931: 279]). One of the best was the answer to the complaint of Sparta's allies about the disproportionately large number of their soldiers, compared to so few of the Spartans, who were continually campaigning on the Spartans' behalf. Agesilaus "gave orders that the allies all sit down together indiscriminately and the Spartans separately by themselves; and then, through the herald, he commanded the potters to stand up first; and when these had done so, he commanded the smiths to stand up next, and then the carpenters in turn, and the builders, and each of the other trades. As

Besides the systematic austerity, the Spartans fortified themselves with encircling barriers of ritual protection and ethnic distinction. Recall that Cartledge spoke of a certain spatial system of Spartan xenophobia—"the centre's separation from and domination of the peripherae"—like Hocart's "inner and upper" versus "outer and lower" form of Fijian concentric dualism. In the Spartan case, the core consisted of the four original communities of true Spartiates (or five, with Amyclai, apparently something like the indigenous people of the land). This mere collection of old-fashioned villages, as Thucydides said, could show no measure of Sparta's fame in the remains she would leave for posterity, whereas the ruins of Athens in time to come would make her power seem twice as great as it actually was (1.10.2). Here was another fifth-century antithesis, which also proves that Pericles' grandiose building program had made its political point. By contrast, Spartan religious politics was more invested in the series of sanctuaries set around the core Spartiate villages, divinely demarcating and guarding them, beyond which lay an extensive cordon of free *perioecoi* communities (Cartledge 2001: 9ff.). (Note that the *perioecoi* were effectively interposed between the Spartans and the sea, which was again rather the opposite of the Athenian insularity.) Another surround of sanctuaries that included the *perioecoi* and excluded the helots of the hinterland marked the borders of Laconia. These were the boundary sanctuaries beyond which it was dangerous for Spartan armies to proceed without divine sanction. Finally, the allies of the Peloponnesian League, supposed to have been constituted by Sparta with an eye to the threat of helot uprisings, formed the outermost enceinte of this secretive state—which still remains largely unknown to the world.

So just who or what was Cleisthenes thinking of in 508, when he proposed a democratic constitution for Athens that would give each of the ten newly created tribes a share of the three main ecological zones of the state (the coast, the city, and the agricultural interior)? As this inclusiveness was also something of the inverse of Sparta's concentric system, could it be relevant that the Athenians hurriedly adopted Cleisthenes' reform in the face of a Spartan attempt to restore the kind of tyranny the Athenians had overthrown not long before? Since Aristotle at least, the scholars have been wont to explain Athens and Sparta genealogically—that is, by deriving

a result, pretty nearly all of the allies stood up, but of the Spartans, not a single one; for there was a prohibition against their practicing or learning an menial calling. And so Agesilaus, with a laugh, said, 'you see men, how many more soldiers we send out than you do'" (ibid., 279).

their constitutions from other, earlier states through some (murky) process of inheritance or diffusion. So the constitution of Athens might be derived from the experimental regimes of certain Greek colonies, and that of Sparta, famously, from Crete. But at least as much attention ought to be given to synchronic processes as to diachronic ones, to the contemporary generation of differences by opposition as to the historical transmission of similarities by descent. Cultural differences, Lévi-Strauss has said, are not so much the product of the isolation of groups as they are of relations between them (1952: 10). The model of the democratic Athenian territorial integration (synoecism) may well have been the Spartan centripetal system of hierarchy, precisely insofar as the former is the negation of the latter. Determination is negation.

In the same connection, the Spartan support of tyranny in Athens around 508 was a transitional moment in the entirely novel antithesis of oligarchy and democracy, which the Spartans and the Athenians respectively championed in the fifth century, especially in the course of the Peloponnesian War. Perhaps nothing could better illustrate the dynamics of complementary opposition, since in the preceding decades, and despite their supposed disinclination for foreign adventures, the Spartans had been intervening militarily against tyrannies in several cities—Athens, as well as Corinth, Naxos, Sikyon, and Samos, among others—an intervention that would be consistent with their own (ideologically) egalitarian regime. But now the two cities had switched identities in the matter of which was the party of the many.[61] As in Corcyra or Thrace during the Peloponnesian War, the Spartans backed the insurgent oligarchs against the Athenian support of the *demos.* Lévêque and Vidal-Naquet say that not enough has been made of this schismogenic reversal: "it has not been emphasized enough that the political reversal [from tyranny to democracy] that took place in Athens under the aegis of Cleisthenes was accompanied by a symmetrical reversal in the Lacedaemonians' foreign policy . . . the first in date of the ideological conflicts that were to develop between Athens and Sparta. It was beginning in 508 that Sparta began to play the role of gendarme for the oligarchies" (1997: 30–31).

As a historiographic principle, however, schismogenesis would have to compete with the longstanding tradition of conceiving Sparta as an an-

61. To follow Lévêque and Vidal-Naquet, the sixth century opposed tyranny to isonomy; at the turn of the century, the latter term was differentiated into its democratic and oligarchic components as Athens and Sparta respectively backed the rule of the many and the few (1997: 18ff.).

cient, self-generated cultural formation, sprung more or less full-blown from the head of Lycurgus four hundred years before the Peloponnesian War, to believe Thucydides, or more like five hundred, to believe Plutarch. "Spartan mirage" this may be, yet it finds its complement in the modern scholarly hypothesis that the distinctive Spartan institutions were developed as instrumental means of maintaining the subjugation of the Messenian helots, conquered in the late eighth century, and definitively subdued about two generations later (c. 660) in a Second Messenian War occasioned by a large-scale uprising. But since the prosperity and trade achieved by Sparta in the aftermath of the Messenian Wars effectively dispels the mirage of a self-enclosed and austere society, at least until the end of the sixth century, it is clear that the helot-domination theory of Spartan uniqueness should also be revisited. Accepting this late development, my own suggestion is to fold the Messenian issue into the schismogenic opposition of Sparta to her foreign adversaries, Argos, Arcadia, and especially Athens. The internal helot threat was largely generated by the external Athenian one. It is in this triadic conjuncture that the Messenians discovered their ethnic unity, and the Spartans and Athenians their structural antipathy.

First, then, to approach the Spartan mirage close enough to make it recede. For if anything, the conquest of Messenia, rather than turning Sparta into a "grand village morose et fermé aux nouveautés" (Ollier 1933–43: 45), on the contrary made it the wealthiest state in Greece. The eighth-century conquest initiated an era of artistic and mechanical production, and of long-distance imports and exports, that changed shape from time to time but did not slacken until the end of the sixth century.[62] This has been known to classicists for some time. Already the excavations of the sanctuary of Artemis Ortheia at the beginning of the twentieth century "proved that the 'austere' Sparta of the myth had no counterpart in reality before the mid-sixth century at the earliest" (Cartledge 2002: 133). Cartledge talks about the initial conquest of Messenia launching Sparta into the Mediterranean orbit of trade in luxury goods and raw materials, and introducing it "to the most progressive ('orientalizing') artistic currents of the day" (ibid., 103). For at the beginning of the seventh century, rich votive offerings of precious materials—gold, silver, ivory, faience, amber—imported from

62. Besides Ollier's (1933–43) debunking of the Spartan mirage, I base this discussion of the Spartan economy primarily on Cartledge (2001: chap. 12; 2002), Hodkinson (2000), and Whitby (2002), as well as Moses Finley's now classic discussion of the "sixth century Spartan revolution" (1975: 161–77)—much of which may be late sixth century and even fifth century.

many parts of Greece and beyond were being presented at Artemis Ortheia; even as the kind of Laconian bronze horse figures found there were also circulating from Italy to Samos. The mid-seventh century, following the Second Messenian War, saw the florescence of Laconian ivory-carving. Made from raw materials imported from the Near East, these fine objects of Laconian craftsmanship were distributed all about the Mediterranean. "Historically and art-historically, what is most absorbing and significant about this plethora of ivory work is the revelation of an almost totally unexpected Sparta, one which—contrary to the literary image—was open both physically and spiritually to the outside world, and especially to the non-Greek Orient" (Cartledge 2001: 176). Hans van Wees argues that the same could be said poetically. The poetry of Alcman (c. 600) reinforces the art historical picture of a seventh- and sixth-century Laconian elite, "engaged in all forms of conspicuous consumption of wealth and leisure characteristic of archaic Greece. . . . Indeed in Alcman's time Sparta appears to have had a reputation for attaching overriding importance to wealth" (van Wees 1999: 3–4). Spartan trade and openness to the outside extended well into the sixth century. Between 575 and 525 the production of pottery and bronzework flourished. Laconian black-figure pottery was distributed from the Black Sea to Spain. Its subsequent and rapid decline is usually attributed to competition from Athenian pottery. But finally, by the end of the century Sparta was approaching the condition of autarky that Lycurgus had supposedly decreed for it hundreds of years before.[63]

Sparta's military and political presence in the larger Greek world lasted longer, however. Sparta was fighting Tegea and Argos on and off during the last half of the sixth century, as well as intervening against tyrannies in Athens and farther afield. Of the two "prominent" peoples in Greece around 550, the Athenians and the Spartans, the latter were more powerful, the Lydian king Croesus determined, and he thereupon proposed an alliance with them (Hdt.1.56ff.). The Spartans maintained their leadership of the Hellenes through the Persian Wars, only relinquishing it to the Athenians in 478—at the time Athens was making its decisive commitment to sea power. This was a critical turning point, then, for both states. The Spartans decided their interests lay elsewhere than in challenging the Athenians on the sea or for the hegemony—and in searching for wealth this way—according to Diodorus Siculus' notice of their deliberations

63. Do Austin and Vidal-Naquet exaggerate? "In fact it would seem from the evidence of archaeology," they say, "that imports to Sparta ceased completely in the course of the sixth century" (1977: 70).

(XI.50). They settled, in effect, for a competition in lifestyle rather than direct military and economic competition. Diodorus (or his principal source, Ephorus) marks a key moment in his account of a meeting of the Spartan Gerousia, the thirty-member Council of Elders, in 475. The meeting was convened to consider making war on the Athenians, "for the sake of regaining the command of the sea." Earlier, in a general assembly on the same issue, "the younger men and the majority of the others were eager to recover the leadership, believing that, if they could secure it, they would enjoy great wealth, Sparta in general would be made greater and more powerful, and the estates of its private citizens would receive a great increase of prosperity." (So much for the ideology of Lycurgan austerity and, for that matter, uniformity and equality—if Diodorus is to be believed.) Diodorus' text continues with the deliberations of the Gerousia:

> Since practically all the citizens had been eager for this course of action and the Gerousia was in session to consider these matters, no one entertained the hope that any man would have the temerity to suggest any other course. But a member of the Gerousia, Hetoemaridas by name, who was a direct descendent of Heracles and enjoyed favor among the citizens by reason of his character, undertook to advise that they leave the Athenians with their leadership, since it was not in Sparta's interest, he declared, to lay claim to the sea. He was able to bring pertinent arguments in support of his surprising proposal, so that, against the expectation of all, he won over both the Gerousia and the people. And in the end the Lacedaemonians decided that the opinion of Hetoemaridas was to their advantage and abandoned their zest for war against the Athenians. (Diod. Sic. XI.50)

So if the Spartans were land-based, helot-concerned, inward-looking homebodies without any interest in maritime and economic prowess, it was a surprise to a great many of them in 475. By way of a footnote it could be added that the identification of Hetoemaridas as a descendant of Heracles (as was Lycurgus), if it was intended to vouch for his credibility, also redoubles the opposition to Athens on the mythological plane, where a contrast between Heracles, ancestor of Spartan kings, and the Athenian king Theseus had been under way for some decades (Calame 1990b: 404).[64] Still, despite the apparent turn of Spartan policy in the 470s, "evi-

64. On the distinction of the descendants of Heracles within Sparta, see Plutarch (*Lys.* 24).

dence of broader Hellenic interests is not lacking." Peter Fleiss observes: "An anxious concern for Megara, . . . attempts to break the power of Thessaly, and action in the more distant island of Zacynthus in the Ionian Sea—all confirm that Spartan leadership was keeping a watchful eye on events beyond its immediate sphere of influence" (1966: 38).

It was from this time, however, that the number of Spartiate soldiers began to decline sharply. Perhaps eight thousand or more in 480, the citizen warriors numbered only about one thousand at the time of the Battle of Leuctra in 371. The argument of Cartledge, Hodkinson, and others is that growing inequalities in land tenure among Spartan male citizens made it impossible for poorer men to contribute to the communal messes, causing them to lose their hoplite status. It is sometimes further argued that the Spartan cult of poverty, uniformity of consumption, and the like was a reaction to this, as a kind of functional cover-up that maintained a necessary solidarity in the face of the growing inequality. Be that as it may, the date of such aspects of the Spartan "revolution" would then be the fifth century, not the sixth. And according to Cartledge (2001), this would also be the time of its ideological corollary, the famous Spartan mirage:

> It was during this period of a hundred years [480–371], as relations between Spartans and Helots, and between Sparta and the outside world, deteriorated, that the mirage was born—or rather manufactured, at first by the nervous Spartans themselves. It was then taken up, for their own domestic purposes, by aggressively oligarchic, especially [dissident] Athenian, propagandists. In its cultural aspect the mirage was not entirely devoid of correspondence with the Spartan reality, but its pseudo-historical underpinning in terms of Lykourgan prohibitions was of course just so much gossamer and gossip. (183)

The issue of present moment is not so much to debunk the mirage but to understand its significance. The question is not so much its historical veracity as the historical conditions of its appearance. In this connection two aspects of Cartledge's statement should attract our attention. First, the mirage develops not in relation to the helot problem alone, but to the correlated deterioration of Sparta's relations with the outside world, the Athenians above all. Second, Cartledge suggests that as of the fifth century, the mirage bears some correspondence to Spartan cultural realities. Of course, it is safe to say—as Moses Finley did of "the sixth-century revolution"—that the Spartan system did not evolve all at once, and also that elements of it—the dual kingship, for example, or the age-grade system—were probably ancient. It is safe to say, too, that no one knows exactly when and in what order specific Spartan practices came into being as cultural realities. But clearly a fair number of these distinctive features, which seem to be systematically interrelated as well, had developed only since the late sixth century, in the context of "the growing power of the Athenians and the fear this inspired in the Spartans." The following would be among these late developments: the suspension of foreign trade; the demonization of commerce generally and the mechanical arts; the suppression of luxury consumption; the near total dependence on agriculture and land-based military force to the exclusion of maritime activity; the publicly enforced equality, simplicity, and uniformity of lifestyle; and the secrecy, restrictions on foreign contacts, and other such defenses against moral corruption—the last an aspect of a general and radical xenophobia, and a correlated disengagement from foreign political affairs and military ventures.

Where, then, does this leave the modern scholarly complement of the mirage, to the effect that classical Sparta is a formation designed to keep down the Messenian helots, who were definitively conquered and enserfed in the first half of the seventh century? This is "the current orthodoxy," as Michael Whitby (2002) says: "The current orthodoxy, certainly in Anglophone scholarship, is that the helots provide the explanation of the whole Spartan system, since not only did their labour underpin the privileged military life of full citizens but their persistent rebelliousness determined the development and operation of the Spartan system, both within Laconia and through the need to supervise and repress the servile population, and in the wider world because Sparta was afraid to divert scarce resources to external ventures" (178).

The consequences of Sparta's victory over the Messenians, as Forrest put it (1968: 38), "determined her history for three centuries and more"; it was, in Andrewes's words, "a large step along the path that made Sparta different from other states" (1971: 63). Where other Greek poleis would have to meet their land needs by colonization, Sparta, so the argument runs, had a great agricultural future in helot manpower and arable land at her doorstep. "At one stroke she committed herself to an almost purely agricultural future and robbed herself of the incentive to look outside her new borders" (Forrest 1968: 38). G. E. M. de Sainte-Croix gave added persuasiveness to the thesis by pointing out the peculiar nature and difficulties of the Spartan domination of the Messenian helots (1972: 89–90). The peculiarity was that the Spartans had subjugated an entire ethnic group in their native territory, and at that collectively, as serfs of the Spartan state (who were only allocated to the use of individual Spartan citizens). The condition of the helots was unlike that of slaves in other city-states, who were ethnically heterogeneous, polyglot, individually owned, and commercially salable—hardly the stuff of slave revolts. But the Messenians never lost consciousness of their identity, or perhaps took even greater consciousness of it in their captivity, and when they were liberated by the Thebans' defeat of the Spartans in 371, they were able to reestablish a state that had lapsed for three centuries. "Only the Spartans," said Sainte-Croix, "lived on top of a potentially active volcano" (1972: 90). So if the Spartans were stay-at-homes for whom it was dangerous to venture abroad, it was because they had constructed a system in which eternal surveillance was the price of their liberty.[65]

One problem is that the greater part of the Spartans' cultural distinctiveness did not happen until two or three hundred years after their subjugation of the Messenians. A second problem is that, for the same period from the Second Messenian War (c. 660) to the helot revolt of c. 466–65, there is no clear indication of slave uprisings in Spartan territory. We have no evidence that the Messenians were always revolting. Neither is there evidence that they were always Messenians. On the contrary, the recent researches of Thomas Figueira (1999) would make the Messenian identity a development of the fifth century rather than a legacy of the eighth: a kind of political ethnogenesis that was aided and abetted by the Athenians in their own anti-Spartan interests. What apparently is at issue here is the constitution of the Messenians as a polis, like other Greek peoples. Such Messenian national identity was especially promulgated among and by the various refugees of the 460s helot revolt who were settled by the Athenians at Naupactus. These "Messenians" continued to be allies of the Athenians through the Peloponnesian War (ibid., 215, 232). Endorsing Figueira's conclusions, Hodkinson (2000: 128) observed that "the main inspiration of a separate Messenian identity—which took place relatively late during the period of her subjugation to Sparta, after the 460s revolt—was external Athenian propaganda, which was firmly resisted by the Spartans."

That the Spartans' Messenian troubles were not independent of their foreign troubles was actually the intuition of the ancients, Thucydides and Aristotle specifically—who are often cited, however, in support of the modern explication of the Spartan order by the functional necessities of control arising from the eighth-century conquest. Thucydides raises the general issue in the context of the Athenian occupation of Messenian Py-

65. Among other expressions of "the current orthodoxy," see Kagan (1969: 29), McGregor (1987: 31–32), and Powell (1988: 98).

los in 424. He relates that the Spartans, fearing now that the Athenians would encourage other helots to rebel, sent seven hundred of them out of the country with Brasidas' army. In combination with another (undated) incident in which the Spartans disappeared two thousand helots by ruse, Thucydides speaks of the Spartans' fear of the helots' "numbers and obstinacy," and of Spartan "policy at all times having been governed by the necessity of taking precautions against them" (4.80.2–3).[66] For his part, Aristotle similarly likened the helots to "an army constantly sitting in wait for the disasters of the Spartans" (*Pol.* 1269). Natural disasters apart, what often seems to escape scholarly notice is the implication (Aristotle) or the indication (Thucydides) of an external *tertium quid* in the master-slave relations of the Spartans and the Messenians—namely, the enemies of Sparta, who were necessary conditions of the possibility of Messenian resistance. Enlisted by the Spartans to help put down the helot revolt of the 460s, in accord with their mutual obligations under a treaty then in force, the Athenians were abruptly dismissed and sent home because the Spartans feared some collusion between the rebels and these "revolutionary Athenians" (Thuc. 1.102.1–4).[67] And as noted before, when the Messenians were finally liberated in 371/370, it was by virtue of the successful Theban invasion of Laconia. In sum, the Spartans' helot problem, which became critical in the fifth century along with the formulation of a Messenian identity, was a *bagarre à trois,* developing in conjunction with the Athenian challenge to Spartan hegemony.

But then, as a species of instrumental reason, the necessity of keeping down the Messenians could never have been an adequate explanation of the Spartan cultural formation. Speaking to desirable effects rather than

66. Jowett's translation of Thuc. 4.80.3 was even more explicit about the helot influence on the Spartan order: "most of the Lacedaemonian institutions were specially intended to guard them against this danger." Likewise Hobbes: "for the Lacedaemonians had even many ordinances concerning how to look to themselves against the helots." Gomme (1956: 547–48), Hornblower (1996: 265), and Cartwright (1997: 186), in their respective commentaries, reject the Hobbes and Jowett reading in favor of one more like Crawley's. But Cartwright goes on to say that "the helots vastly outnumbered the Spartans, who, since the conquest of Messenia, had adjusted their way of life to ensure mastery of their serf neighbours" (ibid.).

67. In describing this event, Thucydides indicates some of the "Messenian" identity issues. After noting that the rebels consisted of "the Helots and the Thurians [a place in Messenia] and Aethaeans [in Messenia] of the *perioikoi,*" Thucydides goes on to say that "most of the Helots were the descendants of the old Messenians that were enslaved in the famous war, and so all of them came to be called Messenians" (1.101.2). Figueira (1999) argues that the Athenians particularly called them "Messenians," the Spartans, "Helots."

determinate forms, such functions as control do not specify such properties as, say, suspension of trade, let alone that any number of other structures could have achieved the same finality. To be convinced of the insufficiency of the function as the *raison d'être* of the form, it is only necessary to turn the explanation around. The Spartans needed to maintain their subjugation of the helots: therefore, they practiced economic self-denial, refused to engage in foreign trade or foreign travel, resisted innovation, broke up the conjugal household, disdained money, enforced a strict egalitarianism, donned the same clothing, ate black broth, institutionalized pederasty, and developed an allergy to salt water!?! That the Spartan solution to the Messenian problem was not the only one possible is confirmed by the fact that other societies—most proximate historically, the Persians and the Romans—conquered and exploited whole peoples, and were menaced by ethnic or slave rebellions, without the benefit of Spartan-like institutions. If anything, the Messenian conquest suggests that the Spartans were already different in some ways from other Greeks—could one not say, Dorian and immigrant?—well back in the eighth century. It was already unusual for one Hellenic people to enslave another, let alone in the particular way the Spartans did. In certain respects, then, the Spartan cultural scheme was a precondition of its functional specifications rather than the other way around. At all events, the necessity of dealing with unruly "Messenians" arose centuries later, and in the context of an ongoing confrontation with Sparta's external enemies. Whatever the internal functional values of Spartan institutions, the Spartans were now involved in a dialogue of complementary differentiation with the Athenians. In the fifth century the Spartans became, in Hanson's phrase, *anti-Athenian:* "Inward, blinkered, reluctant to venture on the sea, Sparta's self-interested conservatism took on the appearance of an anti-Athenian philosophy" (1996: xviii–xix).

GREECE MYTHISTORICUS

In the fifth century Athens and Sparta were making a system of their differences. They joined in schismogenic competition on the principle that each was as good as and better than, the same as and different from, the other. Elegantly articulating this principle, myths were now elaborated in the two poleis, as of Theseus in Athens and Lycurgus in Sparta, which gave the evolving structural differences between them discursive effect in the act of representing them. The Theseus discourse of the Athenians also entailed a certain counterpoint to the Heraclean (cum Dorian) traditions of the Spartans, although the opposition could only be relative, given the pan-Hellenic honors enjoyed by both heroes. Still, in the late sixth century the proponents of the fledgling Athenian democracy were making a specifically national hero of Theseus, by contrast to the regard the recently deposed tyrants had accorded to Heracles (Calame 1990b: 404). The opposition continued to be developed in the fifth century, when the Athenians were facing off against the Spartan state that owed its foundation to the so-called Return of the Heraclids, and whose kings traced their descent to Heracles—thus to the demi-paternity of Zeus.[68] Theseus, by direct contrast, was not only the great unifier of the Athenian polis (the celebrated synoecism) but also the reputed author of the people's democratic power.[69] As Calame put it, Theseus and his legendary exploits were in effect extracted from the traditions of other cities and elevated to the status of an Athenian charter myth (cf. Paus. 1.3.3). This heroization—including the tradition that Theseus had appeared in spirit before the Athenian forces at Marathon—was notably bolstered by the restoration of his (alleged) bones to the city by Cimon in 475, amid joyous processions and celebrations. "Henceforth," observes Robert Parker (1996: 168), "Theseus towered over all other Athenian heroes in cult as well as in story." Several shrines were dedicated to him, including the great one established by Cimon. A large-scale festival, the Thesia, was devoted to him, and a number of other festivals underwent what Parker calls "an *interpretatio Thesaia,*" as they were associated with events of his life (ibid., 169). Most interesting in the present context is the connection, by way of myth, between Athens' turn to Theseus and her turn to sea power: "As a son of Poseidon, he [Theseus] could become a symbol of Athenian heroism by sea as well as by land, and it was with a great sacrifice at Rhion to him and his father (duly commemorated by an inscription at Delphi) that Phormion's fleet celebrated its victories in the Corinthian gulf in 429" (ibid., 169–70).[70]

The traditions of Theseus, as gathered notably by Plutarch, display the schismogenic principle by likening the Athenian hero to Heracles and Lycurgus as the same and yet different, equal and yet better. As the origi-

68. Note that at the end of Euripides' *Heracleidae* (1955), the Argive king Eurysthenes, great enemy of Heracles, will in death become the protector of Athens against Heracles' children's children—among whom were the original kings of Sparta.

69. In *The Suppliant Women* (c. 420–415), Euripides crowns the (anachronistic) tradition of Theseus as founder of the Athenian democracy, the hero proclaiming, "This city is free and ruled by no one man. / The people reign, in annual succession. / They do not yield the power to the rich; / The poor man has an equal share in it" (1958b: lines 405–8).

70. The Roman-period "Arch of Hadrian," built as an approach to the shrine-rich southeastern region of Athens, has carved into its western façade, "This is Athens, the ancient city of Theseus," and on the east, "This is the city of Hadrian, not of Theseus" (Wycherley 1978: 155).

nator of the Athenian democracy, Theseus is comparable to Heracles, the ancestor of the Peloponnesian kings, although precisely as Heracles founded the kingship, Theseus renounced it and gave power to the people. Moreover, Theseus, whose feats inspired the encomium "Here is a second Heracles," was the Spartan royal ancestor's double. Explicitly emulating Heracles, who was his idol, his sometimes companion-in-arms, and his (classificatory) cross-cousin (what Fijians would make of that!), Theseus even duplicated the famous labors of Heracles by doing away with a horde of scourges and monsters on the way from his birthplace in Troezen to claim his royal heritage in Athens. (The Hephaisteion above the agora, which used to be identified as the Theseion, has the labors of Heracles on its front frieze, the labors of Theseus on the two side friezes.) Yet if Theseus was, like Lycurgus, a great lawgiver, the laws he gave Athens were the diametric contraries of those bequeathed by the Spartan culture hero—and of course, so much better from an Athenian point of view. Not only did he set the Athenian people free, but he also opened the city to the world: "to increase the size of the city still further, Theseus invited people from every quarter to settle there on equal terms with the Athenians. In fact, the current phrase 'Come hither, all ye peoples!' is supposed to have originated as a proclamation, employed by Theseus, when he established a commonwealth which endowed all sorts and conditions of men" (Plut., *Thes.* 25). But then, as the foreigners (*metics*) of Athens were famously merchants and craftsmen, Theseus was effectively sponsoring the commercial development of the city—again in contrast to the Lycurgan economic underdevelopment and generalized xenophobia. There are numerous other detailed contrasts in the two traditions, such as the introduction of silver coinage by Theseus and its interdiction by Lycurgus. Suffice it to say that Lycurgus and Theseus, at least in their fifth-century representations, were protagonists in a mythological *agon.*

Autochthony was another diacritical distinction vaunted by the Athenians in the fifth century particularly, in clear counterpoint to the Dorian immigrants of Sparta (cf. J. M. Hall 1997: 53ff.; Cohen 2000: 79ff.). Literary notice of the Athenians as descendants of the earth-born king Erechtheus now appear in Pindar (470s), Aeschylus' *Agamemnon* (458), and Sophocles' *Ajax* (late 440s).[71] The autochthonous theme also appears in

71. Classicists say this fifth-century claim of autochthony entailed a shift in the meaning of the term from something like "indigenous" or "having always occupied the same land" to "born of the earth." However, insofar as the Athenians reckoned themselves descendants of Erechtheus or Erechthonius, both of whom were earth-born, and insofar as the tradition that Erechtheus was earth-born is much older, in Homer (see below), the possibility of this shift is of no great import here. (See Hall 1997: 54, for a similar opinion.)

Euripides' *Ion,* and in its boldest structural form in Plato's *Menexenus,* where Socrates relates his version of Pericles' funeral speech, as he supposedly had it from the real author, Pericles' mistress Aspasia. Speaking of the Athenians:

> And first of their birth. Their ancestors were not strangers, nor are these their descendants sojourners only, whose fathers have come from another country, but they are the children of the soil, dwelling and living in their own land. And the country that brought them up is not like other countries, a stepmother to her children, but their own true mother: she bore them and nourished them, and in her bosom they now repose. It is meet and right therefore, that we should begin by praising the land which is their mother, and that will be a way of praising their noble birth. (Pl., *Menex.* 237.b–c)

It is curious that the received wisdom often downplays or even more often ignores the pointed contrast between Athenian autochthony and wandering strangers related to the land by adoption—such as the Lacedaemonians, for instance—by speculating rather on the internal functional advantages the notion of autochthony could have for the Athenians. It would make them the contemporary ancestors of their Ionian allies, for example; or it would foster the citizens' unity at a time when the heterogeneous foreign population of Attica was growing rapidly; or it would encourage civic pride, equality, democracy, national consciousness—whatever. Following an otherwise stunning showing that Athenian "autochthony" was elaborated in the fifth century in response to the rivalry with the Spartans, Vincent Rosivach then gives away the store by dwelling in conclusion on its local virtues of asserting the unity of Athenian citizens and their superiority to noncitizens (1984: 246–97, 305). This kind of subversion of a complementary opposition by a functional disposition, thus subsuming the structural relations between societies in the contingent necessities of one of them, is common among historians.[72] Even more often, the scholarly discussions of Athenian autochthony do not consider Sparta in this connection, which is all the more curious in light of Edward Cohen's observation that "as with many other ancient Greek terms, the clearest definition of *autokhthōn* arises from its interplay with its antithesis, *epēlys* or 'incomer,' 'immigrants'" (Cohen 2000: 83). So what about Dorian Sparta? Am I missing something?

72. To a large extent, however, exception should be made for the discussions of Athenian autochthony by Loraux (2000) and Detienne (2003)—texts that came to my attention after this book had gone to press.

Classicists also tell us that the early Athenian king Erechtheus was conflated in fifth-century traditions with another son of the soil, Erichthonius—famously born of Hephaestus' failed attempt on Athena that resulted in his seed falling to the ground. And further, that as kings and ancestors, Erechtheus and Erichthonius represent human transformations of certain chthonian serpentine deities of an older cultic dispensation.[73] But leave aside this curiously reversed euhemerism, from god to hero instead of hero to god, and also the broad planetary distribution of chthonian origin myths (Fijian included) that make no such distinctions between men and gods or, for that matter, humans and serpents. To accept the Homeric relation in the *Iliad* (638–42), Erechtheus was indeed an earth-born king who was subsequently deified by Athena: "the strong-built city of Athens, realm of high-hearted Erechtheus, Zeus's daughter Athena tended him once the grain-giving fields had borne him long ago, and then she settled the king in Athens, in her own rich shrine, where sons of Athens worship him with bulls and goats as the years wheel round the seasons."[74]

In the same vein of ancient, earth-sprung people is Herodotus' identification of the Athenians as pre-Greek Pelasgians, who were only in due course Hellenized. "Pelasgian" was something like a generic term for the aboriginal inhabitants of Greece, of which there could also be local variants. The eponymous ancestor Pelasgus, however, was a "son of the soil" in Arcadia, not only according to the likes of Apollodorus, but also according to Hesiod—which together with Herodotus' description of the Pelasgian Athenians seems evidence enough of the antiquity of their sense of autochthony.[75]

Pelasgus of Arcadia was one of several such earth-born original kings and/or first inhabitants described in the foundation stories of Greek poleis.[76] Among them are Lelex of Sparta and Cecrops of Athens, as well

73. On such derivations of the human from the natural in early twentieth-century classical studies—a certain echo of Fraser through Jane Harrison—see Calame (1990a).

74. It is, of course, possible that this verse is a late interpolation, as some would like to believe. Just so, the Erechtheion of the Athenian acropolis is a late fifth-century construction—the successor, however, of other shrines built on the same hallowed site. In the Erechtheion, Erecththeus received sacrifices along with Athena, Poseidon, and Hephaestus, an archaic lot.

75. Pausanias (viii.4) cites a poem of Asios, a seventh- or sixth-century writer from Samos: "and black earth produced god-equalling Pelasgus in mountains with long hair of tall trees that a mortal race might come to be."

76. As already indicated, my main sources in this discussion of origin charters of Greek poleis are Apollodorus' *Library* and Pausanias' so-called *Guide to Greece.* Their original stories are of course fragmentary and uneven, although I think sufficient to discern the general

as Erechtheus and Erichthonius.[77] Because these characters and their descendants often had the same names as natural features of the polis landscape, or gave their names to the territory, some modern scholars have banished them to a kind of pan-Hellenic natural limbo, without connection to the Greek heroes who followed them and initiated a humanized or civilized era. This interpretative schism, however, not only misses out the hierogamic union that connects the earth-born people with the heavenly descended strangers who established the polis society, it seems to misread the sense of the initial occupation, which was not a naturalization of humans so much as a humanization of nature. By homonymic relations between themselves and the territory—notably including the names of natural features and human settlements as these were known to their classical successors—the original peoples constituted the natural world as a cultural order.[78] True, the originals were characterized by a certain wildness or primitiveness—sometimes explicitly including exuberant reproductive powers—that testifies to their earth-born origins. But as such they constitute an essential element of human existence, of which the ordering and civilizing powers of their god-born successors are the complement. Brought together by the union of the earth-born woman and the god-descended stranger, the terrestrial and the celestial combine to make a suitably complete and self-sufficing foundation of the polis.

The Laconian tradition, as transmitted by Pausanias (III.1–2), is exemplary (fig. 1.18). It begins, "The Lakonians themselves say that Lelex who was a child of the earth was the first king in this country, and that the Leleges whom he governed were named after him." Lelex was succeeded as king by his son Myles, and Myles by Eurotas—which happens to be the

---

pattern of this supersession of earth-born kings by divine strangers, as mediated by the hierogamic union of a royal daughter of the indigenous people with the god-descended outsider.

77. Herodotus describes a succession of earth-born kings and their naming (constituting) the country, before Ion, son of Erechtheus' daughter: "The Athenians, at the time when the Pelasgians held all of what is now called Greece, were themselves Pelasgians and were called Cranai; but in the time of their king Cecrops they acquired the name Cecropidae, and when Erechtheus took over the rule they changed their name again, to Athenians; and when Ion, the son of Xuthus [descendant of Hellen], became their commander-in-chief, they were called, after him, Ionians" (Hdt. 8.44).

78. Fijian onomastic practices were similar. Features of this landscape in eastern Viti Levu were named after deeds or parts of the body of Rokomoutu, the senior (male) ancestor of the High Fijian Genealogy. Likewise, much of the landscape and social order of southern Vanua Levu was named from incidents of a voyage there by Rokomoutu's wife, his oldest son, and their entourage.

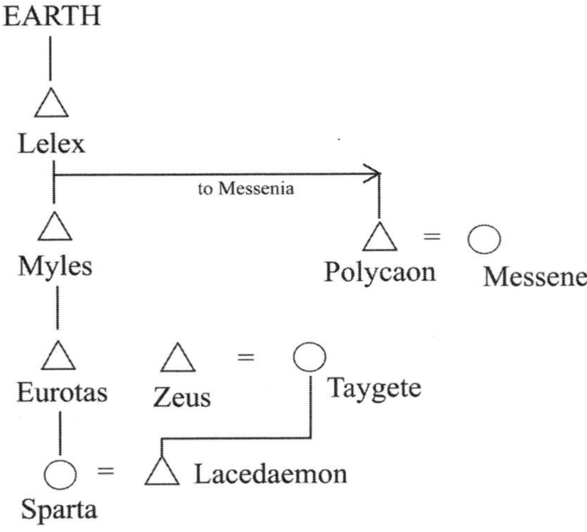

1.18 Spartan origins, after Pausanias

name of the major river in Lakonia. But when Pausanias reports, "it was Eurotas who channeled away the marsh-water from the plains by cutting through to the sea, and when the land was drained he called the river which was left running there the Eurotas," this feat is not so much an allegorical description of a natural process as it is a historicized tradition, in a certain hierarchical form, of a cultural process: the making of the Eurotas valley suitable for habitation and cultivation. (It is curiously reminiscent of the draining of the Rewa marshes by the original Rewa 'land people' [Nadoi].) Eurotas, Pausanias continues, had no male heir, and left the sovereignty to his son-in-law Lacedaemon, "whose mother was Taygete after whom the mountain was named and whose father is supposed to have been Zeus." The daughter of Eurotas, through whom Lacedaemon her husband secured the kingship, was named Sparta—in case there were any lingering doubts about the relevance of the aboriginal people to the constitution of the classical order, or about the link between the earth-sprung aboriginals and the celestially descended peoples who succeeded and incorporated them. Or considering the Pelops' version of this replacement of the indigenous rulers by strangers of divine stamp—a widespread pattern among Indo-European as well as Austronesian peoples, as we have seen—should we not talk of "usurpation"?

The takeover of the land of the original earth-born race by a hero fathered by the Olympian Zeus—or what is structurally the same, the succession of the divine stranger to the kingship through marriage with the indigenous royal woman—amounts to a political re-creation of famous cosmogonic myths. The foundation-tradition of the city resembles nothing so much as the conquest of the earth-born Titans of Cronos by the Zeus-led race of the gods (the offspring of a more anthropomorphic union). Both narratives have the same finality, the inheritance of the self-reproducing earth—whose parthenogenic powers, it is well to remember, are a fact of nature as well as of myth. Yet the battle of the Titans and the victory of the Zeusian stranger-king are but two episodes in a recursive series of similar plots that begins with Gaia's bearing of Uranus, who thereupon covers her: the ritual conjunction of Earth and Heaven that was sundered when their son Cronos, in an oedipal act of replacement, castrated his father. In the sequence of usurpations that follow, everything happens as if progressively more distant and humanized descendants of Gaia and Uranus were attempting to achieve the self-sufficient completeness entailed in their original union. Autonomy was indeed what distinguished gods from humankind, although the latter could aspire to a sub-Olympian translation of it in the political form of freedom. Even the "crimes" that justified each successive overthrow from Cronos in the cosmos to Pelops in Pisa or Lycaon in Arcadia, the many varieties of incest and cannibalism, were also signs (in the codes of sex and food) of the self-sufficiency of the immortals. They were thus as much an argument for the difference between Greeks and their gods as they were for the similarity. Difference and distance are also involved in the widening exogamy of reproductive relations, from the original parthenogenesis and forms of incest among the gods to the brother's daughter and father's brother's daughter marriages that often mark the early generations of dynastic genealogies. A corollary trend is the progressive anthropomorphization of the hero, culminating in the differentiation of humans from their divine ancestors. On the one hand, then, humans are fated to a devolution from that Hesiodic golden age when they shared the company and existence of the gods. On the other hand, as the local traditions tell, successive dynasties cum races benefit from the progressive cultural introductions of royal heroes: a civilizing process that moves from the aboriginal people who are separated from nature, if still in barbarism, to those who supersede them politically while culturally advancing toward the technical and moral refinements of classical Greeks. The devolution from the gods is counterbalanced by the evolution of the human.

Brief as these accounts are, many of the patterns are rehearsed in the traditions of the paradigmatic Pelasgus of Arcadia—or Pelasgia, as it was originally known (fig. 1.19). Son of the soil, Pelasgus, by his introduction

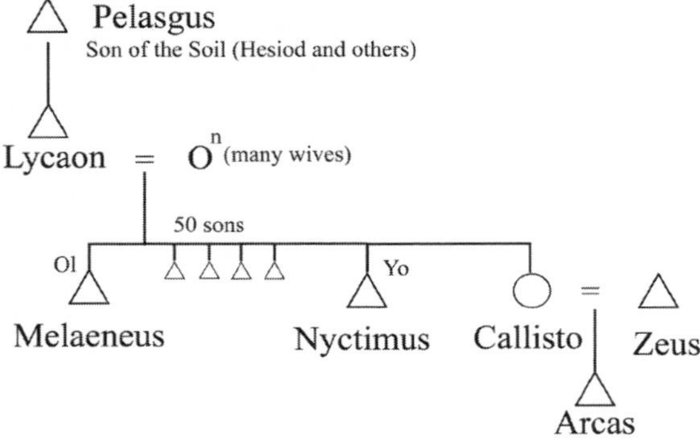

1.19 Arcadian origins, after Apollodorus

of huts and clothing and his interdiction on eating raw grasses and leaves, made the transition from nature to culture for the first people. His son and successor Lycaon, on whom the story of the usurpation pivots, begat fifty sons and sent them to found cities. The motif of the fifty sons has relevant resonances in the broader mythical corpus: it is most obviously reminiscent of the barbarian king Danaus whose fifty daughters married the fifty sons of his brother Aegyptus and killed forty-nine of them. Thus the excessive fertility as well as the deficient morality of the original land people—both of which faults are also attributed to the Pelasgians in the Athenian tradition that tells of their banishment for the rape of Athenian women (Hdt. 6.137–38).[79] In the case of Lycaon, his criminal impiety or that of his sons (depending on the version) lost them Pelasgia. The one or the others killed a human child and offered it as a sacrifice or a sacrificial meal to Zeus. Furious at this act—which evokes the endocannibalistic crimes of his father Cronos—Zeus transformed Lycaon into a wolf and loosed his thunderbolt on the sons, killing all but Nyctimus, who was saved when Gaia stayed the god's hand. Lycaon and his sons, Apollodorus commented, "exceeded all men in pride and impiety" (3.8.1). And in a reprise of the theme of separation from the gods that resulted from Tantalus' serving up his son Pelops to Zeus, Pausanias relates the analogous fate of Lycaon: "Because of their justice and their religion the people of that time entertained gods and sat at table with them, and the gods visibly rewarded their goods with wealth;

79. This story, set later than Herodotus' identification of the Athenians as Pelasgians, presumably refers to Hellenized Athenians expelling the unassimilated aboriginals from Attica.

and in those days certain human beings were turned into gods and are still honoured. . . . So one may well believe that Lykaon was turned into a wild beast" (Paus. 8.2.4–5). In the sequel, by most accounts, Nyctimus lost the kingship to Arcas, the son of his sister Callisto, who was fathered on her by Zeus in one of his frequent liaisons with mortal women. Callisto, however, was turned into a bear by Hera out of jealousy and shot by Artemis. Arcas was nonetheless delivered, and the reign of Zeus-derived kings he fathered was enhanced by his introduction, as it were, of the neolithic period, as he taught the people to cultivate crops, weave cloth, and bake bread. These people became the Arcadians, for the country was renamed after him.

In Laconia, the dynasty of the earth-born Lelex was succeeded by a series of external Zeusian lineages, at least three of them—which effectively distanced the classical Spartans from any autochthonous, maternally derived roots, and from the kinds of claims to authenticity and completeness the Athenians could adduce (fig. 1.20). For the first Zeusian dynasty, the Lacedaemonians, who had succeeded the original sons of the soil, was displaced by a second, the notorious Atreidae, in a transfer of rule mediated by the same process of wife taking. Descendants of Pelops and heroes of the Trojan War, the Atreidae succeeded when Menelaus married Helen, the daughter of the Lacedaemonian king Tyndareus, and their daughter married Orestes—a father's brother's daughter union—who became king of Mycenae and Sparta. But the link to local origins through women was effectively broken when the Heraclid-led Dorians ousted and killed Orestes' son Tisamenus and installed Heracles' descendants in the kingships of the Peloponnesus. Sheerly by force and without benefit of the transmission of primordial earth-powers through the appropriation of the native women, this conquest marked the Dorians as pure strangers.

The Athenians, while stressing their distinctiveness as autochthonous, also maintained their connection to other Greek peoples, including the Spartans, as common descendants of Hellen, eponymous ancestor of all the Hellenes (fig. 1.21a). They appear thus as the posterity of Ion, a grandson of Hellen, in the sixth-century genealogy (from the Hesiodic *Catalogue of Women*) that includes the Spartan ancestor Dorus. But are not these claims to autochthony and Ionian descent contradictory? So it has seemed to some moderns; accordingly, it is said, the Athenians played down their Ionian ancestry in favor of their autochthony in the fifth century, although they could not reject the former altogether because of the purchase it gave them on the Ionian allies of the Delian League. Still, the notion of autochthony, rather than contradictory to descent from Ion, could reinforce

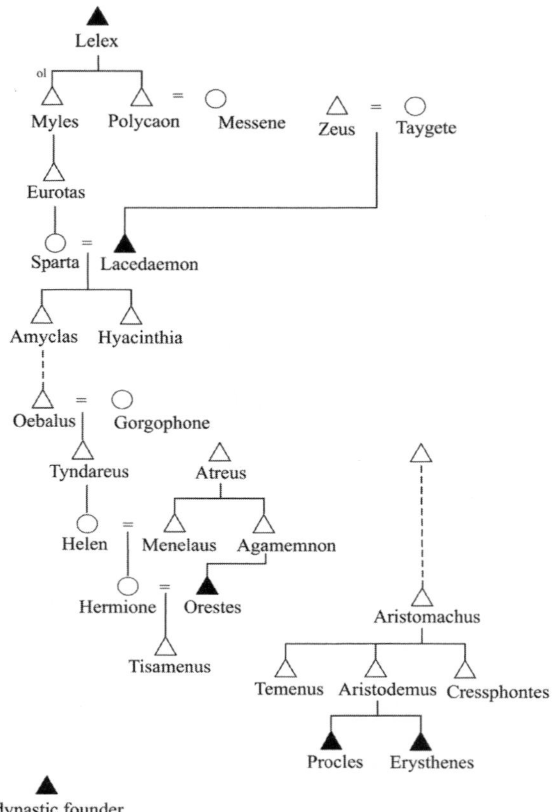

1.20 Dynasties of Sparta

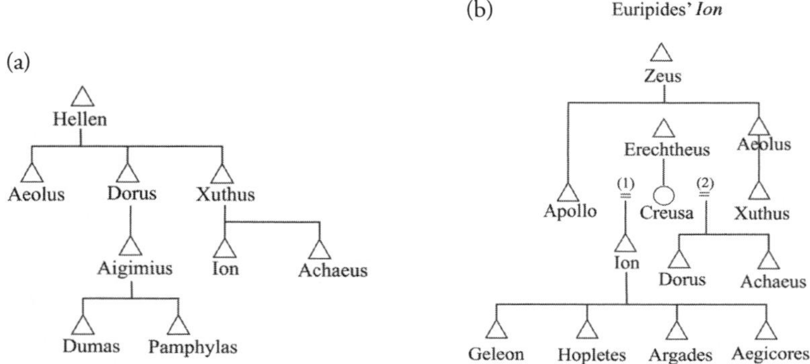

1.21 (a) Hellenic genealogy; (b) genealogy of Euripides' *Ion*

Athens' traditional claim to be "the oldest land of Ionia" (as Solon already put it in the sixth century), thus the homeland of all the Ionians of the Aegean and Asia Minor. The Athenians were mobilizing this argument politically before the Delian League was born. Themistocles used it to rally opposition to the Persians, according to Plutarch. After the Battle of Thermopylae (480), the Athenian statesman sailed along the Thracian coast leaving messages for the Ionians in the Persian host "to come over, if they found the opportunity, to the side of the Athenians, who were their ancestors" (Plut., *Them.* 9). So indeed, when the Ionians became dissatisfied with Spartan leadership of the Hellenic resistance in 478, they "resorted to the Athenians and requested them as their kinsmen to become their leader" (Thuc. 1.95.1). But then, not even genealogically need there be a discrepancy between this Athenian claim to be ancestor of the Ionians, thus descended from Hellen, and sprung from the earth.

On the contrary, when account is taken of the marital and maternal connections of the Athenians to the earth-born Erechtheus, then Ion becomes a pivotal ancestor precisely because he synthesizes their autochthony with their Hellenic ancestry. This synthesis already exists in the usual tradition that Ion was born of the marriage between Xuthus, son of Hellen, and Creusa, daughter of Erechtheus (fig. 1.21a). Ion is a descendant of the soil through his mother. Beside the fact that maternal ancestry is the primordial Greek condition, all gods and men having come from Earth (Gaia), it seems clear that the Athenians traced descent—or perhaps more precisely, they traced ascent to the ancestors—cognatically. They admitted of maternal links as well as paternal, as a basis of membership in determinate houses. Ion would be no less the descendant of Erechtheus, thus of earth-sprung ancestry, than Pericles was an Alcmaeonid—that is, a member of this distinguished lineage, as everyone (including the Spartans) acknowledged, through his mother. While in an abstract genealogy such as the Hellenic pedigree from the *Catalogue of Women,* a code for marking differences and relationships among ethnic groups, a patrilateral reckoning may be preferred, if only for semiotic clarity in measuring kinship distance and seniority, the issue is otherwise when it comes to the affiliation of living people with ancestrally defined houses. Here option is possible, and maternal links may be used in tracing upward to the ancestor, rather than downward or collaterally. The ancestral group is accordingly cognatic or multilineal in composition, and it overlaps with other such groups in membership. The Athenians, by this argument, had no need to abandon their Ionian ancestry in order to assert their autochthony or vice versa. On the contrary: since Ion by many legendary accounts, while indeed a son of Creusa and Xuthus, was the king of Aegialus (Achaea) and only later in life (if ever) returned to

Athens, it was his autochthonous ancestry through Creusa that made him Athenian, and the Athenians thus descended from Hellen. Ion was the necessary condition of both claims.

In the midst of the Peloponnesian War, Euripides retold the story in a way that seems to make the contrast between the Ionians and the Dorians even more invidious—if at the expense of certain contradictions, such as the dissociation of the Athenian ancestor from the received Hellenic genealogy. Still, this ancient charter had put the Spartan descendants of Doros in a privileged position relative to Ion and the Athenians (fig. 1.21a). If we accept Jonathan Hall's argument (1997: 43) that generational status is a measure of hierarchy, the Athenians would be distant junior kin to the Spartans on that score, clearly inferior. But in Euripides' *Ion,* written in the decade 420–10, the Athenians gain the mythical and genealogical high ground on their enemies (fig. 1.21b). The grandson of earth-born Erechtheus by the latter's daughter Creusa, Ion is revealed to be the son of the god Apollo rather than of Xuthus, as in the received genealogical tradition. Xuthus turns out to be an upstart foreigner, an Achaean, who, though awarded Creusa in marriage for feats of war performed on Athens' behalf, will neither gain the kingdom nor sire the heir. He is a stranger-king *manqué.* His ambitions are compromised when it transpires that Ion is Apollo's issue, the fruit of the god's rape of Creusa before her marriage in a cave below the Acropolis. Earth-mothered and god-fathered, Ion succeeds to Erechtheus' throne. His four sons, eponymous ancestors of the four tribes of Ionians, will colonize the Mediterranean. Xuthus' legitimate sons by Creusa, whom Euripides identifies as Dorus and Achaeus, will become kings in the Peleponnesus. But now it is Dorus, the younger son of a mortal father, who is thus junior to his demi-god half-brother Ion. By these ancestral measures of status, Athens is the same as and different from, equal to and better than Sparta.

Some modern scholars find it surprising that Euripides and other fifth-century poets were apparently content to reverse the celebrated triumph of *logos* over *mythos* by spinning out new versions of the gods' stories. Just when the enlightened Greeks, Thucydides above all, were conceiving history as a "human thing," governed by rational interests and knowable by empirical reason, the poets and their countrymen were bringing fresh mythical discourses into historical account. Euripides' *Ion* has been considered war propaganda, but that implies *mythos* still has significant effect on collective attitudes and practical actions. In the same vein, Robert Parker notes that the "exquisite anachronism" of the democratic king Theseus in *The Suppliant Women* demonstrates "the continuing vitality of mythological thought in the late fifth century" (1996: 170). Thucydides said from the outset that he intended to eliminate the marvelous from his *History,* that he would not thus cater to the popular taste. Yet if the Greeks were making history by the marvelous, even as they remade the marvelous by history, wasn't that a mistake on his part?

Not to ignore the inverse relation between *logos* and *mythos:* the obdurate practical realities that promoted an irrational will to power. That happened in the great maritime empire of Fiji as well as in Greece, in Bau as well as in Athens. It did them both in—as we shall now see.

"THAT RESTLESS DESIRE OF POWER AFTER POWER THAT CEASETH ONLY IN DEATH" (HOBBES)

We are inquiring into a certain culture of domination. Again, more is entailed than national character. For Bau and Athens, the domination of others was a necessary condition of their own existence. They had that restless desire of power after power, including wealth, that the Greeks called *pleonexia.*[80] Force was a principal means, but they also ruled by making spectacles of their might, including spectacles of their force. For their supremacy was accomplished without actual rule, without administration. It was hegemony without sovereignty. It relied substantially on a politics of demonstration effects, the power of the signs of power. All the same, both Bau and Athens found themselves in a maritime geopolitics of exponentially increasing costs that generated a corresponding pressure for outward expansion. Eventually, their hubris became irrational. Expanding in order to survive, they succeeded in overreaching themselves. It all ended in death.

The 'kingdom of force' (*matanitū ni kaukauwa*), Bau had a reputation for war, intrigue, and despotism that was unparalleled among Fijian lands, as was its disposition for overturning the conventional relations of hierarchy and legitimacy. "Force rules this world," a Bau chief declared in a petition to the British colonial establishment, and then proceeded to argue that Bau was entitled to the leading position in the colony's system of indirect rule on the same principle of conquest by which Britain had gained its own empire (Wainiu *AY:* 18–19). By that time, the proverbial conspiracy à la Bau (*vere vakaBau*) was more popularly phrased as *politiki vakaBau,* 'politics à

80. Wills makes the same comparison between Athens and Venice: "Once the imperial cities had committed themselves to breathing in life from the sea, they had to keep expanding over it in order to survive. . . . The imperial cities convinced their opponents that they aspired to world domination (2001: 16).

la Bau,' a tortuous derivation from the Greek *polis* that also reminds us of the Bauans' readiness, like the Athenians', to meddle in the affairs of other polities. The war kings of Bau were notorious for interfering in the succession struggles of other lands, especially for backing upstart junior lines and chiefs, in the interest of bringing to power clans or towns that would be dependent on them. But the parvenu local chiefs then stood some chance of being unlucky, because the Bauan notables were famous too for despotic acts of violence and pillage against subordinate towns. The war kings of Bau did not hesitate to procure sacrificial/cannibal victims for ceremonial purposes from peoples within their dominions. For one example, of the ten men killed and eaten in connection with the construction of a new house for Ratu Tānoa (the Vunivalu) in 1839, six were from places under Bauan control (Cross *D:* 1 February 1839).[81] Ratu Tānoa and Ratu Cakobau were both quick to burn and kill in subordinate places that displeased them, especially those that did not comply with their preemptory levies of food or wealth. In the space of barely two months in 1841, the Vunivalu father and son had thirteen men killed for such cause in nearby towns (Cross *D:* 23 September and 27 November 1841).[82] Other high Bauan chiefs took advantage of their female ancestry in certain lands, or sometimes of the general dread of Bau, to commit similar depredations. "It is not at all surprising," Lieutenant Wilkes commented in connection with just such incidents, "but that the chiefs and people of Ambau [Bau] should be so detested by the inhabitants of the group" (1845, 3:149).

In a way reminiscent of Thucydides' characterization of the "revolutionary" Athenians, Rev. John Hunt, speaking of Bau's objectives in the early months of the war with Rewa, warned his fellow missionaries that "*Revolution,* not mere conquest appears to be the object aimed at" (Hunt *L.* to Lyth and Calvert: 28 May 1844). What Mr. Hunt meant was that the Bauan desire for domination, and particularly the ambition of Ratu Cakobau, was moving beyond the normal bounds of Fijian warfare and the constituted relations between Fijian states. The war with Rewa, raising the

81. The six from Bauan-controlled lands were from Kaba, Buretū, and Ovalau. Two weeks earlier, men had been hunted in Moturiki, a Bauan land, for the construction of Ratu Cakobau's house (Cross *D:* 1 February 1839). Some months later, four men from Ovalau were taken as sacrifices for a new temple at Bau (Jaggar *J:* 22 and 23 August 1839).

82. There are a number of such incidents in mid-century missionary records (e.g., Lyth *DB:* 23 September 1849 [3538]; Lyth *J:* 1 July 1850). The whole island of Malake, occupied by a fishing people under Ratu Tānoa, was said to have been wiped out when a turtle caught there was eaten instead of being delivered to the Bau king (Wilkes 1845, 3:210, from Hudson *J:* 523–24).

possibility of eliminating this great rival at the height of its own power, was fueling the sense in Bau that the possibilities of extending its sway were limitless. For not only had the submission of Rewa become conceivable, an explicit war aim, but other lands, small and large, that were never Bauan were now lining up under its hegemony. This included former Rewa allies in the Delta that had gone over to Bau in the course of its early campaigns, as well as important countries to the west that had been traditionally allied with Rewa. The *matanitū* of Nadrogā was one: early in 1845, Mr. Hunt reported it had "come over to Bau" (Lyth *L,* Hunt to Lyth; and Calvert: n.d. [c. 4 January 1845]). In July Mr. Hunt's colleague, Rev. Thomas Jaggar, wrote that nearly the whole of leeward (western) Viti Levu had joined the Bau side (*WMMS/L:* 5 July 1845). Such successes pushed Bauan pleonexia to its only possible conclusion: "the idea of universal domination of the group is gaining ground," observed Mr. Hunt (*L,* to Jos. Waterhouse: n.d. [1844]). And Ratu Cakobau seemed on his way to becoming emperor of the Fiji Islands. "I think if he goes on during the next two years as he has done the last [1844], he will be in every sense the Emperor of Feejee. The whole of Vanua Levu is under him, in one way or another, and Navitilevu [Viti Levu] is bearing its neck to his yoke. If the Rewa wars ends as is generally expected, in the destruction of Rewa, and the death of the king, Thakombau [Ratu Cakobau] might be called Emperor any time" (Lyth *L,* Hunt to Lyth and Calvert: n.d. [c. 4 January 1845]).

Ratu Cakobau was already being called Tui Viti, 'King of Fiji.' The title came in the mail, in the address of a letter from the British consul in Honolulu (Hunt *L:* 25 November 1844).[83] The Methodist missionaries promptly and regularly so referred to Ratu Cakobau in their journals. By 1847 Fijians were using the title as well, according to Reverend Lyth: "Seru (pronounced Saroo) alias Thakombau, Tanoa's son, is now regularly called by his own people and the whites Tui Viti" (Lyth *L:* 26 August 1847).[84] Foreign models were thus being adapted to a growing ambition that had its own, Fijian rationale. Ratu Cakobau had an active interest in expanding the scope and legitimacy of his domination, centrifugal intentions both opened and necessitated by the war. Eventually they pushed Ratu Cakobau

83. Horatio Hale of the U.S. Exploring Expedition, in Fiji in 1840, explicitly said at that time there was no such title as "Tui Viti" (1846: 181).

84. In the cession of Fiji to Britain that Ratu Cakobau negotiated in 1858, he was designated as "Vunivalu of the armies of Fiji, and Tui Viti, etc." (Derrick 1950: 139). The cession was refused by the British government. But in the culmination of a series of Fijian governments headed by Ratu Cakobau and promoted by resident Whites, he was finally and formally installed as "Tui Viti" in 1871.

too far. When he attempted to adopt the monarchical trappings recently affected by certain Polynesian rulers—King George Tupou of Tonga, and before him, Kamehameha of Hawaii—who had acquired European ships as signs of the "universal domination" of their own islands, Ratu Cakobau became engaged in a vain attempt to extend his authority beyond Fijian political reason and his own military capacities (Williams and Calvert 1859: 464). The defeat of a large, sea-borne expedition in northern Vanua Levu in 1852 was not exactly Bau's Sicilian campaign, certainly not in terms of casualties, but it likewise marked the bounds imposed by political reality on visions of universality.

Briefly, the story is this.[85] In 1850, while still at war with Rewa, Ratu Cakobau ordered two expensive European vessels, one from Australia and one from America, promising to pay with cargoes of *bêche-de-mer.* But to do so, he would have to make levies of unparalleled magnitude on ruling chiefs of northern Fiji, the area of the principal *bêche-de-mer* grounds, even though Bau traditionally had little direct authority over these people. Mobilizing his own immediate allies and subject chiefs who did have relations on the north coasts of Viti Levu and Vanua Levu, the Bau ruler exploited every kinship and political connection he could to draw out the *bêche-de-mer.* Through these extended chains of influence—whose links, however, became weaker in proportion to distance—he sent out canvas bags that were to be filled with the cured sea slugs by the local notables and their people. From the beginning, however, the project met with resistance. When Ratu Cakobau sailed to the area in his new ship, the *Cakobau*—which he was purchasing on the never-never—he found the *bêche-de-mer* bags unfilled. They had just been left to rot or else burned. By the end of 1851 he decided he would have to use force, and he would do so in a characteristic way, by making an example of someone who was defying him. For this purpose he chose his most difficult adversary, Ra Ritova, claimant to the kingship of Macuata in northern Vanua Levu. I stress the exemplary value of force, as a punishment to one and a sign to the others. Ratu Cakobau himself explained it that way to Mary Wallis, the wife of the Salem *bêche-de-mer* trader with whom he was negotiating for the *Cakobau.* All the other chiefs were waiting to see how he would take Ra Ritova's refusal to fish *bêche-de-mer,* Ratu Cakobau told her, and if he failed to kill and eat the Macuata chief, "all of Fiji would laugh at him and not acknowledge his authority" (Wallis 1994: 47). Which is about the way it turned out, although Ratu Cakobau had gathered one of the larger armies known to Fijian history: some two thousand or more fighting men, trans-

85. A fuller and documented version can be found in M. Sahlins (1987).

ported to the Macuata coast by two hundred seagoing canoes and the *Cakobau,* where they paraded up and down the beach below Ra Ritova's fortress in a magnificent and vain attempt to intimidate him. (In Fijian terms, the pageantry must have rivaled the splendor of the Athenian armada for Sicily.) This great army, however, had all the weaknesses of its strength: the tenuous control the Bau ruler had over much of it. Like the collection of *bêche-de-mer,* the army had been recruited through indirect claims of authority, which gave Ratu Cakobau limited command over many of the assembled warriors. Clearly, he understood his own vulnerability, for when he finally attacked Ra Ritova, he used only three hundred men, all his own Bauan people—a point taken by some of the inactive allies as a slur on their warrior honor. Worse yet, the Bauans were humiliated: they were driven off with a loss of about ten men, and when a small party made a sortie from the Macuata fort the next morning, the whole confederated army precipitously decamped in their canoes. Nor could Ratu Cakobau succeed in recovering the situation by diverting his forces to fishing the *bêche-de-mer* themselves. One by one his erstwhile allies refused to do so and drifted away, declaring they were fighting men, not menials.

The great *bêche-de-mer* campaign was a turning point in Bau's war with Rewa. Mary Wallis sagaciously understood such to be the case as it was happening. Ratu Cakobau had been climbing in fame for upwards of fifteen years, she noted, "but perhaps he has reached the top of the ladder; by the disgraceful flight of the last week he has certainly descended several rounds" (Wallis 1994: 59). The weeks to come would bring further proofs of decline, such as dissatisfaction among the Bauan forces:

> There seems to be a great deal of dissatisfaction between all the parties. The Bau and Lasakau chiefs [the latter were Bau's great fisher-warriors] say that Thakombau [Ratu Cakobau] has managed very foolishly with the whole affair. Mbete [a local rival of Ra Ritova, siding with Ratu Cakobau] is dissatisfied because he got no dead bodies to feast upon and Elijah [i.e., Ratu Varani of Viwa, a staunch ally of Ratu Cakobau] is dissatisfied because when the pigs were cooked he had no part. The mountaineers of Ovalau [i.e., the Lovoni people, affiliated to Bau through the Viwa chiefs] say that they will never go on another expedition with Thakombau because he prevented them from fighting, and he is a very foolish chief. (Wallis 1994: 67)

When the news of Ratu Cakobau's defeat reached the north coast of Viti Levu, people tore up the Bau *bêche-de-mer* bags for clothing (Wallis 1994: 68). And soon enough, almost all of Fiji was laughing at him: "Bau instead of being feared at present is becoming the [object of] derision of many parts of the coast" (ibid., 74).

The defeat at Macuata in 1852 was not immediately fatal for the Bauans, but it significantly and negatively changed the relationships of the contending forces. Not only was Ratu Cakobau humiliated, but Ra Ritova declared Macuata independent of him and soon was conspiring to join Rewa. The northern chiefs began to negotiate directly with the European *bêche-de-mer* traders on their own account, where formerly this trade was arranged through the chiefs of Bau. And the resident Europeans, likewise put off by Ratu Cakobau's direct intervention in the *bêche-de-mer* trade, fell out with him and entered into collusion with the Rewans and certain disaffected chiefs of Bau who were planning a rebellion. Bau would eventually win the war, with the aid of the English missionaries and Christian Tongan allies. Yet the *bêche-de-mer* fiasco had thus paved the way for the conversion of Bau to Christianity, as well as for the emergence of Europeans as an independent force with their own political agenda, operating now beyond Bau's control.[86] Ratu Cakobau's quest for "universal domination of the Fiji Islands" had opened Fiji to an imperium of even greater pretensions.

Still, for self-undoing fantasies of universal domination backed up by displays of force, it would be hard to beat the Athenians. In 414, a year after they had slaughtered the men of Melos and sold the women and children into slavery because the city refused to bend to the Athenian yoke, and even as the glorious Sicilian expedition was on its course to complete disaster, just in this fateful time of imperial repression and aspiration, Aristophanes produced, in *The Birds,* the comic masterpiece of Athenian hubris. Interposed between heaven and earth, where they could intercept the sacrifices made by men, the avian Athenians of Cloudcuckooland were thus able to starve the gods themselves into negotiation and submission. Allegorical readings of *The Birds* have been numerous and sometimes farfetched, but the parody of the Athenians' o'ercrowing ambitions is right on top. As William Arrowsmith says:

> Put an Athenian among the Birds and he will be an imperialist with wings and fight the gods. . . . Cloudcuckooland is a visible parody of the Athenian Empire. . . . I wonder what Athenian could fail to notice the

86. Previously, the leader of the European settlement at Levuka was widely recognized as the "Envoy to Bau" of that place, and he did not hesitate to use his Bauan status on his own as well as the Bauans' behalf (Wilkes 1845, 3:184–86).

> way in which, point for point, the policies and strategies of imperial Athens toward the member-states of her empire are adapted to Cloudcuckooland's campaign against the gods. . . . In Aristophanes' eyes, the logical terminus of Athenian aggressiveness is that man should become god, wear wings and rule the world. (Arrowsmith 1994: 176–78)

It only needs to be added that as a mythologist, Aristophanes showed he was the equal of the ancients. In depicting the downfall of the gods, he uses the time-honored myth of the stranger-king who usurps the sovereignty through a union with the native princess. It is the same topos we saw in the charter traditions of cities, where the god-fathered stranger appropriates the earth-descended princess, except that here the synthesis is worked out in reverse: through the acquisition of the celestial woman by a usurper of terrestrial (human) ancestry. Cut off from the sacrifices, the gods accord the leading bird-man Pisthetairos their "Divine Princess"—was she not Athena?—and he thereby becomes the ruler of the world.

Reading Thucydides—an exercise in hard-headedness rather the opposite of Aristophanes, *Realpolitik* land rather than Cloudcuckooland—reading Thucydides, Jacqueline de Romilly arrived at the similar conclusion that for the Athenians power became an end in itself. By its "very nature," she said, Athenian ambition could discover no limits (Romilly 1963: 65). From the beginning of the empire in 478 to its downfall in 404 at the end of the Peloponnesian War, each Athenian victory, each expansion of Athenian power, only seemed to make the objective of all this activity recede even further. Further and further, one might say, into pure abstraction: power as such, for its own sake. What the Athenians finally wanted, observed de Romilly, was "the greatest possible power and the domination over all other countries; and if we are to take as a sign the feeling to which the imperialist leaders chose to appeal, this final aim is less the desire to possess something than the ambition to exercise authority" (ibid., 78–79).

In Thucydides' *History,* Cleon and Alcibiades were the main avatars of this pleonexia. Especially Alcibiades in the debate over the invasion of Sicily, when he argues that Athens must collapse if she cannot expand: "We cannot fix the exact limit at which our empire shall stop; we have reached a position in which we must not be content with retaining what we have but must scheme to extend it for, if we cease to rule others, we shall be in danger of being ruled ourselves" (Thuc. 6.18.3). Note for further reference that the imperialist animus is not just an internal impulse, but is set in a political context of opposition—of rule or be ruled. It is also notable that the pleonexia was not just a late development, contingent on the progress of the war and fanned into flames by a few belligerent orators. According to Plutarch, the judicious use of force that Pericles practiced and preached in the 430s, before the war, was in reaction to the Athenians' intoxication with their own power. The conquest of Sicily was already envisioned back then. There was also talk of recovering Egypt and attacking the seaboard of the Persian empire. "There were even some who dreamed of attacking Carthage and Etruria, and, indeed their hopes were not altogether ill-founded, when one thinks of the extent of Athenian domination at that time and the full tide of success which seemed to attend all their undertakings" (Plut., *Per.* 20).

The darker complement of Athenian domination was the resentment it provoked among the allied Greek cities, whose subjugation was increasing over time even as freedom, the sub-Olympian version of divine autonomy, remained the supreme political value of the Hellenes.[87] As the Persian threat receded and Athens turned the allies into subjects whose tributes subsidized the power she held over them, resistances appear in this erstwhile federation, the Delian League, which was fast becoming an outright Athenian empire. "Of all the cause of defection," observed Thucydides, "that connected with arrears of tribute and vessels, and with failure of service, was the chief; for the Athenians were very severe and exacting, and made themselves offensive by applying the screw of necessity to men who were not used to and in fact not disposed for any continuous labor" (1.99.1; cf. Plut., *Cim.* 11). The impositions on recalcitrant cities included the installation of Athenian garrisons in their territories, the appropriation of land for Athenian settlement (cleruchies), the promotion of local democratic governments, the posting of Athenian inspectors, and the augmentation of the annual tribute obligations. Diodorus Siculus speaks of "most of the allies" reacting to the severity of Athenian rule by "discussing rebellion with each other" (11.70.2). But rebellions, of which a number are recorded from the early 460s, were met by harsh repressions and additional impositions.

The Peloponnesian War brought new possibilities of rebellion by the allies, and repression by the Athenians, because it involved a third party, the Spartans, who could in principle abet the first and relieve the second. The empire was becoming a tyranny for the tyrannizers. Rallying the Athenians

87. "In a world where freedom is so highly valued, the Athenian Empire, excellent as it was and highly worthy of a Funeral Oration, could not have been in any sense popular. All its institutions, all its methods of stopping the allied states getting their independence, must have been resented" (Cawkwell 1997: 103).

after a second year of Spartan invasions, Pericles warned that they were in peril not only of losing their empire but of suffering "from the animosities incurred in its exercise. . . . For what you hold is, to speak somewhat plainly, a tyranny; perhaps it was wrong to take it, but it would be dangerous to let it go" (Thuc. 2.63.1–2). Making the same point three years later, in relation to the revolt of Mytilene in Lesbos, Cleon was (characteristically) even more direct. "Your empire is a despotism and your subjects disaffected conspirators," he told the Athenian assembly in what would have amounted to a self-fulfilling argument for punishing the Mytileneans by exterminating them. As it happens, Mytilene escaped such a fate, but not so Torone (captured by Cleon), Scione, or, most famously, Melos. Many years later, in 339, Isocrates lamely excused these Athenian atrocities on the grounds that even the gods were known to do it—and the Spartans to do worse (*Panath.* 62–63). In referring to the Spartans, Isocrates' case for Athenian supremacy thus reproduced rhetorically the condition of his city's reputation for brutality a century before: another *bagarre à trois,* where the unrest of internal subjects was exacerbated by the presence of external enemies, thus necessitating repression of the former in some proportion to the menace of the latter. In 432 this dynamic had been explicitly understood, at least by the Athenians who were trying to dissuade the Spartan assembly from opening hostilities against them. They spoke of how they had taken up the leadership of the Hellenes when Sparta let it go after the second Persian war; how honor and glory thus combined with interest to promote their empire; and then how, when the Spartans turned against them, rebellions in the subject cities threatened their defection to Sparta, and so the end of empire: "And at last, when almost all hated us, when some had already revolted and been subdued, when you [Spartans] had ceased to be the friends you once were, and had become objects of suspicion and dislike, it no longer appeared safe to give up our empire; especially as all who left us would fall to you" (Thuc. 1.75.4).

The past is not just a foreign country. It is relationships among countries.

THE *ARCHĒ:* HEGEMONY WITHOUT SOVEREIGNTY

Athens and Bau developed an imperium of a distinctive kind—and one distinctively disposed to brew up a volatile mixture of fear and attraction among the peoples dominated by it. Their hegemonies were not like the European empires of modern times, where the foreign-colonial power directly imposed its own state on other territories and societies. Gained by invasion and maintained by occupation, such colonial regimes were actually sovereign over the subjugated peoples, governing them with all the necessary means of administration, regulation, and coercion. But neither Bau nor Athens had created their empire by conquest, and neither directly ruled it. They exercised hegemony without sovereignty.[88] This did not mean that their rule was mild, however, only that it relied on awe and fear—which is to say, on a reputation for power, confirmed by strategic displays of it. Rather than mild, the Athenians and Bauans could be all the more brutal, so that they would be known for it.

Yet, as I say, they were not conquerors: both Bau and Athens in effect inherited their supremacy, as successors of previous hegemonic regimes. Military force was certainly involved in their respective ascendancies, but it was mainly the demonstration of force against powerful others—Athens against the Persians, and Bau against the predecessor kingdom of Verata—that gave them a kind of elective leadership. They were able to realign preexisting political allegiances in their favor, as weaker lands, with the sort of voluntarism that is driven by the fear of a worse fate, submitted to them for their own protection.[89] Thus the innocence the Athenians were able to assume in their aforementioned plea before the Spartan assembly in 432. They did not really merit the unpopularity their empire had brought them, they said, for "that empire we acquired not by violence but because you [Spartans] were unwilling to prosecute to its conclusion the war against the barbarian, and because the allies attached themselves to us and spontaneously asked us to assume command" (Thuc. 1.75.2).

We have seen that many of the allies could justify their allegiance by kinship to Ionian Athens, something that was also known in the Bau hegemony. When Bauan attacks on Verata induced the subject lands of the lat-

88. It is said that crimes in the allied cities that involved capital punishment were obligatorily tried in Athens (Hornblower 1991a: 29). This would certainly be an infringement of sovereignty of a critical sort, the denial of the monopoly right over life and death that is a hallmark of state. Starting in the 440s, the Athenians attempted to impose their own coinage on subordinate cities, but this apparently failed to take (Picard 2000: 85–87; Kagan 1969: 116–17).

89. Hocart notes the relationship between the nonadministrative character of Fijian dominance and the indeterminacy of political boundaries; what he says of the "tribe" in this regard could certainly go for the sovereignties of Bau, Rewa, and other kingdoms: "The reality of the tribe is not so definite; it is not always easy to say where one tribe ends and another begins, because the foundation of Fijian society is not administration, but allegiance, and allegiance may vary infinitely from ritual subservience combined with political independence to complete serfdom" (1968: 75).

ter to defect, they normally did so by forming strong kinship relations between their own rulers and the Bauan chiefs: either by asking for a ranking Bauan woman as wife to their own paramount; or by 'begging a chief' (*kere turaga*), that is, asking for a Bauan notable to assume their own ruling title (cf. M. Sahlins 1994). However, the quasi-voluntary character of these imperial systems, together with the kinship ties, implied that at a certain relatively low level of material exaction or political imposition, the exercise of hegemonic authority could meet with subaltern resistance. For the core relationships of the empire were not just the ideological means and mystifications of hegemony. Or if they were, they were not too functional in such respects. Specifying at a relatively low level of imposition the point at which the economic and political pressures of the dominant power are experienced as oppression, they were ready-made formulae of resentment. Resentment in the core: here was another source of imperial pleonexia, of the impulse to bring more lands under control.

I am arguing that what historically counts as exploitation by a dominant power is neither self-evident nor a direct expression of the material or physical coercion involved. The same goes for what counts as force. For the amount of exaction or coercion on the part of the dominant power is only one aspect of the political significance; the existing relationships between the parties and the sense and value of autonomy on the part of the oppressed group are also relevant. Neither exploitation nor force is politically meaningful in itself. As Paul Veyne put it: "Relationships of force, whether symbolic or not, are not invariable. . . . Their transhistorical appearance is an analogical illusion. Their sociology is set within the limits of an arbitrary and historical program" (1988: 59).

Hegemony without sovereignty: how to designate this kind of imperial order? Thucydides referred to the Athenian empire as the *archē,* a nominalization of the verb for "command," and some classicists, recognizing the distinctiveness of the case, have adopted his usage. Olivier Picard for one: *empire,* he says, might be suitable in reference to the dominions of the Persian king, but the originality of Athenian power is such "that modern vocabulary does not furnish an appropriate name for it; and lacking as well are other examples with which it could be compared (except perhaps the Venetian *puissance*)" (Picard 2000: 10; cf. Kallet 2001). Let us add Bau to this small number of *archē* formations, maritime powers all, that dominate many other self-organized polities distributed over wide distances, without, however, assuming the rule of them. Indeed, the great disproportion between the size, manpower, and domestic resources of these thalassocracies, on one hand, and the scale of their supremacy, on the other, is a fundamental characteristic of the *archē.* It is the condition of another particularity of their hegemony—namely, that they control others largely by demonstration effects, by displays of power and superiority that, to adopt a Hobbesian phrase of governance, "keep them all in awe." Of course, I do not claim that displays of power are techniques of rule unknown to other imperial systems, those that directly administer their empires, only that in the *archē* such display is the principal instrument of domination, both of acquiring and of maintaining it. The necessity of always showing their power goes some way toward accounting for the Athenians' and the Bauans' obsession with it. The *archē* is in significant respects an empire of signs: signs of power, magnificent, draconian, or both at once, that bring other peoples into submission, perhaps for their own advantage or protection, but surely on pain of their destruction.

In the empire of signs, force too is a sign of force. Not to say that force is "just symbolic," or that the Bauans and Athenians did not employ it to coercive effect to subdue rebels and add to the extent of their *archē.* But at the same time, such uses of force were more broadly governmental, deliberately taken with an eye toward their demonstration effects on parties other than the victims, for which purposes they could be even more cruel than the situation required. *The violence was the greater for being symbolic.* Athenian force was terroristic, as de Romilly says, just because there was no administrative or political structure of it (Romilly 1968: 215). In the same way that Ratu Cakobau in Fiji could make the worst sort of cannibal end of a defiant chief, the Athenians were swift and pitiless in their reprisals on rebel cities or those that resisted inclusion in the *archē.* The violence employed in such cases was not only repressive but deliberately excessive. It was designed to objectify and disseminate a reputation for unbeatable power. "Punish them as they deserve," said Cleon, arguing in favor of massacring the rebellious Mytileneans, "and teach your allies that the penalty of rebellion is death" (Thuc. 3.40.7).

The famous debates in the Athenian assembly over the fate of Mytilene in 427 and Melos in 416 hinged decisively on the question of exemplary force. The defection of Mytilene, a ship-providing ally rather than a fiscal tributary, was a multiple blow to the Athenians. Initiated by the few (the party of the oligarchs), the rebellion was supported by a Peloponnesian fleet, which implied not only a concerted operation of Athens' enemies but a challenge to her control of the seas in her own Ionian backyard. After an initial decision to exterminate the Mytilenean lot, however, the Athenian assembly reconvened to reconsider this brutal measure. Arguing against reversal, Cleon warned his fellow citizens that they must not give way "to the three feelings most fatal to empire—pity, sentiment and indulgence" (3.40.2). His insistence that death was the lesson the other allies must be taught was coupled to the observation that the fate of other cities whose rebellions had been suppressed (less brutally) had been "no lesson" to the Mytileneans (3.39.3). All the same the decision was reversed—on the same principle of demonstration effects by which it was initially approved. The assembly was persuaded by the counterarguments of one Diodotus. "Where Cleon was so positive as to the useful deterrent effects that will follow from making rebellion a capital offense, I who consider the interests of the future quite as much as he, as positively maintain the contrary" (3.44.3). For the demonstration, said Diodotus, would only prove to would-be rebels that they might as well fight to the death, since such would be their fate if they lost, even as it would send the wrong message to Athens' natural friends in other cities, the democratic many, by killing their like in Mytilene for the crimes of the oligarchic few (3.45.46). Taking this argument, the Athenians decided to spare the many; only the aristocrats were killed.[90]

For Melos, which claimed to be an ancient Sparta island colony, the ending was less happy. The Athenians offered to lift their siege if the Melians would come over to them; when the Melians refused, asking to remain neutral instead, they were wiped out. Thucydides' placement of the Melian episode just before the Athenians' ill-fated Sicilian expedition is generally taken by the commentators as a moral point: the Athenians paid dearly for their cruelty. Yet the Athenians were practicing their customary politics of reputation. They could not accept the offer of neutrality, they told the Melians, because "your friendship will be an argument to our subjects of our weakness, and your enmity of our power" (Thuc. 5.95). And again, "if any maintain their independence it is because they are strong, and if we do not molest them it is because we are afraid; so that besides extending our empire we should gain by your subjection; the fact that you are islanders and weaker than others rendering it the more important that you should not succeed in thwarting the masters of the sea" (Thuc. 5.97). Hoping vainly for aid from the Spartans or, because their cause was just, from the gods, the Melians refused to surrender. All the men were killed, and the women and children were sold into slavery.

In both the Melian and Mytilenean events, the presence of the Spartans, actual or virtual, and their threat to Athenian sea power, indicates the

90. Thucydides says more than one thousand were killed (3.50.1); by other readings, the toll was much less.

growing complexity of the field of forces and the growing difficulties facing the Athenians in maintaining their hegemony. Add in the possibility of collusion among rebellious cities, and one can see why a draconian response to those who dared oppose them would seem in their interest. But there were also other ways of keeping others in awe.

"Polychrome Athens," as Gary Wills calls it. Athens was a spectacle: a force of cultural attraction and source of cultural radiation that had value as a politics of the *archē* by other means. In his excellent ethnography of Old Comedy, Victor Ehrenberg wrote that "even contemporary society realized that Athens, 'the most brilliant of cities,' stood out among all the Greek states for its beauty and spirit. Athens provided the best soil for every kind of intellectual and artistic endeavour. The comic poet derides the man who does not know Athens, or if he knows her, does not love her, or if he loves her, does not stay there" (Ehrenberg 1951: 278).

A fine comparison Athens made, too, with fundamentalist Sparta. Recall Thucydides' prediction that in time to come no one would be able to perceive Sparta's power from the poverty of her material traces, although one would be likely to overestimate Athens' from the monumentality of hers. Such ideas of the relation between pomp and power are echoed in Alcibiades' boast about the civic virtues of his unprecedented seven-chariot entry and one-two-four finish at the Olympic games of 416: "The Hellenes, after expecting to see our city ruined by war, concluded it to be even greater than it really is, by reason of the magnificence by which I represented it at the Olympic games. . . . Custom regards such displays as honorable, and they cannot be made without leaving behind them an impression of power" (Thuc. 6.16.2).

Such was the politics of this glory that was Greece: of the magnificence of her architecture and art, the brilliance of her theater, the glittering processions and ceremonies, the gymnasia and the symposia. Even those who never saw Athens could know her superiority by the reputation of her poets and philosophers, her politicians, and her athletes. Yes, a "tyrant city," but still "the school of Hellas."[91] By means of her numerous and admirable spectacles, "some passing all bounds in outlay of money," Athens made a point of drawing the world to her: "our city throughout all time,"

91. On "the school of Hellas," Isocrates echoes Pericles (Thuc. 2.41.1) in boasting of Athens's intellectual contributions to the world: "And so far has our city distanced the rest of mankind in thought and speech that her pupils have become the teachers of the rest of the world" (*Paneg.* 49–50).

Isocrates concluded, "is a festival for those who come to visit her" (*Paneg.* 46). Subject peoples notably visited her with their annual tributes at the time of the important religious festival, the City Dionysia, which was also the theater season.

If Bau, by contrast, offered no particular architectural spectacle, it was nonetheless the most dramatic island in Fiji, the scene of almost constant festivals of its power. Life on Bau was a more or less continuous pageant of subjugation and superiority. It was a series of ritual demonstrations of Bauan might that for speech, gesture, song, dance, bodily adornment, displays of food and wealth, crowds of people, and general excitement represented Fijian culture, one is tempted to say at its highest, but in any case at its most highly appreciated. Spectacle attended the tributes that came from places near and far, small and large. As we have noted, some were first-fruit offerings, especially of yams and tree crops, while others were annual or semi-annual offerings of the wealth of distant kingdoms. There were also the extraordinary levies on subject lands, and the voluntary gifts therefrom to one or another Bauan chief with some favor in view. None of this could pass without ceremony, and much was accompanied by festivity. Basil Thomson gives us a glimpse of the day-to-day demonstrations of hierarchy during the early colonial period, as seen from the vantage point of the ruling war king:

> A European, staying with a great chief such as the Vunivalu of Mbau, is astonished at the number of minor presentations. Several times, perhaps, during the course of the day the *tama* [ceremonial greeting approaching the house of the ruling chief or the god] is shouted from without the house. The chief's *mata* [*matanivanua,* 'herald'] looks out, and announces the arrival of some subject clan with an offering—a roll of sinnet, a bale of [tapa] cloth, a turtle, and the inevitable root of kava. A few of the household step out to listen to the speech of presentation and clap their hands in the prescribed form, but the chief himself scarcely deigns to check his conversation to listen. The merchandise is carried to a storehouse, where in due course it will be doled out to some chief deserving it, for the use of his numerous dependents, or to be used in the tangled political negotiations on which the safety of the federation depends. (Thomson 1908: 282)

One may judge something of the more important festivals of authority from Rev. Thomas Williams's general description of "tax paying in Fiji," considering that such scenes were considerably more frequent in Bau than elsewhere:

> Tax-paying in Fiji, unlike that in Britain, is associated with all that the people love. The time of its taking place is a high day; a day for the best attire, the pleasantest looks, and the kindest words; a day for display: whales teeth and cowrie necklaces . . . the scarlet frontlet . . . the newest style of neckband . . . the most graceful turban. The coiffure that has been in process for months is now shown to perfection; the body is anointed with the most fragrant oil, and decorated with the gayest flowers. . . . The weapons also—clubs, spears, and muskets—are all highly polished and are unusually gay. The Fijian carries his tribute with every demonstration of joyful excitement, of which all the tribe concerned fully partake. Crowds of spectators are assembled, and the King and his suite are there to receive the impost, which is paid with a song and a dance, and received with smiles and applause. From this scene the taxpayers retire to partake of a feast provided by their King. Surely the policy that can thus make the paying of tax as "a thing of joy" is not contemptible. (In Williams and Calvert 1859: 30–31)

In Bau, moreover, such joyous scenes of taxation were complemented by frequent rites of war: before battle, after battle, and sometimes, as displays of force during sieges, in place of battle. From their station near Bau, English missionaries saw fleets of war sailing from the island some sixteen or seventeen times between October 1839 and June 1841. These expeditions were often as large as thirty or forty canoes and sometimes coordinated with movements of warriors on the Viti Levu mainland. Reviewing soldiers for battle, dedicating and eating the human sacrificial victims taken in war, consecrating the man-slayers and their weapons, and thanking the gods and allies with feasts some time after the victory were usual concomitants of such actions, especially the large ones. Hence, one may take from such notices of Bauan engagements some idea of the ritual intensity entailed by its belligerence. Nor were all the rituals solemn or terrible. The jubilation over the bodies of cannibal victims, including the sexual bacchanalia that went on through the night as the bodies were roasting in the earth ovens, was at least as pleasurable to the victorious Fijians as it was disgusting to many Western witnesses.[92] In any case, these events were always stratifying,

92. See Clunie (1977: passim) on the rites of war, including cannibalism and the celebration of the man-slayers.

making political points. The speeches, prestations, kava rites, and other aspects of the ceremonies represented and communicated the supremacy of the Bauan chiefs. Those who came to visit Bau were thus treated to festivals of power they could absorb in marked bodily experiences that ranged from pleasure to dread. There was no theater season in Bau, but there were more or less continuous performances of its hegemony.[93]

* * *

It is not as if a system of hegemony without sovereignty, likewise functioning on the creation of compliant regimes and demonstration effects of the murderous and the marvelous, were unknown to the contemporary world. If one requires a familiar example of an *archē* like Athens, similarly built on exemplary force, cultural spectacle, and the export of democracy, how about the modern American empire?

THE GEOPOLITICS OF PLEONEXIA

In 451 Cimon the Athenian general and statesman, having recently ended the so-called First Peloponnesian War by concluding a five-year peace with Sparta, led a large expedition of two hundred triremes against Cyprus and Egypt (Thuc 1.112).[94] According to Plutarch, soon after the peace was established, it became clear to Cimon that "the Athenians were incapable of settling down quietly but were bent on a policy of constant activity and expansion of their empire through foreign expeditions" (*Cim.* 18). The Persian-held parts of Cyprus and Egypt were chosen as targets, because Cimon did not want to provoke the other Greek states by cruising around the islands or the Peloponnesus. "His plan was to keep the Athenians in constant training through their operations against the barbarians, and to allow them to profit as they deserved from the wealth they took from their natural enemies and brought to Greece" (ibid.)

93. Reverend Calvert gives us a glimpse of what going to Bau with tributes was like from the other side, that of the tribute-bearers: "When people of small towns are going to Bau, they will present offerings to their Gods, begging for safety, that the Bau chief be well-disposed towards them, feed them well, and give them good property in return for food or property which they take. If the [local] priest [possessed by the local god] is dissatisfied with neglect of him, in not offering pigs, first-fruits, or regular [feast-]puddings & kava, he will report that the god is angry & that they will be in danger. Their visit is postponed until the proper offering can be made" (*Missions:* 22 January 1855).

94. The Athenians not long before had been driven out of Egypt by the Persians.

One is reminded of Thucydides' comment on the general enthusiasm for the Sicilian expedition, cited earlier: "The idea of the common people and the soldiery was to earn wages at the moment, and make conquests that would supply a never-ending fund of pay for the future" (6.24.3). In fact, Cimon's policy already had many essentials of the enduring geopolitics of Athenian pleonexia. I refer to costly adventures at the peripheries of the empire, which were motivated by growing material demands at the center and the necessity of avoiding undue impositions on the allies and Athens itself. There was a certain deflection of exploitation and expansion outward—the way Cimon steered clear of "the islands," thus of Athens' allies, while also avoiding her erstwhile Peloponnesian enemies. By contrast to the taxation and resentment that could accumulate in the core of the *archē,* military actions at and beyond its limits promised new revenues and resources, booty (especially slaves), and, for the participants, livelihood while in naval service. Cimon's expedition of two hundred triremes, in providing "constant training," must have also provided constant pay for many thousands of Athenians—even assuming something less than the usual complement of two hundred men per vessel. Since much of this disbursement would come from public funds, and some from the contributions (liturgies) of rich men who assumed the maintenance of particular ships, such adventures must have envisioned considerable returns, including the long-term returns of trade and tribute. In Cimon's case, however, the expedition probably amounted to a net loss, including the loss of his own life. The latter misfortune caused the Greeks to break off their siege of Cyprus, and apart from one victory, the squadron returned home with little to show for its large efforts (Thuc. 1.112).

The geopolitical dilemma of the *archē* is that a thalassocracy of this type, subject to a cumulative increase in costs as it expands, then discovers a like necessity to increase its exactions from its own people or from subject peoples—or else, find new peoples to exploit. Subsidizing the maritime expansion generates demands on the resources and manpower of the hegemon in something like an exponential rather than a linear fashion. Situated at the center of a sphere of domination that extended outward in many directions, Athens could find its interests and expenses multiplying by something like the square of its distance to an expanding circumference times 3.14159. The problem was even more acute than geometry suggests, inasmuch as the major sources of Athenian grain supplies were situated at the far reaches of her power, in the Crimea particularly. Keeping the trade routes open required considerable naval presence and periodic military action: continuous patrols of eighty ships for eight months of the year, according to Plutarch (*Per.* 11). Ehrenberg summarizes: "We may take it for certain that the mere task of keeping the corn routes free from interference was in itself a matter of high policy and frequent military measures. The necessity and difficulty of getting grain and other vital supplies for the state and people afforded a means by which politics could influence economics, and even more, economics could affect politics" (Ehrenberg 1951: 325; cf. Thuc. 2.69.1; Casson 1991: 111–12).[95]

The critical "politics" part of this geopolitics had to do with the risks of putting the escalating material burdens of the *archē* onto its core populations, the people of Attica and the allies of long standing. The risks were sedition at home and rebellion abroad. Rebellions we already know about; the potential sedition inheres in the condition that the rich and powerful were under the greatest obligations, morally as well as legally, to support the state. The navy was to some extent created and funded by liturgies: the public duties assumed by rich private citizens of constructing, equipping, maintaining, and paying crews' wages for triremes, over which they also enjoyed the (nominal) command at sea. (The exact extent to which the Athenian navy was supported by liturgies in the fifth century and the extent to which liturgies were legally enforced are unknown.) In a recent work on the financing of the Athenian fleet, Vincent Gabrielson (1994: 12) remarks on the great interest taken by the state "in the preservation and goodwill of its primary object of taxation," that is, the rich: "Its interest was economic *and* political: economic because any abuse would lead to declining cooperation on the part of property owners, or even worse to exhaustion of their financial potential; political, because unlimited fiscal demands would be found to cause social unrest or even *stasis* (civil strife)." Here, among the potentially rebellious rich and the formally independent tributaries, were the centrifugal pressures that deflected the Athenian predatory gaze to the hinterlands of their *archē,* as far off as Sicily and Cloudcuckooland.

The Peloponnesian War made everything worse: more taxation of the Athenians, heavier levies on the allies, tribute-collecting expeditions to the borders of the *archē.* And after the Sicilian disaster, all this was not enough to prevent widespread rebellion abroad and an oligarchic coup at home.

95. Regarding the Black Sea, Kagan writes: "The importance of this region to Athens is often seen in purely economic terms, but its economic significance was subordinate to its strategic role. The entire security of Athens rested on its independence of local food supplies. The long walls turned Athens into an island obtaining all its requirements by sea. An enemy who could cut off her access to the Black Sea could bring her to her knees" (1969: 180).

Thucydides' first notice of extraordinary taxation of the Athenians already shows the correlation with the tendency to increase exactions from the outskirts of the *archē*. In 428, needing money to sustain a siege of Mytilene in Lesbos, Athens for the first time levied a war-tax on its citizens. But the 200 talents this raised was not enough, whereupon twelve ships were dispatched to "collect money from their allies" (Thuc. 3.19.1). Such tribute collections were armed excursions. In this case, after collecting monies from places that could be reached by sea, the commander of the expedition marched inland, into the Carian region of Asia Minor, where he and many of his soldiers were killed in an attack by the local people (3.19.2). Two years earlier the same fate was visited in the same general region on another Athenian force dispatched to collect tribute and discourage piracy (2.69). Including two other, similar missions mentioned by Thucydides, all these tribute-collecting excursions of Athenian fleets in the 420s were targeting areas at the extremes of Athenian hegemony, and apparently sometimes beyond, from the Carian and Lycian areas in Asia Minor, through the Hellespont, and to Eion in Thrace (2.69.1; 4.50; 4.75). In 425, moreover, the Athenians raised the tribute rates throughout the empire. At least some allies saw their assessment doubled; indeed, Moses Finley claimed that the Athenian revenue demands more than trebled (1972: 24). And then, in the dire circumstances of 413, the Athenians resorted to new measures of taxation. Pinned down at once in Syracuse and in Attica (by the Spartan occupation of the strategic fort of Decelea), the Athenians "imposed upon their subjects, instead of tribute, the tax of a twentieth of all imports and exports by sea, which they now thought would raise more money for them; their expenditures being now not the same as at first, but having grown with the war while their revenues decayed" (Thuc. 7.28.4). Within the year, the allies/subjects were revolting: Lesbians, Euboeans, Chians, the Hellespont cities, and many others, some aided by the Spartans, some conspiring with one another (bk. 8, passim). So too were the Athenian rich, "the most powerful citizens, who also suffered most severely from the war," and who "now had great hopes of getting the government in their hands" (8.48.1). The government they wanted was an oligarchy, which they got for a short time, until their coup was reversed, largely by the democratically inclined army. But the end of the Athenian *archē* was near.

The Fijian *archē* of Bau faced a similar geopolitics, and, as noted earlier, its accompanying pleonexia had a similar dénouement—including, in fact, a failed coup attempt. But then, from the beginning, Bau likewise was disposed to fight for wealth and power at the extremities of its sphere of domination. It took a series of provocations extending over two years for the

Bauans to engage in the showdown with nearby Rewa, and even as the great Polynesian War was finally about to begin, the Bauans, or at least some Bauan chiefs, still preferred as enemies the distant, prosperous lands of northern and eastern Fiji, with which they had been at war on and off for years, like Cimon picking his targets in Egypt and Cyprus.

In the late 1830s and early 1840s, under the command of Ratu Cakobau, Bau had undertaken repeated forays of war or tribute exaction against the major kingdoms of Verata, Macuata, Namena, Cakaudrove, and Lau. The Bau fleets or those of their allies sailed far and often to recover the domination the kingdom had enjoyed in the 1820s under the Vunivalu, Ratu Naulivou, but which was threatened and weakened during the stasis of 1832–37, which saw the exile of his successor Ratu Tānoa. Now the old kingdom of Verata attempted to assert its former ascendancy by attacks on Bauan canoes, a move that endangered Bau's control of the islands, many of which were once Veratan lands. Moreover, in return for the refuge afforded him in 1832 in Somosomo, Ratu Tānoa had ceded Bau's rights of tribute collection in Lau to the king of Cakaudrove (Hale 1846: 59). Becoming quite full of themselves, the Cakaudrove ruling chiefs then ceased sending their own tributes to Bau. By the end of the decade they had persuaded the rulers of Macuata to do the same, and to enter into an exchange relationship with Cakaudrove instead of enriching Bau. The Çakaudrove chiefs also conspired with certain Viti Levu peoples (Namena and Telau) to join them in hostilities against Bau. In sum, the kingdom of Cakaudrove had aspirations of replacing Bau as the hegemonic power in Fiji—until Ratu Cakobau essentially repeated the persuasive demonstrations of force that had sustained Bauan power at the beginning of the century.[96]

Bau and Cakaudrove never came into direct conflict, although a state of war existed between them from 1839, and Cakaudrove was repeatedly agitated by rumors of an imminent Bauan attack. Rather, Bau first moved to subdue Verata. Bau canoes sailed against Verata towns nine or ten times between October 1839 and November 1840, engaging the enemy on several occasions, and finally forcing a formal submission (*i soro*) by the Verata chiefs in December 1840. In one of Ratu Cakobau's subtlest and most suc-

96. So Mr. Hunt wrote in 1839: "I have already spoken of the manner in which the Somosomo [Cakaudrove] chiefs are said to have obtained power over their neighbors. I may here add that they think themselves little less than gods because of the prosperity they have had. They are now about to make war with Bau, or rather Bau with them, but they speak of their past successes as being certain proof that they shall never be conquered. They have lately heard that many towns belonging to Bau are favorable to the cause of Somosomo, which lifts their heads very high" (in Lyth *N:* 332).

cessful conspiracies (*vere vakaBau*), the lands of Namena and Telau suffered a massacre of their warriors in 1839 while on a friendly visit to Viwa Island, near Bau—which he followed up by several sea-borne attacks on Namena proper (northeast coast of Viti Levu). Occupied thus with its Viti Levu enemies, Bau did not have the means to confront Cakaudrove directly. Instead Ratu Cakobau sent a fleet of Viwa and Tongan warriors—some five hundred Tongans lived in Bau for six months in 1840—to attack Macuata. After Verata capitulated, however, the Bau Vunivalu led an unsuccessful expedition to defend the Taveuni town of Vuna against Cakaudrove, and another, triumphant foray against Macuata that continued on to the northeastern point of Vanua Levu, terrorizing many towns along the way. These demonstrations of Bauan power, together with a revolt of Cakaudrove's warrior allies (Natewa), convinced the Somosomo chiefs to sue for peace at the beginning of 1843. Soon after, an impressive, tribute-bearing flotilla was on its way from Cakaudrove to Bau, and a visit by Ratu Cakobau to Lau restored the customary levies of Bau on these prosperous islands. To complete the geophysical dimensions of this historic recovery of the Bauan *archē,* we need only mention that the subject islands—especially Koro, Moturiki, Ovalau, and Nairai—contributed significant resources for mobilizing the Bau armies, sustaining them on campaign and rewarding their successes. Such levies on Bauan subjects, however, were not always designed to encourage their loyalty. Tradition records that after a successful attack on two Verata towns by a large force of Bauans and their Viti Levu allies, Ratu Cakobau told his people to sail to the islands of the Koro Sea and seize pigs and wealth (*i yau*) willy-nilly for the great feasts of victory (Anon. 1891 [4]: 11). The securing of the marches of the *archē* had been achieved at the expense of the inner subjects and the center: losses that presumably would be compensated by returns from the peripheral conquests.[97]

This geopolitics of pleonexia was not a simple geographical thermodynamics, however, either in Greece or in Fiji. The physical forces were set in motion by a strategy dictated by the nature of the *archē,* the system of hegemony without sovereignty. The interests, resistances, ambitions, and other intentions of political action, including the irrationalities thereof, derived their motivation from a specific structural context, a determinate scheme of relationships and values. One cannot read the *archē* politics simply or directly from universal human dispositions, such as desires for power

97. The Bauan reconquest of 1838–42 can be followed from the numerous entries in that period in the journals of Messrs. Cross, Jaggar, Hunt, and Lyth, primarily.

and gain, the way Thucydides recommended—and too many have since followed.

THE HISTORIOGRAPHY OF HUMAN NATURE

> *Melians:* And how, pray, could it turn out as good for us to serve as for you to rule?
>
> *Athenians:* Because you would have the advantage of submitting before suffering the worst, and we should gain by not destroying you. . . .
>
> *Melians:* You may be sure that we are as well aware as you of the difficulty of contending against your power and fortune, unless the terms be equal. But we trust that the gods may grant us fortune as good as yours, since we are just men fighting against unjust, and that what we want in power will be made up by the alliance of the Spartans, who are bound, if only for very shame, to come to the aid of their kindred. . . .
>
> *Athenians:* Of the gods we believe, and of men we know, that by a necessary law of nature they rule wherever they can. And it is not as if we were the first to make this law, or to act upon it when made: we found it existing before us, and shall leave it to exist forever after us; all we do is to make use of it, knowing that you and everybody else, having the same power as we have, would do the same as we do. Thus, as far as the gods are concerned, we have no fear and no reason to fear that we shall be at a disadvantage. . . . The Spartans, when their own interests or their country's laws are in question, are the worthiest men alive; of their conduct towards others much might be said, but no clearer idea of it could be given than by shortly saying that of all men we know they are most conspicuous in considering what is agreeable, honorable, and what is expedient, just. (Thuc. 5.92–93, 104–5)

These excerpts from the famous "Melian Dialogue" would be strong testimony for the claim that Thucydides was the true father of history—Western history, that is. "The first page of Thucydides is, in my opinion, the commencement of real history," wrote David Hume. "All preceding narratives are so intermingled with fable, that philosophers ought to abandon them, in a great measure, to the embellishment of poets and orators" (1985: 422). It was appropriate praise from a philosopher who believed that "in all nations and ages . . . human nature remains the same in its principles and operations. . . . Mankind are so much the same, in all times and places, that history informs us of nothing new or strange on this particular" (1975: 83). One might fairly judge from this that Thucydides was the end as well as the beginning of history, since he had already identified the relentless self-interest that enlightened Western philosophers, from well before Hume up to the present, have likewise considered the universal mainspring of historical action.[98] To be more precise: of the Augustinian "triple libido," the three lusts of sex, gain, and power that have dominated our native anthropology for millennia, Thucydides concentrated on the gain and power. Sex was largely neglected—as were women nearly altogether. Of natural human aversions, the principal one in Thucydides was fear. (Again, you can see where Hobbes was coming from.)[99]

Here, then, was the brilliant origin of the unhappy Western consciousness of history as the expression of the worst in us (Orwin 1988: 832). There have been plenty of debates about other aspects of Thucydides' historiography. Classicists seem to have said just about everything that could be said about it, including the opposite of everything. Thucydides was a pragmatist and a mythologist, objective and subjective, a prose poet and a scientific historian, really a moralist and an amoral realist, a man of his time, a modernist before his time, and—why not?—a postmodernist (Connor 1977). Still, on the two major principles of the kind that must have appealed to Hume, Hobbes & Co.—the intention to write a history of universal relevance and the referral of historical action to a self-regarding human nature—there has been wide agreement about Thucydides' historiography. I would only add the assertion that a history based on such foundations is decidedly anticultural—and in the same measure antihistorical. The resort to human nature depreciates the cultural construction

98. Regarding the usual comparisons with Herodotus, Crane's remark is pertinent: "Thucydides was not the first person to analyze historical events in terms of self-interest and the calculus of forces, but his *History* does so with greater intensity and thoroughness than any earlier surviving document" (1998: 146). On self-regarding human nature in Thucydides, see, among others, Cawkwell (1997: 6, 19), Connor (1984: 144), Guthrie (1971), Palmer (1992), Romilly (1967).

99. Connor comments on a passage from the so-called "Archaeology": "The cause of the growing prosperity in the time of Minos was not courage or heroism, but something much deplored in the aristocratic literature of early Greece—the profit motive, *kerdos:* 'Desiring profits the weaker put up with the "slavery" imposed by the stronger and the more powerful having surpluses subjugated the lesser cities' [1.18.3]. Here we encounter the dynamic represented [by Thucydides] as a cause of many phenomena in early Greek history. The developments Thucydides describes are not the result of heroes or heroism but of desires that had often been deplored in early literature. Self-interest, the desire for profit, and even fear lead to the growth of power and security in Greece and to an escape from the squalor and danger of early times" (Connor 1984: 25–26).

of forms of human life. If Thucydides was the true father of history, then history began by the taking of true anthropology out of it. Or to follow Thucydides' own phrasing, it began by the elimination of the marvelous, in the interest of making his history relevant to all times, so long as people are what they naturally are:

> And it may well be that my history will seem less easy to read because of the absence in it of a romantic element. It will be enough for me, however, if these words of mine are judged useful by those who want to understand clearly the events which happened in the past and which (human nature being what it is) will, at some time or other and in much the same ways, be repeated in the future. My work is not a piece of writing designed to meet the taste of an immediate public, but was done to last forever. (1.22.4)[100]

Thucydides' modest intellectual ambitions involved a double humanization of history, a secularization and a universalization, which he then confounded although they do not necessarily entail each other. By eliminating the "romantic," Thucydides meant to get rid of divine intervention as a cause of historical events. He would make history understandable as a human creation, and he has been much celebrated for it—notwithstanding the ethnographic cardinal sin of ignoring what the people thought important. Yet to make the Greeks humanly responsible for their own history is not the same thing as making their own history a model for humanity. On the contrary, to make Greek history universally applicable, one would have to subtract whatever was distinctively Greek from it, whatever specifically conditioned it, and ground its intelligibility instead on a generic human nature. Eliminating the marvelous thus became a prescription for devaluing the cultural in favor of the natural for the sake of the universal.

Human nature: this animalization of the rhetoric of history is the counterpart, argues David Grene (1965), of its humanization in fifth-century Athenian consciousness. Taken from the control of the gods and delivered to human decision, politics was thus delivered to bodily desire: "Because

100. I have used Warner's rather than Crawley's translation of this passage, as most commentators agree that the "human thing" (*to anthrōpinon*) here designated refers to human nature, as is more literally the case in the parallel passage on the revolt in Corcyra: "The sufferings which revolution entailed upon the cities were many and terrible, such as have occurred and always will occur long as human nature [*physis anthrōpōn*] remains the same" (3.82.2; cf. Cook 1985: 43). See also Luginbill (1999: 30n, 32n) on the virtual identity of "the human thing," or as he puts it, "the human condition," with human nature in Thucydides.

the greatness of Athens' empire was in the eyes of its inhabitants man-made and based on its exploitation of material resources, almost exclusively, because there is no attempt to believe in a divinely imposed task or a more than human duty or the perfectibility of man, political rhetoric in fifth-century Athens develops a theory of human nature based essentially on nothing but animal desires and their satisfaction" (28).

In the historiographic event, it is not just the gods' doings and humanity's better sentiments that get intellectually sidelined; so too does culture, inasmuch as human meanings and rules cannot stand up to the powerful forces of natural desire. If history is a "human thing," as it was for Thucydides, then it comes down to an unequal contest between changeable words and implacable bodies. In his history, *nomos,* 'convention,' was no match for *physis,* 'nature.' *Nomos* was to *physis* as the contingent to the necessary and the mutable to the unchangeable. "In short, it is impossible to prevent," says Diodotus in the Mytilenean debate, "and only great simplicity can hope to prevent, human nature doing what it has once set its mind upon, by force of law or by any other deterrent force whatsoever" (3.45.7). The list of cultural practices and institutions that are one way or another subject to human nature in Thucydides, whether overcome by it or dependent on it for their own characteristics, is quite impressive. It includes kinship, friendship, ethnic affiliation, empire and traditional social institutions in general; law, morality, honor, treaties, and justice in general; the gods, sacredness, and religion in general; and not least, language, the meaning of words in general. All of these are nothing in comparison to human desires, either in the sense that self-interest will subvert them—as in the Corcyraean revolution or the Athenian plague—or in the sense that self-interest is the real reason for their existence—as in the pursuit of gain and power that made the Athenian empire or, more specifically, led to the destruction of the Melians. Note, then, the remarkable explanatory power of Thucydides' invocations of human nature. The argument will account both for order and for disorder, for structure and for anomie, for the construction of culture and for its deconstruction. An enviable, no-lose debating stance, still found in reductionist anthropologies of human nature, the procedure explains everything and its opposite.[101]

Even so, Thucydides' reliance on human nature was in trouble from the

101. So on successive pages Robert Kaplan (2002: 48–49) speaks of "power and self-interest" as motivating Athenian imperialism (as in the Melian dialogue), even as "power and affluence blinded Athens to the bleak forces of human nature that lie just beneath the veneer of civilization, threatening its good fortune."

beginning insofar as it did not sit well with the differences between Spartans and Athenians as expounded by the Corinthians in Book One. I mean the national temperaments that Thucydides made so much of. The way these contrasts in national character are set up specifies that in exactly the same conditions, the Spartans and Athenians behave in exactly opposite ways (cf. Bagby 1994: 137–38). I take an example that has dramatic echoes in Thucydides' several discussions of human nature. Addressing the Spartans, the Corinthians observe that while the Athenians "are adventurous beyond their power and daring beyond their judgment, and in danger they are sanguine; your wont is to attempt less than is justified by your power, to mistrust even what is sanctioned by your judgment, and to fancy that from danger there is no release" (1.70.3). Consider, first, the differential response to "danger," because danger meets the Thucydidean condition for the unleashing of natural instincts. Danger is what causes self-interest to wreak havoc with established institutions, especially in the Corcyraean revolt. So one is directly entitled to question how it is that, human nature being the same all over, the Spartans and Athenians react differently in the same circumstances? These were the very conditions—similarity of circumstance and identity of human nature—that were supposed to make Thucydides' history a treasure for all time. Of course, one could say that the self-interests of the land-based Spartans and the thalassocratic Athenians were different. But apart from the tautology, what this really says is that their interests depended on their cultural schemes. Their values and utilities, and accordingly their motivations and actions, derived from the cultural and not from the natural order. Peoples differ by what they love, as Saint Augustine put it.

And then there is the relation to "power" noted by the Corinthians: the Athenians are ambitious, as for domination, even beyond their power; the Spartans attempt even less than they could accomplish. This is hardly the only instance in which the Spartans are human-nature challenged, or where the Athenians turn out to be the exclusive paragons of universal human dispositions. The voluntary alliance of autonomous states with equal voting rights in which Sparta was the only *primus inter pares,* an alliance lacking the tributary exactions and the other privileges of domination Athens enjoyed in her empire, the Spartan confederacy is testimony enough to its leading state's deficits in *libido dominandi.* Yet the will to rule where one can is a law of human nature, often enough expressed by Thucydides. Recall the Athenians telling the Melians that they were not the first to make this law, nor would they be the last to act on it, that all they did was use it, "knowing that you and everybody else, having the same power as we have, would do the same as we do." Yet it was already clear that the Spartans, having the same power, would not always do the same (as you guys). Moreover, in this instance the Melians also proved lacking in the appropriate universal-natural inclinations: they did not know how to fear for their own preservation. Choosing to fight—while hoping, also against all odds, for divine or Spartan intervention—they were destroyed. If their failure to perceive their interests, as so clearly laid out in the dialogue, ironically confirms the Thucydidean point that *logos* is no proof against human passions, it also supports the rather antithetical point that hope does not respond rationally to reality—"for it is a habit of mankind to entrust to careless hope what they long for, and to use sovereign reason to thrust aside what they do not desire" (4.108.4). Allowing their wants to interfere even with their perceptions—hope and greed, "although invisible agents, are far stronger than the dangers that are seen" (3.45.5)—men are not then inclined to follow the course of their best interests. The deceptive gift of Pandora, hope thus neutralizes the interest-thing by making calculations on it impossible. Instead, it leads people to act on considerations of another kind, such as gods, justice, or kinship with Spartans—all of which, Thucydides also says, are supposed to be less powerful than human nature, especially in a crisis. This is again the best of all possible worlds of historical theorizing, where it is only human nature to act contrary to human nature, in which event human nature becomes the unbeatable world champion of historiography.

But just whose interests are at stake in this history? Not those of women certainly, nor of the suffering peasants of Attica, to judge from Aristophanes. Not the interests of the Spartans' helots, surely. Yet in 422 the Spartans were anxious to make peace with Athens in order to rescue 120 of their men captured on the island of Sphacteria (Thuc. 5.15.1). Ah, but these were true Spartiates and of the "first families" of the city. So what are "first families," in this famous society of "the peers," and why do they rate so highly?[102] Clearly, we have to do with socially and politically differentiated schemes of interest and power, which is also to say, schemes of differential historical agency. But Thucydides was writing in the early stages of what was to become the vast Western delusion of conceiving society as a collection of autonomous individuals: as if there were nothing to consider in the making of history—as in the making of economy or polity—other than the

102. On the differentiations of Spartan society by wealth, descent, and other factors, see Hodkinson (1983).

interplay between *sui generis* individuals and the undifferentiated totality called society. Everything is reduced to man and the city (as Leo Strauss put it), as if there were nothing in-between and articulating them, and as if the historical issue hinged on negotiations between the city's interests and individual interests (as Pericles put it).

The strategy of laying the whole analysis on an opposition between these curiously abstract historical subjects is perhaps already apparent—as it has been apparent to the many modern historians who have made valiant efforts with limited resources to fill in the cultural vacuum of Thucydides' natural history. "Did Thucydides ever envision a time," asks Simon Hornblower, "when civilized human beings would not speak what we call classical Greek?" (1987: 96). Missing from Thucydides' account is the whole set of mediating institutions and values involved in the constitution of historical agency: the complex relationships, both conjunctural and systematic, that give authority to certain persons and groups, thus confining the collective destiny to their particular dispositions. Recent works by classicists suggest that what has been left out of the account of fifth-century Athens is—fifth-century Athens. Absent are the clans (*genē*), demes, tribes, and cognatic houses (in the Lévi-Straussian sense); the marital relations, friendship networks, political clubs, and followings; or in general, the economy (for the most part), the religion (for the most part), and the organization of the *archē* (for the most part). In this connection, Thucydides, as Albert Cook observes, "leaves Herodotus' ethnographic inquiries almost totally behind. He does not need these particulars" (1985: 2). Maybe he didn't feel the lack, but what the scholarly world ever since Thucydides has been trying to put into his account is precisely the ethnography he missed out.[103]

The reason is that, peoples being culturally distinct, and acting differentially in and on the world, it will be necessary to know their schemes of value and relationships in order to understand their histories. Otherwise, in a historiography without anthropology, our accounts are reduced to the

103. "Life in Athens was organized through complexly multiple, sometimes overlapping, sometimes distinct institutions and groupings: cult associations, self-help *eronoi,* political subdivisions, migrant social groups, business associations, groupings of messmates, and funerary associates, religious congregations, 'houses' and households, brotherhoods, kin groupings, family organizations and many others—loci of significance and epicenters of authority often impacting, supplementing, superseding, negating the formalistic political organization of the male politai" (Cohen 2000: 8, cf. Connor 1992; Ehrenberg 1951; Hornblower 1992).

indeterminacies of a generic human nature or the implicit common sense of the historian's own tribe—the ethnocentricity of the latter, in the form of rational self-interest, often taken for the universality of the former.

Still, what all these exercises prove is that if Thucydides got us into this mess, pondering his immortal pages can help get us out of it. Apologies to Thucydides, then. We owe a lot to the old man.

CHAPTER 2

* * *

CULTURE AND AGENCY IN HISTORY

Take Thucydides' foundational text on the Peloponnesian War: who exactly is acting here? Who, or what, are the agents of this history? City-states? Peoples? Certain persons? The same puzzles of agency are present in Herodotus. I venture to guess they vex almost every history ever written, despite the attempts of the *Annales* school to banish individuals in favor of structures, at least for certain histories of the *longue durée.* As it appeared in antiquity, the historiographic problem runs something as follows. In relating the Peloponnesian War, Thucydides moves freely and without apparent motivation between two different kinds of historical agents: between collective subjects, such as the Athenians, the Spartans or the Corinthians, and prominent individuals, such as Pericles, Brasidas, or Alcibiades. So in a famous passage about the "truest cause" of the war—as distinct from the incidents that set it off—Thucydides spoke of "the growing power of the Athenians and the fear this inspired in the Spartans." Collectives were the movers and shakers. In the same totalized register were the characterological differences between the derring-do Athenians and the conservative Spartans, which supposedly accounted for important differences in their respective military strategies and imperial hegemonies. Yet it was the sagacious Themistocles who made Athens a maritime power, the ambitious Alcibiades who engineered the grandiose Sicilian expedition—and the superstitious Nicias who screwed it up. In what W. Robert Connor calls "commander narratives," individuals here get all the historical credit, as opposed to the passages in which the city-states, or more precisely the peoples thereof, act as collective bodies (Connor 1984: 54–55).

Connor notes that these two types of historical subject alternately dominate Thucydides' text—exception made for the complex story of competing persons and factions in the Athenian stasis of 411—but he offers no general principle for the historian's oscillation between them. W. D. Westlake (1968) and more recently Simon Hornblower (1987: 145–46) suggest something of a reason, based on the observation that individuals are more salient and more fully described in later books of Thucydides' *History* than in earlier ones. They believe Thucydides increasingly became aware of the historical significance of individuals as the war and the writing of it went on. But this rather begs the question, supposing we already understand that significance, hence when and why history should be narrated individually and when collectively. The great Arnaldo Momigliano seems to have supposed likewise when he tried to account for the "disturbing presence" of particular persons in the historical texts of fifth-century Greece—"disturbing" in light of the evident powers of the city-state in the determination of political action and its privileged place in political thought (Momigliano 1993: 40–42). Because the important decisions were taken by the city in assemblies or councils, this "produced or at least reinforced the impression that military and political transactions were in the hands of collective bodies." But for all that, says Momigliano, despite that the city was both the principal subject and subject matter of history, the chroniclers could not ignore particular people, such as Pericles and other Athenian generals cum statesmen (*strategoi*)—because they were there: "No history, however bent on emphasizing collective decisions, can manage to get rid of the disturbing presence of individuals: they are simply there." Still, however sufficient as a reason for climbing mountains, this fact of mere existence does not seem good enough for writing history.

Momigliano's argument about political decisions does speak to an unusual custom of Athenian historians, notably Thucydides and Herodotus. The ancients were disposed to identify the collective subject as the people of the city or the state, rather than the state itself. Athens, Sparta, Corinth, Persia, et al. are not, as such, the historical actors in these texts; they are not the grammatical subjects of active or passive verbs. The actors are the Athenians, the Spartans, the Corinthians, the Persians, and their like (Finley 1984: 26). The "truest cause" of the Peloponnesian War was not the growing power of Athens and the fear this inspired in Sparta—although the passage is often so translated—but "the growing power of the Athenians and the fear this inspired in the Spartans." In our own common usage—and I believe this is true in many other places, even in the Fiji Islands—the nation, the city, and other such collectives are readily anthropomorphized: they appear as entities in historical and other talk with the character and capacities of nonhuman persons. "America" can be belligerent or feel threatened, intervene or turn its back to a crisis, enjoy a period of prosperity, struggle against its AIDS epidemic, and so on. But not so classical "Athens"—because, it is usually said, of its democracy. In democratic Athens, with decisions taken in the assembly of all citizens and most offices filled from the *demos* by lot, the history of the city was perceived as the people in action. The citizens and the state were one. The Athenian state, as Ehrenberg says, "was called neither 'the Republic of Athens' (like the *res publica Romana*) nor was it called 'Attica' (like a modern territorial state), but 'the Athenians.' The citizens, they and they alone, made up the State which was embodied in the person and idea of Demos, the people" (Ehrenberg 1951: 337). It could be that such inhibitions on perceiving the state as an entity of and for itself are corollary to, and have the same basis as, Thucydides' only limited reflections on Athenian social and cultural order as such.

But we are still left with the question of the historical subject: when should it be Themistocles, and when the Athenians? And behind such historiographic questions are structural ones, likewise remaining to be answered: what are the structural and situational conditions by which now totalities, now individuals are empowered as history-makers? "Who is to decide," asks A. B. Gallie, "and on what grounds could it possibly be decided, whether the following of general trends or the following of individual motives and reasons is of greatest importance in history?" (1963: 175). Yet this slightly different phrasing, substituting "general trends"—a form of change—for the collective agents of history, may well suggest how the question "could possibly be decided." The suggestion, broadly, is that collectives are to trends what individuals are to events; in other words, that the choice of historical subject depends on the mode of historical change. Such is the argument I examine in this chapter, starting with an apparently curious example from the annals of American baseball.

BASEBALL IS SOCIETY, PLAYED AS A GAME

In the late 1960s the Yale historian J. H. Hexter wrote a revelatory essay on "The Rhetoric of History," the centerpiece of which was a crafted response to the question, "How did the New York Giants happen to play in the World Series of 1951?"[1] Since the so-called World Series of that time matched baseball teams all the way from the Mississippi River to the East Coast of the United States, and from the Canadian border to the Mason-Dixon line, you will appreciate the world historical significance of the question. If not, you are probably not a fan, and I must apologize to you for this commentary on Hexter's text. Apologies especially to people other than Americans, Canadians, Japanese, Dominicans, Venezuelans, and Cubans, who are not baseball fans and probably couldn't care less—although anyone who is an athletic supporter of some sort should be able to transpose the narrative to a league sport of another kind. I can offer the consolation that the story of how the New York Giants defeated the Brooklyn Dodgers for the National League championship, which is how they got to play in the World Series, also has elements of class warfare, inasmuch as it pitted the patrician Manhattan followers of the Giants against the plebeian Brooklynites. In any case, it will be useful to suffer through the account of the 1951 Giants' pennant, together with the comparison Hexter draws with the American League championship of 1939 won by the New York Yankees, because the two stories not only feature individual and collective agency, respectively, they also motivate the narratological difference by contrasting kinds of historical change.

There are structures *of* and *in* history. It's not all tricks the living play on the dead. The history of the '39 Yankees' pennant was developmental, where that of the '51 Giants was evenemential. The first was evolutionary, the second a kind of revolutionary *volte-face.* The Yankees dominated the 1939 season from beginning to end, April to October, steadily pulling away from the second-place team. The Giants won at 3:58 P.M. (EDT) on 3 October 1951, when Bobby Thomson hit the famous home run that defeated the Brooklyn Dodgers in the last half of the last inning of the final game of a three-game playoff for the title—the teams having been tied at the end of the regular season. Hexter chose to compare the two seasons because in contrast to the narrative mode appropriate to the Giants' victory, which he calls "storytelling," the Yankees' championship is better understood by "analysis": an account simply of their attributes as a team, without the necessity of referring to individual exploits or particular games. So to compare small things with great ones, again as Thucydides would say, here also are histories of competition that, by their specific forms, variously

1. Originally appearing in the *Encyclopedia of the Social Sciences* in 1968, the essay is reprinted in Hexter (1971: 15–76).

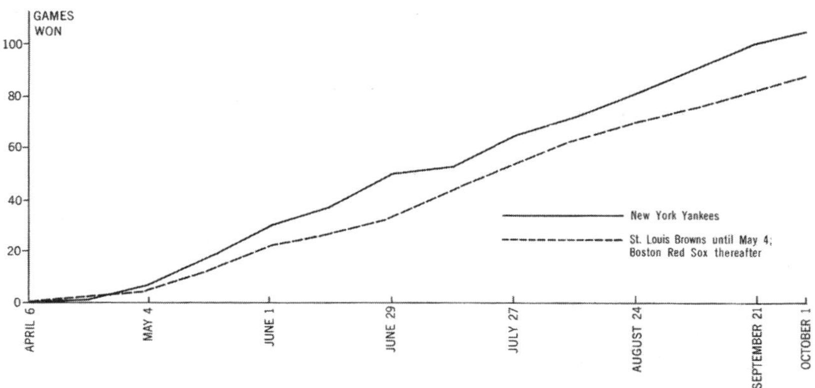

2.1 New York Yankees' Pennant run, 1939

motivate a collective recounting or the intervention of difference-making persons. Even more, Hexter's baseball comparison affords a principled reason, grounded in the nature of the history at issue, for the temporalities or periodizations by which we relate it. Eureka! Contrary to the prevailing epistemological mood of pessimistic self-reflection—which is too often self-reproach for laying presentist concerns on a past that seemingly offers no resistance to the historian's manipulations—the structures of and in history impose some strong limits on our hubris.

There was no pennant race in the American League in 1939, no turning point, no contest (fig. 2.1). Minor day-to-day fluctuations apart, right from the beginning the Yankees progressively distanced themselves from the competition, to end the season with an extraordinary seventeen-game advantage over (who else?) the Boston Red Sox. For the same reason, there were no decisive, pennant-winning acts or heroes. Although certain Yankee players had outstanding years, and one or another may have made an outstanding play to decide a particular game, neither any individual performance nor any specific event can adequately respond to the question (in effect) posed by Hexter, how did the Yankees come to win the pennant? To understand this history of progressive domination, it suffices to demonstrate the Yankees' superiority as a team, over the whole season, in the critical baseball functions of hitting, fielding, and pitching. The historical subject is the collective, and accordingly the relevant historical factors are its properties as a collective. Or as Hexter put it: "There is nothing to do but analyze the betterness of New York [the Yankees], to seek out its ingredients and render them intelligible to the reader" (1971: 39–40). At this point, any baseball fan becomes a cliometrician, adducing the readily available statistics on team play: batting average, fielding percentage, home runs, runs scored, earned run average of starting pitchers, saves-to-blown-saves of relief pitchers, and so on. That's why the Yankees won the pennant. Yet not to overlook the shape and measures of Hexter's diagram of the season. They tell the history in a certain temporality as well as a certain agency.

The form of historical change at issue here, a long-term developmental change, valorizes one or another scheme of periodization, as most suitable to describe it. Although Hexter does not explicitly discuss the choice, the time periods he adopts to diagrammatically relate the 1939 season are equal, precisely so that they can show the Yankees' domination as a long-term trend. Moreover, they are of sufficient duration, four-week intervals, to ensure that this trajectory is neither exaggerated nor obscured. Longer periods would have misleadingly represented the Yankees' success as a rocket launch. A day-by-day account, by its oscillations, would not answer directly to the question of why the Yankees won out, inasmuch as no particular game or stretch of games decided the pennant. In contrast, the Giants' victory of 1951 was precisely another "story."

To explicate the Giants' victory, says Hexter, one has to conform to the logical rules of "storytelling"—which he proceeds to do in practice, without explicitly telling us what the rules are. He does say that fiction can serve as a guide: an observation that Don DeLillo recently confirmed (if rather in reverse, art following life) by making the story of the decisive game between the Giants and Dodgers the opening chapter and repeated refrain of his novel *Underworld* (1997). Perhaps Hexter remained reticent about the rhetorical logic he adopted because he did not ask the question that would motivate it. The critical question was not the one he posed, "How did the New York Giants happen to play in the World Series of 1951?" The critical question was: How did the Giants overtake the Dodgers to win the pennant (and thus play in the World Series)? For what happened, again, was a specific kind of historical change: the overthrow, at the last possible moment and thus in dramatic fashion, of a longstanding relationship between the two teams or, if you will, the competing collective subjects. Here was a reversal of the order of things, a structural change that qualifies Bobby Thomson's home run as a historic event, even as it qualified him as a hero, a history-maker. And it is from this revolutionary dénouement, working backward, that we discover and rhetorically motivate the tempos, turning points, and agents of our history. The structural reversal in the story is the determining principle of historical value and relevance, a *telos* that rules

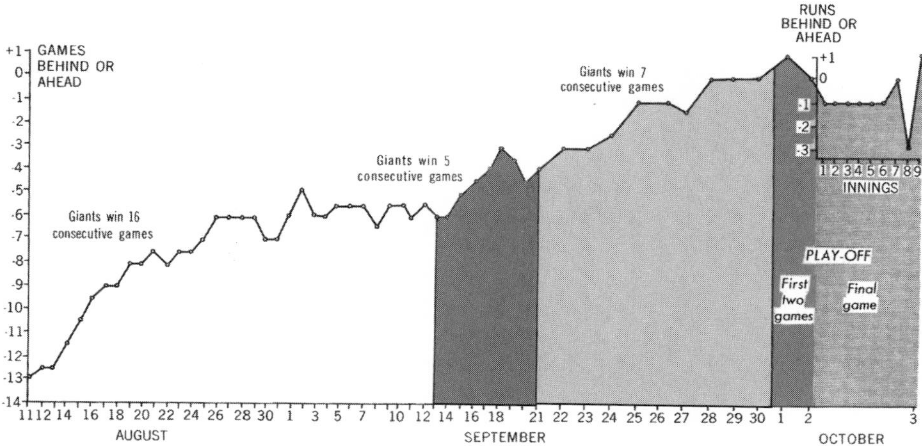

2.2 New York Giants' Pennant run, 1951

the organization of the account. Historical storytelling is the retelling from the beginning of an outcome already known, that knowledge guiding the selection (from the archive) of the successive events of the narrative. It is as François Furet said: "every evenemential history is a teleological history; only the end of the history permits one to choose and understand the events of which it is fabricated" (1982: 75; cf. Gallie 1963: 168; Veyne 1984: 31).

So Hexter chose to begin his story of the 1951 pennant race more than halfway through the season, on 11 August, because this was the turning point, the beginning of the reversal, although no one could have known it at the time (fig. 2.2).[2] Indeed, around this time Charlie Dressen, the Dodgers' manager, made his famous pronouncement, "The Giants is dead." At the end of play on 11 August the Dodgers held a thirteen-game lead on the Giants, the most they would ever attain. The next day the Giants began a sixteen-game winning streak, cutting the Dodgers' advantage to six games. Note that although Hexter does not diagram it, he does remark that the Dodgers' performance in the several months prior to 11 August resembled the Yankees' pennant run of 1939. Presumably it would be periodized appropriately as a long-term trend and explained analogously

2. The book about the 1951 pennant race authored by Bobby Thomson (with others) also starts here, on 11 August, for "it was only then that the real story of the 1951 season began to unfold" (Thomson et al. 1991: 7).

by the Dodgers' "betterness" as a team. From 11 August, however, the appropriate historiographic form changes from "analysis" to "storytelling," a difference of narrative mode marked by corollary differences in temporality and agency. Time is progressively magnified. The account that began in months will end in moments, ultimately one final moment of perhaps ten seconds, *the* home run. And at a certain point in time, individual subjects replace collectives. The account that began with the relative performances of the Dodgers and the Giants will end with Bobby Thomson at the plate.

Beginning on 12 August the historical tempo picks up, and Hexter accordingly periodizes it in shorter and shorter stretches of time. (This is represented in his diagram by the lengthening of daily intervals along the horizontal axis [fig. 2.2].) By "historical tempo" one usually means something like the density of events over a given time span, recognizing that the condition for what counts as an event is the pertinence of the happening to the final outcome. In the present instance, then, what should motivate and demarcate the historical periods are the times when the relationship between the teams changed substantially—that is, when the Giants made significant ground on the front-running Dodgers. As Hexter indicates, there are a couple of reasonable alternatives, but one cannot go wrong in choosing: first, a span of about a month, from 12 August to 14 September, when the Giants closed to and maintained a position about six games back; and second, the period from 15 September to the end of the season on 30 September, when two Giant winning streaks allowed them to catch and tie the Dodgers. The league season ends in a draw. The teams move into a best-of-three series for the pennant.

Since each game of the playoff significantly affects the teams' positions, we change now to a day-by-day account. On 1 October, the Giants win, 3 to 1, but the next day the Dodgers tie the series, winning 10 to 0. The whole season now devolves upon the final game of 3 October. This sort of structural compression is a hallmark of evenemential history: the working out of a long history in a short time and of macro-relationships in micro-acts. Indeed, it is the event, by the changes it effects, that brings time past and greater social order to bear—that, as it were, reifies them and embodies them in particular actors. History indeed becomes what Alcibiades did and what he suffered. Or, in this case, what Bobby Thomson did and Ralph Branca suffered.

With everything riding on the one game of 3 October, we are virtually down to an inning-by-inning description. More precisely, the narrative tempo shifts to a changing-score-by-inning account, since that would be a succinct indication of the two teams' pennant chances. Brooklyn goes ahead, 1 to 0, in the first inning and holds the lead until the bottom of the seventh, when the Giants tie the score. One whole season, two playoff games, and seven more innings: they are still deadlocked. But the Dodgers score 3 in the top of the eighth and carry the lead into the bottom of the ninth, the Giants' last bats. Of course, individual players could have been introduced into the narrative of this game thus far: as DeLillo does, for example, although sparingly. But until the final inning, the whole season did not come down to what particular players did. Now it does.

(Need I remind you of the U.S. presidential election of 2000, where the outcome likewise, by virtue of the structure of the conjuncture, was decided by what a few people did or did not do? Authorized as difference-makers were the likes of Katherine Harris, the Florida secretary of state, and Antonin Scalia, the U.S. Supreme Court justice who used the advantage of his two votes to the other justices' one to enforce the opinion that if the Florida vote were recounted, it would damage the legitimacy of Dubya's presidency—presumably by showing that Al Gore won.)[3]

Last of the ninth, Don Newcombe, who started the game, still pitching for the Brooklyn Dodgers. The first man up for the Giants, Al Dark, singles to right: a ground ball that barely eludes the Dodger first baseman, Gil Hodges. Man on first. Hodges—or the manager, Dressen—elects to hold the runner on instead of moving to a fielding position between first and second, where the next Giants batter, Mueller, promptly hits a ground ball single, Dark going to third. (History does not record who decided to hold the runner, but as the cognoscenti know, and the consequences show, it was a bad baseball decision, since Dark was no threat to steal second in that situation, down 4 to 2 with the heart of the order coming up.) Monte Irvin pops out. Then Whitey Lockman, a lefthanded hitter, strokes an opposite-field double over third base, Dark scoring, Mueller stopping at third. (Hurt sliding into third, Mueller is carried off the field and replaced by a pinch runner.) It is 4 to 2 Dodgers, one out, Giants' runners on second and third, Bobby Thomson the next scheduled batter. Dressen decides his pitcher Don Newcombe is out of gas and replaces him with Ralph Branca. On the advice of his bullpen coach, which ordinarily Charlie Dressen never even solicited, much less took, Branca was chosen to replace Newcombe rather than Carl Erskine, who was also warming up. Dressen used

3. The man who broke another notable tie of the 2000 election, U.S. senator James Jeffords of Vermont, whose defection from the Republican Party gave the Democrats control of the Senate, was interestingly aware of the conjunctural order that empowered him and made him a celebrity. "'I was in a position to turn things around,' he said. 'So I used those actions and forces'" (*Chicago Tribune*, 7 June 2001).

Branca despite that Thomson had homered off him in the first playoff game—indeed, ten of the seventeen homers Branca had allowed that season were by the Giants, as well as five of his eleven losses. Obviously, such decisions, including the positioning of Hodges after Dark's leadoff single, were crucial. We could go behind them, but that way lies chaos (theory), since all previous acts were necessary to the outcome and none as such won the pennant for the Giants.[4] What won the pennant was Bobby Thomson's home run. So stepping in against Branca, "the Scot from Staten Island," the third baseman Thomson, born in Glasgow, hitting a respectable .292 percentage for the year with a team-leading thirty-one home runs. And as we thus focus in on the ultimate actors, we go into slow motion.

In the final extension of time, it is pitch by pitch. The first pitch is a waist-high fastball that Thomson lets go for a strike. It was a good hitter's pitch, but Thomson unaccountably did not offer. The next is a high inside curve. Thomson tomahawks it into the lower left-field stands (figs. 2.3, 2.4). A home run. Three runs score. The Giants win the game. The Giants win the pennant. Over the uproar, the astonished Giants' radio announcer, Russ Hodges, shouts it again and again: "The Giants win the pennant! The Giants win the pennant! The Giants win the pennant! The Giants win the pennant!" The Brooklyn announcer, the incomparable Red Barber, in what has been called the most eloquent description of baseball ever broadcast, falls completely silent for fifty-nine seconds. Next day the famous sportswriter, Red Smith, anticipating Don DeLillo, writes that indeed henceforth, art can only follow life: "Now it is done. Now the story ends. And there is no way to tell it. The art of fiction is dead. Reality has strangled invention. Only the utterly impossible, the inexpressibly fantastic can ever be plausible again" (*New York Herald Tribune:* 4 October 1951).

4. Of course there is no need to resist the "going behind" when the tributary stories are so entertaining. For example, Charlie Dressen's moves. You have to know that Leo Durocher, the Giants' manager, had managed the Dodgers as late as 1948 with Charlie Dressen as a coach and his righthand man. Now Dressen had something to prove about his capabilities relative to those of the more famous and flamboyant Durocher. "Thus, each meeting between the two teams had the potential for a myriad of managerial moves and decisions that would be more conducive to a tactical chess match than a baseball game" (Thomson et al. 1991: 9). But as for the general point about necessary contingencies, Thomson, reflecting on all the events of the previous few years that put Durocher, Dressen, and the various ballplayers in their respective 1951 places, asked, "What if Durocher hadn't been suspended in 1947? . . . What if Stoneham hadn't agreed to let Durocher deal his sluggers and pursue the likes of Dark and Stanky? What if Ashburn hadn't made a good throw and Cal Abrams had been safe at the plate [in the final game of 1951]? Just one change, one piece out of place . . ." (ibid., 76).

2.3 Bobby Thomson's home run. (© Bettmann/Corbis)

The Giants' implausible season became "The Miracle of Coogan's Bluff" (the site of their ballpark, the Polo Grounds). Bobby Thomson's home run was "the shot heard round the world." Every red-blooded American baseball fan of a certain age remembers where he or she was when listening to the broadcast of Thomson's great feat—just as they remember the news of Pearl Harbor, the death of Franklin Roosevelt, the assassination of President Kennedy. After first writing that sentence, I came across the following passage on Bobby Thomson's home run in Jules Tygiel's *Past Time: Baseball as History* (2000: 144):

> "It was likely the most dramatic and shocking event in American sports and has since taken on the transcendent historical character of Pearl Harbor and the Kennedy assassination," observed journalist George W. Hunt in 1990. "Anyone alive then and vaguely interested can answer with tedious exactitude the question 'Where were you when you heard it?'"

Perhaps we have underestimated sport the way we underestimate talk about the weather, as the integument of an otherwise divided and only imagined

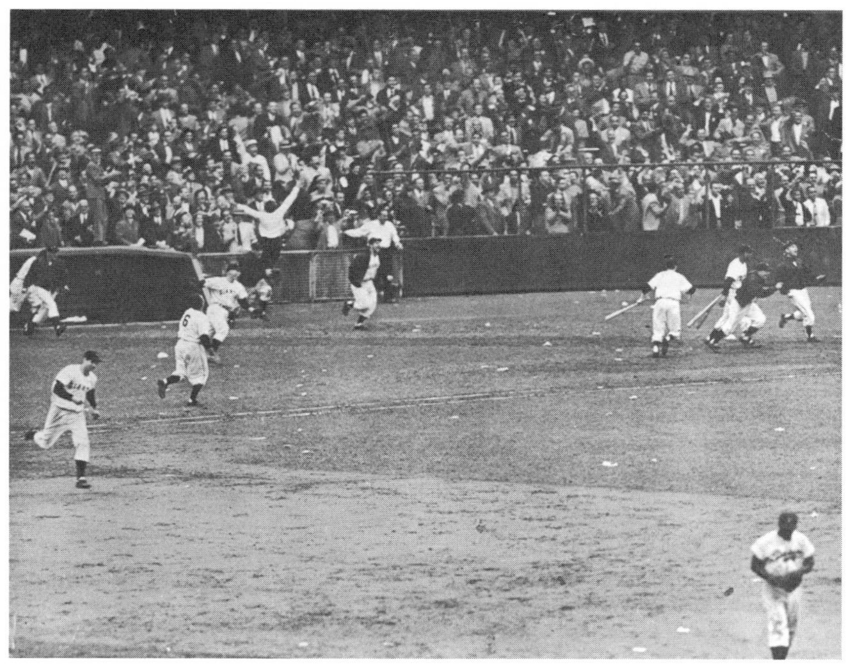

2.4 Thomson rounds the bases. (National Baseball Hall of Fame Library, Cooperstown, NY)

community. Tygiel notes DeLillo's musing on this score: "Isn't it possible that this midcentury moment [i.e., Bobby Thomson's homer] enters the skin more lastingly than the vast shaping strategies of eminent leaders, generals steely in their sunglasses—the mapped visions that pierce our dreams?" (ibid., 144–45).

So is it truly chutzpah to put "the shot Heard round the world" on the same plane as the Peloponnesian War or the 2000 U.S. presidential election? Hexter said Thomson's homer was "the equivalent (in its sphere) of the defeat of the Armada, the battle of Stalingrad, the Normandy landings" (1971: 42).

Or else, in the same hyperbolic vein, it was the equivalent of the Copernican Revolution. The difference between the types of historical change we have been discussing seems much like Thomas Kuhn's famous distinction between revolutionary "paradigm shifts" and "normal science"—the first described in such terms as "breakthrough" and "transformation," the second as "progressive" and "cumulative"—as much in their respective temporalities and agencies as in their dynamic forms (Kuhn 1970, 1977, 2000).

Like the Yankees' 1939 pennant, normal science is the working out of a developmental trend, as initiated by a breakthrough scientific discovery or theoretical formulation. The filling-out of the periodic table of the elements, for example. So the historiography of normal science, in Kuhn's treatment, is much like Hexter's "analysis." The historical subject is likewise collective and by and large anonymous, being "the scientific community," "the profession," or sometimes "normal science" itself. This community "knows" what the world is like, shows "willingness" to defend its assumptions, or else "goes astray," to the point that it can no longer "evade" the experimental anomalies that "threaten" it, and so forth—again, a collective, nonhuman person (e.g., Kuhn 1970: 5–7). But when Kuhn speaks of scientific revolutions, the narrative register shifts to actual persons. Paradigm shifts indeed take individual proper names—Newtonian dynamics, Copernican astronomy, Einsteinian relativity. True that Kuhn confesses to certain regrets about "the unfortunate simplification that tags an extended historical episode with a single and somewhat arbitrarily chosen name (e.g. Newton or Franklin)" (1970: 15). And he has related misgivings about the event-character of paradigm shifts. Considering the discovery of oxygen and the end to phlogiston-thinking, for example, he denies that the breakthrough can be dated to a specific moment or attributed to a particular person—although by his own account it is datable to a finite period of a few years (1774–77) and concerned a restricted cast of characters (Priestly, Lavoisier, Scheele, and Bayen) (1977: 166–67). In any case, and in contrast to the progressive trends of normal science, a paradigm shift is "relatively sudden," as Kuhn says (2000: 17), and "emerges first in the mind of one or a few individuals" (1970: 144). Now we are into "storytelling" à la Hexter, and indeed, in some passages, observations something like the folkloric traditions of culture heroes: "Sometimes the shape of a new paradigm is foreshadowed. . . . More often . . . the new paradigm or a sufficient hint to permit later articulation, emerges all at once, sometimes in the middle of the night, in the mind of a man deeply immersed in crisis" (Kuhn 1970: 89–90).

We seem to be on to something. Going back to Thucydides, it would be extravagant to suppose that the appearance of individuals and collectives in his *History* always marks the difference between turning points and progressive changes, if only because such actors serve various other narrative functions besides agency, notably including identity.[5] The issue is better

5. It may likewise be extravagant to note the correlation between the two relevant types of historical change—evolutionary and revolutionary—and the Aristotelian distinction between essential (or natural) and accidental (or violent) notions. But there it is.

understood the other way round, whether or not the two kinds of historical change are marked by this difference in the historical subject. It would seem so, considering the anonymity or near-anonymity that attends Thucydides' descriptions of the development of the Athenian *archē* or the cyclical Spartan invasions of Attica and other such indecisive maneuvers, by comparison to Themistocles' or Pericles' maritime strategies, Brasidas' extraordinary victories in Thrace, the roles of Alcibiades, Nicias, Hermocrates, and Ephemus in the Sicilian campaign, and other such interventions of particular persons that altered the political course or changed the correlations of military force. Even Thucydides' identifications of speechmakers seem to follow the rule. They are collective and anonymous, "the Athenians" or "the Melians," for example, when it is a question of rehearsing the received policies of the cities they represent; or again, when arguing for the continuation of a certain status quo—e.g., the Athenians who tried to convince the Spartans to maintain the peace in 432. But when it is a question of going to war or deciding on a fateful strategy, the speakers are generally individually identified. Even Diodotus, the one who convinced the Athenians not to exterminate the Mytileneans: he seems to prove the rule, since it was only by virtue of this speech that his name has passed into history; otherwise, we know nothing about him. So without making greater claims for the relationships between types of historical agency and modes of historical change, allowing that we have hardly exhausted and vastly oversimplified the issue of the acting historical subject, the seeming correlation does raise interesting questions about the situational and organizational conditions that empower one or another kind of history-maker.

Or are we just mired in the old epistemic murk of "the great man theory of history" and the even more ancient quicksands of "the individual versus society"? It is worth taking time out to do some archaeology of these questions: not exactly a Foucauldian excavation, but at least something like a surface survey.

EXCURSUS: DEAD WHITE WHALES, OR FROM LEVIATHANOLOGY TO SUBJECTOLOGY

The "Great Man Theory of History" was a nineteenth-century problem, it is said. Yet it is still with us in the twenty-first century.[6] Nor does it look to

6. "At its crudest, political history remains stuck in a late nineteenth-century mould: narrating 'great events' and passing judgment on 'Great Men' (or their flipside, 'Really Awful Men')" (Arnold 2000: 80).

be resolved so long as its generic form, the opposition of the individual and the society, continues to be irreconcilable in the human sciences. No doubt it will be with us so long as the late "late capitalism," now neo-liberalism, continues to interpolate the conflict between personal freedom and societal constraint into the everyday practices and native consciousness of the culture. The argument, as it has come down to us, takes a weaker form and a stronger one. The weaker form, famously championed by Count Tolstoy, is that the real power of history-making resides in the mass of the people rather than their leaders; accordingly, we should put aside our stories of kings and battles in favor of "bottom up" histories. But taking Marx's point that the concept of a population without reference to its organization—mode of production, class system, political system, and so forth—is an empty abstraction, the stronger opposition of individual agency versus the societal order, or the individual versus the culture (in its anthropological version), is where the historiographic battles have been more significantly joined.[7] If anything, positions are more than ever polarized between the idea that people are creatures of some great social machinery, on the one hand, and on the other, the notion that individuals are autonomous and self-moving, society being nothing but the residue, in the form of relations between them, of their self-regarding projects.

Still, this is a Western hang-up of the very long run. The opposition of man and the city is already there in Thucydides, in the explicit form of conflict between personal and polis interests. Also already present is the grounding of interests in a human nature driven by relentless desires of power and gain. Much as in the *Protagoras* or *Gorgias* of Plato, people debate in Thucydides' pages whether public or private interests actually do, and morally should, prevail in the affairs of the polis. Pericles, who as so-called first citizen of an egalitarian democracy already incarnates the antithesis, tries to reconcile it on the principle that individual interests will be best served by promoting the public good. Hence his famous exhortation to the Athenians to the effect of "Love thy city as thou makest love thyself." Since the public good was the Athenian empire, acknowledged to be a tyranny for those who ruled it as well as for those ruled by it, Pericles' policy was rather the inverse of the lesson in Mandeville's *Fable:* here Pub-

7. I do not wish to join here in the issue of whether "society" or "culture" is the appropriate antithesis to the individual. I have elsewhere made the point that since the specific structure of the society is a symbolically constituted order, it is ontologically a cultural formation, thus an aspect or dimension of culture (M. Sahlins 2000). For present purposes, and given the received formulation of the historiographic problem as individual versus society, I will take that as synonymous with individual versus culture.

lic Vices were Private Virtues. Yet Thucydides' framing of the individual / society opposition shares with Mandeville—and many others between and since—what can only be described as the simple-minded sociological dualism of an unmediated relation between them. Individual in particular and society in general confront each other over an empty social space, as though there were no institutions, values, and relationships of diverse character that at once connect and differentiate them. As we shall see presently, the same thing happens even in advanced notions of societal constraint such as Gramscian hegemony or Foucauldian power. True, these speak to intermediate institutions, but mostly to assign them the function of transmitting the larger order of society into the bodies of individuals.

Modern versions of the individual /society opposition also incorporate the sense of a fateful struggle between social coercion and personal freedom that was picked up by the classical dualism as it passed through a Christianized anthropology. Only that in the Christian dualism, where the earthly city was not Athens but the residence of inherently sinful man, the positive value was all on the repressive, social side. For Saint Augustine, the social control of unruly bodies—of the child by the father as of the citizen by the state—was a necessary condition of human survival in this contemptible world of Adamic self-pleasers. Otherwise, men would devour each other like beasts. "Not even lions or dragons," said Augustine, "have ever waged with their kind such wars as we have waged with one another" (*De civ. D.* XII.22). Or again, like fish: "How they mutually oppress, and how they that are able do devour! And when one fish hath devoured, the greater the less, itself also is devoured by some greater" (in Deane 1963: 47). The rapacious fish metaphor is good testimony to the longevity of the concept of self-interested, unruly man. Present in the rabbinical tradition that antedates Augustine, it was still proverbial in the Middle Ages, according to Huizinga (1954: 229): "les grans poissons mangent les plus petits." To this day "big fish eating little fish" remains a popular one-line description of corporate capitalism. But for a comprehensive secular translation of the same anthropology, together with its providential political resolution, see Hobbes. Translator of Thucydides, Hobbes, in a way analogous to Saint Augustine, found the remedy to the state of nature in the nature of state: the institution of a monopoly power that could check the antisocial ravages of the human libido, and "keep them all in awe." (If that reminds you of Freud and the superego, it is not only because *libido* was the word Augustine also used. I mean this is really bedrock Western folklore—that is, social science.) Thus, the "Leviathan" of Hobbes, a reference to Job 40–42:

Behold now behemoth, which I made with thee . . .
His bones are strong pieces of brass; his bones are
Like bars of iron.
He is the chief of the ways of God . . .
None is so fierce that dare stir him up;
Who then is able to stand before me? . . .
Upon earth there is not his like, who is made without fear.
He beholdeth all high things: he is a king over all
The children of pride . . .
Then Job answered the Lord, and said,
I know that thou canst do everything, and no thought
Can be withholden from thee.

Note that this is the same kind of "interpellation" ("Who is able to stand before me?"), likewise from the Old Testament, that Louis Althusser (1971: 127–86) would make into a grand theory of the social fashioning of the individual. For Althusser, the subjugation of the subject by the Subject (God) is the model of the way that individuals, enlisted into "the ideology of the ruling class," are thus constrained to reproduce "the relations of production and of the relations deriving from them" (ibid., 182–83).[8]

8. *Interpeller* [Fr.], 'to summon preemptively,' as by the police, considered more broadly as an act of subjectivization, refers to the process by which individuals are recruited as social subjects by imperative discourses or practices. In Althusser's paradigmatic model, the Lord calls Moses by name, and Moses replies that it is really "I. I am Moses, thy servant; speak and I shall listen." Moses realizes himself as subject/subjugated through interpellation by the Subject *par excellence,* the One of himself: "I am that I am." Theology thus provides Althusser with the essential working of hegemonic ideology, directly translatable into the constitution of subjects by and for the reproduction of the economic infrastructure. God creates men in his own image, or in Christ duplicates himself as man, a mirroring that reciprocally allows men to recognize themselves in Him, which is also a guarantee that on the condition of their submission they will ultimately participate in Him. So then, says Althusser, "let us let the words slip"—into submission to the relations of production. "What is needed," he asks, "if things are to be what they must be? . . . If the reproduction of the relations of production is to be assured, even in the processes of production and circulation?" The answer, like Saint Augustine's, is the transposition of Zion to Babylon, a move at once providential and adulterating, that realizes and mystifies the power of God in the constraints of society. "Indeed, what is really in question in this mechanism of the mirror recognition of the Subject and of the individuals interpellated as subjects, and of the guarantee given by the Subject to the subjects if they freely accept their subjection to the Subject's 'commandments'? The reality in question in this mechanism, the reality which is necessarily *misrecognized* (*méconnue*) in the very forms of recognition . . . is indeed, in the last re-

I think the reason Emile Durkheim was able to find god in society, the latter as the coercive force that men figure as the former, is that He was already there in the received Western anthropology (cf. M. Sahlins 1996: 407–11). Not only did the state represent divine providence in its subjugation of the unruly subject, but in the long struggle with the Church it proceeded to usurp much of the latter's authority and functions. In any case, like Saint Augustine and others, Durkheim understood the social fact as a necessary constraint on an undisciplined humanity. Man is double, he said, double and divided: composed of a moral and intellectual self, received from society, struggling to hold in check an egocentric and sensual self that is essentially presocial. So Durkheim, too, is not really modern. His idea of man as half-angel and half-beast retains something from the anthropological dark ages. "Modern" is the view that attempts to appropriate one side of the old dualism totally within the other, subsuming the individual in society or assuming the society in the individual, so that in the end only one has any independent existence. Either society is no more than the sum of relations between enterprising individuals, as Jeremy Bentham and Margaret Thatcher would have it, or individuals count for nothing, nothing more than personifications of the greater social and cultural order, as in certain advanced notions of the construction of subjectivity that amount to the death of the subject. It seems that the development of capitalism and its discontents gave the ancient anthropological dualism still another twist, specifically political—and consequently dialectical. Right and left pushed each other into complementary and extreme theories of individual and cultural determinism. On the right: rational choice theory and other such brands of *radical individualism,* all content to resolve social totalities into the projects of self-fashioning individuals. On the left: concepts of the cultural superorganic and other such species of *leviathanology,* draconian notions of autonomous cultural behemoths with the powers of fashioning individual subjects in their own image.

Not to spend a lot of time on radical individualism, which it is easy to understand as our own bourgeois society taking consciousness of itself. From rational choice theory to sociobiology, these utilitarian problematics are able to encompass the social in the individual by endowing the latter with an operating principle of maximization from which the arrangements of the former seem to follow. Extreme versions, such as that practiced by

---

sort, the reproduction of the relations of production and of the relations deriving from them" (Althusser 1971: 182–83).

University of Chicago economists, are able to explain cultural and historical phenomena of every shape and form—from juvenile delinquency through suicide and the fall of the Soviet Union—as so many collective effects of people husbanding their "human capital." The secret here, as Louis Dumont discovered, is precisely to presuppose the structures and values of the society in the dispositions of the individual, as though he or she were their author. Dumont (1970) explains: "The kingdom of ends coincides with each man's legitimate ends, so the values are turned upside down. What is called 'society' is the means, the life of each man is the end. Ontologically, the society no longer exists" (9–10). I said the political tango between the social and the individual became dialectical, and as this passage implies, the assertion was not altogether playful. In radical individualism, the society is preserved in its negation, included as the source of the values, "the kingdom of ends," that appears in consciousness and economic science as the intentions of individuals. Society gets mystified as the preferences and satisfactions of individual rational volition in order to reappear as the result thereof.

Leviathanology is the symmetric inverse of radical individualism. Its thesis is that the individual does not exist as such but only as the expression of an all-powerful system—variously identified as society, culture, or hegemonic discourse, or some form thereof, such as capitalism, nationalism, or colonialism. The famous liberal ideology of the Invisible Hand had already presaged this negation of the subject by the system in its obeisances to the transcendent social mechanism that mysteriously transformed the good that people did for themselves into the well-being of the nation. Here was something *sui generis,* powerful and mechanical, something that could encompass the self-interested acts of individuals in a collective and providential way. Again Dumont: "This something is the mechanism by which particular interests harmonize: a *mechanism* . . . that is, not something willed or thought by men, but something that exists independently of them. Society is thus of the same nature as the world of natural objects, a nonhuman thing" (1977: 178).

So if Adam Smith & Co. could argue singularly for the freedom of individuals to indulge their natural propensity to truck and barter, on the ground that the social good would automatically follow, the critique of capitalism countered by rendering visible this self-subsisting Great Pumpkin with the power of encompassing and conjugating the behavior of people in ways beyond their knowledge and control. Thus Marx, in a well-known passage from the preface to *Capital:* "Here individuals are dealt with only insofar as they are the personifications of economic categories, embodiments of particular class-relations and class interests. My standpoint, from which the evolution of the economic formation of society is viewed as a process of natural history, can less than any other make the individual responsible for relations whose creature he socially remains, however much he may subjectively rise above them" (1967: 10). Not to leave out the working class: "It is not a question of what this or that proletarian, or even the whole proletariat, at the moment regards as its aim. It is a question of what the proletariat is, and what, in accordance with this being, it will historically be compelled to do" (Marx and Engels 1956: 37).

This sort of resolution of the subject to the system of class relations—and (in the good old "final analysis") to the forces and relations of production—is what has come to be called, by partisans of emancipatory causes that cannot be reduced to class relations, the "anti-humanism" of Marxism. Engels, Plekhanov, and Trotsky made notable attempts to carry it off historically, to subsume history-making persons in suprapersonal forces that had their own laws of motion. Trotsky especially, in his breathtaking analysis of the parallel personalities of Nicholas II, Louis XVI, and Charles I: all victims of regicide, whose shallowness, affability, laziness, hypocrisy, and indecisiveness were not so much a mark of their individuality as what the decline of absolutism had made them (Trotsky 1980: 112ff.). Iconic of decadence, these characteristics—shallowness, affability, laziness, hypocrisy, and so forth—would seem to make a convincing argument did they not also make a very possible description of George W. Bush, not to mention numerous other politicians, some university administrators, and many used-car salesmen. One among the numerous problems of such correlations of personal dispositions with structural forms or historical changes, whatever the direction of the arrow of causation, is that there are not enough generic dispositions available for the indefinite number of cultural variations. But this never stopped Trotsky from privileging "the great moving forces of history, which are suprapersonal in character," and arguing that "the 'distinguishing traits' of a person are merely individual scratches made by a higher law of development" (ibid., 73).

One is reminded of A. L. Kroeber's and Leslie White's early twentieth-century ideas of the "superorganic," an anthropology of subjects without agency, merely reflecting and expressing an omnipotent cultural order. Kroeber (1917) was slightly more generous to individuals than White (1949). For him culture was like a great coral reef, a vast edifice built up by millions of tiny microorganisms, each of which secreted an almost imperceptible addition to this enduring exoskeleton whose scale and organization by far transcended it:

> Lives of great men all remind us
> We can make our lives sublime,
> And in passing leave behind us . . .
> A small deposit of lime.

White's "superorganic," however, was even more dismissive of individuals. Altogether under the control of the great cultural entities, people were more like its secretions. Or again, the individual, he said, is like a pilotless aircraft controlled from the ground by radio waves (White 1949: 157). Here was a primary source of that unhappy anthropological consciousness of culture as an authoritarian prescription of conduct, especially self-defeating conduct, as in the so-called culture of poverty or the "traditional culture" that supposedly prevents underdeveloped peoples from becoming happy just like us! As the term *superorganic* suggests, these conceptions of cultural domination preserve the subjectivity they negate by reproducing them on the level of the social or cultural totality.

But the cultural superorganic was only one of several species of leviathanology to evolve in the twentieth century, culminating in such advanced forms as Althusserian-derived interpellations, Gramscian-inspired hegemonies, and power-laden Foucauldian discourses. All retained characteristics of their ancient ancestors, including the pervasive sentiment of repression virtually without mediation in the construction of subjectivity without agency. For the mediating institutions between the social totality (as organized in the interest of the ruling classes) and the subject existed merely to transfer the values of the former in the process of constituting the latter. Again, the making of individual subjects is synonymous with their subjugation. "The individual," says Foucault, "is in fact a power effect, and at the same time, and to the extent that he is a power-effect, the individual is a relay: power passes through the individuals it has constituted" (2003: 30). Here is the essentialized social subject, trapped in the belly of the whale, fashioned in image or for the reproduction of the social totality by embodying and expressing its ruling interests in his or her own dispositions.

There is an awful lot of culturological terrorism going on these days, in the humanities and social sciences both, the complement it seems of the popular academic notion that culture is basically power. Power turns out to be the secret (that is, the function) of almost any institution an anthropologist could name (M. Sahlins 2002: 20–23). The symbolic capacity that is the essence of culture—and without which human bodily dispositions would be indeterminate in their object and human relationships lacking in pattern—appears solely as an imposition, a hegemonic trip laid on people by and/or for whatever powers that be. Yet without culture, people would be, as Clifford Geertz put it, "unworkable monstrosities, with few useful instincts, fewer recognizable sentiments and no intellect: mental basket-cases" (1973: 49). Evolution has produced a creature whose ability to satisfy organic needs depends on the ability to meaningfully organize them—the way sex is organized by kinship systems, hunger by determinations and preferences of edibility, and dominance, if it is indeed a necessity, by football. But having thus confined the body to the symbolic organization of existence, the human being, without culture, does not survive. In this light, culture is fundamentally empowering. And in any case, it is never as monolithically repressive as current anthropologies of hegemony would make it. I mean the texts that speak of ruling ideas that "accumulate the symbolic power to map and clarify the world for others," generating meaningful categories that "acquire not only the customary power of dominance over other modes of thought, but also the inertial authority of habit and instinct."[9] Never mind that every use of a word in and for a world we do not control is a risk to its meaning. Some would even separate an unreachable realm of hegemony that, as a world-constituting ontology, is able to colonize the rest of the culture as much by determining what people cannot think as by prescribing what there is. It is a wonder that anthropologists believe this, since it makes their profession absurd. As victims (as much as anyone else) of such a hegemonic order, they would not be able to think what other peoples are thinking. In this and too many other ways of late, anthropologists seem hell-bent on demonstrating anthropologically that anthropology is impossible.[10]

All the same, the most terrible transubstantiation of that old Holy Ghost, the Invisible Hand, into an all-controlling culture at large would have to be Foucault's pancratic vision of power. (It hasn't seemed to bother cultural students that Foucault's leviathanology was originally meant to apply to the modern West: the idea has been spread about wholesale, ethno-

9. This is Stuart Hall (after Gramsci) in the enlightening discussion by Jean and John Comaroff (1991: 18–19), which goes on to discuss the hegemonic as the unthinkable.

10. Like the way anthropologists now "diss" culture, leaving them a discipline without an object.

graphically and historically.) Here is power as irresistible as it is ubiquitous, power emanating from everywhere and invading everyone, saturating the everyday things, relations, and institutions of human existence, and transmitted thence into people's bodies, perceptions, knowledges, and dispositions. "Subject-bashing," as J. G. Merquior calls it (1985: 82). The argument is more hegemonic than Gramscian hegemony, where the selectivity of dominant definitions of reality, in a historical context, rather ensured the coexistence of residual and novel forms. Foucault rightly denies also that he is a structuralist, since all that is left of structuralism in his problematic is its avoidance of human agency. His position is indeed "poststructuralist" inasmuch as it theoretically dissolves the structures—families, schools, hospitals, philanthropies, technologies, and so forth—into their functional-instrumental effects of discipline and control.[11]

Is the family simply an institution of power, one of a number of social arrangements for making the individual a "power-effect" of the modern capitalist society? Of course, it is true that the family (our family) is patriarchal. But patriarchy is a precapitalist relation. Indeed, the family—with its unpaid labors, its allocation of work and resources by solidary social relations, its flows of values from the haves to the have-nots, in brief, its kinship economy, not to mention the emotions associated with all this—the family is structurally an anticapitalist system. To adapt a phrase from old Lewis Henry Morgan, it is more like "communism in living"—from each according to her ability, to each according to his need. (I said it was patriarchy.) But in the Foucauldian perspective the family is a way of dumping on people. As in other functionalisms, then, cultural matters are known not for what they are but for their supposed purposes, not for their order but for their ordering. So it's not only "cut off the king's head." Power is a more generalized version of academic Terror, the instrumental death of cultural form and content both.[12]

11. Stuart Hall cites L. McNay: "Foucault steps too easily from describing disciplinary power as a *tendency* within modern forms of social control, to positing disciplinary power as a fully installed monolithic force which saturates all social relations. This leads to an overestimation of the efficacy of disciplinary power and to an impoverished understanding of the individual" (Hall 1996: 12).

12. Michael Walzer on Foucaultian functionalism: "The disciplinary society is a *society,* a social whole, and in his account of the parts of this whole, Foucault is a functionalist. No one designed the whole, and no one controls it; but as if by an invisible hand, all its parts are somehow fitted together. Sometimes Foucault marvels at the fit: 'This is an extremely complex system of relations, which leads one finally to wonder how, given that no one person can have conceived it in its entirety, it can be so subtle in its distribution, its mechanisms, reciprocal controls and adjustments'" (Walzer 1986: 57).

Ironically, then, with this dissolution of cultural forms into subjugation effects, the only thing left standing is the subject. The only object substantively remaining to historical and anthropological analysis is the subject into whom the cultural totality has been interpolated, the one summarily interpellated. Subjectivity, which was once deemed the most elusive of ethnographic knowledges, becomes the critical site of culture and history. Thus Foucault on the Reformation: "All those movements that took place in the fifteenth and sixteenth centuries, which had the Reformation as their main concern and result, should be analyzed as a great crisis of the Western experience of subjectivity and a revolt against the kind of religious and moral power that gave form, during the Middle Ages, to this subjectivity. The need to take direct action in spiritual life, in the work of salvation, in the truth that lies in the book—all that was a struggle for a new subjectivity" (Foucault 1994: 332). Institutions, structures, relations, and their like are here figured as modes of subject-making power. They give subjectivity its form. But in the event, as the structures become their power functions, *only subjectivity would have form.* Foucault allows that subjectivity stands in reciprocal relations with Marxist verities such as "forces of production, class struggles, and ideological structures that determine the form of subjectivity." But such institutions do not enter into the Foucauldian account as such: there is no accounting for their attributes, their relationships, and their transformations. They are given to the historical analyses, like the modern state that completed the movement from otherworldly to this-worldly salvation of the individual—a god from the machine in more than one sense. And with this reduction in focus, they are comprehended not as formations, historical or institutional, but by and as their subjugation/subjectivization effects, as if this were what religion, the state, the family, and so forth consisted of, were all about. Their power function serves for their constitution. What is then left with the privilege of being historicized, of being the veritable locus of history and even its effective mainspring, is the subjectivity of the subject. I say this is ironic because the original project of leviathanology was to reduce the individual subject to nullity. But in the end, the system having been dissolved in the acid bath of instrumentalism, we are locked into the metaphysics of the subject, which the analysis was originally meant to foreclose.[13]

13. Terence Turner makes a similar point about the related reduction of social and political analysis to the "body": "The body has filled the vacuum created by the general evacuation of the social, cultural and political content of theorizing about the human condition, above all in the modern/postmodern era" (1995: 144).

Still, modern subjectology is not just the residue of a decadent structuralism. A complementary positive valuation of the subject, coupled to a political opposition to any sort of superorganic systematicity, has attended the emancipatory movements in the human sciences, including cultural studies, that have flourished since the 1960s and 1970s. I mean not only feminism and queer studies, although these have often taken the theoretical lead in setting a subject-oriented agenda. Even in the former anthropological province of the indigenous peoples, now usually redefined as the colonized and postcolonial peoples, the emphasis has shifted from an apparently detached interest in different ways of ordering human life that now seems politically feckless—if not complicitous in their destruction—to the ethnography of domination, suffering, and resistance. Notions of cultural systematicity take a battering when they appear as the political cum intellectual enemy. They can hardly survive when they are referred to the alienated, impersonal world of structures associated with men and the powers that be, as opposed to the experience-near, embodied world of excluded subjects, demanding their own identities and contesting the authoritative narratives of the larger society—whose reality as a coherent, bounded, totalized, essentialized system must then become problematic. In this mood of the academy, better Lacanian psychoanalysis than any sort of structural analysis.

In any case, in whatever the form, subjectology has arrived. The pages of the advanced journals are filled with all kinds of subjects, subjectivities, and selves, differentiated by a prefixed species identity, thus the "bourgeois subject," "postcolonial subjectivity," "the Cartesian self," and their like. The effect is an anthropology in the genre of allegory, telling tales of cultural forms and forces in terms of abstract persons. Replacing institutions, relations, customs, and so forth is a whole new *dramatis personae* of bourgeois subjects, colonial subjects, nationalist subjects, late-capitalist subjects, modern subjects, postmodern subjects, and postcolonial African subjects, not to forget the easily recognized wounded subject of the neo-liberal state; also in play are the alienated self, the neo-liberal self, the Melanesian self, the socialist self, and the consumerist self; then there are the various subjectivities, including the gendered, the racialized, the globalized, the hybridized, the democratized, and the modernized, among many other such characters. It is a brave new anthropological world that has such creatures in it. Or else a quaint old one. Just as archaic mythologies may represent cosmic forces in anthropomorphic guises, so in the pages of our scholarly journals the personifications of cultural macrocosms now strut and fret their hour upon the stage, doing . . . what?

If not exactly nothing, not a whole lot, it seems—not all alone, without the cultural order that has been lost in the translation. Slippery in its definition, subjectivity becomes a black hole as well as a black box. Occasionally there are inflated claims, such as those made for a certain "late socialist subject," which according to an article in *Public Culture* was the "source" and "inner logic" of the collapse of the Soviet Union (Yurchak 1997). Or promises such as those of "progressive social theory," which are "concerned with the status and formulation of the subject, the implications of the theory of the subject for a theory of democracy." But how can all this compensate for the historical formations and movements that have thus been functionalized, subjectivized, and ontologically traduced? What we get is colonial subjects who are disciplined and repressed—how? in what ways?—and accordingly resist—again, in what form?—or bourgeois subjects who are alienated—like you and me?—and consume—how much of what?—and other species of this same tautological genus. To do some anthropology or history of this, one will have to go back to the specific cultural formations and relations that were "disappeared" in the translation to indeterminate subjective dispositions. Nor will the invocation of "multiple subject positions" solve the problem. Either the multiplicity dissolves into pure individualism, since in principle there are as many subject positions as there are individuals, or it replicates leviathanology by generating a school of whales, a pod of abstract collective persons, instead of one giant one. Either way, subjectology ends with the anthropological tautology with which individualism began: with an abstract, ideal subject in whom resides the whole kingdom of social ends, mystified as his or her own private ends. This is the return of the repressed individual, now harboring the plague of both houses—with the old essentialism thrown in in the bargain. For now it is the essentialized individual, the one who embodies the cultural totality in his or her own being: the common, average, bourgeois subject, for example, whose personal characteristics express the defining characteristics of bourgeois society. The very essentialism that is fashionably denied these days to the culture thus creeps back into the individual-as-microcosm. The univocal, atemporal, totalized system of categories and relationships, unwanted in the culture, has been transposed to an ideal subject.

What are we to conclude of this going around in ever decreasing hermeneutic circles? Perhaps that, to paraphrase Marx, culturology has never gone beyond the antithesis between itself and individualism, and the latter will accompany it as its legitimate negation up to their bitter end.

The problem is hardly that subjects, at least concrete ones, or subjective dispositions, even shared ones, are irrelevant to the histories of societies.

(There will be occasion shortly to adduce instances to the contrary.) The problem is the attempt to reduce general social forms to subjective dispositions, or vice versa, as if they were in some kind of mimetic correspondence. Leviathanology and subjectology both ignore what Paul Ricoeur (1984: 193) calls "the epistemological break" between them: between the social entities with which history is concerned—nations, city-states, classes, tribes, governments—and the subjectivities of the people concerned. One could speak of multiple breaks, basically ontological, that make it impossible to resolve the social to the individual, thus to encompass or determine the one directly by the other, whether in one direction or reciprocally. One is the difference of phenomenal order between social cum cultural phenomena, as constituted by symbolic attributes, and the dispositions of individual subjects. Divine kingship, the Democratic Party, the New York Yankees, the difference between parallel and cross cousins, Protestantism, the Reformation, the rise and fall of the Athenian empire: these cultural formations and transformations cannot be predicated, in their own characteristics, from attributes of subjects. Neither is the culture adequate to the description of the subject, in the sense that the former is wholly or isomorphically replicated in the latter. The cultural order (even if it were monolithic) functions in an intersubjective field. Individuals have partial and differential relations in it—for which reason, incidentally, the argument that the cultural categories are fuzzy or cultural logics indeterminate because people have contrasting and negotiable versions of them does not seem cogent. For present purposes of understanding historical agency, it is especially relevant that there is no standard bourgeois subject or others of such ilk, persons who are nothing and do nothing but what their class, country, or ethnic group has made them. The concrete individual, whose relations to the totality are mediated by a particular biographical experience in familial and other institutions, must thus express the cultural universals in an individual form. This individual is a "historic complex *sui generis,*" as Alexander Goldenweiser put it in response to A. L. Kroeber's influential 1917 article on "The Superorganic."

> The term "individual," in this context requires specification. It is not the biological individual, nor is it the abstract being of general psychology, nor is it this or that more or less gifted individual, it is not even the average individual who partakes of the given civilization. The individual who counts here may be designated as the biographical individual. He is a historic complex *sui generis.* Neither biological nor psychological, nor civilizational factors exhaust his content. He has partaken of the culture

> of his social environment, but only of certain aspects of it, and these have come to him in a certain individual order, received and absorbed by a psyche that was unique. This is the concrete individual of historic society. (Goldenweiser 1917: 449)

The process Goldenweiser described of individuals partaking of the cultural universals selectively and uniquely, in a differentiated social environment, is similar to what Sartre later argued under the term *mediations.* Sartre likewise insisted on the singular ways that persons live the culture, its ruling forms and mentalities—the nation, relations of production, class relations, Christianity, science, democracy—by virtue of the filtering of such generals in and through interpersonal relations and particular experiences, especially through family life. Living the culture in a specific way, a person will also uniquely express it, which is as it were a going-beyond-it while still being-in-it (cf. Wagner 1973). "Summed up and for this reason universalized by his epoch," the human being "in turn resumes it by reproducing himself in his singularity" (Sartre 1981–93, 1:ix). In fundamental respects, the notion is the opposite of Althusserian interpellation or Foucauldian subjectivization, including notably the structural resistance of the interpersonal realm to the hegemony of the larger social order. Sartre's *Search for a Method* (1968) is a sustained critique of abstract subjects and their essentialized subjectivities, as if these could account for the works of society and history. "Valéry is a petit bourgeois intellectual," as Sartre says, "no doubt about it. But not every petit bourgeois intellectual is a Valéry" (1968: 55–56).

Nor did every petit bourgeois intellectual gain the readership of the bourgeoisie for his apparent antibourgeois realism, like Gustave Flaubert. Here was another literary history-making intellectual who, as Sartre described in tedious detail (1981–93), lived the larger relations and contradictions of his time in a family whose organization and dynamics gave these greater collective forces novel, specific, and intimate dimensions. I simplify enormously. Born in 1821, Flaubert was in one sense a child of the Restoration and the July Monarchy and of their correlated conflicts between a rising bourgeoisie and a revived Ancien Régime of king, clerics, and noble landowners, between anticlerical utilitarian liberals and pious *ultras,* as also between materialism and faith, science and Christian doctrine. But most proximately, Flaubert was the second surviving child of an eminent Rouen doctor and hospital director who had risen to middle-class status from a rural, peasant-dominated background—his own father was a veterinarian—and a mother who had some pretensions to nobility by virtue of matrilineal links to a rather prominent family of magistrates and clerics. The father, Achille-Cléophas Flaubert, who put his wealth into land while maintaining his friendships and clientele among the industrial and mercantile bourgeoisie, had his own contradictions. Most fateful for his sons was his use of a tyrannical patriarchal authority, peasant in origin and feudal in character, to instill in them his fervent liberal, positivist, materialist, and anticlerical opinions—though he was circumspect about the last in public, outwardly demonstrating a respectable relation to the Church. Sartre's claims about the piety of Flaubert's mother have been disputed and apparently refuted,[14] but whatever her old-regime values, she, as wife cum daughter under Achille-Cléophas' *patri potestas,* did not contest his analytic-rationalist teachings. For Gustave, all this was further complicated by his older brother Achille, the anointed successor of their father—feudal primogeniture as the mode of scientific reproduction—who indeed made the great doctor's career the model of his own, but with whom poor Gustave was unable to compete. On the contrary, by comparison with his accomplished older brother, Gustave's apparent slowness and disengagement as a child, including what Sartre argues was a resistance to learning to read, brought upon him the suspicion of being "the family idiot."

Discussing the dynamic of this family, Sartre is careful not to perceive its members as simple embodiments of greater structures—as bourgeois subjects, feudal subjects, or the like—since each of them internalized all the relevant universals in distinctive ways, "giving these structures the unity of his person." The Flaubert family was not riven by personal cleavages that directly corresponded to and instantiated the greater forces of social contention. "The antagonistic forces that were tearing France apart and tearing [Gustave] apart were not embodied, at [his home in] the Hôtel-Dieu, by people" (Sartre 1981–93, 1:487). Of course, it was critical to Flaubert's status as a petit bourgeois intellectual unlike any other that his father was the rising bourgeois scientist and his mother the pious one of fading noble memories. Had the oedipus complex been lived the other way around, the history of French literature would have been different. But as Sartre put the dynamics: "To understand Flaubert, it need never be forgotten that he was forged by the fundamental contradictions of the period, but at a certain social level—the family—in which they are masked

14. Sartre's position on Mme. Flaubert's religion does not seem to me as dogmatic (either on his part or hers) as his critics seem to believe. "Her religion without the Church, her God without obligations or sanctions who was manifest only to justify and envelop her with a tenderness her husband hardly lavished," and so on (1981–93, 1:493).

in the form of ambivalences and ironic twists" (ibid., 488). It is ironic that Achille-Cléophas uses his "sovereign authority" to impose his "liberal ideology" on his sons as a "categorical imperative." He deploys his divine authority and the adoration of his sons to disabuse them of any reverence for God. Except that the de-Christianization cannot succeed for Gustave, precisely because it worked so well for his brother. Unable to compete with Achille, Gustave is unable to identify with his father, and all his life he remains ambivalent about a god he ostensibly renounced (in the name of the father). But at the same time, he renounces this world of the father in favor of an imaginary one in which, unlike many other authors in conversation and complicity with their readers, he aims to be "like God in the universe, present everywhere and visible nowhere."[15] Aesthetically, it is pure writing, for itself, an art-for-art's-sake that is complemented and sustained by bitter anti-bourgeois sentiments and generalized contempt for humanity. "Axiom: hatred of the Bourgeois is the beginning of virtue," he wrote to George Sand. "But for me the term 'bourgeois' includes the bourgeois in overalls as well as the bourgeois who wears a frock coat" (Steegmuller 1953: 211).

This was no simple bourgeois intellectual, and *Madame Bovary* was surely a new species of idealism—which the bourgeoisie mistook for realism and were quick to buy up despite (or because) it got Flaubert indicted on a charge of corrupting public morals. Sartre thinks the popularity of *Madame Bovary* was the result of a fortuitous conjunction of personal and collective chronotypes ("programmation"), which matched Flaubert's anti-bourgeois attitudes with the going bourgeois guilt, always capable of being evoked by the proletarian gaze, for having betrayed the working class in the events of 1848. Perhaps so, but the phenomenon of bourgeois, anti-bourgeois authors whose works have wide appeal to a certain fraction of the bourgeois public has been recurrent in the last two hundred years, during the high culture of Christian capitalism. Christian capitalism: a contradiction in terms involving the elaboration of original sin—pleasing oneself in the flesh, in defiance of God—into a way of life. Not to forget the dual existence of "the bourgeois subject" in a family that in critical respects was opposed to the economics and sentiments of the larger society.

15. "Gustave, between the ages of thirteen and fourteen, was converted to literature when he understood that he could use it in an attempt at countercreation, which would make him the imaginary equal of God, and that the enterprise of writing would at last give him his being—that he could construct himself in the process of constructing" (Sartre 1981–93, 2:304).

STRUCTURES OF AGENCY

Focusing now on individual historical agency, I examine some of the structures of history that authorize it.[16] For granted that individuals may have historical effect, they have to be in a position to do so, as Raymond Aron reminds us, and "position" means a place in a set of relationships, whether institutional, conjunctural, or both. We have to overcome certain received ideas of an unbridgeable opposition between cultural order and individual agency—now reinforced by the latest subjectologies and leviathanologies—together with the correlated antitheses of the sociological and the psychological, the objective and the subjective, the lawful and the contingent, the universal and the particular, and their many like. It is true these contrasting aspects of human existence are irreducible the one to the other, which is one reason why historians and social scientists are often motivated to argue the inconsequentiality of either structures or persons. But what all this manichaeanism ignores is the way persons can be empowered to represent collectives: to instantiate or personify them, sometimes even to bring them into existence, without, however, losing their own individuality. Or in other words, what is not sufficiently considered is how history makes the history-makers. Here I speak of two such structures of agency, again, as it were, polar types: *systemic agency,* like that enjoyed by Pericles, Napoleon, or the kings of the Fiji Islands, and *conjunctural agency,* like that of Bobby Thomson or Scalia, Harris & Co.

For some reason, Napoleon has been a more popular example in discussions of historical agency than Bobby Thomson. Some of this discussion, especially by Count Tolstoy and J.-P. Sartre again, I find revelatory of the institutional empowerment of the great man, or what I am calling systemic agency. I do not mean Tolstoy's famous arguments in the epilogue to *War and Peace* (1962) on history-from-below. In the course of a complex exposition of this populist thesis, Tolstoy introduces a third term to the polarity of leader and masses. He speaks of the relationship between them, thus of institutional or structural forms of empowerment, phenomena that

16. A caveat about *agency* as used in the present context of individual action. By this term I designate interventions that affect the history of social collectivities, thus specifically "historical agency." I do not argue for or against "agency" in the sense of one's personal responsibility for one's actions as opposed to the responsibility of the collective or the milieu. In any case, this sense of agency is not at issue here, inasmuch as my position is that the complex biographical determinations of the individuality of history-making persons are not specified by the larger structures of the conjuncture that authorize and realize his or her social effects.

are different in quality from the historical persons as such, either individual or en masse. The *tertium quid* became relevant when Tolstoy pondered how Napoleon was able to command the whole force and destiny of France. Napoleon had the power to raise an army of six hundred thousand men and send them off to war: but just what and whence, Tolstoy asked, was that power? (Note, parenthetically, that it included the power to screw up badly by a futile invasion of Russia—just in case one were tempted to believe that the world historical Napoleon was truly an exemplar of the cunning of reason. One of the values of conceiving agency as constituted by a cultural order of which it is an idiosyncratic expression is that we can then understand a history that turns out to be a tragedy and forget the panglossian anthropologies—from so-called cultural materialism through structural-functionalism, cultural ecology, rational choice theory and international relations realism—that are always on the lookout for the best or most rational of all possible worlds.) Used for good or evil, Napoleon's power was not personal, Tolstoy argued; it did not emanate from his own physical or moral being. Of course, dealing with a military situation where so many commands go awry, Tolstoy could be doubly convinced that the power to make things happen lay outside the person apparently exercising it. Rather, power was "in those relations which the person possessing it stands to the masses" (Tolstoy 1962: 1110). What, then, is power? "That relation of the commanding person to those he commands is indeed precisely what is called power" (ibid., 1118). But now, speaking of the *relationships* of those in command to those commanded, we are in the realm of cultural order. It follows that commander narratives are motivated by systemic relations of empowerment: by structural relays of the larger organization of society to particular persons of authority.

Sartre complements this argument by emphasizing the dialectic of the universal and the singular that necessarily follows: the historical effects of persons empowered by cultural orders, which they live, however, in their particular ways. Citing Plekhanov to the effect that if someone other than Napoleon had come to power, the revolutionary outcome would have been the same, Sartre says that this passage has always made him laugh. The only differences would have been the bloody Napoleonic wars, the influence of the revolutionary ideology on the rest of Europe, the occupation of France by the allies, the return of the landowners, the economic regression of the Restoration, the White Terror, Victor Hugo (whose father was a general of the empire), *et des choses comme ça.* All this, Sartre puts in apposition to a golden paragraph on the dialectics of structure and agency, a passage that has been for me a capital statement on this issue:

> We . . . must consider in each case the role of the individual in the historic event. For this role is not defined once and for all: it is the structure of the groups considered which determines it in each case. Thereby, without entirely eliminating contingency, we restore it to its limits and its rationality. The group bestows its power and its efficacy upon the individuals whom it has made and who have made it in turn, whose irreducible particularity is one way of living universality. . . . Or rather, this universality takes on the face, the body, and the voice of the leaders which it has given itself; thus the event itself, while a collective apparatus, is more or less marked with individual signs; persons are reflected in it to the same extent that the conditions of the conflict and the structures of the group have permitted them to be personalized. (Sartre 1968: 130)

We are left, then, with the question: what governs the extent, obviously variable both culturally and historically, to which groups and their struggles allow themselves to be personified? Can we say something more general about these structural transmissions of the macrocosm to the microcosm, about how particular people are authorized to make the histories of collectivities? The possibility that we can is the secret of the apparent madness of juxtaposing Napoleon Bonaparte with the likes of Bobby Thomson or Katherine Harris. They are contrasting forms of the structuring of agency. Thomson is a good example of conjunctural agency, Bonaparte of systemic agency.

Bobby Thomson was circumstantially selected for his heroic role by the relationships of a particular historical conjuncture; Napoleon's historical powers were prescribed by the office he held in an enduring institutional order. For Thomson, it was the situation alone that allowed him to determine history. The situation put him in a position to make a significant difference, and the situation constituted the significance of the difference he made. Such was the rationality of that contingency. But Napoleon's singularity was historically empowered by his supreme position in collective entities—France, the army—that were hierarchically organized precisely to transmit and implement his will. True, institutional positions were in play in Bobby Thomson's case, localized relationships that always enter into conjunctural agency. It was the rules of the game and his place in the batting order that allowed the whole season to devolve at that moment on Thomson's shoulders. But the power of deciding the pennant was not as such a specification of Thomson's place in the order—any more than holding the office of secretary of state of Florida prescriptively specified that Katherine Harris should determine who should be president of the United

States. Bobby Thomson's agency depended on the felicity of his act under the circumstances. If he had struck out, he would not even be a footnote to history (not unless the next batter hit a home run, as Thomson would have been the second out). By contrast, Napoleon's acts, empowered by his institutional position, would be fateful whatever strategic decision he took: whether he invaded Russia or not, he would have thus influenced the course of history. Indeed, if Bobby Thomson's heroics were made such by the situation, Napoleon made the situation as such, insofar as he brought about a certain relation of the collective forces and to that extent was responsible for the outcome—even if his plans and commands went awry.

Located in the institution, a command authority over history such as Napoleon enjoyed endures as long as the person holds the position. By contrast, Bobby Thomson was only a momentary hero, erupting for an instant from an ordinary place in the larger scheme of things, and sinking back into relative obscurity after his inning in the sun. (Indeed, total obscurity, since he was soon after traded to the Chicago Cubs.) Thomson's historical presence was as ephemeral as it was conjunctural: ephemeral because it was only conjunctural. True, he would be long remembered for what he did. In *social memory* such one-time heroes may enjoy more than their allotted fifteen minutes of fame—something like fifteen minutes of immortality. Inventors especially may turn out to be the beneficiaries of what could be called the "*post-factum* event," as what they did, and accordingly their stature, grows over time in proportion to the social consequences of their invention. The Wright brothers' experiments at Kitty Hawk or Alexander Graham Bell's first telephone conversation may have been little noted at the time, but they have been long and well remembered in proportion to the development of aviation and telephonic communication. By contrast, the immortality of Bobby Thomson's fifteen minutes comes only from its memorial recycling when for some reason, usually extraneous to the event itself, the country is given to a bout of nostalgia over baseball or the decade of the 1950s. This happened in 2001, the fiftieth anniversary of the shot heard round the world, which was marked by a spate of newspaper stories and a one-hour HBO special about it. There was even a fresh controversy, sparked by a story in the *Wall Street Journal* claiming that the Giants had been successfully stealing their opponents' pitching signs in games at the Polo Grounds, up to and including the fateful final game. An article in the *New York Times* countered with a statistical argument that if so, this was of no particular help to the Giants since their road record in the critical period was better than their home record—not to mention that the day before Thomson's home run they had been bombed

10 to 0 in the Polo Grounds. Interviewed in connection with the alleged sign stealing, Bobby Thomson denied it, although unconvincingly, as it seemed to some. Ralph Branca, who has long since become Bobby Thomson's friend, co-star on the banquet circuit, and co-vendor of signed baseball memorabilia, was quoted to the effect that "he still had to hit it." But such questions of social memory aside, the conjunctural hero, unlike those who institutionally command history, disappears more or less rapidly from public view once his or her historical moment has passed. Only occasionally does she resurface in a "human interest" story of the genre, "Where is Monica Lewinsky? And what is she doing now?" (And for that matter, who cares?)

MAKING HISTORY: DIVINE KINGS OF THE FIJI ISLANDS

On the other hand, everyone, every morning, knew where the sacred kings of nineteenth-century Fiji were, since every morning the king solemnly recreated the society by taking the part of the god in the principal temple, thus making the people's existence possible. I want to discuss here the large cultural work entailed in relaying the social destiny to key individuals, both in systemic and conjunctural agency, taking the god-kings of Fiji as an example of the first and the saga of Elián Gonzalez for the second.

Fijian sacred kings were in many ways the structural conditions of the possibility of the countries they ruled. By their presence and action, they evoked the collective existence of the kingdom as such, its own reified presence and corporate action. Without the king, the polity knew a distinct tendency to disaggregate into its several unrelated parts: its 'different peoples' (*dui kaikai*), as Fijians say. These were the several localized ancestral groups, often designated in the ethnographic literature as 'clans' (*mataqali*) or 'lineages' (*yavusa*), but colloquially known as the 'So-and-so people' (*Kai* + proper noun). Distinct in origins, these clans were also differentiated in status and specialized in function, as we have already seen in the earlier discussion of Bau and Rewa. They were chiefs of various kinds, or priests, heralds, fishers, farmers, carpenters, navigators, or warriors. The differences in function did not reflect a strict division of economic labors, since most of the groups farmed and otherwise provisioned themselves; rather, they represented the diacritic services the several clans respectively contributed to the king. Indeed, the "different peoples" of the kingdom often seemed to have little to do with one another in their daily existence. The several causeways (usually four) leading through the moat of traditional Fijian towns connected the different clans to their respective lands and bathing pools (according to modern informants), and the domestic compounds were fenced about, at least in chiefly places, so that one did not readily or easily move about in the village precincts of unrelated people.[17] In effect, the kingdom had a dual structural mode, alternating between the one and the many: between the *matanitū* (kingdom) as an entity and the different peoples going their own ways. Rather than some Durkheimian organic solidarity, the Fijian system was characterized by a hierarchical solidarity in which the relation of the different groups to one another was a function of their common subordination to the sacred king. If what the king did then made history, it was because the manifestation of his presence or will performatively made the kingdom. So likewise by his absence or death could the king make history, since without him things fell apart (M. Sahlins 1985).

Thus making and unmaking society, the king was the human, visible form of divinity. "There does not seem to be much difference between their presenting an offering to their god and making a present to a chief," the missionary Rev. John Hunt noted in his journal. "The great and just difference observed by Christians between approaching men and god seems not to be known by this people" (Hunt *J:* 1 September 1840; cf. Hocart 1912: 447). It is somewhat paradoxical that Christians, as worshipers of a god in human form, should make such a fuss about this "great and just difference"; yet Mr. Hunt's observation was not altogether amiss. The kings of the great lands of eastern Fiji—including Bau, Rewa, Verata, Cakaudrove, Macuata, and others—were indeed *kalou tamata,* 'human gods.' "The great chiefs would sometimes say 'I am a god'; and they believed it too" (Waterhouse 1866: 402). Or, to select one Fijian witness among many: "The chiefs: they are the gods of Fiji" (Rabuku 1911: 156). Fijians generally did not have religious images in their temples, rarely if ever in the principal temples of the state gods. "Though they worship false gods," said Mr. Hunt, "they have no idols" (*J:* 28 October 1843). Rather, installed in the principal temples were the priests, whom the gods possessed on occasion, and sacred kings, the likes of the Roko Tui Bau, who were abiding embodiments of the great, invisible deities of the land.

17. In Mary Wallis's observation (1851: 211), the isolation pertained especially to chiefly men; women, who were residentially intermixed by natal clan affiliation, were more collegial. So where women were often seen in parties, "parties of chiefs, however, do not associate. We shall never see [Ratu] Cakobau visit any place with his father, or any chiefs of high rank in the company of either." Of course, men did associate in temple rituals and kava circles.

The Fijian sacred king was a twinned being or a duplex person, rather of the kind Kantorowicz described for medieval Europe in *The King's Two Bodies* (1957). He had a human form by nature that embodied a divine form by consecration—in Fiji, by the solemn ceremonies of the royal installation (Hocart 1969). This specifically does not mean that the king was himself, in his own mortal body, the god. As Hocart says, "That is a claim which is occasionally put forth by monarchists, but only in the intoxication of autocracy that invariably precludes its downfall: it is a symptom of decadence" (1933: 244–45). For all his harboring of divinity, the king did not thereby lose his humanity, his individuality, or his mortality, any more than the god's being would be exhausted by his instantiation in the king. Hocart says the ruler is the "*locum tenens* of the god" (ibid.). Fijians sometimes say he is the god's 'successor' (*i sosomi*), meaning he takes the god's place among humanity (Rokowaqa 1926: 31). Gods could also be 'embodied' (*vakatolo*) in certain animals or other nonhuman beings, as well as in the priests whom they entered (*curumi koya*) in temple rituals—in which condition the priests were considered and addressed as 'gods' (*kalou*). So it could be said that the king's godliness was like that of any ritual principal. But then, what distinguished the king from any other who might be the vessel of the god in the course of ritual is precisely that "his whole life is one course of ritual" (Hocart 1933: 245). All the king's activities and the objects thereof, from the ceremonies of his birth to those of his death, passing by way of his everyday life, testified to the duality of his person. This is the point the Cakaudrove man was making to Hocart when contrasting the king to spirits that were only occasionally manifest, as in the rituals of war, when they temporarily entered their priests:

> "In olden times," said a Fijian to me, "it was the chief who was our god." "Only the chief," said a subject of the Lord of the Reef [Tui Cakau, sacred king of Cakaudrove], was believed in [*vakabau*]; he was by way of a human god [*kalou tamata*]. Spirits [*tevoro*] were only useful in war; in other things, no." (Hocart 1952: 93)

Indeed, at the beginning of every day, in consuming the offering of sacred kava presented by the chieftains of the land, the king not only succeeded the gods to whom this kava had just been presented, but he thereby assumed the divine function of instituting human social life. Making human society, he thus demonstrated a sublunar vision of divine power (*mana*). Of course, I am speaking here of the first king of the diarchy: even in Bau, where the war king (Vunivalu) ruled *de facto,* the sacred king (Roko Tui Bau) received the kava in the principal temple.[18] So also did the paramounts in other great eastern Fijian kingdoms (such as Verata, Rewa, Macuata, and Cakaudrove) and evidently also in many prominent lands (such as Tokatoka, Nakelo, and the Waimaro polities).[19] In these places, until the ruler received the offering of kava at sunrise in the main temple of the land, all human activity was effectively suspended. The total silence and immobility imposed on the king's town by the call of the herald (or in some places the priest) at daybreak marked the time (out-of-time) when the god's presence superseded the people's existence—in order to make the latter possible. In principle, talk was not allowed, or the crying of children, the barking of dogs, or the crowing of cocks. No work could be done. It was prohibited to go about on land or sea. Gathered in the temple, the heralds, priests, and clan chieftains prepared and presented the ceremonial kava to the gods and royal ancestors, praying for prosperity and victory. An early American trader, Warren Osborn, described the prayer as "a long yarn requesting the favour of the spirits so that they may have a good yam season, that their enemies may die, that many ships may visit their coasts & get cast away that they may have the whites property and more good natured wishes to the same effect" (Osborn *J:* 25 March 1835). The offering was then served to the king. Immediately the king drank—that is, immediately the sacrifice was accepted—a cry was sent resounding through the capital town, picked up and amplified on every hand, signifying that normal activities could be resumed.[20] At the same time, the several clan chief-

18. In Bau's principal temple, Navatanitawake, the first cup of kava was the privilege of the Roko Tui Bau, whereas in the houses of the town, that honor went to the Vunivalu (Hocart *FN:* Bau; cf. Capell 1973: 240 [tū]). I believe in this connection that the large man's house, Naulunivuaku, was the more secular counterfoil to the temple, and here the war king presided—just as one of his titles, "Tui Levuka," referred to the "native" people (Levuka) with whom this house was originally associated.

19. The principal sources on the king's daily kava in various lands include Williams and Calvert (1859: 111–15), Lyth (*TFR:* 13), Williams (1931, 2:319, 322; *MN,* vol. 1), Sinclair (*J:* 15 August 1840), Jaggar (SC/Y), Toganivalu (*TkB*), Lester (1941–42), Hocart (*FN:* 310), Hale (1846: 69), Diapea (1928: 93), testimony of Komaitai (CSO/MP 5947/17), MacGillvray (*J:* 12 October 1854).

20. Another early trader cum beachcomber, the irreverent "Cannibal Jack" (also known as John Jackson, William Diapea, and William Diaper) thought the manner of raising the tabu by shouting was a peculiarity of the Cakaudrove capital, Somosomo. He said of it, "The habit they adopted when Tue cakau [Tui Cakau], the king, had imbibed his morning drink of 'yagone' [*yaqona,* kava]—always about half-past 7 A.M.—to screech and halloo aloud from house to house, inside and out, echoing, and re-echoing all over the place, till at last it became—to me at least—perfectly disgusting (Diapea 1928: 93).

tains in the temple were served kava in order of rank, in this way reproducing society in its hierarchy and diversity. As the people went to work, the king and chiefs continued to sit around the grog bowl discussing kingdom affairs great and small. Thus, by the offering appropriated by the king, all the functions of society were reinstated, together with its order.

Conversely, the death of the king was a crisis of society. This could mean more than the ritual suspension and/or inversion of the social order that, as in many hierarchical societies, follows upon the death of the king. The death of the Rewa king, Ratu Qaraniqio, in 1855 snatched defeat from the jaws of victory and issued in the complete surrender to Bau in the greatest war Fiji had ever known—the great Polynesian War of Bau and Rewa. By late 1854 the Rewans had completely reversed the losses they had suffered since 1843, including the sacking of their capital twice over by the Bauans, the death of Ratu Qaraniqio's royal predecessor at the enemy's hands in 1845, and a debilitating civil war of several years' duration. Having recuperated these losses and more, Ratu Qaraniqio now had the Bauans in a seemingly inescapable vise.

Not that the Rewans' success had been all of their own doing. A lot was the undoing of Ratu Cakobau, the great war king of Bau.[21] You will recall Ratu Cakobau's failure to extend his political and economic reach over northern Fiji in the ill-fated *bêche-de-mer* expedition of 1852 against Macuata. The embarrassing battle with Macuata not only cost the Bauans the control of the *bêche-de-mer* trade, but set the unified forces of the White traders and the Rewans, together with former Bauan towns and a rebel party within Bau itself, against the humiliated Ratu Cakobau (cf. Derrick 1950: 108–9; Calvert *J:* 15 May 1855; Williams and Calvert 1859: 471–72). The peoples of Fiji's northern coasts began to trade independently with Europeans, while the White residents of Levuka (Ovalau), in collusion with the visiting *bêche-de-mer* vessels, effectively put an embargo on Bau, causing a serious shortage of ammunition and other valuable goods. At the same time, the cantankerous American consul John Williams publicly denounced Ratu Cakobau in a Sydney newspaper, calling upon the "civilized nations" to destroy him. The various White parties—the Methodist missionaries excluded, as Cakobau had strategically converted on 30 April 1854—were soon conspiring with and supplying the Rewans as well as the

21. The discussion of the plight of Cakobau and the death of Ratu Qaraniqio can be followed in Waterhouse (1866: 251–52), Derrick (1950: 103–4), Calvert (*J:* 26 January–15 May 1856 and passim), Calvert (1856: 6–8), Williams and Calvert (1859: 358–59), *CL* (Mathieu: 10 March, 27 April 1855), Marist Anonymous (*HM:* 65–68), Moore (*J:* 25 January 1855), Deniau (*HF2*), Rougier (*FL*).

rebels in and around Bau. Led by a classificatory brother of Ratu Cakobau, the uprising mobilized internal enemies of the Bau war kings of long standing and a recurrent disposition for usurpation. All these enemies established a central stronghold at Kaba, on the peninsula near Bau (map 1.1). The loss of Kaba itself was a blow to Ratu Cakobau, not only because it was the eponymous homeland of his own clan (Tui Kaba), but because he had stored there, besides a large war canoe and a cache of arms, the schooner *Thakombau,* one of the two European vessels whose acquisition had led to the *bêche-de-mer* fiasco of 1852. In addition to Kaba, a number of other towns with similarly strong ties of kinship and allegiance to the Bau war king joined the alliance of his Rewan, foreign, and Bauan foes. Then, early in early March of 1854, much of Bau burned down, and what remained was flattened by a hurricane two weeks later.

Meanwhile, Ratu Cakobau himself was ailing, apparently despondent in mind as well as afflicted in body by a "fistula in Perineo," according to the missionary doctor, Rev. R. B. Lyth (*DB:* 19 July 1854). Already in November 1853, Mr. Lyth had noted, "Bau is now hemmed in by enemies. The proud rebellious city with its head Thakombau [Ratu Cakobau] seems on the verge of war or revolution" (*J:* 5 November 1853). His colleague Rev. James Calvert, who was preaching on Bau at this period, had a similarly gloomy view of Ratu Cakobau's personal condition and military situation: "He was peculiarly and severely affected. The current was strong against him. Gods and men were united to bring him low—in body, circumstances & mind, he suffered" (Calvert *J:* 15 May 1855). The Methodists, notably Mr. Calvert, maneuvered hard to deliver their prize convert from his numerous dangers. By bribery and threat, they helped keep the powerful warrior-fishers of Bau, the Lasakau people, on Ratu Cakobau's side. They were also instrumental in bringing to his aid the army of the Christian ruler of Tonga, King George Tupou.[22] The combined Tongan and Bauan forces defeated the Bau rebels at Kaba in April 1855. But by then Ratu Cakobau's greatest enemies, the Rewans under their king Ratu Qaraniqio, were out of it.

22. MacGillvray of HMS *Herald* commented on the Protestant missionaries' machinations after Ratu Cakobau's conversion: "Throughout these missionaries (Mssrs. Moore and Waterhouse, but especially Mr Calvert) have been unremitting in their endeavour to bring about a reconciliation between Thakombau and those opposed to him. Although there is no doubt that the settlement of the 'difficulty' in the manner in which the missionaries propose [the submission of the Bau rebels to Ratu Cakobau] would vastly increase their influence, as the other would diminish it, yet I would not impute any other motive to them than which ought to activate Christians and Ministers" (*J:* 12 October 1854).

All the advantages Rewa had gained in the last years of bitter war with Bau were dissipated when Ratu Qaraniqio died, unexpectedly and rather suddenly, on 25 January 1855. Negotiations for a surrender to Bau began within days, and were concluded with Ratu Cakobau's acceptance of the offering of submission (*i soro*) on 9 February. Yet not many weeks before, Ratu Qaraniqio had built a temple in which to celebrate his imminent victory over Bau, having disdained several messages from Ratu Cakobau indicating he was ready to make peace. Everything happened as if the great lament raised in Rewa at the king's demise (according to the resident Catholic missionary) were true: "The chief has fallen! Our great chief has fallen. Bati Vundi [Bati Vudi, another name of Ratu Qaraniqio] is no more! Alas!, alas! We are all lost" (Rougier *FL*).

The shock of Ratu Qaraniqio's death may have been the greater for being something of an official surprise, even as the immediate circumstances of it were not conducive to a smooth succession—and thus the continuation of the war. According to the resident Methodist missionary, Rev. William Moore, who for some weeks had been treating Ratu Qaraniqio for severe dysentery, the king was concealing his illness, "fearing to let his people know." "You know," he wrote to Reverend Lyth, "a chief's health is all important in war time" (Lyth *L:* 7 June 1855). The implied (Frazerian) correspondence between the health of the king and the well-being of the body politic helps make intelligible the collapse of collective resolve that set in at Ratu Qaraniqio's fall. Another factor, much credited by the Protestant missionaries, was that Ratu Qaraniqio had been unconscious for some hours before, and passed away mute, without giving the charge of war to his chiefs or a successor. Indeed, it was only after the customary ten-day mourning that Ratu Rabici, the son of a deceased brother of the king (Ro Bativuaka), a young man not yet twenty, arrived from Kadavu Island and apparently claimed the rule. Ratu Rabici, together with certain priests, several fighting-allies (*bati*) of Rewa, and many others, including the Catholic missionaries, blamed the Methodists, Mr. Moore in particular, for killing the king. It was said that the medicine Mr. Moore gave him was a poison, or else that the missionary put certain Bauans in his own entourage up to the dirty deed. If nothing else, the accusation does reflect the fact that the Protestants' neutrality had been compromised by the recent conversion of Ratu Cakobau. Nor would Mr. Moore give the Rewans reason to think him innocent by urging them, after the king's death, to make peace with Bau. The immediate consequence was that Mr. Moore's house was burned down: for which deed, it was widely believed, Ratu Rabici was responsible.

But this was the best the young successor of Ratu Qaraniqio could do.

I suspect the disarray that followed the king's death was due to more than the shock of it. Rewa's northern allies (*bati*) favored continuing the war, and apparently so did Ratu Rabici, but not the other chiefly powers that be. I question too whether they favored Ratu Rabici, not only because of his youth, but also because he could be a contentious choice of successor in a ruling kindred notorious for generations of patricidal and fratricidal strife over the kingship. Whether by the circumstances of Ratu Qaraniqio's death or by the lack of an immediate legitimate successor, Rewa in late January was without an effective ruler. Ratu Qaraniqio was buried in the temple he had built to thank the gods for a victory over Bau that was, instead, entombed along with him. Father Rougier wrote his political epitaph: "Whether he died a natural death or not, it is certain the only powerful & really formidable enemy [of Bau] fell in him. Rewa, without its head, could not direct its army upon Bau. Considering Fijian customs, it was quite impossible" (Rougier *FL*).

The death of Ratu Qaraniqio was thus an evenemential turning point, another historical reversal of the kind we have been discussing. And though in this case it did not lead to anything as momentous as who got to play in the World Series, it did sediment relations of domination and opposition between Bau and Rewa that continued into and through the period of Fiji's colonization (1874–1971)—and are still discernible in the turbulent politics of the postcolonial nation.

There follows another example of turbulent politics, but one that rather features the construction of conjunctural agency.

THE ICONIZATION OF ELIÁN GONZALEZ

One of the lasting images of the Elián Gonzalez affair is the untitled cartoon showing the head of the young Cuban boy attached to the body of a chess-piece pawn (fig. 2.5).[23] Discovered drifting at sea on 25 November 1999, Thanksgiving Day in America, Elián was the survivor of an ill-fated attempt to reach Miami that cost the lives of his mother and ten other Cubans. Almost immediately he became a *cause célèbre*. Until 22 April 2000, when he was seized by federal agents and restored to his father, little Elián was used as an argument, not to say a pretext, by a variety of political interest groups arrayed in complex relations of opposition in principle and alliance of convenience. What is conveyed by the image of Elián as a pawn

23. Bibliography on the Elián Gonzalez affair, most of it referring to Internet sites, appears in a special section at the end of the general bibliography.

is the interpolation of these greater national and international struggles into the family conflict over custody of the child: a meaningful-structural magnification of the interpersonal relationships that gave them correspondingly large political effects (cf. Rowe 2002).

Within days of Elián's installation in the Miami household of his great-uncle, Lazaro Gonzalez, the Cuban exile community in Florida and the Cuban government apparatus in Havana had each made Elián's cause their own in the struggle with the other. The question of whether a minor who has lost his mother comes under the custody of his father, easily resolvable in American law, had been translated into ideological contraries as irreconcilable as they were abstract.[24] In Miami, the argument of why Elián should not be returned to his father was democratic freedom versus communist dictatorship; in Havana, the reason he should be returned to his father was revolutionary morality versus capitalist perversion. Soon both sides were objectifying these values in daily mass demonstrations. Large crowds gathered outside the Gonzalez house nightly and all day on weekends, chanting the boy's name and beseeching his appearance—which they greeted with joy bordering on adoration

2.5 The pawn. (Taylor Jones/*Los Angeles Times;* © Tribune Media Services, Inc. All rights reserved. Reprinted with permission)

24. So far as it was a custody case, and not an immigration case, the Justice Department report held that "it would be a substantial intrusion into the realm of parental authority for a distant relative to be able to trigger government procedures concerning the parent's 6-year-old son that could seriously disturb the parent-child relationship and family stability" (*ABC:* 24 April 2000). Indeed, had Elián's mother survived, she could well have been indicted in federal court for kidnapping, since she took the child to America without his father's permission. This happened to one Arletis Blanco, who was sentenced to three years' probation for "international parental kidnapping" in October 2001 in Florida. Ms. Blanco had fled Cuba in a boat with her boyfriend and her daughter and son the previous November, leaving the boy's father in Cuba—a case singularly like the Elián affair. The boy was returned to his father (*NYT:* 25 October 2001).

2.6 Crowds gather daily at the Gonzalez house. (sk/Susan Knowles/UPI/Landov)

(fig. 2.6). Cuba answered with demonstrations rallying people in the thousands all across the island, complemented by several hours of television coverage and discussion daily. "Here in Cuba," came the report, "it is all Elián, all the time" (*WP:* 17 April 2000). In Miami, the "miracle child" (as Elián was widely known there) was given the seat of honor at the annual Three Kings Procession. In Havana, the "boy martyr" (as Elián was widely known there) shared the limelight in absentia in the annual celebration of José Martí's birthday. *Granma,* the Communist Party daily, also compared Elián to Che Guevara, saying the boy "had been converted forever into a symbol of the crimes and injustices that imperialism is capable of committing against an innocent" (*MH:* 29 January 2000). The comparison could only confirm the Miami Cubans' worst fears for Elián, were he to be repatriated. Not long after he did return to Cuba, one of his Miami relatives observed, "They're teaching him to be like Che—an assassin and an asthmatic" (*MH:* 25 May 2000). In Miami, as already implied, the ideology of liberation was more messianic than revolutionary, associating the boy with Christ and Moses rather than Che Guevara and José Martí.

Together with the politics of Elián, these ideological and performative associations are of central interest here, as so many structural relays of the macrocosm to the register of the familial and the personal. International affairs are thus played out in domestic relationships. Accordingly, the Elián affair raises not a few questions of historical agency. Among them is how certain, quite ordinary people can become big-time historical movers and shakers. Defying federal court orders and the U.S. Immigration and Naturalization Service—thus the Justice Department, the attorney general, and ultimately the president—the Gonzalez family of Miami was able to hold Cuban-American relations hostage to their own intransigence. Moreover, there would be long-term and large-scale historical residues, not excluding (as it happened) the decisive effects of the Elián affair on the U.S. presidential election of 2000. (So to relate anthropological theory again to chaos theory, not without some justification: no Elián, no war in Iraq.) Here are fateful conflations of different cultural registers or structural levels, with the dialectical effects of endowing national-political issues with the character of family values, and family issues with national-political consequences. The relations between states, which ever since Thucydides we have believed to be governed by *Realpolitik,* are entangled in sentimental dramas of kinship.

Call it, then, *historical melodrama.* Nationalism is the more easily propagated when the imagined community is recognized as a real family. Actually the current hip term is *méconnaissance.* But if we must have French dressing on our theoretical salad, I prefer the Rousseauian *pitié:* experiencing the pains and pleasures of creatures like ourselves as feelings of our own. Britain recently went through a season with the tribulations and death of Princess Di. Of course, as we already know, royal families have a head start as signifiers of the totality. But in the sad aftermath of the events of September 11, 2001, every body recovered from the debris of the World Trade Center was wrapped in an American flag—whatever the person's actual nationality. The crafted *New York Times* stories on the everyday personal lives and virtues of the victims made each one seem like another verse of "God Bless America."

Such syntheses of the national with the personal are also familiar from anthropological studies of soap operas, notably including the very popular Latin American *telenovelas*—which are probably metonymically as well as metaphorically pertinent to the Elián case. "In the *barrios* of Washington and other cities across the country, Latinos are following the saga of Elián Gonzalez like a real-life soap opera, one full of political intrigue and family strife. They know all the characters—the father Juan Miguel, the uncle Lasaro, Cuban dictator Fidel Castro looming in the background—and they understand the plot all too well, particularly how immigration can separate parent from child" (*WP:* 9 April 2000).[25] Just so, in the *telenovela,*

25. However, the same article in the *Washington Post* noted that the non-Cuban Hispanics were more interested in the human drama than in the Cuban American political

social categories and universals on the order of the state, classes, and ethnicities, as well as general moral principles, all take on the emotional charge of the human relationships in which they have been instantiated. The collective categories and customs are then narrated allegorically, and their destiny is configured as the dénouement of a poignant story of private lives. Speaking of the crowds that came to catch a glimpse of Elián, the mayor of Miami-Dade, Alex Penelas, observed that "what you see here in the faces of these people is over 41 years of persecution. . . . These are real family emotions. . . . This is real pain" (*MH:* 14 April 2000). There were many such reports of great emotionalism over Elián in Little Havana, a fervor for which the Anglo community had as little sympathy as it had understanding. But for Miami Cubans, the symbolic transfers between the political macrocosm and the familial microcosm were right on top, enough to be explicitly articulated, as by the popular local priest Francisco Santana. "I am absolutely certain that communism began in Cuba by dividing the family," he said, "and communism is going to end in Cuba when this family is reunited." His argument was that "if the boy's battling family, his communist father and his anti-communist Miami relatives, can make peace, then Castro will fall" (*WP:* 21 April 2000). Or again, in another take of Rousseauian *pitié:*

> People see in Elián's plight their own tragedy [said Ramon Saul Sanchez, leader of the Democracy Movement, one of the most vocal Cuban exile groups]. They see the disintegration of the Cuban family, and the human drama of a small child having experienced losing his mom. And there is also another issue: They see a defenseless human being faced with the enormous powers of a world power like the United States and a Cuban dictatorship intent on utilizing him as a political chip. (*WP:* 1 April 2000)

At the same time, similar political capital was being made of the plight of "kidnapped Elián" in Cuba. Kidnapping of children, not incidentally, has a specific resonance in Cuban historical memory: the legendary tales

---

cause per se. "It's like a telenovela or a soap opera. They're following it as a human drama rather than a political drama. The interest hasn't translated into strong political views." Perhaps relevant here is a certain disconnect between the Florida Cuban Americans and other Hispanic groups, there being some resentment among the latter of the powers and privileges acquired by the former. The political friction may be judged from the fact that the non-Cuban Hispanic vote in the 2000 presidential election ran 2 to 1 in favor of Gore, while the Cuban American vote was 3 to 1 for Bush.

of the capture and sacrifice of White children in 1904 to the Santería deity Changó by Afro-Cubans—though the true antagonists, by Stephan Palmié's reading, were the Spanish and American colonialisms intent on kidnapping Cuba's future (cited in Rowe 2002: 144).[26] Even more directly related, as it was mentioned in connection with Elián by Gabriel García Márquez (Commondreams.org 2000) among others, was the notorious Operation Pedro Pan of 1960–62, which made "false orphans" of thousands of Cuban children. Under the auspices of the Catholic Church in America—working in secret agreement with the U.S. government—over fourteen thousand Cuban children between the ages of six and sixteen were separated from their parents and shipped to the United States, where they were placed in foster care. It is widely believed that the CIA was responsible for the terrible rumors being circulated by the Cuban Church and Radio Swan to induce the parents to part with their children: that the Castro regime was going to take the youngsters away from them for political indoctrination, or else send them to Russia for that purpose. Among the "even crueler lies" spread about was that "the most appetizing children would be sent to Siberian slaughter houses to be returned as canned meat" (ibid.)—a cannibal refrain that would be revived in Miami as the probable fate of Elián if he were to be sent back to Castro. Operation Pedro Pan was shut down in 1962 by the Cuban missile crisis, which also suspended migration to the United States, leaving the children already there separated from their parents for years (many of them still are). So as it turned out, thousands of Cuban children had indeed been coercively taken from their parents by an alien power for political cum cultural indoctrination, successfully enough that many later emerged as witnesses to the cause of preventing Elián from returning to the terrible communist regime in Cuba. Yet the memories of their own "kidnapping" were also resurfacing in Cuba, precisely in testimony to capitalism's "disregard for the most fundamental of human relationships." In both cases, the key ideological move was to collapse the political abstractions into the pathos of a family torn apart and a child bereft. After Elián had been repatriated, the president of the Cuban National Assembly told the *New York Times* correspondent that regrettably the agitation of recent months would have to be scaled back: "You cannot ask the people to have the same emotional level about a boy without a mother, separated from his father, for a discussion of the [U.S. immigration] adjustment law" (5 July 2000).

26. The memory would also be revived by stories circulating in Miami that Castro would have to recover Elián and sacrifice him to a Santería deity, as we shall see.

Damian Fernandez, professor of political science at Florida International University, sums up the historical-melodramatic significance of the shipwrecked Elián: "To understand the Elián case, you really must understand it symbolically. Elián is a metaphor for the Cuban nation, and it's a nation in crisis, a shipwrecked nation. And both sides, here in Miami and there in Havana, are fighting for the nation of tomorrow" (*PBS:* February 2001).

Here, then, is another critical point about these interchanges between the collective and the personal: not just any old story will do. It has to be a good old story, structurally speaking—which this one was, in several ways. As often remarked in the American press, the whole Elián affair would have been over in an instant, passed without public notice, if it had been the child's father who was lost at sea and his mother who remained in Cuba. Who could have made a cause of keeping the child from his loving mother? In the American psyche, the father-child relationship is less compelling than the mother-child bond, rather as the merely cultural is to the fundamentally biological.[27] Another felicitous aspect was Elián's youth, hence the innocence and helplessness that could be an argument either for restoring him to his father or for protecting him against brutal governments, whether American or Cuban. Not to forget the beauty of this kid, his photogenic appeal—or his race (fig. 2.7). That Elián was white, not black, was a condition of the possibility of his iconization, not only in the Anglo population, but also in the Miami Cuban community whose demographics reflected a racially selective immigration process: "Indeed, racism among Miami [Cuban] exiles, nearly 90 percent of whom are white, is not uncommon, and it has been widely speculated that had Elián Gonzalez been black—as are some 50 percent of Cubans on the island—'he would have been tossed back into the sea,' as one caller put it to a Miami talk radio program" (*George,* May 2000: 67).[28]

27. Writes Lance Morrow in *Time* (17 April 2000): "It's disturbing how blithely some Americans have resolved the dilemma by dismissing, even denigrating, the father—and even the role of fathers. If it had been Juan Miguel Gonzalez who had died in the Straits of Florida and the mother who waited back in Cuba, Elián would have been sent back to her immediately, on the premise that the mother-child bond trumps politics. It's natural. But the father. . . . That's different. . . . Americans operate as if fathers were secondary and essentially dispensable."

28. Said Elena Freye, director of the moderate Cuban Committee for Democracy, "This child was not some ugly black kid from Haiti. This child was an adorable-looking [white] boy—very photogenic" (*PBS:* 26 April 2000). The Haitian boy comparison was apparently common fare: see "Race Called a Key in Elián Saga" (*AP:* 8 April 2000). In this connection, the Elián affair did not lessen the opposition between the African American and Cuban

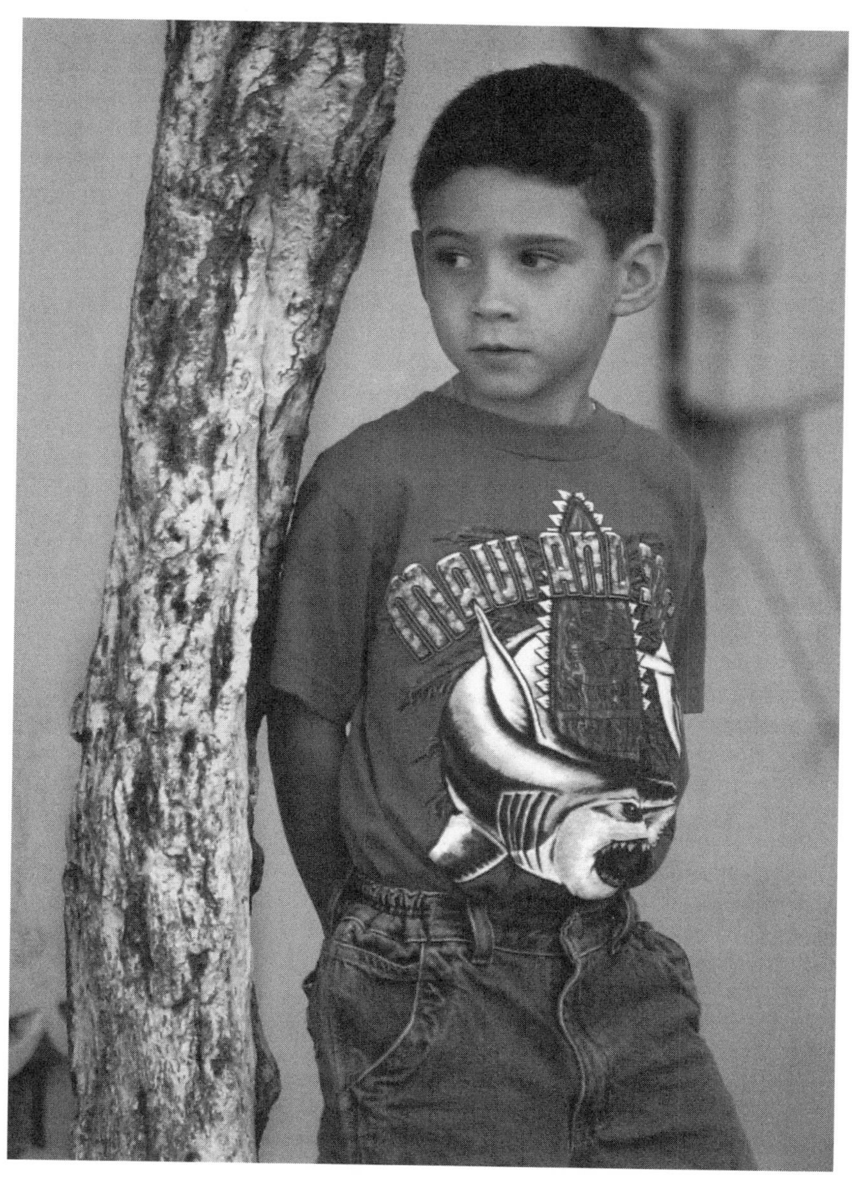

2.7 Elián. (© AFP/Corbis)

Then there were the structural virtues of the focus on close kinship, an apparent common ground for all the parties concerned, upon which they could proceed to develop their working misunderstandings. For Cubans, this was a somewhat different and larger issue than for Anglos: an all-too-familiar one of an extended kindred torn apart by immigration. (In this respect, the Gonzalez people shared something with Fidel Castro, who had once won a similar custody battle over his own son, and whose own nephew, U.S. Rep. Lincoln Diaz-Balart [R.-Fla.], gave Elián a Labrador puppy, among the other strenuous arguments he made to keep the boy in America.) From the Cuban vantage, the relationships of the people involved in the custody of Elián were at least four generations deep, including one great-grandmother, grandparents, and their siblings and distant cousins. Americans were fixed singularly on the nuclear kinship of mother, father, and child—"primary ties" that by their "sacredness" could make the claims to guardianship by Elián's collateral relatives seem all the more frivolous. Indeed, it passed almost without notice in the American media that while two of Elián's great-uncles, Lazaro and Delphin Gonzalez, were fighting to hold him in the country, their brother Manuel, also in Miami, believed the boy should go back to his father—which only made Manuel a lonely and heckled man on the streets of the city, a "*communista* and a traitor" (*WP:* 6 April 2000). Nor was it much noticed that although Elián's mother had "sacrificed herself for his freedom" (as Miami Cubans said), her own mother, living in Cuba, came to America to lobby for his repatriation to "Communist Cuba."[29]

The *dramatis personae* of this historical melodrama should also occasion some reflection on just who gets to be a history-maker, and in what circumstances. Clearly, the structural goodness of the story is more critical than the character of the historical agents it empowers. The devolution of international relations on the likes of Lazaro and Delphin Gonzalez would

---

communities in Miami, the former put off by the privileges and power enjoyed by the latter. Black Americans generally, and Black American congressional representatives notably, favored the repatriation of Elián. By April 2000, 92 percent of the African Americans in Miami-Dade favored returning Elián to Cuba (*WP:* 15 April 2000).

29. The necessity for a "good old story," structurally speaking, was underscored by the more recent failure of the Cuban government to whip up enthusiasm over five "heroes of the revolution" convicted in December 2001 of espionage in the United States. As reported in the *New York Times:* "As with Elián Gonzalez, the shipwrecked child ultimately reunited with his father in Cuba, the [Cuban] government has made them the focus of rallies, televised discussions and appeals to the international community. But diplomats say it has proved difficult to generate much sympathy for grown men who admitted to having worked for Cuban intelligence. Arrest, they point out, is a normal risk in that line of work" (*NYT:* 17 October 2002).

not seem to be a sterling example of the Hegelian cunning of Reason. One is reminded rather of Marx's remark about Louis Napoleon in his preface to the second edition of his *Eighteenth Brumaire of Louis Bonaparte:* that the class struggle in France had "created circumstances and relationships that made it possible for a grotesque mediocrity to play a hero's part." But that was a case of systemic agency. Neither born great nor empowered by office, the Gonzalez clan of Miami were, a number of them, rather dubious characters to have greatness thrust upon them.[30] It has to be admitted, however, that on the score of past DUI charges, the great-uncles Lazaro and Delphin had almost as many qualifications for heroic leadership as George W. Bush and Richard Cheney. And Lazaro, an unemployed auto mechanic, did have the gumption to hold off the American powers that be, finally forcing the feds to seize Elián in an armed raid (fig. 2.8). This defiance fit the macho image he sometimes adopted for appearances in U.S. courts, dressed up in a shiny black shirt with a shiny purple tie—another working misunderstanding. Marysleysis, Elián's second cousin once removed (by standard American reckoning), was popularly considered his "surrogate mother," apparently because she had primary care of the boy—when she was not being rushed to the hospital for one of her frequent "anxiety attacks" (*Salon:* 29 June 2000; *MH:* 26 May 2000). A dropout from the local community college, twenty-one-year-old Marysleysis was in and out of the emergency ward six or eight times during Elián's stay (fig. 2.9). Taken as a sign of her spirituality and her sufferings, her faintings made her all the more beloved in the Little Havana community. But a disposition that many Anglos perceived rather as hysterical, while it brought her a lot of television time, did not garner a lot of sympathy from the larger American audience. Indeed, the U.S. media generally held Marysleysis in some contempt, called her "the actress" or worse, according to Gene Weingarten of the *Washington Post* (6 April 2000). Weingarten's three-part piece, "A Modern Play of Passions," is the best reportage I have seen on the Elián saga, although his observation of Marysleysis's behavior could be reminiscent of the uncomprehending missionary accounts of the funerary rites of South Seas islanders. "Marysleysis often seems cold and haughty, and overly made up and flagrantly fingernailed, and she can sometimes be seen laughing with friends moments before turning to the cameras and crying over Elián" (*WP:* 6 April 2000).

From the mainstream American perspective, the supporting characters

30. Notices of the guardians of Elián in Miami may be found in Lopez-Calderon (geocities.com, 2 April 2000), *Salon* (17, 26 April, 12 May, 8, 29 June 2000), *ABC* (10 February 2000), *WP* (6 April 2000), *Newsweek* (17 January 2000), *MH* (30 January, 10 February 2000).

2.8 Lazaro Gonzalez. (Patrick Ward/UPI/Landov)

of the Elián melodrama were even more problematic. The twin cousins who often came over to play with the boy, Jose and Luis Cid Cruz, were both felons with long rap sheets. One was under indictment for an armed robbery committed a half-mile from the Gonzalez house. Besides strong-arm robbery, the police dossiers of these two included felony firearms charges, resisting arrest with violence, grand larceny, petty larceny, burglary, and failure to pay child support. Then there was the media-famous

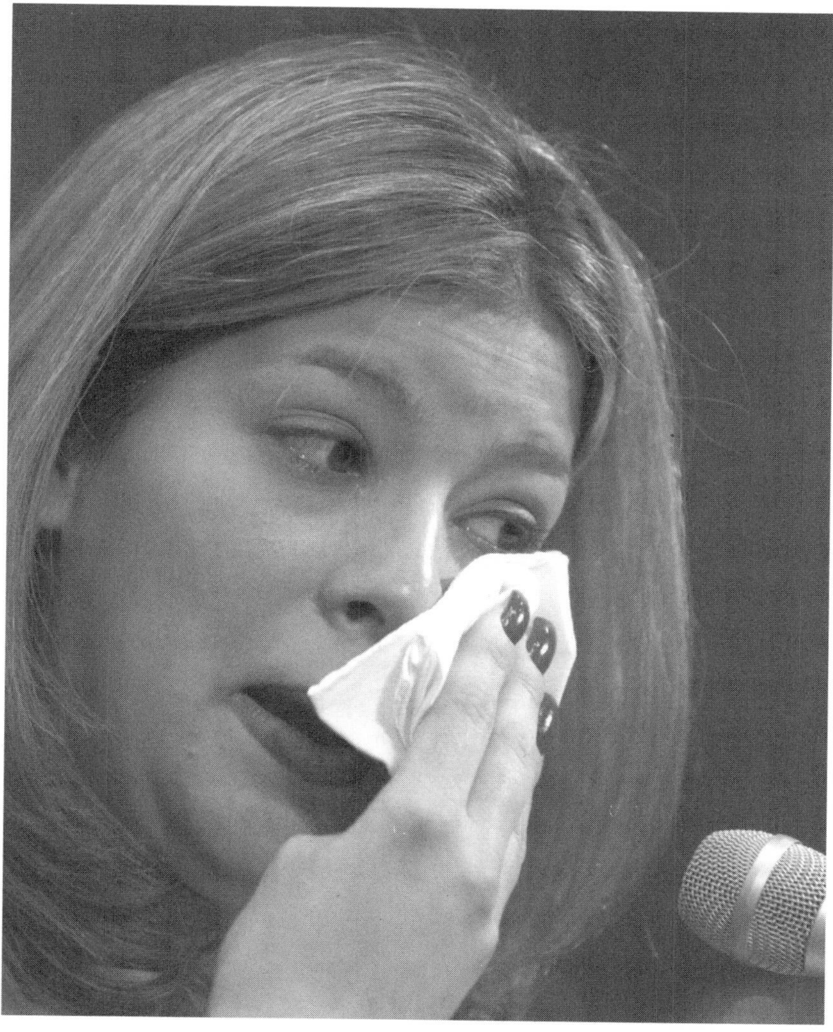

2.9 Marysleysis Gonzalez. (rg/lw/Ian Wagreich/UPI/Landov)

"El Pescador," the "fisherman" who helped rescue Elián. Capitalizing on this repute, he became a frequent visitor at Lazaro's house and a hero in the neighborhood—although in truth he was neither fisherman nor Latino. Donato Dalrymple was a guy of Scotch Irish and Italian parentage from Poughkeepsie, New York, who cleaned houses for a living, and who happened that day to go on a fishing trip for the first time in his life when his cousin asked him to come along to drive the boat. Otherwise, however, with two arrests for domestic violence and three failed marriages, El Pescador did rather fit the profile of Elián's guardians. His many eager appearances on TV earned him, on one hand, personal congratulations from the likes of Oliver North (of pro-Contra notoriety), and, on the other, unflattering characterizations such as "the Fonz" and "the bombastic buffoon" from the more liberal press (*Salon:* 29 June 2000). "800,000 Cubans love me," he told Michael Leahy of the *Washington Post.* "Yeah, I could see myself walking through that door and maybe running for mayor or maybe that lower office, you know, what is it? Commissioner or something?" (*WP:* 26 April 2000). Gene Weingarten observed that the Elián story "has made several people unlikely celebrities, and the unlikeliest may be Donato Dalrymple" (*WP:* 7 April 2000). "Unlikely celebrities"—that's the historiographic point.

But as I say, considerable political effort had gone into making such unlikely historical agency. In Havana and Miami, Cubans in both camps were moved to raise the political stakes in Elián by the declining fortunes of their foundational political causes. A tired revolution in Cuba faced off against a waning counter-revolution in Florida, the hard-liners on each side sensing the decline of political commitment among their younger people especially. Prominent in the drive to keep Elián in Miami was the conservative Cuban American National Foundation (CANF), notorious for its anti-Castro activities. The CANF is widely credited with having set off the Elián affair by having a propaganda poster made of the child for display at the World Trade Organization meeting in Seattle, where Fidel Castro was scheduled to appear. Fidel did not show up, but the poster did, not only in Seattle, but thereafter all over the streets of Miami. "Before Elián," observed the political scientist Dario Moreno, "we were growing up, moving to another stage, less extreme, less passionate. Elián Gonzalez allowed the old guard to reestablish control over politics, because Elián was the perfect symbolic cause" (*WP:* 7 April 2001; cf. *PBS:* Frontline, February 2001; *NYT:* 16 January, 2 September 2000). So too in Havana: "A small boy bails out the old dictator," as the echoing headline of *The Guardian* read (12 April 2000).

Clearly, what helped make Elián "the perfect symbolic cause" was the felicity of his plight for fashioning a politics of youth (*CT:* 24 June 2001). Accordingly, schools became prominent sites of agitation on both sides of the Florida straits. In Cuba, schoolchildren were turned out *en masse* to demonstrate their solidarity with "the boy hero." While Elián was in Miami, his empty desk in Cuba was used as a symbol of perfidious capitalism; when he returned to Cuba, his empty desk in Miami became a symbol of perfidious communism—indeed, his Miami classroom was dedicated to him with a plaque, and plans were made for a permanent display of his schoolwork. In statements that likewise mirrored each other, spokesmen on both sides commented afterward on the political silver they had gained in recuperating their younger people—a "silver lining" in the one case, if a "silver platter" in the other. Miami Cubans consoled themselves for the loss of Elián "with the commitment to the cause of young Cuban Americans previously uninterested in Cuba" (*MH:* 23 November 2000), even as a prominent Havana politico told the *New York Times:* "They gave it to us on a silver platter. This is a battle of ideas we clearly appreciate. . . . Those several months have allowed us to discover new forms, methods and actors—a lot more youth above all" (*NYT:* 5 July 2000).[31]

The mobilization of the Miami Cubans intersected in complex ways with American national politics, producing new alignments of the political forces, including several of the strange-bedfellow variety. Ridiculed sometimes in late-night TV talk shows, criticized often by print journalists, and strongly opposed by the Democratic Clinton administration, the Cuban American cause was by all accounts running poorly in the nation at large. To believe the public opinion polls, the sentiment for returning Elián to his father increased progressively from December (46 percent in favor, 33 percent opposed) to April (59 percent in favor, 33 percent opposed) (*ABC:* 2 April 2000). Popular sentiment to end the trade embargo on Cuba was also mounting. At the same time, an interest in controlling immigration to the United States gave Presidents Castro and Clinton common cause for returning Elián. On the other hand, Sen. Joseph Lieberman, soon to be the Democratic vice-presidential candidate, was prepared to join certain conservative Republicans in circumventing the Immigration and Naturalization Service by endorsing a congressional bill that would make Elián an honorary U.S. citizen. A very rare congressional act, such honors had heretofore been reserved for the likes of Winston Churchill and Mother Theresa. "I don't think it's in [Elián's] best interest to send him to a place where the government can tell him what he thinks and what he'll become," said Republican senator Connie Mack in sponsoring the bill that would have the U.S. government decide Elián's best interest and what he would

31. A similar report, citing the director of the North American desk of Cuba's Foreign Ministry, reads as follows: "It [the Elián affair] was an affirmation of the Revolution. It got people involved. . . . Young Cubans weren't born during the Soviet period, during the Bay of Pigs, during the Cuban missile crisis. But they felt part of this sad story" (*CT:* 24 June 2001; cf. *NYT:* 2 September 2001).

become (*WP:* 16 January 2000). Lieberman, incidentally, had been a darling of the Cuban American community since 1988 when he ran for the Senate against the independent Lowell Weicker, who favored an opening to Castro. Early in 2000, when he was standing for reelection to the Senate, Lieberman received a campaign contribution of at least ten thousand dollars from the Free Cuba Political Action Committee. Despite all this, and Al Gore's pandering to the Cuban American vote by advocating that Elián be kept in America, when the Clinton administration repatriated the boy, the Florida Cubans came out *en masse* in the presidential election with the aim of "punishing the Democrats." The Gore-Lieberman ticket of 2000 got roughly fifty thousand fewer Cuban American votes than the Clinton-Gore ticket of 1996. Add Elián Gonzalez to the numerous unnecessary and sufficient reasons why Al Gore lost Florida and the presidency. Still, many liberal Democrats had been opposing measures such as the Elián citizenship bill from the beginning—on conservative Republican principles. The way that Maxine Waters, African American congressional representative from California, arguing on national television for restoring Elián to his father, invoked the sacred Republican cows of "family values" and "natural rights" (*CNN:* 4 January 2000).

Of course, the American political right had its own contradictions, of which its commitment to "family values" represented one side and libertarian anticommunism the other. Its ensuing dialectical contortions at once weakened the right's hand politically while pushing it to shrill ideological extremes of possessive individualism. On the one hand, a significant number of prominent Republicans stood firm on family values. "It's a no-brainer," said Rep. Steve Largent, of Oklahoma, a former football star. "He should be sent back to his father" (*CT:* 22 January 2000). Or Kathleen Parker, conservative columnist: "The primacy of parents' God-given right to nurture their own children must always prevail over politics" (*CT:* 19 January 2000).[32] On the other hand, then, the radical right, forced to abandon the family values high ground, fell back on the bedrock position that individual freedom is the greatest good: a right of the self to the self that must take priority over any parental claim. For months, the talk radio shows, the downchannel TV stations, and the Internet were indulging in paroxysms of libertarian fundamentalism, linking the Elián case to every major and minor threat to free enterprise and the American way of life.

32. Jill Nelson, in *USA Today* (7 January 2000): "hostility to Cuba doesn't trump the bond between parents and children. . . . Elián's return to the arms of his father will be a small victory for the much-touted notion of 'family values' that American politicians love to bandy about" (cf. *CPD:* 22 December 1999; *WP:* 1 January 2000).

Here are some examples from the over-the-top Internet right-wing site "capitalismmagazine.com." Authored by heirs of Ayn Rand, this net magazine kept up a running commentary during the events called "Keep Elián Free." The general thesis was that it would be "a sin" tantamount to "child abuse," or even "regulating Bill Gates," to send the boy back to the "tropical prison camp" of Castro's Cuba where he would become "a slave of the state"; for in such cases, "a father's right can never supersede those of a child," and in any case, if the father is a committed communist, "that disqualifies him from being a parent." The latter, far-out reflections on parental rights come from interviews with one Edwin Locke, a professor of business and psychology at the University of Maryland, who also thought that returning Elián to his father was just the kind of thing encouraged by the relativist multiculturalism now running rampant in America. For multiculturalism, Locke said, "maintains no way is right and everybody has his own opinion. If you accept multiculturalism, then everybody is equal. Castro is no different than Thomas Jefferson" (*cm.c:* 25 March 2000). In another article (co-authored with Richard Salsman), Locke indicates one could hardly expect justice from the attorney general, Janet Reno, who in a matter of months had not only managed to "sentence a boy to slavery in a dictatorship," but (referring to tobacco liability cases) "to destroy a whole industry" and (referring to Microsoft) "to crush America's most successful company." Regarding the damage suits against cigarette manufacturers, Locke thought it "preposterous to abrogate the rights of sellers because buyers abuse products that give them pleasure" (does that go for heroin dealers?), even as it is preposterous to penalize Microsoft because some "resentful laggards" convinced the government to give them a competitive advantage that "they could not earn by their own effort." Hence the obvious connection to Elián Gonzalez, who was similarly dispossessed of the freedom to maximize his own interests: "Whether the issue involves a whole industry, a single company or a single individual, the fundamental principle is the same. Either people possess the right to their own life, which includes the right to trade freely with other men, or they do not" (*cm.c:* 23 April 2000). Thus Edwin Locke. For possessive individualism, John Locke could not have said it better.

Another value contradiction stirred up by Hurricane Elián swept all across the political spectrum. Some of the American opposition to keeping Elián was fundamentally self-critical. It came from the uncomfortable and not always subtle doubt, based on experience of the contemporary U.S. youth culture, that Elián's future as an American kid would be as beneficial as the champions of his "right to freedom" were claiming. It could be even worse here than there. Nor were the images broadcast of an Elián loaded down with toys and other goodies—including the toy guns he liked to shoot off—reassuring to a lot of Americans coping with problems of teenage violence and self-indulgent drugging (fig. 2.10). The Elián story broke in the same year as the massacre perpetrated by two teenage students at Columbine High in Colorado. Consider, then, the opinion of a fair-average conservative journalist: "Under the cloak of freedom we have lavished [Elián] with toys, made him a celebrity, handed him a puppy, taken his picture, raised his hands in a victory sign, and then asked him if he wants to go back to icky old Cuba." Imagine a foreign country keeping your child "because our society is permeated with drugs, sex and violence?" (Parker, *CT:* 19 January 2000). Gabriel García Márquez (commondreams.org 2000) noted that photos taken of Elián on his sixth birthday, 6 December 1999, showing him in a combat helmet, surrounded by model weapons and draped in an American flag, occurred shortly before a child of the same age killed a schoolmate with a revolver in Michigan—thus motivating Márquez's observation that Elián's real shipwreck was not on the open sea but on dry land, where he had fetched up.

2.10 Elián in Miami. (© Reuters/Corbis)

The extravagant consumerism of it all: the houseful of battery-operated toys including the dune buggy Elián could drive himself, the wristwatches, cell phones, sporting equipment, clothing, and so on (fig. 2.11).[33] "You think it's been easy keeping up with all his presents?" asks the Floridian novelist and commentator Carl Hiaasen. "Every day something new gets unwrapped, some expensive goody the boy would never get to own if he lived in Cuba" (*MH:* 30 January 2000). Most of the stuff was given by Miami Cubans. And no doubt the abundant gifts had local meanings and functions,

33. The dune buggy was among the many Christmas presents Elián received. "This week a group of Miami city officials, including one dressed as Santa Claus, brought Elian a battery-powered purple, yellow and red dune buggy, an aluminum bat and a baseball glove and ball" (*WP:* 25 December 1999).

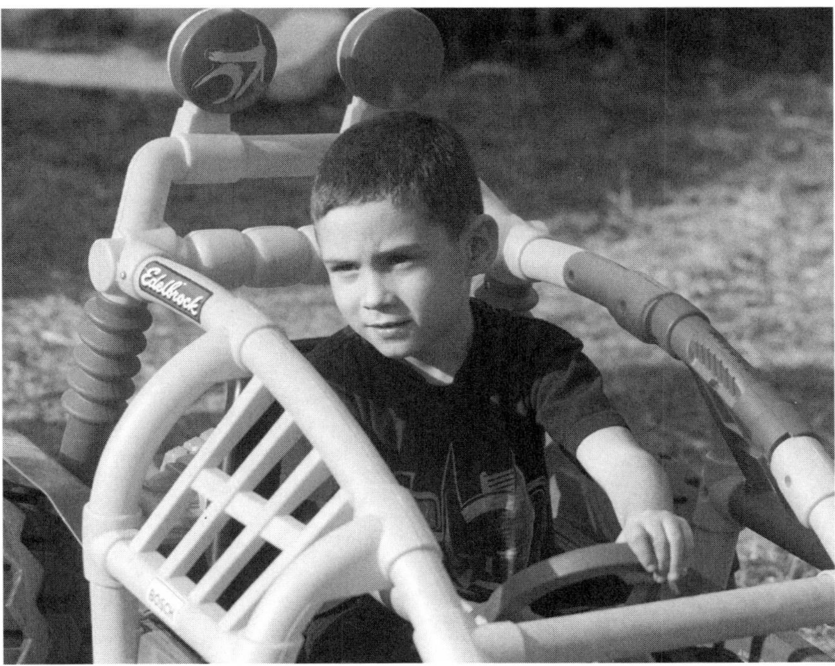

2.11 Elián and toy buggy. (Michael Bush / UPI / Landov)

ranging from bribing Elián's affections to affirming his status as a "special child," something approaching King of the World. The message was clearly, as Hiaasen put it, "Who needs Dad when you've got a closet full of Star Wars Legos?" Elián was taken to Disney World barely two weeks after his rescue, where, according to a local Cuban journal, he "was personally received by Mickey Mouse . . . at 11:00 A.M." (Libre 2001: 16).

Yet the images of a super-indulged Elián could have different meanings for middle Americans. A cartoon in the *New Orleans Picayune* by Walt Handelsman shows Elián literally surrounded by boxes of toys, as a figure of Uncle Sam standing nearby says, "We've put up a blockade to keep Cuba from getting him back" (fig. 2.12). Another, by Joe Heller in the *Green Bay Press-Gazette* (fig. 2.13), shows Elián with a playmate from whom he has taken what appears to be a G.I. Joe doll, while in the background are a man and woman identified as Elián's relatives and a caricature of Janet Reno labeled "Feds." Elián shouts at the other child à propos of the doll: "You can't have him back! He's mine now! You're never going to get your hands on him! Not now! Not ever!" At which one of his relatives says, for

2.12 Keeping Elián in America. (Walt Handelsman/*New Orleans Picayune;* © Tribune Media Services, Inc. All rights reserved. Reprinted with permission)

Reno's benefit, "See? Elián truly is one of us!" Speaking of similar representations, on PBS *Newshour,* the journalist Richard Rodriguez considered that they reflected a certain embarrassment among Americans about "the people they had become": "a cartoonist in the morning paper, mediocre talent, who every time he had a chance to draw Elián would put him in sunglasses with his Nike shoes, you know the consumerist Nike child. And I think, if you were really to ask a lot of American parents, would this boy be better off in Havana or would he be better off in South Beach on rollerblades with sunglasses, a lot of Americans, in our middle-aged caution, would say we would not want Elián to grow up like our own children" (*PBS:* 26 April 2000).

The politics of the Cuban Americans had its own contradictions and ironies. The position of the majority that freedom for Elián trumped parental rights was ridiculed by the moderate minority for what was thus being touted as "freedom" and "democracy" in Little Havana. "Whenever they use freedom as a reason to do something, I laugh," said Francisco

2.13 Elián, the American kid. (Joe Heller/*Green Bay Press-Gazette*)

Aruca, a commentator on Miami's Radio Progreso.[34] "They" were the hardline anti-Castroists who monopolized power in the Cuban community: a network of controlling organizations and godfather-like figures, whose ideology was disseminated without possibility of dissent in the principal Spanish-language media. For decades, marching to this drumbeat had been a necessary condition of economic opportunity and personal tranquility in Cuban Miami.[35] For the so-called moderates—also pejoratively called *dialogueros* because they wanted to open communication with Cuba—the local system of domination and repression was no exemplar of American democratic virtues. On the contrary, "what they've done here," said Aruca, "is to eliminate the American constitution from Miami." Said another liberal intellectual, Max Castro: "In a post-communist world

34. Extensive *Frontline* interviews with Aruca and other Cuban-American "moderates" on the subject of Elián can be found in *PBS* (2000).

35. Lisandro Perez, professor at Florida International University: "In order to understand some of the dynamics of the Cuban community here and how it functions politically, you have to understand that in many ways, it's like a small town. The community is economically very strong. It generates a lot of employment, and it generates a lot of business for itself, for its members. And one of the things you don't want to do is be ostracized on the basis of your political ideology, because you disagree with some of the basic tenets of the community" (*PBS:* 2000).

where Marxist-Leninism has imploded as an ideology and the Soviet bloc has disappeared, the [Cuban] exiles often end up looking more authoritarian, more out of touch, than the Cuban regime" (*PBS:* 26 April 2000). Some of the contradictions of the "freedom" promised Elián are already embedded in the identity of "exiles" generally assumed by the expatriate Cubans—that is, "exiles" in contradistinction to "immigrants." For in thus clinging to a prerevolutionary legitimacy, they are also claiming the heritage of the authoritarian Bautista regime. Moderates say there is indeed a family resemblance.

Break here for an anthropological reflection on order in culture. This whole involuted complex of political positions, with its chiasmatic relationships and dialectical oppositions, should be of some relevance to the current postmodern disposition to "always disconnect." I mean the perverse satisfaction that many in the human sciences, following the lead of certain cult-studs, seem to derive from finding incoherence in culture and cultures. You know, the celebrations of contested categories, fuzzy boundaries, polyphony without harmony, the impossibility of master narratives, and the other sly delights of deconstruction. I wonder, however, as does Julian Barnes in an analogous context, "When a contemporary narrator hesitates, claims uncertainty, misunderstands, plays games and falls into error, does the reader in fact conclude that reality is being more authentically narrated?" (1984: 89). In this connection, the question raised by the politics of Elián is whether there is anything systematic going on. Certainly, when we look at the dialectical schisms in the American right between individual freedom and parental rights, or the reservations about growing up in America in a certain fraction of the middle class, or the emphasis on youth in Havana and Little Havana, the answer seems yes: the positions are hardly random; they are neither structurally nor symbolically aleatory. Perhaps we have been too quick to equate differences, as of "conflicting discourses," with disorder. It then becomes all too easy to call off the search for relationships *in* and *of* the differences—to call off the search *a priori*, on the grounds that such systematicity is impossible. I prefer Bourdieu (quoting Goethe) on this tactic: "Our opinion is that it well becomes a man to assume that there is something unknowable, but that does not have to set any limit to his inquiry" (1996: xvii). I am arguing something more than that the political positions taken on Elián are, as differently situated subject positions, coherently motivated by the respective interests of these parties—although that is already saying something systematic, as Bakhtin tells us. These subject positions stand in specific logical and sociological relationships to one another, and thus imply a larger, complex order, marked

2.14 The cosmology of Elián, a Miami folk mural. (Joe Raedle/Getty Images)

by a dynamic of contrasting moral and political doctrines. Yes, Jim (or George, or whoever), there is a culture. There would even be a master narrative, though with its diverse cast of characters and complex plot, it could never be a simple one. End of theoretical break.

Meanwhile, back in Miami, one of the regulars outside the Gonzalez house said that "if Elián were just a child, Fidel would not have bothered him. Fidel knows he is divine, and wants to destroy him" (*NYDN:* 9 April 2000). The national political storm spreading out from Little Havana was being continuously whipped up by a powerful religious afflatus. "The Miracle Child" (*El Niño Milagro*), or indeed "The Child King" (*El Niño Rey*), Elián had come to redeem the sufferings of the Miami exiles, to destroy their pharaonic or herodic oppressor Fidel Castro, and to restore them to their homeland.[36] "I have the feeling he will be the one," said Marta Rondon, a woman who had joined one of the vigils of people anxious to see Elián (*MH:* 10 January 2000) (fig. 2.14). Resembling the ritual processions

36. The supposed medical miracle, testified to by doctors at the hospital to which Elián was taken when rescued, was that the boy showed hardly any signs of exposure after twenty-four to forty-eight hours adrift in the sun on an inner tube. The "miracle" was naturally credited in the Miami Cuban community, but doubted by some elsewhere, on grounds that the length of time Elián had been afloat was exaggerated.

of saints' images, the nightly parades of the child around the Gonzalez family's yard, carried on high before an adoring crowd, were a regular feature of the Elián phenomenon. This time, when the boy finally emerged on the shoulders of Delphin Gonzalez, making V signs with both hands and then pretending to douse the crowd with an empty water gun, Marta was overcome: "I feel such emotion, such warmth in my heart for him. He's a special child. Definitely, he's a special child" (ibid.). Many of the Cuban Catholic clergy thought so, too—although the Anglo hierarchy in Miami was skeptical of the supposed miracle and disinclined to join in Elián's canonization. "Herod—Castro—is waiting in Cuba," said Rev. Jose Luis Mendez, pastor of Corpus Christi Church. "Pontius Pilate is washing his hands in Washington, and that is President Clinton. And the suffering of this child is the suffering of the Cuban people" (*WP:* 20 April 2000). Or, to put it succinctly, as on one of the banners outside the Gonzalez house, "Elián is Christ. Castro is Satan."

The correlated buzz on Miami Spanish radio and in the Cuban coffee shops—as well as the official Elián web site—was that the boy had been saved by dolphins that encircled the rubber tube in which he was floating and protected him from sharks. "Any Cuban would know this is a story right out of the Bible," another follower told a *Miami Herald* reporter (*MH:* 8 January 2000). Actually it isn't in the Bible, although it is in Aristotle. Indeed, "shipwrecked sailor saved by fish," or something similar, is a worldwide mythical topos: "Escape from sea on fish's back" (Stith Thompson motif B541.1); "Fish carries man across water" (B551.1); "Sea beast allows voyager to land on his back" (B556); or "Magic salmon carries hero over water" (B175.1), among other analogous themes (B256.12, F1088.3.2, B551.5).[37] Similar stories are told of Cuba's patron saint, Our Lady of Charity: of how she miraculously intervened to calm a storm and save a fisherman, or how she brought one fisherman, or three fishermen, or a little boy safely to shore in a storm. Poems were written about the dolphins' rescue of Elián: "And the child sailor was protected by dolphins / Who resembled little angels hovering over the little rafter" (Jose Manuel Carballo, *MH:* 23 January 2000). Cartoons, paintings, and murals depicted Elián floating in the sea encircled by dolphins who were being benignly directed from the

37. "'I think the dolphins love him more than his father,' said Sonia Espinosa, a Nicaraguan American at the [Three Kings] parade. 'They took care of him when he was alone, orphaned in the ocean. He is a miracle'" (*MH:* 10 January 2000, "Three Kings"; cf. *MH:* 23 January 2000). I am indebted to Gregory Schrempp of Indiana University for the Stith Thompson references.

heavens by flying angels, Our Lady of Charity, or the hand of God. A more elaborate folk mural (fig. 2.14), synthesizing Christological and Santería motifs with icons of the political struggle, is described in *Religion in the News:* "Elián floating on the sea in his inner tube with Our Lady of Charity, Ochun [The Orisha], and Eleggua [son on Ochun] in the tube with him. Three dolphins circle around, while overhead preside the hands of God and a tiny Virgin and Child. The scene is framed by a larger scale of justice in which repose the head of Pope John Paul II on one side and that of President Clinton on the other. In the background hover two shadowy images of Fidel Castro, a grim-faced Statue of Liberty, Jesus himself and an archangel holding another scale" (*RIN:* 2000).

Talk of raising the historical stakes of a family melodrama! Part Jesus, part Moses, and part orisha, to name only the most salient identities, Elián was iconized as a messianic hope, and thus gave cosmic significance to the kindred relations and political conflicts in which his fate was being worked out. More than ideological reflexes, these religious representations were, as I say, structural relays, motivated mediations by which the history of the national was interpolated in the interpersonal, so that in the event what the Gonzalez folk did *became* the event.[38]

We have had some indication already of the Christological aspect. "Elián did the stations of the cross to get out of hell," said the Miami weekly *Libre.* Signs of Elián as Jesus were often sighted in the crowd around the Gonzalez house, such as the poster that read, "After the crucifixion, Elián and Cuba will rise up too" (*WP:* 20 April 2000), or the homemade crucifix with a baby doll displayed after Elián's repatriation, together with the sign, "Clinton, Reno crucified Elián" (*RIN* 2000). Some credited Elián with divine healing powers: parents lifted their sick infants over the Gonzalez family's fence in the hope of effecting a cure (BBC News: 29 January 2000). As might be expected from the circumstances of Elián's survival as well as the religious tradition, the theme of Elián-as-Christ was also marked by Marian symbolism. Elián's own dead mother was celebrated ritually and enshrined in bricolage altars. On the day Elián was sent back to Cuba, a woman was heard to say, "Maybe his mother will show up and this will be over" (*MH:* 28 June 2000). The Virgin Mary had already shown up twice: as an image on the mirror of Elián's bedroom in the Gonzalez house,

38. The religious dimensions of the Elián affair were widely reported. See, among others, *Chicago Tribune* (17 January 2000), *MH* (8, 10, 23 January, 26 March, 10 April, 14 May 2000), *WP* (22 January, 6, 14, 20 April 2000), *CNN* (28 March 2000), *NYDN* (9 April 2000), *RIN* (Summer 2000), Lopez-Calderon in geocities.com (2 April 2000).

and more publicly on the window of a bank a few blocks away. The bank's image was unmistakable, according to a teller, Maria Rodriguez, even though "you could not see the body or the face" (*WP:* 6 April 2000). This Virgin of Totalbank, 468 NW Twenty-seventh Avenue, attracted varying degrees of veneration, ranging from the mothers who came to press their babies against the windowpane to the skeptic who declared that the so-called Virgin was a residue of Windex (*MH:* 26 March 2000; *Newsday:* 9 April 2000). Perhaps the unbelievers were convinced some time later, not long after Lazaro Gonzalez had purchased the famous house at 2319 NW Second Street, when 2-3-1-9 hit on the Florida lottery, paying five thousand dollars each to 192 ticket holders, most of whom must have been Cuban.[39]

Of course, the mother figure also played in the topos of Elián as Moses (*CT:* 17 January 2000; *WP:* 22 January, 20 April 2000; ReligiousTolerance .org). "A Cuban Moses" reads the caption on the back cover of a local Spanish-language magazine (*RIN:* Summer 2000). "God's will is absolutely inscrutable to man's mind, but the characteristics of this case point to Elián being something like Moses," according to a former political prisoner of Castro's (*WP:* 20 April 2000). A deft exegesis of Elián's story by José Marmol, a columnist of a Miami Cuban paper, made the point-for-point case for a second coming of Moses. Moses' mother too had set him adrift in hopes of sparing his life, said Marmol. And then, "the daughter of the pharaoh took in Moses and this changed the history of the Hebrews. . . . Moses lived to lead his people out of Egypt to the promised land of Israel after a captivity of 40 years—about the same as our exile from Cuba" (*CT:* 17 January 2000).

The logical motivation of such symbolic amplifications of Elián is impressive. It extends also to the boy's incorporation in Santería as an Eleggua (or a son thereof): the trickster orisha whose powers appropriately include the opening and closing of roads. (This identification was not necessarily contradictory to Elián's figuration as the Christ Child, since the latter is one of Eleggua's many forms.) Santería, moreover, had the general value of making a direct and malevolent link to Castro. Like Santería itself, Castro was outside the established Church, and thus could be credibly perceived as under the influence of the orishas and their priests, or even a secret adherent. A piece of paper furtively passed to the *Washington Post*'s

39. In October 2001, this house was converted into a shrine in Elián's honor (Unidos en Casa Elián).

Gene Weingarten by a demonstrator outside the Gonzalez house seems to say it all:

> It is indeed astonishing. It says that Fidel is a devotee of the mysterious Afro-Cuban religion of Santería. It alleges that the Cuban dictator fears he has run afoul of the mighty Santería saint Eleggua. It says he has consulted snail shells, and "thrown coconuts," and sacrificed monkeys and goats and bulls and sheep, to no avail. It alleges that he believes Eleggua has taken up residence in the body of Elián Gonzalez, and that for Castro's luck to change, to save his regime, he must get Eleggua back. It implies that when he gets him back, Elián will be sacrificed to the god that inhabits him. (*WP:* 6 April 2000)[40]

Despite the furtiveness, Weingarten subsequently learned that this document was no secret. It was available all over Miami as the lead story in a Spanish tabloid under the headline, "The Boy and the Beast." The newspaper was free. Weingarten picked up a copy from the giveaway stack in the office of the Hon. Alex Penelas, the mayor of Miami-Dade County. But then, according to Jonathan Alter in *Newsweek* (24 April 2000), the U.S. Congress heard sworn testimony that Castro would eat Elián on his return to Cuba.

Some of the ritual performances of Elián's sanctity were even more public. Not so much the Santería sessions or the countless personal prayers, of course, but certainly the many Sunday church services and, by the end of Elián's stay, the nightly services in and around the Gonzalez house. Six nights a week a mass was held inside, thanking God "for the miracle that brought 6-year-old Elián Gonzalez safely to them," while outside in front of the house from 5:30 to 11:30 P.M., six Catholic and six Evangelical pastors, "numbered like the 12 apostles," took turns leading a prayer service—except on Friday, the day of the crucifixion, when all twelve officiated jointly (*MH:* 10 April 2000). Given the well-known oppositions of Catholics and charismatics, the ecumenicalism was another miracle attributed to Elián. It did not, however, extend to the more liberal American Protestants

40. A similar furtive note, this passed by Lazaro Gonzalez to one Sister O'Laughlin for delivery to Elián's grandmothers, had an influence on the course of events when the nun failed to deliver it and became a public spokesperson for keeping Elián upon reading it. The note warned that Castro wished to make "a witchcraft sacrifice" of the boy (*MH:* 31 March 2000). On Santería, see also *Washington Times* (4, 15 April 2000), *SFC* (9 April 2000), *WP* (20 April 2000).

70
22
30
54
90
SOME CUBANS SWEAR ELIAN IS THE MESSIAH; THAT WHEN
HE WAS RESCUED HE WAS SURROUNDED BY DOLPHINS.

2.15 The Dolphins save Elián. (Don Wright/*Palm Beach Post;* © Tribune Media Services, Inc. All rights reserved. Reprinted with permission)

who, as represented by the National Council of Churches, actively supported Elián's repatriation. Although the religious enthusiasm in Little Havana helps account for public opinion polls running as high as 83 percent in favor of keeping Elián, the same could be a turnoff in the Anglo community, as witness the accompanying *Miami Herald* cartoon (fig. 2.15).

Still, the miracle could reach some Anglo hearts—of a certain conservative bent. Peggy Noonan, Republican intellectual and former speechwriter for President Bush the First, filled the *Wall Street Journal* with banal pieties about the Elián story—a story, she said, that was marked from the beginning by "the miraculous" (*WSJ:* 24 April 2000). For it was "a miracle that when he was tired and began to slip, the dolphins who surrounded him like a contingent of angels pushed him upward."[41] A miracle, too, Noonan wrote, that Elián was saved on the American Thanksgiving Day, even as it was a sign of Democrat blasphemy that he was abducted by federal agents on the day before Easter. "Too bad Mr. Reagan was not still

41. For the record, the presence of dolphins in the vicinity of Elián's inner tube could not be confirmed from the reports of the Coast Guard rescuers or the changing and conflicting stories of the fishermen who discovered Elián.

president," she said. "Mr. Reagan would not have dismissed the story of dolphins as Christian kitsch, but seen it as possible evidence of the reasonable assumption that God's creatures had been commanded to protect one of God's children." There you have it. Miracle! Miracle! Read all about it in the *Wall Street Journal*—a tract that had always been a firm believer in the Invisible Hand in any case.

Then, finally, there was Tom DeLay, the Republican majority whip in the House, who called Elián "a blessed child" on *Larry King Live*—prompting the *Star Tribune* to editorialize: "And it came to pass that Tom DeLay the Righteous appeared to Larry the King in a dream. And Larry said unto him, 'What dost thou make of the boy Elián snatched up by agents of the Emperor Bill?' And DeLay the Righteous said unto Larry, 'This is a blessed child. Two days he was in the waters and the great fishes bothered him not, neither did they devour him. Neither did the hot sun blister him'" (*RIN:* 2000). All this piety in high places convinced the journalist Richard Cohen that Elián had truly been saved for a purpose—which was "to make fools of politicians" (ibid.).

And thus, to make history.

CHAPTER 3

* * *

THE CULTURE OF AN ASSASSINATION

Reacting to the storming of Paris by Marxist theory in the years following World War II, Raymond Aron found in Thucydides a tactical counterexample of how history should be written. Following Thucydides, history should be written in the mode of "human action as such, and by that I mean the action of one or several men engaged with one another" (Aron 1961: 103–4). Certainly that goes for the political and military history by which the fate of societies is decided. To believe Aron, Thucydides, by his eye singular to the actions of individuals rather than social forces, indeed presented us with a historiographic treasure for all times, just as he had intended.

Aron allows that Thucydides did leave out a lot in the way of sociological description—but legitimately so, he thought. Unlike Aristotle or Xenophon, Thucydides took little interest in the constitutions of cities, nor was he much concerned with their economic regimes, their colonial histories, or even the going forms and rules of military combat. It follows that—unlike many of Aron's own contemporaries—Thucydides had no use either for general laws of economic and political functioning. In effect, the culture in general ought to be left out of it, Aron argues. A history of political events, be it of classical Greece or modern Europe, cannot be resolved into the history of societies. The collective conditions neither predicate, nor *a fortiori* can they predict, the wills and words of the particular orators who swayed the assemblies or the generals who commanded the battles:

> The history of events is irreducible to that of societies, classes or economies. It was thus irreducible in the 5th century before our era; it is irreducible in the 20th century after Jesus Christ. . . . The event, in the sense we give the term, that is to say *the act accomplished by one or several men, localized and dated,* is never reducible to the [situational or structural] conjuncture, unless we eliminate, by thought, those who have acted and declare that anyone else in their place would have done the same. (Aron 1961: 116)

Aron's argument is a radical although not atypical brief for the disengagement of event from structure, of intentional action from cultural order—and so, beyond that, of narrative history from historical ethnography. Not that it would be altogether wrong for some purposes, he admits, to transcend events in order to attend to the larger movements of society. Thucydides was correct to do so in Book I, where he undertakes "to sketch the grand lines of an evolution"—the "Archaeology" so-called—outlining the development of the Hellenes from their primitive beginnings. Concerned with political and military affairs, however, the succeeding books were appropriately written in the entirely different genre of event-history, marked by the intervention of difference-making persons. Aron does not choose to notice that even in the "Archaeology" there are some historically significant individuals, notably those whose doings prefigured or contributed to the emergence of Athens as a maritime empire. Nor were the following seven books on the war without their collective historical subjects—that is, the contending peoples acting according to their rational interests or national characters if not exactly their cultural formations.[1] But these exceptions are consistent with Aron's assertion that even where general social laws are in play, and even where these laws make certain human

1. Appearing in Book I as precursors of the Athenians in the development of navies, conquests, and colonies were the likes of Minos of Crete and Cyrus of Persia (1.4.1, 1.8.2, 1.13.6). Themistocles also appears, of course. And even one Ameinocles, a shipwright of Corinth, who built the first triremes (1.13.3).

decisions more probable than others, in no case can they specify the acts and intentions that actually determine the course of history. No one man may have willed or thought the Peloponnesian War in advance, "but more than the cities, the regimes or the necessities of combat, it is man himself, the eternal man, driven by constant motives who is revealed in this tragic event, the work of men conscious of their acts but unconscious of their fate" (Aron 1961: 114).

Note that Aron's argument is at least dual, and to some extent self-contradictory, as it invokes by turns the uniqueness of the history-making actors, their absolute individuality, and "the eternal man" acting on motives common to all humanity. Freedom and human nature. On the one hand, Aron needs to emphasize individuality as a condition of the irreducibility of history to social laws or collective circumstances. Here everything turns on ontological incommensurabilities, as between real acts and abstract laws, from which follows the legitimacy of a history that privileges the doings of "one or several individuals." On the other hand, Aron needs universality—as the condition of the intelligibility and applicability of Thucydides to the twentieth century A.D. as much as it was to the fifth century B.C. Historical agency then slips away from individual actors. Consider this passage: "To write the history of the Peloponnesian war is to recount how the Athenians, carried away by pride, and the will to power, having defied the counsels of Pericles, finished by succumbing, despite their heroism and superhuman efforts" (Aron 1961: 105). Now the historical subjects are indeed collectives, the Athenians rather than Pericles, and true to Thucydides' own doctrine, they are driven by generic human dispositions—in this instance, pride and the will to power. Here Aron mobilizes Weber against Marx: history becomes the rational project of attaining such ends as power and glory with the available means. Yet contradictory as Aron's two arguments may be, the one proceeding from the universal qualities of human action and the other from its individual particularities, they have the common function of banishing the cultural order beyond the historiographic pale.

But Aron implicitly gives away the argument when, in the attempt to recuperate basic economic changes within the political—thus infrastructure within superstructure, another anti-Marxist move—he says such economic changes are also essentially political inasmuch as they are authored by individuals "capable *by reason of their position* of affecting the lives of their fellow citizens" (Aron 1961: 118; my emphasis). But "position," as we know from Tolstoy, if not from Saussure, is a differential place in a community of relationships.[2] Aron is speaking of structural empowerment. Implied is the "position" in a system or a social situation that transmits the acts of certain authorized persons into fateful consequences for the community as a whole. "Position" will always entail a larger cultural scheme of persons, things, and values empowering the history-makers and giving efficacy to their doings—even though the results may not be what they intended.

This chapter is an attempt to substantiate these assertions by the examination of a fateful political assassination, occurring in 1845, that dramatically affected the history of the Fiji Islands, with effects still apparent to this day. The discussion attends particularly to certain schemata of Fijian culture that constituted the historical situation and organized its dénouement—without, however, determining what actually happened. Nothing in the larger structure could have prescribed that the assassination would turn upon the would-be assassin, making the latter instead the historic victim.

THE LEADING CHARACTERS

On or about 5 August 1845 Ratu Raivalita, a high-ranking chief of Bau Island, Fiji, was killed by the order of his paternal half-brother, Ratu Cakobau, apparently acting on the command of, certainly on behalf of, their father Ratu Tānoa. Titular war king (Vunivalu) of Bau, the aging Ratu Tānoa had largely given over the functions of rule, including war itself, to Ratu Cakobau. Like other major Fijian countries (*vanua turaga,* or 'chiefly lands'), Bau had a dual kingship, consisting of a so-called sacred king, the Roko Tui Bau, and the war king, upon whom devolved many executive functions. In most Fijian kingdoms, the war king was subordinate; he 'carried [the] rule' (*cola sau*) for the sacred king, the paramount figure of the diarchy. However, as we know, in Bau the *de facto* rank of the two kings had been reversed, at least since the beginning of the nineteenth century and probably for much longer (see above, chapter 1). For all practical purposes, including even ritual purposes outside the principal temple of the kingdom, the Vunivalu ruled in Bau. The sacred king 'just abided' (*tiko ga*)—albeit indispensably so, as the 'man-god' (*kalou tamata*) of the kingdom, the spiritual condition of its integrity and prosperity (see above, chapter 2).

Within the war king's family, the same contrast between an active ruler

2. "Community" is usefully taken here in the double sense of a social totality and of a Kantian judgment (much like a Saussurian structure) of a whole having many parts that are comprehended as mutually determining.

and an abiding title-holder had progressively characterized the relationship between Ratu Cakobau and Ratu Tānoa since the late 1830s. By 1845, when the assassination of Ratu Raivalita assured Ratu Cakobau's preeminence, it seemed to Rev. Thomas Jaggar that the aging Ratu Tānoa had "little to do with the affairs of government, excepting through his son, Thakombau [Ratu Cakobau]. The old man is evidently failing. He stays much at home through infirmity" (*WMMS/L:* 5 July 1845).

The "old man" would hold on for another seven years, often enough disapproving of the adventurous wars undertaken by his relentless strong-arm son. Once a formidable warrior himself, Ratu Tānoa, like many ambitious younger sons of kings, had cultivated a reputation for violence and cruelty during the reign of his older brother, Ratu Naulivou (d. 1829), as Vunivalu. Here again, the rivalry of the siblings would differentiate them as it were along the lines of the *gravitas* and *celeritas* aspects of Fijian chiefship, the title-holder maintaining the royal dignity and his fraternal rival trumping it by displays of outrageous force. According to the information gathered by the *bêche-de-mer* trader William Driver (*J:* 6 October 1827), Ratu Tānoa, whose "cannibal disposition" had occasioned several disputes with his brother, at one point decamped for the Lau Islands together with a large part of the Bau population. Ratu Naulivou sent a party after them, although we do not know to what effect, punishment or reconciliation. In any case Ratu Tānoa would bear the "fearful scars" of these fraternal differences into his old age: the impressions of two war-club blows to the head behind his right ear, said to have been inflicted by Ratu Naulivou (Cargill *J:* May 1839). In public, Ratu Tānoa wore a large turban of barkcloth, distinctively arranged to conceal the damage (plate 1).

Lieutenant Wilkes's description of Ratu Tānoa in 1840 is characteristic of several European reports of the period (1845, 3:56). The Bau king was then about sixty-five or seventy, tallish at perhaps five feet ten inches, but bent by his years, rather thin if not fragile, vainly trying to disguise the effects of age by blackening his face, chest, and fulsome beard. Lieutenant Wilkes thought that Ratu Tānoa had earned the sobriquet of "Old Snuff" among the Whites because of this "begrimed look." But others attribute it to the speech impediment that left him with a high and squeaky voice, as though he were speaking through his nose, rather difficult for Europeans to decipher (Eagleston *UD,* 1:283; Jackson 1853: 459).[3] For all that, there

3. If Fijian custom in the matters of chieftainship held in the mid-nineteenth century as it did in much of the twentieth, Ratu Tānoa's speech and other distinctive characteristics were no doubt the subject of private ridicule in Bau. Officially and publicly, however, ruling chiefs are paragons of the human form.

was a certain shrewdness and intelligence in the old man's countenance, Mr. Wilkes thought, and "his mind is said to be quite active" (Wilkes 1845, 3:56). Nor was he entirely out of the picture, politically, however much his warrior son Ratu Cakobau railed against his decisions, circumvented them, or else maneuvered the old man into compliance with his own projects.

Missionary accounts and other journals from the late 1830s onward repeatedly show Ratu Tānoa less ready than Ratu Cakobau to enter into conflicts with powerful lands such as Rewa, Macuata, and Cakaudrove. The old warrior was also circumspect in his treatment of Europeans, especially visiting men-of-war, to the extent that he was usually described by them as "friendly" and sometimes as "timid" (Pickering 1846: 155).[4] Fijian chiefs know well how to give pleasure to foreign interlocutors, being masters of the politics of politesse, but still there was some contrast in such respects between Ratu Tānoa and his blunt-spoken son. During the great war with Rewa, Ratu Cakobau got into serious tangles with certain Whites, with the small European community in Ovalau Island collectively, and with the mercantile shipping, all to his military and political disadvantage. The way he held the missionaries, Catholic as well as Protestant, out of Bau gave rise to some of the more amusing passages of recorded Fijian history. Indeed, the Methodist missionary Reverend Waterhouse took some delight in Ratu Cakobau's disrespect for the passing "Popish bishop" who wanted him to receive a French missionary. The bishop had asked Ratu Cakobau if he knew why the English missionaries had failed to gain a foothold on Bau. It was because, the bishop explained, "the Virgin Mary was keeping Bau for the Catholics," and when Ratu Cakobau became a Catholic, he would order the converted Protestants to change their faith. "Whereupon the king told the bishop to leave him and his city to the care of the Virgin, and to come again when the Virgin had converted them" (Waterhouse 1866: 196). But the pages of Reverend Waterhouse's *The King and People of Fiji* are unselfconsciously peppered with the equally contemptuous views Ratu Cakobau took of his own windy preaching: "I found the high-priest sitting at the right hand of Thakombau, whilst the priest's offering of a very large root of *kava* lay at the royal feet. For two hours I expostulated with the prince; but in vain. When, in conclusion, I reminded him that we three would meet together once more before the judgment-

4. It was reported at the time of the coup against Ratu Tānoa in 1832 that one of the causes was his undue protection of the European shipping. He is said to have prevented the Bauans from taking the ship *Glide* in 1831 and two schooners in July 1832 (Eagleston *UD,* 1:438).

seat of God, he said, in derision, 'O! I suppose a vessel from the other world has arrived in England. You seem to be well up in information on the day of judgment'" (ibid., 192). Nor did the reputed tortures of Hell with which he was repeatedly threatened by the Protestants faze Ratu Cakobau; after all, he said, "it is a fine thing to have a fire in cold weather" (ibid., 103).[5]

In 1845, at the time Ratu Raivalita fell by his order, Ratu Cakobau was about thirty-five years old, or a little more, and near the height of his power, both personal and political. The death of his brother and rival chief was one more testimony to his prowess, since it was he who was the intended victim of the assassination and Ratu Raivalita the would-be assassin. We will find as the story unfolds that turning the assassination plot around also made a turn in Bau's ongoing war with Rewa. Ratu Raivalita's mother was from Rewa, while the mother of his half-brother Ratu Cakobau was a high-ranking woman of Bau. Ratu Raivalita accordingly was the leader of "a Rewa party at Bau" (Derrick 1950: 85). His conflict with Ratu Cakobau was a familial microcosm of the larger war with Rewa, and the outcome of the former struggle had serious effects on the course of the latter.

Ratu Cakobau had been demonstrating his extraordinary political and military abilities, including his gifts for making and undoing conspiracies, for over a decade. Conspiracy went with the territory, with the position of Vunivalu of Bau, and Ratu Cakobau was especially good at it. During Ratu Naulivou's own reign as war king, his conspiracies, it was said, numbered "a hundred times a hundred." In the late 1830s Ratu Cakobau pulled off two spectacular ones that were truly worthy of his uncle and predecessor. One was the counter-coup of 1837 that restored Ratu Tānoa to the title: it involved a sudden uprising against the usurpers, managed by a dissembling Ratu Cakobau even as he was living in Bau, thus amidst his father's enemies. A second shocker was the massacre in 1841 of a large number of enemies (from Namena and Telau Island) who were invited to a ceremonial feast at Viwa, an island near Bau. Viwa was the site of the mission of Rev. William Cross, who was an astonished witness to the event (Cross *D:* 19–29 May 1841). Even the paramount chief of Viwa (Ratu Namosimalua) was surprised when the Bauan army led by Ratu Cakobau, ostensibly mounting a charge on Viwa itself after blatantly threatening it for days, was instead let into the town by prearrangement with the chief's nephew (Ratu

5. Ratu Tānoa likewise, for all his friendliness to *Papalagi,* would not consider conversion to Christianity. As he told Lieutenant Wilkes, "To be a Christian would not make him White or give him ships, so what the good would be, he could not tell."

Varani), upon which the combined forces of Bau and Viwa turned upon and slaughtered the unsuspecting visitors. This feat was only one of a series of campaigns undertaken far and wide by Ratu Cakobau to reclaim the hegemony of Bau over eastern Fiji that had been slipping during the exile of Ratu Tānoa in the 1830s.

In leading the drive to restore Bauan domination in the late 1830s and early 1840s, Ratu Cakobau was indefatigable. It must have been particularly galling personally as well as significant politically when the fisher-warriors of Verata attacked a Bauan canoe around the middle of 1839, killing a prominent chieftain and several others. Verata, as we know, was the leading kingdom of Fiji before Bau, and Bau's legitimacy as hegemon still depended on noble Verata's recognition of, and submission to, its *de facto* superior power. Verata's current belligerence implied that it meant to profit from Bau's weakness to reclaim its ancient superiority. It was thus imperative to answer Verata's attack. Tradition has it that the Bau warriors, still reeling from the recent civil war, had no stomach for the fight, but Ratu Cakobau confined them all in a large men's house night and day for eight days until they agreed to do so (Anon. of *Na Mata* 1891 [5]: 10).[6] For the next thirteen months, Bau fleets set out in numbers to attack various Verata towns, until the Veratans, after one aborted attempt to surrender—desired by Ratu Tānoa but thwarted by his bellicose son—finally got the Bau rulers to accept their capitulation (*i soro*) in late November 1840 (Cross *D:* 12 March, 22 November 1840). Lieutenant Wilkes, who was in Fiji while this conflict was in course, reported that Ratu Tānoa had asked him, when he saw Ratu Cakobau, "to talk hard to him, and give him plenty of good advice, for he was a young man, and frisky; but he himself was old, and saw things that were good and bad" (Wilkes 1845, 3:59). But *gravitas* could not hold back *celeritas.* Ratu Cakobau accepted Verata's surrender only because he wanted to get on with attacking Macuata and Cakaudrove in Vanua Levu. About a year after Lieutenant Wilkes's departure he received a communication about Ratu Cakobau's activities from David Whippy, the leader of the small colony of Whites at Ovalau Island, the conclusion of which was that "the islands are becoming worse every day, for the tyrant Seru [Ratu Cakobau] is depopulating them, and will do a great deal of harm if his career is not stopped. He is, in fact, king, for Tānoa does not dare to act without Seru's permission" (Wilkes 1845, 3:362).

Descriptions of Ratu Cakobau around this time by Lieutenant Wilkes

6. In December 1839, Reverend Cross heard that many Bauans were tired of the war with Verata, but were being pushed by Ratu Cakobau against their will (*D:* 27 December 1839).

and other *Papalagi* indicate that he had all the physical and mental presence of his considerable political attainments (plate 2). He was a tall and imposing man, six feet or over, light complexioned and heavily bearded, whose customary habit of a chiefly loincloth of tapa exposing a powerfully built body gave the Europeans an added sense of his likewise powerful disposition—as he must have known. Sometimes playful, usually dignified, and always "proud," he displayed, as one early report had it, "high royal feelings" (Eagleston *UD,* 1:386). A visiting missionary spoke of a certain "consciousness of power, which oozes out at all points" (Lawry 1850: 47). "Charismatic," one might say nowadays; "every inch a king," said Captain Erskine of the Royal Navy (1853: 186). All were impressed by his political adroitness. Reminiscing about Ratu Cakobau after his conversion to Christianity had ostensibly worked some change in him, Reverend Calvert wrote that "formerly there was not his equal in Feejee in planning, scheming, managing Feejean affairs. He was very clever at treachery" (*J:* 15 May 1855).

Certainly his brother Ratu Raivalita, who plotted to kill and replace him, proved not his match in scheming and treachery.[7] "A young chief of considerable spirits, but not of equal talents," said Reverend Hunt of the ill-fated Ratu Raivalita. The earliest notice we have of him, in 1835 when he was a boy of about twelve, already shows his over-the-top "spirits." The trader Warren Osborn encountered him at Rewa, where he was living with his mother Adi Qereitoga. As the latter was the sister of the sacred ruler of Rewa (Roko Tui Dreketi) as well as the "favorite wife" of Ratu Tānoa, the ruling war king of Bau, Ratu Raivalita enjoyed the prerogatives of a great *vasu* (*vasu levu*) in Rewa, the privileged uterine nephew of the kingdom. A personage of such status is accorded liberties that if assumed by anyone else would be considered injurious, which helps explain Osborn's description of the boy as a figure of high rank in Rewa, who was "treated with respect" and given to sauciness. Although he was compelled to behave when within his mother's reach, his "pranks" were otherwise not much noticed, said Osborn, who thought that in any case disrespect of parents was common among Fijian children (*J:* 31 January–25 February 1835). Ratu Raivalita's pranks, however, would soon escalate into something more serious, and take on a certain significance in the context of Bauan politics.

By 1840, when Lieutenant Wilkes saw him ("fine-looking young man of about 18 years of age"), Ratu Raivalita's despoiling of defenseless villagers was in the American officer's view a prime example of the "outrages"

7. In Fijian sources, Ratu Raivalita is commonly found under another of his names, Doviverata or Ratu Doviverata.

Bauans were "in the habit of committing" and why they "should be so much detested by inhabitants of the group" (Wilkes 1845, 3:149). While obviously not unique among the Bau elite, Ratu Raivalita's 'despotism' (*sau katakata*) was distinctive enough to earn him a place in Bauan tradition as an especially bad type; indeed, "a villain of first order," according to the historian Ratu Deve Toganivalu, and even worse than Ratu Cakobau (*TkB*, n.p. [5]; cf. Anon. of *Na Mata* 1891 [7]: 14–15). Ratu Deve condemns Ratu Raivalita as a man prepared to brutally punish those who failed to punctiliously carry out his orders: subjects of Bau, for example, who did not prepare a feast to his liking—for which harshness the young chief earned the sobriquet of "Hot Food" (*Buta Katakata*). As Ratu Deve was something of an apologist for Ratu Raivalita's rival, Ratu Cakobau, the historian's judgments might be considered extreme, were they not supported by contemporary accounts. Indeed, the partisanship of the source gives added political significance to Ratu Raivalita's violence—namely, that it needs to be understood in relation to his rivalry with Ratu Cakobau. The demonstration of terror, outrageous and divine, is the characteristic challenge of a younger son or brother to the authority of the senior. And Ratu Raivalita was a terror.

Lieutenant Wilkes learned that shortly before he met him, Ratu Raivalita had summarily burned down a town on Ovalau Island because the inhabitants fled with their valuables when he approached, fearing he was going to take everything from them (1845, 3:149). Wilkes also reported that Ratu Raivalita had killed a "nephew" (probably a sister's son) of the important Bauan ally, the chief of Levuka: apparently accidentally, when the young Bauan intercepted a Levuka fishing party in order to despoil them of their catch. Mutilating the victim's face to disguise it, Ratu Raivalita brought the body to Bau to be eaten. However, Ratu Tānoa prevented it, and sent a whale's tooth and the sacrificed little finger joints of some Bauans in propitiation to the Levuka chief (ibid., 3:103). A few years later, the beachcomber John Jackson saw the like from Ratu Raivalita when accompanying him "on a kind of excursion to the tributary towns of Bau." Given insufficient notice of the chief's coming, the people of Batiki Island had not had time to cook his feast properly before it was demanded by his "tasters and aides-de-camp, &tc., whom I found were the cause, in a just measure, of the tyrannical usage of the people." These henchmen were quick to inform Ratu Raivalita that the food presented by the harried Batiki people was quite raw, observing "that it was an old offence of that place in particular." Assembling the offending Batiki islanders on the beach, Ratu Raivalita abused them royally, saying that killing them would be too good for them, and adopting instead the punishment suggested by one of his men to the effect that the offenders, hardened slaves as they were, could more easily make a meal of the pumice stones on the beach than the chief could eat the undone pork. Ordered to thus eat the stones, they did so at such a rate, said Jackson, you could see the beach visibly diminishing (Jackson 1853: 456). "Hot Food," indeed.

Ratu Raivalita was practicing his tyranny on the subjects of Bau, dependent villages in no position to resist him. His roving depredations were the moral equivalent of Ratu Cakobau's conquering violence, although they were nowhere near the same in scale or effect. Nor in 1845, when he was in his early twenties, did his attempt to assassinate Ratu Cakobau match the counterstroke of his intended victim. Instead, Ratu Raivalita was dead. "That was the flaw in his philosophy" (as Joseph Heller said of Colonel Clevinger).

DEATH IN BAU

"There are many tales," said Rev. John Hunt about Ratu Raivalita's death. Stationed in nearby Viwa Island since September 1842, the best informed among the English missionaries about the affairs of Bau, Mr. Hunt penned a report of the event a few days after, in a letter to his colleagues, Reverends Lyth and Calvert at Lakeba (in Lyth *L:* 9 August 1845; cf. Lyth *J:* 9 August 1945). Some months later, he added further details and reflections in an account of the first two years of the great Bau-Rewa war.[8] Mr. Hunt must have received his information from local sources, but he does not name them. Another near contemporary narrative, even more detailed than Mr. Hunt's, was composed by Mrs. Mary Wallis, the wife of an American *bêche-de-mer* trader. Her informant, "Tommy," was a Rotuman in the service of Rev. Thomas Jaggar, who had recently joined Mr. Hunt at Viwa. Others among Mr. Hunt's Methodist colleagues would later have occasion to describe Ratu Raivalita's death in letters and in print, probably in part on information received from him or Mr. Jaggar, although Messrs. James Calvert and Joseph Waterhouse also had the opportunity of hearing Bauan retellings when they were on the island in the early 1850s. An interesting complement to the Methodist writings from Bau is provided by Catholic priests stationed at Rewa, who relate crucial testimony of the involvement

8. This account of the war was inserted in Mr. Hunt's journal following the entry for 19 October 1845, but it was written at a later date, as it includes a description of the fall of Rewa in December 1845.

of the Rewan powers that be in Ratu Raivalita's conspiracy. Finally, to complete this *aperçu* of the primary sources, mention should be made of the Bauan traditions, as stabilized and published, however, some fifty years or so afterward.

In the letter written shortly after Ratu Raivalita's death, Mr. Hunt reported that the chief had been carrying on a conspiracy against Ratu Cakobau and had been betrayed by some of his own party (in Lyth *L:* 9 August 1845). Mr. Hunt's observation that there were "many tales" referred more to this penumbra of intrigue enveloping the event than to any uncertainties about how it unfolded.[9] How it unfolded can be reasonably reconstructed from his own and Mrs. Wallis's texts, especially. They recount that Ratu Raivalita was clubbed down in Bau in late July or early August 1845, shortly after returning from a voyage.[10] Ratu Raivalita was in the company of his boon friend, a certain Selemi, who by his own request was to be his companion also in death. (*Selemi* is the Fijian for "Salem," home port of many of the American residents and merchants trading in the islands since the 1820s, including David Whippy and Captains Wallis and Eagleston.)[11] Ratu Raivalita was following appropriate Fijian custom by going to the house of his father Ratu Tānoa upon coming ashore—this house "Muaidule" (fig. 3.1) was near the principal canoe landing—to announce his return and secure his welcome by an offering of kava (*i sevusevu*). Made through the offices of his herald (*matanivanua*), the presentation of the kava in principle would include a rehearsal of the events of the young chief's journey. Not only customary, the offering would have been

9. So in his later narrative, Mr. Hunt told of a "plot" against Ratu Cakobau, of which Ratu Raivalita was "at the head," and that the latter had "a strong party in his favour." Others suffered when Ratu Raivalita fell, "but it is not known whether all who were engaged in the plot were found out. Some think that there was in reality no plot, but that the young chief was falsely accused by his enemies, and died innocently" (*J:* 19 October 1845). We will see, however, that more light can be thrown on the plot, its reasons, and who was involved, from other contemporary sources.

10. Ratu Raivalita was coming from Somosomo, according to Mrs. Wallis (1851: 101), but the Bauan tradition that he was returning from Ovalau is more likely. Ratu Raivalita had led a large Bauan party to Somosomo in March; they were escorting home the old Cakaudrove king, the Tui Cakau (Lyth *J:* 31 March 1845). In company with one Selemi and a Bauan chief, Ratu Nayagodamu, he remained in Somosomo about three months, leaving in May. (See Williams 1931, 3:322–23, where Ratu Raivalita appears under his other, frequently used name, Doviverata, or in Williams's orthography, "Droiverata"). Still, confusion remains about Ratu Raivalita's comings and goings just before his death because of an entry of Mrs. Wallis's for 17 April 1845, indicating he visited her at Viwa on that date—when according to Reverend Williams, he was in Somosomo (Wallis 1851: 80).

11. Selemi's Fijian name was Matanibukalevu (Williams 1931: 324); his relationship by kinship or clan affiliation to Ratu Raivalita is not known.

3.1 "Muaidule," the house of Ratu Tānoa. (Painting by Conway Shipley, 1851)

all the more necessary if, as both Mr. Hunt and Mrs. Wallis reported, Ratu Raivalita knew his life was at risk in Bau, for the acceptance of the sacrifice at the hands of the old ruler ought to have afforded him some security. Yet as the war kings of Bau were often inclined to violate custom—such indeed was their custom—so in this instance, Ratu Raivalita's gesture did not gain him either the pity or the protection of his father. By most accounts, the decision to kill Ratu Raivalita was the old man's, even as it was widely believed that Ratu Raivalita intended to do away with him as well as Ratu Cakobau.

The kava presentation concluded, Ratu Raivalita begged leave not to drink it with Ratu Tānoa but to proceed to his own house "Naisogolaca," across the town from "Muaidule" (fig. 3.2). Along the way he was seized: some say by Ratu Cakobau himself, but most say by another (classificatory) brother of theirs, Komainaua (Ratu Wainiu). Komainaua, a descendant also of war kings and a *vasu* (uterine nephew) to the ruling house of the Cakaudrove, was thus a chief of substantial importance in Bau. Which is usually to say, he was a man of substantial talents for maneuver and intrigue: just a few years earlier, for example, he had been an arch-enemy of Ratu Cakobau, scheming with his Cakaudrove kinsmen to make war on Bau. However, Bau and Cakaudrove had been reconciled since 1842, or

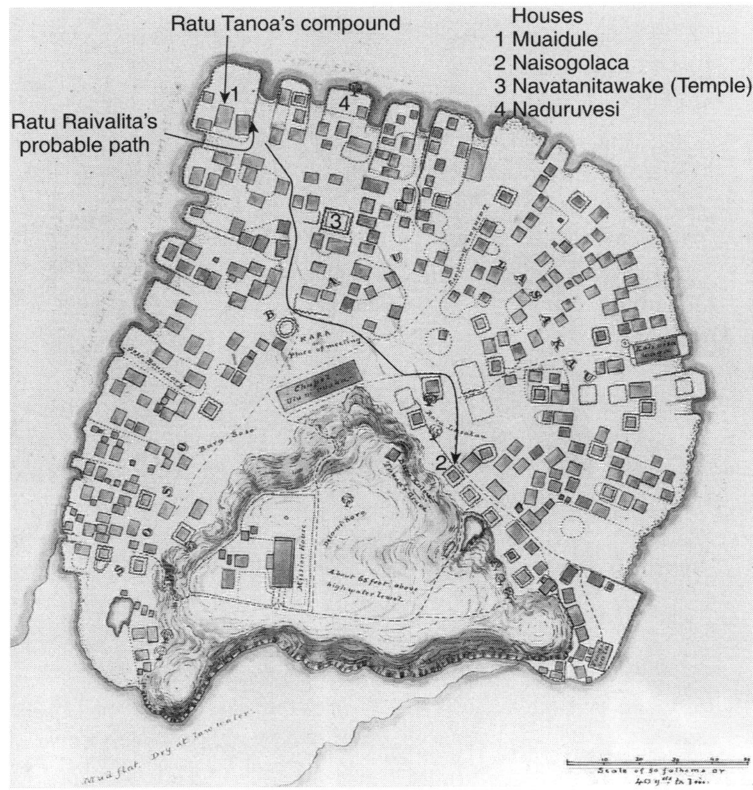

3.2 Ratu Raivalita's fateful course in Bau

more precisely Cakaudrove was reconciled to Bau's dominance, which may help explain Komainaua's apparent good relations with his royal brother.[12] For now he was something of Ratu Cakobau's designated executioner, not only in this instance but a few months later when he was commanded to do the same job on the king of Rewa—which order he refused, however.

On the present occasion, Komainaua leveled Ratu Raivalita with a club to the head. Just before, as the doomed chief was being held in the grip of Ratu Cakobau and pleading for his life, he denied plotting against the lat-

12. Just a year or so after Ratu Raivalita's death, however, Komainaua was reported to be again plotting to bring down Ratu Cakobau (Hazelwood *P*, Lyth to Hazelwood: 7 November 1846). He was again in the report of a conspiracy in 1850 (Lyth *J*: 4 March 1851). Neither of the reputed plots came to anything.

ter: "My enemies have told you lies," he is supposed to have said (Wallis 1851: 104). The protestation was apparently taken for what it was worth, under the circumstances. ("What an unmerciful thing is heathenism," commented Reverend Hunt [*J:* 19 October 1845].) The blow that followed, however, was apparently not lethal. A popular story is that the stunned Ratu Raivalita was buried alive, some say in the floor of his own house, and for two days he could be heard moaning from under the ground. But Reverend Waterhouse seems more credible: he says that shortly after being clubbed, Ratu Raivalita was strangled to death "in the usual form," and buried that night near the house of Ratu Cakobau, "where his enclosed grave still stands as a beacon to any who may hereafter conspire against the powers that be" (Waterhouse 1866: 110).[13]

Two missionary sources—both further removed from the scene than Mr. Hunt or Mrs. Wallis—tell of an additional actor in the story of Ratu Raivalita's death (Waterhouse 1866: 109; Williams 1931, 2:322–23). This was a certain unnamed Whiteman, who took the unfortunate young chief's part, endangering both Ratu Cakobau's life and his own. Sufficiently different to indicate that they were compiled from different sources, the reports of Messrs. Williams and Waterhouse cannot be dismissed out of hand, though they cannot be confirmed either from other documents. Many high-ranking chiefs of the time did have foreigner 'pets' (*manumanu,* lit. 'birds,' 'animals') in their entourage, performing a variety of services from repairing muskets to distilling whiskey and providing personal protection. Such a one, an Englishman, was sitting beside Ratu Raivalita when he was clubbed, according to Mr. Williams. The *Papalagi* promptly drew a loaded pistol and aimed at Ratu Cakobau, only a short distance away. But the pistol misfired. Ratu Cakobau ordered the Englishman clubbed, but no one dared do it. A conversation ensued between them, the upshot of which was that Ratu Cakobau, admiring the man's courage, offered to take him into his own service (Williams 1931, 2:323). Mr. Waterhouse's account, most likely from local Bauan sources, has the *Papalagi* accompanying Ratu Raivalita as he leaves Ratu Tānoa's house. When two chiefs seized Ratu Raivalita, the foreigner drew his pistol, but upon one of the chiefs commanding him to desist by a wave of the hand, he held fire.

13. In Bauan traditions of fifty or so years after the event, while Ratu Cakobau's descendants were still in power, he himself is given no personal role or responsibility for Ratu Raivalita's death (Anon. of *Na Mata* 1891[7]: 14–15). To believe these accounts, even though Ratu Raivalita is said to have made five attempts to shoot him, all misfiring, Ratu Cakobau remained unconcerned (*sega soti ni bau yalo lailai kina*). Rather, it was the other Bau chiefs or else Ratu Tānoa who were held responsible for Ratu Raivalita's death.

Ratu Cakobau does not enter into this narrative. Instead, the Whiteman, weeping, runs to tell Ratu Tānoa of the attack, who sends someone to see what is happening (Waterhouse 1866: 109).

A brief Bauan tradition (Toganivale 1912b: 171), recorded much later than the missionary accounts, likewise speaks of a *Papalagi* companion of Ratu Raivalita who rushed to the scene with a pistol when the young chief was seized by Ratu Cakobau's people. By this version, the Whiteman ran off and escaped when Ratu Cakobau called out for someone to club him down.

What to make of these reports? Their truth value is difficult to establish, except perhaps for one implication, itself conditional: Ratu Cakobau could also have been killed that day. However much we limit historical contingency by the cultural analysis to follow, we shall not eliminate it.

Returning to the immediate testimony, in the aftermath of Ratu Raivalita's death, his companion Selemi voluntarily met his. Selemi chose to accompany his chief—although not professing innocence himself, but on the contrary disclosing a widespread plot against Ratu Cakobau. After the chief was struck down, Selemi went home to have his people appropriately dress and adorn him for the strangling cord. Ratu Cakobau was then invited to the scene: perhaps as witness but certainly to hear Selemi confess the plot, which involved several prominent Bauans and allied chiefs. Thereupon, Selemi shared the fate of his chief—by custom the strangling is done by close kin of the person—and "the spirits of the friends were reunited, who shall say where?" (Wallis 1851: 105). Dying with the chief, symbolically or actually, is a pervasive theme of the old Fijian culture. Indeed, the whole country symbolically dies in the acts of self-mutilation, the circumcision rites of young men, and the general disorder that follow the death of the king—to be revived and reconstituted by the emergence of his successor. There were also the actual deaths of wives and of retainers such as Selemi, killed in order to accompany the chief in the afterworld (*Bulu*), where he would be thus equipped to continue ensuring the prosperity and otherwise controlling the destiny of his people.

Something is to be said about "companions" (*i tō*) of ruling chiefs, like Selemi in the present context, for they evidently had significant roles in the making and unmaking of conspiracies: arranging them, spying them out, and defending their chief against them. For younger chiefs such as Ratu Raivalita and Ratu Cakobau, their entourages probably represented the continuation into political life of youthful gangs that had before played together, pranked together, and eaten and slept together in a house dedicated to their own use (*bure ni sā*). Such a cohort of young men accompanied

Ratu Cakobau on a visit to Wilkes's ship in 1840 (Wilkes 1845, 3:66–67). What made these groups functional politically is that they were not exclusively recruited from the clan (*mataqali*) of the high chief who was their natural leader. Rather, these companions (*i tō*) were affiliated with various clans; in some cases—such as Ratu Varani of Viwa, an important partisan of Ratu Cakobau—they came from other, allied lands. Sometime in the 1840s Reverend Lyth (*RC:* 13) compiled a list of some nine men whom he labeled "The Companionate of [Ratu] Cakobau" (*Ai Tokani i Cakobau*). It is difficult to determine the clan affiliation of some, as they are all identified by warrior titles (*koroi*) rather than their proper names—an interesting fact in itself, indicating that they were all recognized man-slayers. The five I have been able to trace come from four different clans of Bau: none of them from Ratu Cakobau's own people, but three from groups that were their hereditary enemies. In a society as clanic as the Fijian, where loyalties were generally organized by descent and marital alliance, the chiefly entourage amounted to an unusually flexible instrument of political action. Established chiefs had their hereditary heralds, priests, and warriors to do their business—though a lot of their business was keeping the chief company around the kava bowl. But for younger bloods the likes of Ratu Raivalita and Ratu Cakobau, the more personal and pragmatic attachments they formed with active young men of their own inclinations gave them opportunities for political intelligence and mayhem that were likewise beyond the structural norms. The coteries were thus the social form of the *celeritas* powers of rising and ambitious chiefs. We have already seen from the stories of Ratu Raivalita's depredations that they were not exactly nice guys.

THE CONSPIRACY

In his retrospective narrative, Mr. Hunt spoke of a "strong party" in Ratu Raivalita's favor, though "it is not known whether all who were engaged in the plot were found out"—albeit there were also those who thought the young chief was innocent of any conspiracy and had been framed (*J:* 19 October 1845). Among the many corroborating reports, however, were too many confessions of participation to doubt the reality of the conspiracy, which indeed, as disclosed by Ratu Raivalita's companion Selemi, was extensive and formidable. Even so, he did not tell the whole of it. Named by Selemi in the plot to kill Ratu Cakobau were the paramount (Roko Tui Viwa) of Viwa island, Ratu Namosimalua, and his son Mai Sapai; the paramount (Roko Tui Veikau) of the land of Namara, an important fighting ally (*bati*) of Bau, traditionally affiliated with the sacred king of Bau (Roko Tui Bau); the two leading chiefs (unnamed) of the Lasakau sea warriors of Bau, the clan of "dangerous men"; and the two leaders (also unnamed) of the powerful shore warriors, the Soso people (Wallis 1851: 105). The list stands up well to other evidence, but it already recommends itself because it fingers certain longstanding adversaries of the Bau war king's family, participants in the uprising that had exiled Ratu Tānoa a decade earlier. Another of Ratu Raivalita's close companions, Ratu Nayagodamu, who had recently accompanied him to Cakaudrove, had a similarly suspicious background. In the coup of the 1830s, his father's brother had replaced Ratu Tānoa as the Vunivalu of Bau. The enmity between his own house and Ratu Tānoa's would be proven again in the early 1850s, when Ratu Nayagodamu was again a prominent member of the faction in Bau that tried to overthrow Ratu Cakobau. Nor was he the only one of the inveterate enemies of the ruling war kings who was repeatedly involved in attempts to do them in: confrontations that, we shall see presently, go back to the eighteenth century.

Another important Bauan, the notorious 'strong man' (*qāqā*) Ratu Gavidi (plate 3), played an ambiguous role in Ratu Raivalita's plot. The leading chief of a moiety of the Lasakau sea warriors, whose own road to power had been paved by the assassinations of rival kinsmen, Ratu Gavidi in all probability was one of the two Lasakau chiefs implicated as co-conspirators in Selemi's confession. Although Mrs. Wallis, who reported that confession, also had information that Ratu Gavidi had been in on the caper for months, she believed nonetheless that his conduct in the end exonerated him. As she understood, Ratu Gavidi, having learned of the plan from Ratu Raivalita, thereupon disclosed it to Ratu Cakobau, for which good offices the latter promised him one of his own sisters to wife (Wallis 1851: 103). (The gift of a royal sister, it should be noted, was one of the most effective of Fijian political transactions: it would not only make the heir of the wife-receiving chief a privileged sister's son or *vasu* of the ruling house, but would pretty much guarantee the succession of that royal uterine nephew to the leadership of his father's people.) But Ratu Gavidi hardly deserved the high marks in character and loyalty Mrs. Wallis was naively prepared to give him. Let us not forget Mr. Hunt's report that Ratu Raivalita was betrayed "by one of his own party." Knowing Ratu Gavidi's history of treachery, it is likely he was again playing a double game—which he was bound to win whoever killed whom—if he was not just selling out Ratu Raivalita for the advantages (the royal woman) he could gain by Ratu Cakobau's survival. Five years later Ratu Cakobau would be widely suspected of putting

Ratu Gavidi out of the way by having him shot in the back during a Bauan attack on Verata.[14] "Fijian politics is as mysterious as the black art," Mr. Hunt once observed, "and indeed bears some resemblance to it. It is almost impossible to learn what their intentions are, especially the Bau chiefs" (*WMMS/L:* 26 February 1845).

A surviving fragment of a contemporary missionary journal implies that Ratu Raivalita's conspiracy was not all that secret, and that it had been in the works for some time. So one may read what Ratu Namosimalua of Viwa told Mr. Jaggar—on the authority of Adi Vatea, a half-sister to Ratu Cakobau himself: "Namosemalua told us this morning that Dovevarata [Ratu Raivalita] told Vatea that he and Luke [probably Ratu Mualevu of the ọld Bauan enemies of Ratu Tānoa's house] were not coming to Vewa [*sic*] because they say they are vereing [conspiring] together that N is trying to turn Dovev" (Jaggar *PJ:* 9 September 1844; "N" may refer to Ratu Namosimalua or to Ratu Gavidi, sometimes "Ngavindi" in European accounts).

Almost all the contemporary documents single out the Viwa Island notable Ratu Varani as having unmasked the intentions of Ratu Raivalita, whoever else may have also forewarned Ratu Cakobau. Although he had recently been converted to Christianity and forsworn war, this erstwhile fighting companion of the Bau war king had not altogether retired from the political machinations in which he had long distinguished himself. *Varani* is a transliteration of "France," a name the chief received for taking a leading part in the capture of the French brig *Josephine* by Bau and Viwa people in 1835. Ratu Varani was the brother's son of the ruling chief of Viwa, Ratu Namosimalua, and virtually as prominent because of his military exploits and his offices in organizing the *bêche-de-mer* trade on Bau's behalf. In 1845, his otherworldly concerns notwithstanding, he went to some effort to protect Ratu Cakobau. According to Mrs. Wallis's information, Ratu Varani had overheard Ratu Raivalita "talking over the affair" with the aforementioned Ratu Gavidi on board the *bêche-de-mer* brig *Gambia* (Capt. Joseph Hartwell). Indeed, Ratu Varani ("Frene") is noted in the *Gambia*'s log as having come aboard the ship off the north coast of Viti Levu in mid-December 1844, apparently as the agent of Ratu Cakobau's in-

14. On this occasion, Mrs. Wallis was convinced of Ratu Gavidi's enmity to Ratu Cakobau: "It has been ascertained that he had been planning to kill Thakombau [Ratu Cakobau] and it is most likely that his life was the penalty for his offence" (1994: 10). Evidently, Ratu Nayagodamu was in on this conspiracy too, as was Komainaua (Lyth *J:* 4 March 1851).

terest in the trade (Anon. of *Gambia* Log: 15 and 16 December 1844). By Mrs. Wallis's account, Ratu Varani sent a trusted man to spy out the scheming taking place on the *Gambia.* The man immediately determined it to be a conspiracy or " 'vere' to murder Thakombau [Ratu Cakobau], Verani [Ratu Varani] and one other," upon which "Revelete [Ratu Raivalita] was to be king of Bau" (Wallis 1851: 103). As the story goes, when Ratu Varani's man later disclosed the plan to Ratu Cakobau, the latter supposedly did not believe it and dismissed the informant. But that seems to have been Ratu Cakobau's usual *modus operandi,* one of the stratagems of Bauan politics that made it "impossible to know what their intentions are," certainly not what intentions he had formed when Ratu Raivalita came ashore at Bau in August next.

Ratu Cakobau would have reason to suppose that the conspiratorial forces ranged against him were greater than the several chiefs who were exposed when the attempted assassination backfired. A deep fault line runs through the Bau polity: not the constituted division of Bau into moieties headed respectively by the Vunivalu and the Roko Tui Bau, although these relationships were certainly in play, but a historic rupture between factions whose internecine struggles for control of the kingship, especially the war king title, had been troubling the island from the prehistoric period and would continue to do so into postcolonial times. Basically the split was between the old Bauan nobility (as we shall call them), including the houses of former war kings and the Roko Tui Bau People, and the upstart war kings, the Tui Kaba People of Ratu Tānoa and Ratu Cakobau, who had only recently gained the Vunivalu title and the supreme rule—together with the resentment of the groups they had deposed. Observing this political scene in 1840, Horatio Hale spoke of two "parties" of chiefs divided by a recent history of usurpation, with the rest of the Bau people adhering to one or another as it suited their interests (Hale 1846: 60–61). Opposing the Vunivalu crowd, the "Ruling House People" as Hale called them (*Kai Vale Levu*), were a group he identified as the "Mbatitombi"—that is, Batitobe, who are also commonly known as Nabaubau.[15] The Batitobe, Hale learned, "formerly possessed the supreme power, of which they were deprived by the grandfather of the present king" (ibid., 60). Lieutenant

15. *Nabaubau* and *Batitobe* are equated or else used alternately for the same group in several Fijian sources. For example, in Bauan tradition, as related to the Native Lands Commission: "The Batitobe; that is, they of Nabaubau [*na Batitobe, a ya iratou mai Nabaubau*]" (NLC/TR [Tailevu North (Yavusa Kubuna)]). In Lands Commission records of the 1890s, Batitobe and Nabaubau are alternate names of subdivisions of the ruling Tui Kaba people. In other texts, Nabaubau is identified as a division or house of Batitobe.

Wilkes more specifically identifies the usurper as Ratu Banuve, in a passing reference to "the family of Mbatitombe [Batitobe], who reigned at Ambau [Bau] before Bamiva [Banuve], the father of Tanoa, succeeded in gaining the kingdom" (Wilkes 1845, 3:131). But Hale, in any case, had grasped the key dynamic of the recurring Bauan political crises: the readiness of the older chiefs, nursing grudges of ancient and recent memory, to support any challenge to the usurping war king crowd—including challenges that came from within the ruling house, as in the case of Ratu Raivalita. Beyond that, on the principle that the friend of my enemy is my enemy, the old nobility of Bau made war on the Rewa when they harbored Ratu Tānoa during the coup of the 1830s; while on the principle that the enemy of my enemy is my friend, the same people were a drag on Ratu Cakobau's campaigns against Rewa a decade later.

A further word about these contentious chiefly groups of Bau. It is significant that the Nabaubau, the Roko Tui Bau, and their aristocratic like, as former sovereigns, were on that score the truer chiefs of Bau, by contrast to the arriviste Tui Kaba of Ratu Tānoa et al. The current war kings were essentially descendants of the aforementioned usurper Ratu Banuve, the Vunivalu in the late eighteenth century (d. 1804)—or else, by other genealogies, the usurper was Ratu Banuve's father. Yet as it was put to the Native Lands Commission early in the twentieth century by an obviously partisan Bauan, "This Ratu Banuve, it is not very clear who his father was" (NLC/TR [Tailevu North (Yavusa Kubuna)]). The statement appears in one of three tangled and conflicting histories of the Bau kingship recorded by the commission—to which other, no less contradictory versions, collected before and after, could easily be added. Many of the problems reside in structural and polemical issues of genealogy: the customary foreshortening of pedigrees to six or seven generations' depth, beyond which is the era of divine culture heroes; the existence of different names for the same person and the same names (and sometimes the same stories) for different persons; and, of course, contestable manipulations of chiefly ancestry. On the other hand, the history that is codified on the ground—by the presence of distinct local groups whose possession of their own gods and temples is testimony to their close kinship and independent origins—that history is somewhat less difficult to decipher. Reading it, one finds that the prominent enemies of the ruling Tui Kaba people fall into two categories: (1) former war kings, lineages once holding the Vunivalu title, of which the most prominent in the nineteenth century were the Nabaubau or Batitobe noted by Horatio Hale, together with their allies by marriage inside and outside Bau; and (2) the people of the sacred king, the Roko Tui Bau, together with certain clans, also inside and outside Bau, that traditionally recognized him as their chief. Including at least three other clans besides the Nabaubau, the category of former war kings is testimony to a whole series of ancient usurpations and lingering antagonisms, but it had some collective existence and coherence in opposition to the Ratu Tānoa crowd.[16] The Nabaubau people led this coalition, not simply because they were the last to hold power, but because, for the same reason, they had the greatest network of political support. Nabaubau women had been widely sought in order to give chiefly houses elsewhere the cachet of *vasu,* or privileged sister's sons, to Bauan royalty. As it was put by a modern, knowledgeable man from a town subject to Bau: "The story of 'Nabaubau' says that in the olden days, all the high chiefs and ladies in Bau came from 'Nabaubau,' their mothers and mothers' mothers were usually from 'Nabaubau.' . . . You can see that all the great names are existing in Bau today, both chiefs and ladies" (Rosenthal *FN;* cf. Lyth *DB,* 4:40b).

An interesting number of the greatest Fijian chiefs of the nineteenth century were indeed uterine nephews to the Nabaubau aristocracy, the sons of ranking Nabaubau women. Included were two chiefs implicated in Ratu Raivalita's coup attempt, the paramounts of Viwa and Namara. (Ratu Cakobau himself was a *vasu* to Nabaubau, although his mother died when he was an infant, and the relationship hardly served him in 1845; in the 1830s uprising against Ratu Tānoa, however, it did figure in securing his survival, as will be seen presently.) The Nabaubau were important partisans of every major uprising against the parvenu war kings of Tui Kaba, from a rebellion around the turn of the eighteenth century that aimed, unsuccessfully, to restore the supremacy of the sacred Roko Tui Bau, to the rebellion, also unsuccessful, against Ratu Cakobau in 1854–55.[17] Likewise prominent par-

16. The four main groups of former war kings opposed to the Tui Kaba were Nanukurua, Nabaubau, Naisoro, and Dewala. They are collectively known as "Lower Tui Kaba" (*Tui Kaba i Ra*), in contrast to the ruling "Upper Tui Kaba" (*Tui Kaba e Cake*) of Ratu Cakobau et al., though this may have been a usage of the colonial period. In the colonial scheme these four groups ("Batitobe" sometimes replacing "Nabaubau") were designated segments (*i tokatoka*) of the clan (*mataqali*) of the Tui Kaba. Collectively and colloquially, the groups opposing the Tui Kaba proper are often called "Rokodurucoko" or "Dewala." Each of these four noble lines had its own god and god-house, except Naisoro, which shared those of the Tui Kaba—suggesting that the Banuve crowd entered the Bau ruling circles by affiliation to the Naisoro, apparently as wife-takers therefrom, hence *vasu* thereto (Wainiu *BK*).

17. The Nabaubau or Batitobe people are indeed sometimes identified as the Roko Tui Bau or sacred kings in tradition and by modern Bauan informants. It is possible that the Nabaubau people functioned as a segment of the Roko Tui Bau clan in the early nineteenth

ticipants in at least three of these movements against the ruling Vunivalu People (in 1800, 1832, and 1854) were the hereditary land warriors (*bati*) called Vusaradave, a very large clan of Bau affiliated specifically with the Roko Tui Bau kings—and their historic grievances. So although we do not know the full membership of the "strong party" in Ratu Raivalita's favor, the warrior chiefs of Vusaradave and the old nobility of Bau would certainly qualify as the usual suspects.

Certain other notable sister's sons of the old Nabaubau nobility—namely, the rulers of Rewa—not only were involved in Ratu Raivalita's plot but, to believe some chronicles of the time, they were its prime movers. As maternal uncles of Ratu Raivalita, the Rewa king Ro Kania and his brother Ratu Qaraniqio had a direct kinship with the assassination scheme: they were something more than the friends of Ratu Cakobau's enemies. Not that the Rewans were simply moved by the customary sentiments or obligations they owed Ratu Raivalita as his *vasu* due. Rewa was in all-out war with Bau in 1845, and under the circumstances this already marked relationship between maternal uncle and uterine nephew took on the added value of a tactical advantage. It became a salient structure of interest and action. Indeed, even as the Rewa rulers were backing Ratu Raivalita in Bau, their Bauan counterparts, Ratu Tānoa and Ratu Cakobau, were exploiting a virtually symmetrical schism in the ruling house of Rewa.

The war with Bau was hardly a few months old when Ro Cokānauto, a paternal half-brother to Ro Kania and Ratu Qaraniqio of Rewa, defected to the enemy—who happened to be his mother's people.[18] His mother was a daughter of Ratu Tānoa, and he was thus a 'sister's son to Bau' (*vasu ki Bau*), just as Ratu Raivalita was to Rewa (fig. 3.3). Taking a number of loyal towns and clans with him to the Bauan camp, Ro Cokānauto split Rewa nearly in two, and seriously weakened its military position. He moved to a town in the south of the Rewa Delta, Nukui, which was soon invested with Bauans and used to harass Rewa by land and by sea. At the instigation of Ratu Tānoa, his rebel grandson Ro Cokānauto was installed as sacred king of Rewa, Roko Tui Dreketi, thus setting up an alternate government.

---

century, hence came under the general identity of Roko Tui Bau people. The principal herald of Bau told me in 1988 that the Nabaubau were indeed Roko Tui Bau people at one time, and were later taken into Lower Tui Kaba, being *vasu* to the latter.

18. All of these Rewan notables had several names, and accordingly they are variously identified in European and Fijian texts. The king Ro Kania is also known as Ratu Banuve; Ratu Qaraniqio also appears as Dakuwaqa, Bativudi, and Lagivala ('Longfellow'); Ro Cokānauto is more commonly "Phillips" in Western literature, named after the employer of the Salem *bêche-de-mer* trader, Capt. John Eagleston.

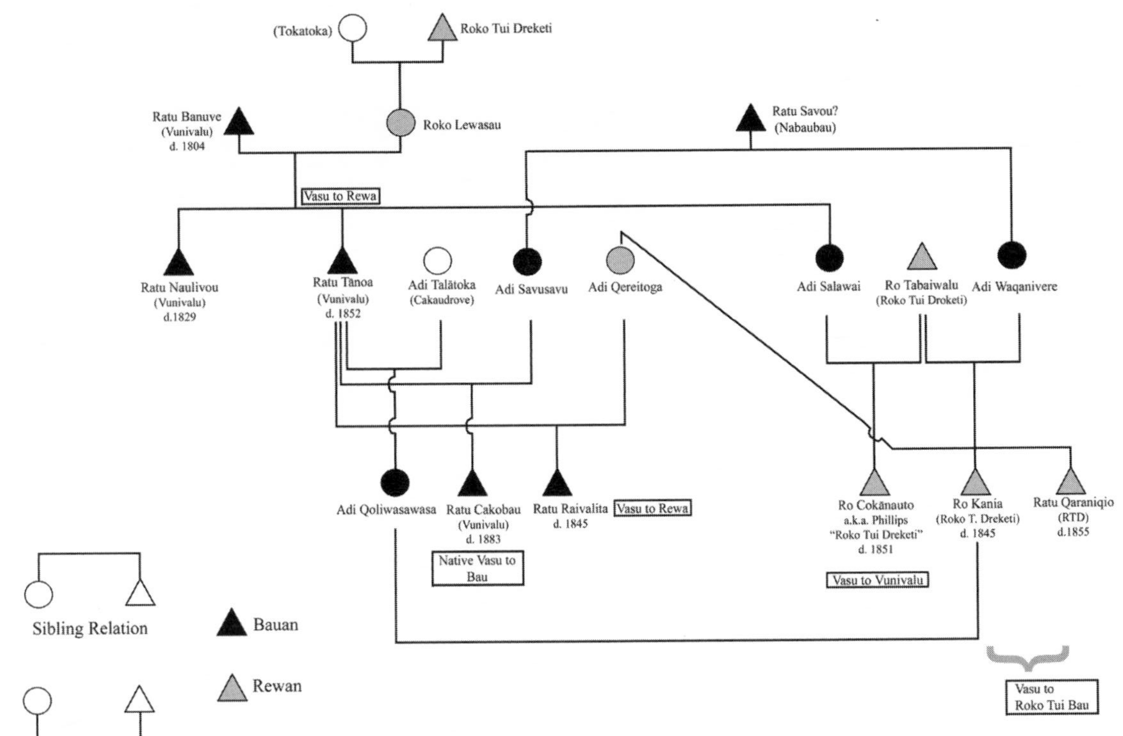

3.3 Relations of the rulers of Bau and Rewa

Hence, it would hardly be unprecedented for Ro Kania of Rewa to attempt to do something similar on behalf of his sister's son Ratu Raivalita in Bau—especially when he was being so hard-pressed militarily and politically.

A few years afterward, Ratu Raivalita's royal kinsmen of Rewa, as represented by Ratu Qaraniqio, not only admitted participation in his assassination plot, but wanted the credit for it. Ratu Qaraniqio told the French Catholic missionary Père Mathieu in 1851 that his brother the Rewa king was behind it all: "Before . . . my brother Ratu Banuve, Roko Tui Dreketi [Rewa's royal title], raised a war against Cakobau. He plotted with Raivalita, *vasu* to Rewa, who would help him. But the famous Varani, the assassin of the commander of *L'Aimable Josephine,* having heard of the plot, went to inform Cakobau. The next night, the latter had his brother put to death" (in Deniau, *HF2*).[19]

The implication that the project of taking out the Bau rulers originated in Rewa is even clearer in Mr. Calvert's version—which by date and religious conviction had to be independent of the Catholic father's. On Calvert's assessment, the prime motivation for the conspiracy lay in Rewa's unfavorable strategic situation in the war with Bau: "Hitherto Rewa, though much the weaker, had been obstinate in keeping up the war, resting in the hope of assistance from [Ratu] Raivalita, their *vasu,* who had engaged to kill his brother Thakombau [Ratu Cakobau], on condition that Rewa would become tributary to him on his assuming the government of Mbau" (Williams and Calvert 1859: 350).[20] In other words, the Rewa rulers were willing to settle for their survival at the small cost of a tribute to Ratu Raivalita as Vunivalu of Bau—tribute that could hardly be differentiated from, or much more significant than, his customary right as their *vasu.* In that event, the political situation would have been restored to its antebellum condition: on the whole amicable, with the ruler of Bau the great *vasu* to Rewa, Ratu Raivalita simply replacing Ratu Tānoa in that relationship.

There is some contemporary evidence that Ratu Raivalita was indeed in Rewa conspiring with his royal kinsmen in the months before his death. Being their *vasu,* Ratu Raivalita would in principle enjoy free passage between Bau and Rewa despite the ongoing hostilities. According to Mr. Calvert (Williams and Calvert 1859: 350), the Bauan was sending messages to

19. P. Mathieu's interview with Ratu Qaraniqio—here referred to as Bativudi—is reported in quotation marks by Deniau, that is, as he had it from P. Mathieu. The conversation between the missionary and the Rewan chief took place in Levuka, Ovalau.

20. Mr. Calvert (or the printer) incorrectly dated the assassination of Ratu Raivalita in this text as "mid-1846" instead of 1845 (Williams and Calvert 1859: 350).

Rewa by night. The missionary also heard that Ratu Raivalita had personal contact with his maternal uncles, the Rewan king and Ratu Qaraniqio. The log of the aforementioned *bêche-de-mer* brig *Gambia* lends some credence to these claims. While cruising off southeastern Viti Levu in November 1844, the *Gambia* was met by some canoes from Rewa. In one that came alongside was "Roveleet [Raivalita], a chief of Bau" (Anon. of *Gambia* Log: 8 November 1844). The log indicates that certain unspecified "negotiations" were held with Ratu Raivalita. If they had to do with the *bêche-de-mer* trade, here would be a hint that Ratu Raivalita could back his regicidal ambitions with some ammunition. In any case, it is clear enough that the interests of the Rewan enemy were relayed, by transpolity kinship relations, into the contentious politics of Bau kingship.

Events then unfolded on two levels, as a dialogue of the two struggles. Ratu Raivalita's attempt to seize power articulated a collective struggle for supremacy between rival kingdoms with an interpersonal contest for succession between royal kinsmen. Each conflict was lent a surplus of intensity and historical effect by its interpolation in the other. Endowed with the animus of the war between Bau and Rewa, the enmity of Ratu Cakobau and Ratu Raivalita—inherent in the relations of Fijian chiefship, as will be argued presently—was then carried to a murderous extreme. Conversely, the fratricide further destabilized Rewa's military situation, and almost literally opened the gates of the city to the Bau forces. The agon on the individual level at once responded to and fairly decided the course of the larger war.

But if history indeed works on this kind of integration between the collective and the interpersonal, something more needs to be said about the structural relays that transmit the impulses of the one to the other. The effort will also be worthwhile because it helps to establish the rationality and thus the limits of contingency—the indeterminacy involved in who would wind up killing whom—while also endowing it with determinate historical effects. The mediating institutions, such as the Fijian *vasu* custom, in their own right comprehend a synthesis of the universal and the particular, something like the similar effect they achieve in historical action. Referring to the distinctive relations among brothers and sisters and their respective offspring, what he called "the cross cousin system," A. M. Hocart (1933: 253) pointed out that much more is entailed than the classification of relatives. There is here, he said, "a whole theology" (Hocart 1970b: 237). To understand our narrative of discrete events and particular personalities, we have to take a break here of cosmological proportions.

THE SISTER'S SON (*VASU*)

> *Vasus* cannot be considered apart from the civil polity of the group, forming as they do one of its integral parts and supplying the high-pressure power of Fijian despotism. . . . However high a chief may rank, however powerful a king may be, if he has a *vasu,* he has a master.
>
> THOMAS WILLIAMS, in *Fiji and the Fijians* (Williams and Calvert 1859)

A Fijian short answer to the reasons for Ratu Raivalita's death would probably be "look at the *vasu* relationships." The distinctive status of the uterine nephew goes a long way toward explaining the enmity of Ratu Raivalita and Ratu Cakobau, as well as why the war between Bau and Rewa devolved upon their personal animosity. For what opposed these two sons of the Bau war king Ratu Tānoa was the same thing that connected their personal fates to the fortunes of the warring kingdoms—*vasu* relations. Ratu Raivalita was a great *vasu* to Rewa, a tabu uterine nephew to the whole kingdom, because his mother was the sister of the ruling Roko Tui Dreketi, here the supreme as well as the sacred king (fig. 3.3). Ratu Cakobau's mother was of the Nabaubau, a house of former royal glory in Bau; although the Nabaubau dynasty was now superseded, that made him all the more honored as a 'native sister's son' (*vasu i taukei*). (Ratu Tānoa had wives to spare, and no doubt the mother of Cakobau was meant to neutralize the hostility of the deposed Nabaubau people.) By their respective maternal ancestries, then, the two brothers had different strategic values in Bauan politics: advantages and disadvantages that were, however, subject to change with the changing relations between Bau and Rewa. Good relations with Rewa would favor Ratu Raivalita's career in Bau; enmity with Rewa would be better for Ratu Cakobau.

The *vasu* relation is the main structural form of Fijian practical politics. In contrast to the inflexibilities of common descent and of groups organized on that basis, the sister's son–mother's brother relation, as a function of marital alliances, is much more readily adapted to shifting conditions of force and fortune. Marriage is at once an arrangement allowing of some choice and a promise of an enduring bond of loyalty and obligation between the son of the woman and her brothers and fathers, her natal group. Here is a space of relative freedom in the system, a historically open dimension of the cultural order, allowing the fashioning of new alliances of political utility apart from the ascribed solidarities of common descent and hierarchies fixed by seniority of birth. In this normatively patrilineal order, marriage and *vasu* relations are where the action is. The *Realpolitik* is in connections between men established through women and, therefore, established *by* women to the extent they are able to shape these relations between their husbands, brothers, and sons—which is often considerable, as we shall see in the case of Ratu Raivalita. Here it is important to note that *vasu* is more a political term than a personal kinship term proper, for it designates the relation between a person and a group, his mother's brother's people. The proper kinship term for one's sister's son is *vugo* (plus possessive suffix), which is used reciprocally (in reference) for mother's brother. But *vasu* is a kinship title, as Hocart (1929: 40) put it, referring to the status of a man relative to his mother's paternal relatives collectively—and in the case of mothers' brothers who are ruling chiefs, to their countries and their subjects as well.[21] Nor would any of these maternal kinsmen (or their subjects) refer to the *vasu* with a first person possessive form: one could not say "my *vasu,*" only "our *vasu*" (*neitou vasu*). It is this character of the *vasu* relation as a bond between a man and his mother's people, as a status he holds among them, that makes it the privileged structure of the politics of betrayal as well as alliance, and of usurpation as well as succession. And it is so practical just because it is theological.

The Cosmology of Cross-Kinship

It will be convenient to speak of a category of "cross-kinship," referring to people related through a brother-sister (cross-sex) pair. Cross-cousins are the children of a brother and sister, or from my point of view, my mother's brother's and father's sister's children (fig. 3.4). It happens in the Fijian case that the pun on the English "cross-kinship" is pertinent, for an element of hostility attends what is otherwise a relation of extreme respect.

Let us begin with an ethnographic experience of Fijian cross-kinship—an explication of it in local terms—that implies its politics in the same breath as its theology. Here is a man of Keteira village, Moala Island, in 1955, explaining to me the differences between his kinship relationships to and through his sister and those in his paternal line or natal house, as represented by his brothers. Taka, the man in question, develops a double contrast: at once between the novelty of cross-kinship by comparison to the stability of fraternal bonds, and between the 'sacred' (*tabu*) nature of the

21. Hocart says the term *vasu* is applied to men only, thus not to sisters' daughters. I believe this is true of the unmarked use, and may have generally been true in the early twentieth century and before. However, I have occasionally heard women so referred to, provided the referent was clear.

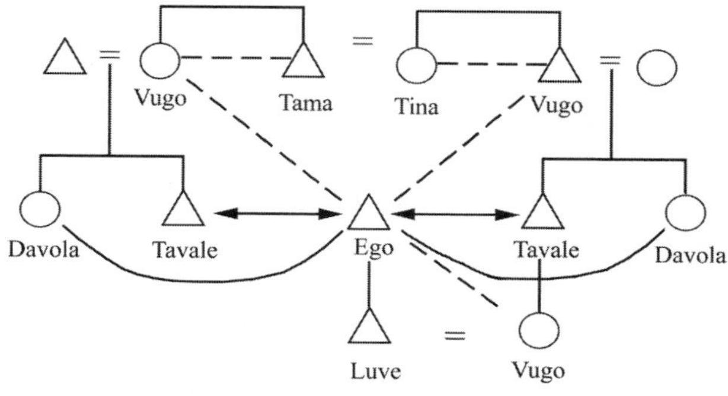

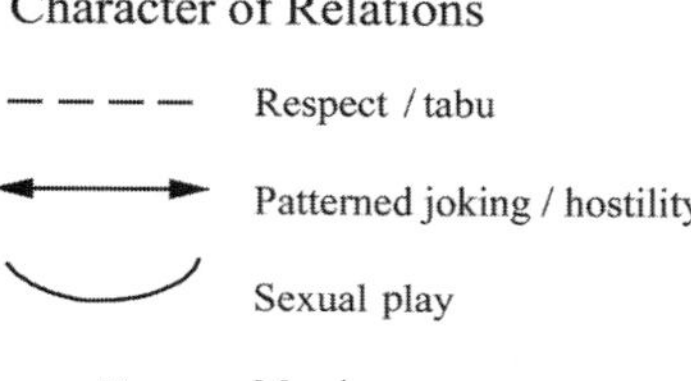

3.4 Fijian cross-kinship

former by comparison to the unmarked character of the latter. All his kin through his sister and his father's sister, said Taka, were 'sacred blood' (*dra tabu*) to him, above all his sisters. And, he continued, "my sister's son is very serious [*dredrē*]. It is my blood; my sister went to give rise to that man. Brothers are only brothers [*veitacini sa veitacini ga*], but the sister's child is a new path. Your daughter or your sister makes a new line [*kawa*]. Brothers are only in the house; they have been there from the past to today. But the descent of my sister is a new line" (in M. Sahlins 1962: 168). We can already sense here the political virtues of the cross-kin, that they are able to trump the constituted groups and relations of lineage. Indeed, various expressions of the power of the sister and the sister's son suggest an alternative mode of political legitimacy. Seniority of descent has its own sanctity, but in relation to it, the *vasu* embodies an extravagant divine force—something beyond normal human sociality.

We have already seen the like in the uterine nephew's violation of the sacrifice, his seizure of what is offered to the god of his mother's brother's people, in effect taking the god's place (see above, chapter 2). Recurrent versions of the *vasu*'s high-handed breaches of the normal rules, with the same implication of a usurpation of authority, appear in several different cultural registers: from customs of ceremonial exchange to charters of kingdom formation, passing by way of everyday kinship interaction. Extending from the interpersonal level through the cosmic, such structural replications would thus be relevant to the historiography of Ratu Raivalita's death, precisely as it involved the folding of collective forces into individual rivalries through the mediation of *vasu* relationships. A similar *glissando* from the cosmological to the register of social action, involving the resolution of sacrificial offerings to material utilities, can be seen in the practice Fijians know by the transitive verb *vasuta,* 'to *vasu* [something], to take an object by *vasu* right.' These seizures of property always entail some sense of the "sacred blood" of the uterine nephew. In any case, it would be difficult to differentiate the divine from the mundane when it concerns the nephew's expropriations of the valuables received by the maternal uncle in ceremonial transactions, since in traditional custom all such goods are ritually presented first of all to the gods of the recipients and thus have the character of offerings. From this to the ordinary *vasu*-ing of the maternal uncle's crops, pigs, or movable goods is only another small and not-too-different step.

In proper custom, however, such seizures of the uncle's things, without permission and typically without warning, should be done in moderation and when the *vasu* is a child. In principle it would be beneath the *gravitas* of adults and particularly of chiefly persons.[22] This did not prevent some Bauan chiefly hotheads of mature years from making reckless demands, even for women, on their royal maternal uncles—as Ratu Cakobau's classificatory brother and future rival, Ratu Mara Kapaiwai, was wont to do in Lau.[23] Not that the exercise of the *vasu* prerogative would always pass with-

22. Rev. Thomas Williams tells of an exemplary exercise of the *vasu* privilege that took place in July 1846 at or following a temple ritual in Somosomo, where Bauan forces had gathered for a combined military action with Cakaudrove. A son of Ratu Tānoa, "a little lad," took possession of a double canoe and twenty-one single ones "by virtue of his being a *vasu* to this place" (1931, 1:351). Speaking of the same incident, Mrs. Wallis commented (no doubt on missionary information) that such acts are "mostly done while they [the *vasu*] are children, as when the '*vasu*' becomes older, they are ashamed to help themselves this way" (1851: 217). On the other hand, some adults must have put the kid up to it—twenty-two canoes, after all.

23. Some of Ratu Raivalita's infamous depredations when he was a young man may have been backed by *vasu* right. In 1839 Rev. Thomas Jaggar, stationed at Rewa, lost some pigs by virtue of Ratu Raivalita's *vasu* claims on the whole of the Rewa kingdom. He reported that Ratu Raivalita had "*vasu*'d our pigs" being raised in Dreketi, a subject land to Rewa (*J:* 10 Nov 1839). Also on *vasu* and pigs, Captain Eagleston related an occasion in 1838 when

out resentment. On the contrary, a certain sense of violation is present in the practice. One could say, with Hocart, it is essential to the practice (1929: 235). Recall that when the *vasu* expropriates the prestation to his mother's people (or their god), his maternal uncle's sons, his cross-cousins, have the right to pummel him—although they do not recover the goods. As one of Hocart's interlocutors from Bau told him, "If *wekana* [his relatives] know [the] *vasu* well, they hit him and his people; but it is no matter, he gets the *i yau* [the valuables]" (*FN:* 2777).

Interesting how, if one follows the norms of conduct among these various relations—brothers and sisters, maternal uncles and uterine nephews, cross-cousins—they chart a course of interactions over time analogous to the archetypal ritual of *vasu*-ing the sacrifice. The sequence of interactions and transactions among cross-kinsmen is like a narrative, spanning three generations, of the constitution and dénouement of the *vasu* right. The "whole theology" starts with conduct appropriate between brother and sister. If (as Taka of Keteira said), the sister carries with her the "sacred blood" of her lineage, then the prescribed avoidance between her and her brothers, prohibiting direct address, bodily contact and sexual reference, ensures the alienation of the divine powers she embodies, her reproductive powers, to the house into which she marries. Her brothers lose the active powers of reproduction and growth. Passing beyond their (human) control, these powers become incarnate in their sister's son, their transgressive *vasu.* Hence the *vasu*'s tyranny over his maternal kinsman—spiritually, ritually, materially, and politically—is in some sense legitimate, for he now detains the "sacred blood" of their line. The *vasu,* Fijians sometimes say, is their 'sacred land' (*vanua tabu*)—just as, inversely, some Fijian gods are *vasu* to the land of their worshipers (Hocart *HF:* 445; on Gau).

Throughout the generations, what remains at issue between a woman's natal house and the house into which she marries is the latter's gain of reproductive power at the expense of the former. The kinship system is a generations-long agon of alienation and final reconciliation, marked by successive stages of exaggerated respect and exaggerated hostility, all revolving about the contest over sexual cum spiritual prowess. So like the interaction between brother and sister, the relationship between the maternal uncle and the sister's son is again marked by avoidance tabus on sexual references. Overtly signifying great respect, what Fijians call a 'heavy kin

---

he could not procure provisions in pigs in Rewa because the king had tabued them for a feast. Eagleston resorted to shooting them while walking in the king's presence, at which the latter exclaimed, "My my, a *vasu* at Rewa" (*UD,* 2:101).

relationship' (*veiwekani bibi*), the behavior also leaves unspoken, and thus secures, the transfer of woman-power to the *vasu*'s house. What is protected by avoidance and respect is the asymmetrical privilege of the *vasu:* "however high a chief may rank, if he has a *vasu* he has a master." A ritual showing of the child *vasu,* along with a prestation of wealth, by his father's people to his mother's brother's legitimates these uterine nephew rights. The *vasu* may thereupon aggressively exercise his claims to property against a *gravitas* maternal uncle who is enjoined to endure it (*vosota ga*)—or even, acting in a chiefly manner (*vakaturaga*), to welcome it.

In the next chapter of this kinship narrative, however, the covert hostilities surface in the form of a prescribed antagonism between the *vasu* and his mother's brother's sons, that is, his cross-cousins (Hocart 1915, 1923). The alienation of powers entailed in the passage of a woman from one house to another now finds expression among the men of the succeeding generation. The archetypal ritual pummeling of the sister's son by the sons of his maternal uncle in retaliation for his theft of the sacrifice has realizations in various forms of practice—what David Graeber has called "the exchange of bads" (by opposition to the exchange of goods). The cross-cousins may indeed steal from one another. Or in a verbal analogue to the ritual fight, they engage in a classic "joking relationship" whose good humor (in the double sense) is the ostensible manner of an exchange of insults, notably including sexual insults. This sexually marked abuse evokes the initial alienation of the woman, as if to confirm or redress it. So too is the enjoined flirtation that the cousins engage in with each other's sisters. Their explicit banter in terms of endearment may lead to sexual intercourse, but traditionally in the coastal kingdoms, marriage between first cross-cousins was discouraged. The preferred union was between second cross-cousins, precisely the children of the mutually taunting *vasu* and his mother's brothers' sons.

Here, in the union of second cross-cousins was the dénouement of the kinship drama and the beginning of its repetition. The marriage could be said to sublimate the feud of the *vasu* and his mother's people (his mother's brother's sons), except that, if it repeated the original union of two generations earlier, it would reestablish the same relationships—the same hierarchy and underlying antagonism. There is no rigid rule here; the wife-takers and wife-givers need not repeat their earlier roles. But depending on the stability of the political context, there is a tendency to do so, at least among chiefly houses. The noble lines of Bau, for example, repeatedly revisit former alliances, gaining at least some of their wives from the same lands again and again. Of course, the continuity of these arrangements would be affected by the political fortunes of the intermarrying groups, even as their political fortunes could depend on continued intermarriage. Such were the theological politics of kinship.[24]

Another expression of the same was the foundation of kingship as a relation of sister's son to the people of the land. As was observed earlier (see above, chapter 1), a recurrent charter of dynastic origins in many Fijian countries involves the advent of a stranger-prince who secures the rule by marrying the daughter of the indigenous chief and sires a successor who is thus the *vasu* of the native people (*vasu i taukei*). As the Lauan man said to Hocart, "The chiefs come from overseas; it is so in all countries of Fiji" (1929: 129). This union of the overseas chief with the indigenous woman combines the master dichotomies of Fijian cultural order: the correlated oppositions of sea and land, foreign and native, chief and commoner, heaven and earth. Synthesizing these polarities, the royal offspring hierarchically encompasses the society, incarnates its totality. Yet his status and powers are always ambiguous: inside the polity and yet a foreigner by origin, above the people but in some sense their junior, a source of prosperity and a force of destruction. The ruling chief is honorably addressed as 'child chief' (*gone turaga*), an honor that is also a reminder that the chief is the offspring of the native woman, and the indigenous people are his 'elders' (*matua*). Legends tell of the beneficence of kings and their creative acts: how they gathered the scattered settlements of the native people into a unified and ordered polity, for example. But there remains about the ruling chief a residual aura of the usurper, and beneath his gravity and dignity lurks a threat of violence. In other words, the chief has the persisting character of the *vasu*. Buell Quain provides a good ethnographic observation of the ambiguities of Fijian chiefship, this from the interior of Vanua Levu:

> A good chief disapproves of violence and discourages it among his subjects. He disregards personal slights and never raises his voice above a mild, polite, conversational tone. Such restraint befits a chief; in itself it pleases the ancestors and encourages "a good soul" among all the people who, as ordinary mortals, are incapable of learning such thorough self-control. But a male chief must also be a "man." . . . If he satisfies his own

24. Technically speaking, there seems to be an implicit four-class system in Fijian kinship, as would be implied by continuing FMBSD or FFZSD marriage. Men sometimes repeat their FF marriage to a given house—indeed, *grandmother* (*bui*) is an alternative term for one's wife. The same is encoded in the sometime practice of repeating proper names in alternate generations of chiefly lines. (F = father, M = mother, S = son, Z = sister, D = daughter, B = brother.)

desires and overrides all social regulations, people will say that he is "bad," but they will also say that he is "indeed a chief." Ratu Seru [another of this name, not Ratu Cakobau], who uses a "strong arm" on his women and whose lack of modesty shocks the village, is indeed a chief; people will speak in voices hushed with awe and admiration of a certain chief of Rokowaqa, long dead, who used to wait near the child's bathing place so that he could choose a particularly fat child to bake for his supper. (Quain 1948: 203)[25]

The Sister's Son (*Vasu*): Politics

Given the authority and privileges of the sister's son among his mother's people, the negotiations of the marriages by which these *vasu* relationships were established, above all the marriages of the great chiefs, were at the center of Fijian politics. Along with conspiracies, of which they were often a part, these negotiations were a high Fijian art. Calculation had to take into account the structural permutations in the *vasu*'s powers, which depended on the status of the intermarrying chiefs, together with strategic practical demands of the moment. Nor would it always be possible to maximize the marital advantages because there were likely to be contending interests within the house of any given ruling chief—namely, the divisive concerns of the chief's several wives about the marital fate of their children, concerns in which their respective brothers also had a share. To understand the praxis of marriage and the *vasu* relation, then, we have to first examine the structural principles by which they are negotiated.

First principle: the political scale of the *vasu*'s claims depended on the chiefly standing of the sister's son and his maternal uncle in their respective countries. This is in itself complex, since it involved the *vasu*'s mother's rank as well as his father's, but what I draw attention to is the variation in the social scale of the *vasu*'s rights according to rank. A man may be a *vasu* simply to another house, or thereby to a whole clan, land, or even kingdom, depending on his own rank and that of his mother's kindred. At one extreme, among people of no particular political account, the *vasu* relationship and its prerogatives pertain only to the immediate principals involved: the sister's son, his mother's brothers, and the households of the latter. At the other extreme—say, the son of a Bau war king (Vunivalu) whose mother is the sister of the sacred king of Rewa (Roko Tui Dreketi)—the

25. Quain went on to indicate that the legendary cannibal dispositions of the Rokowaqa chief should not be taken literally, that the story was retailed with evident enjoyment of its shock value and as a boast of the ancestor's powers. But it clearly conveys another kind of truth about ruling chiefs.

Bauan is *vasu* to the kingdom of Rewa as such. He is a 'great *vasu*' (*vasu levu*) or a 'chiefly *vasu*' (*vasu turaga*). Here the *vasu* indeed holds a kinship title, a status relative to an entire corporate group. What makes it possible, structurally speaking, is the hierarchical encompassment of the group in the person of its chief—in this instance, the chiefly mother's brother—such that his personal relationships must implicate all the people who acknowledge his rule. The chief's sister's son is his people's *vasu*. Ratu Raivalita, son of the Rewa king's sister, was a '*vasu* to Rewa' (*vasu ki Rewa*), a 'great *vasu*' (*vasu levu*) whose claims to honor and property extended to all the places subject to his royal maternal uncle. By the same principle, a uterine nephew of great rank engages his own people in his *vasu* status. Not that they exercise *vasu* privileges themselves, but they participate in the alliance and its benefits. Hence the political values of chiefly marriages and, most particularly, the critical strategic interests in certain royal women.

High rank conjugates the *vasu* relation in another way, potentially extending it temporally, over the generations, as well as socially and spatially. *Vasu* status was in some cases heritable. Certain influential Bauans have been known to claim *vasu* privileges by descent—bilateral descent at that—from ancestors two or three generations past. Consider the following, written in 1913 by Ratu Joni Madraiwiwi, the son of a famous rebel chief closely related to Ratu Cakobau, justifying his rank against his father's old enemies in a letter to the British colonial government:

> My father [Ratu Mara Kapaiwai], having been born truly of the Vunivalu family, and also my mother having been the eldest child of the Vunivalu [Ratu Tānoa] and the Radini Levuka [the title of the war king's principal wife, Adi Talātoka of Cakaudrove], she [his mother] was the lady of highest rank of all the daughters of the Vunivalu of Bau and Bau lands, therefore I am *vasu* to Bau (the whole of it) and the whole of Bau lands. Therefore, my rank is the highest of us, the Vunivalu family, who are now living. . . . I am also a high chief in Cakaudrove because of my mother [the daughter of Adi Talāloka of Cakaudrove] and could make levies there indiscriminately at proper times . . . likewise [in] the whole of Lau on account of my father [the son of a woman belonging to the former ruling house of Lau, Cekena], and could make levies there indiscriminately, as my father used to do. (Ratu Joni Madraiwiwi FM/MS 629: 26 August 1913)[26]

26. I have only an English-language version of this letter. "Family" probably translates the Fijian *mataqali*, which I have been loosely calling "clan." "Lady" is no doubt *marama*, a 'chiefly woman.'

Ratu Madraiwiwi does not mention that his father, who indeed took property and women indiscriminately from the Lauans, often got into trouble with them because of it. For present purposes it is notable that Ratu Madraiwiwi could act as a *vasu* to Lau because his father was *vasu* there, and to Cakaudrove because his mother's mother was of the ruling family there.[27] But also worth remarking is the status he claimed as a native *vasu* (*vasu i taukei*), the offspring of a high-ranking woman of his own land.[28] Here is another structural value that enters significantly into practical political negotiations.[29]

A high-ranking member of the ruling group of Bau—the Vunivalu People, or the Tui Kaba clan—Ratu Madraiwiwi doubles his prestige as their sister's son as well, his mother being the Vunivalu's daughter. Ratu Madraiwiwi is thus a titular sister's son to his own father's people, with a prescribed right to lord it over them. He is a native *vasu,* although not the most honorable of that description. The most honorable would be one descended of former kings of the land, its ancient and true royalty. Hence the importance of the union of the stranger-king—"the chiefs come from overseas"—with the daughter of the indigenous ruler in the charters of kingdom formation. The practice is seen in other usurpations, as where a chiefly lineage is deposed by a *vasu* belonging to the same land, as well as in the rituals of surrender in war, marked by the gift to the victorious chief of a basket of earth and a daughter or daughters of his defeated chiefly adversary. We have seen this marital tactic practiced by Ratu Tānoa's house, which had usurped the war king title and assassinated the sacred king a

27. Ratu Joni Madraiwiwi himself married the daughter of a former ruler of Lau, Adi Litiana Maopa, thus repeating his grandfather's (father's father's) marital path and making his son, Ratu Sir Lala Sukuna, again *vasu* to Lau. That he acquired *vasu* rights through his mother's mother is another indication of an underlying four-class marriage system.

28. I translate *vasu i taukei* as 'native vasu'; more often it is translated as 'home *vasu.*' The highly charged term, *i taukei,* has meanings ranging over the English "indigenous," "first occupant," "authentic person of a place," "native to a place," "owner of a place," and so forth.

29. A. M. Hocart reported on, and was somewhat puzzled by, the superiority of the native *vasu* in Lau, particularly the uterine descendants of the Cekena people, the same former kings from whom Ratu Madraiwiwi claimed his standing there: "The great prestige of the home nephew (*vasu i taukei*) points to a time when the highest form of marriage for a nobleman was with a lady of the land. . . . It is difficult to understand why the son of a lady of a comparatively obscure clan like Thekena or a low caste village like Waitambu should be a greater man than he who could boast of a mother from Thakaundrove, one of the premier states of Fiji" (1929: 234). But Hocart was on target when he concluded that "obviously, it was not mere rank that counted but the combination of noble and land."

generation before. One of Ratu Tānoa's wives, Adi Savusavu, is variously said to have been a daughter of the old Nabaubau nobility or of the sacred Roko Tui Bau, and the offspring of this great woman (*marama levu*) was Ratu Cakobau himself. As native *vasu* to Bau by descent from its authentic rulers, Ratu Cakobau was thus completely identified with the kingdom, through his mother as well as his Vunivalu father—by invidious contrast, in the circumstances of 1845, to the great *vasu* of the Rewa enemy, Ratu Raivalita.

Finally, in the matter of structural permutations, the *vasu*'s powers are inflected by the respective political standing of his own and his maternal uncles' land. Where a woman marries down (or hypogamously), as a noble Bauan woman might be sent to marry the paramount of a subject village, the *vasu* status of her son is attenuated by the lowly rank of his father. Such a *vasu* would be an 'honorable man' (*tamata dokai*) in Bau, and his country might be protected against onerous tributes and depredations, but he could not have the material prerogatives or the political influence of the *vasu* in the inverse situation. In the inverse situation, where the woman marries up (hypergamously), as a woman from a subject land taken to wife by a high Bauan chief, she is likely to give birth to a sister's son who is something of a monster, so far as the exercise of his *vasu* rights. These are the sort of young chiefs who go about terrorizing their maternal kinsmen, making excessive demands on their property and labor. Bau and Rewa were particularly known for such tyrannical *vasu*.[30] In Cakaudrove, sons and brothers of the king were wont to live in subject lands where they were *vasu*, and virtually take them over.[31] Early in the colonial period, at the Council of Chiefs instituted by the British government, one member accounted for the mischief Whitemen were making in Fiji by supposing they must be "Vasus to Heaven" (Council of Chiefs, *Proceedings*, 1876: 14).[32]

30. In 1840 one of Lieutenant Wilkes's ships captured Ro Veidovi, paternal half-brother of the Rewa king, for having masterminded an attack on the crew of an American vessel at Kadavu a few years earlier (see below). Later, when visiting Kadavu, Wilkes was told by a local chief "that the people of Kantavu [*sic*] were glad he [Ro Veidovi] had been taken away, for he was continually making exactions on them for all kinds of articles, under his authority of vasu" (1845, 3:289).

31. Ratu Lewenilovo, a son of the Cakaudrove paramount (Tui Cakau) and great *vasu* to the subject land of Bouma, went to live there for a period in the 1840s because of a conflict with his father. Reverend Hunt observed that Ratu Lewenilovo "has as much power perhaps at Bouma as the king has at Somosomo [the capital of Cakaudrove]" (*J:* 8 February 1842).

32. Another pragmatic variation in *vasu* standing is occasioned by the customary polygyny of title-holding chiefs and the equally common indeterminacy of succession among

Vasu and the Marital Politics of Bau

Given the significance of the *vasu* system, marital strategies were the continuation of war and peace by other means. This was especially so in Bau, because of its distinctive combination of poverty and power (see above, chapter 1). I have heard it said of Bau that chiefly women were its main export. In truth, the best known Bauan valuables (*i yau*) were highly decorated bridal skirts, but insofar as these would accompany out-marrying daughters and sisters, the implication is similar. Nor would it violate Fijian categories to speak of ranking women in this way. On the contrary, virgin or "raw women" along with human sacrificial victims or "cooked men," together with sperm whale teeth, were so many commutable 'great things' (*ka levu*), the highest of Fijian values (M. Sahlins 1983). One might say, in a Radcliffe-Brownian vein, that their extraordinary value lay precisely in their powers of organizing and reorganizing society: in the alliances they made and unmade, the assassinations and the successions, the wars and the submissions. And then for Bau, always busy in such affairs, there were the added material problems of supporting its large population and finding the wherewithal of its numerous politico-ritual transactions (see above, chapter 1). For *vasu* relations were of value, too, in such provisioning. Although the spectacular prerogatives of the uterine nephew involved seizing canoes, pigs, or other property of his mother's people, more important were the long-term claims that could be made on their land, labor, and produce. Bau, as we have seen, thrived on goods flowing in from all over the Koro Sea and the adjacent Viti Levu mainland, and some significant part of the traffic was based on ancient and recent *vasu* connections. This means that women were coming into Bau, to produce sister's sons to other lands, as well as going out as "great things."

How the strategic decisions of marriage were being made in Bau is not easy to know. Clearly the palavers were proceeding in two different spheres: among ranking men in the kava circles of temples, men's houses, and chiefs' houses; and in the domestic sphere, where chiefly women had powerful voices, and the relations among them, as well as between them and their husbands, could decide the issue. In this connection, the historical record highlights two dyads functioning respectively in these two spheres: in the

---

their sons by different mothers. While the father is alive, the sons of many of his daughters may enjoy *vasu* status to his house. But unless the full brother of any given daughter succeeds their father, the *vasu* loses some privilege, if not also status, as his mother's brother has been excluded from the title, a fate that may well extend to the latter's direct descendants (see fig. 3.1). This sort of change has played a role in historic episodes we will be considering.

larger arena, the control of the king's herald over the unions of his daughters; and in polygynous households, the influence of noble mothers on the careers of their chiefly sons. It is possible to interpret these common references in the literature as indicating the normal (unmarked) cases, ignoring the influence of the royal heralds on the marriages of the ruler's sons and of royal wives on their daughters' unions. What they contrastively single out are the different immediate interests bound up in sons' and daughters' marriages. At stake in royal daughters are the interests of their father's land, the distribution of *vasu* claims upon it—about which one ought to be politically canny and a bit defensive. But the royal wives' involvement in their respective sons' conquests, marital and otherwise, affects the fortunes of their own natal lands, the sons' maternal kinsmen. It is good to have a *vasu* in power in a powerful kingdom.

In Bau, the 'face-of-the-land' (*matanivanua*) or royal herald, titled the Tunitoga, was the adviser, executive, and master of ceremonies of the war king, the Vunivalu; the sacred Roko Tui Bau had his own such aide, the Masau. Called 'face-of-the-land-in-the-house' (*matanivanua e vale*), by contrast to the outside heralds who represented the people with respect to the king on the ceremonial ground of the town, these inside men were in effect priests of the living gods, the counterpart of the priests who served the invisible gods in their abodes, the temples (Hocart 1913).[33] Giving royal women in marriage to the chiefs of other lands was an aspect of their ritual offices (Rabuku 1911: 157). Based on his experience in Bau, Rev. Joseph Waterhouse said that the great herald, the Tunitoga, was the "natural guardian" of all the daughters of the king and chiefs; that he "disposed absolutely" of them; that proposals of marriage came first to him; that his will on these matters was superior to the parents' and his decision final (1866: 15). One need not take the reverend's word for gospel on this. It is clear that men of the power, will, and acumen of Ratu Tānoa and Ratu Cakobau knew how to make their own moves with the women under their control: witness Ratu Cakobau's gift of a sister to the Lasakau chief Ratu Gavidi for betraying Ratu Raivalita. It is also clear that the Vunivalu's herald did not dispose of the daughters of many chiefly houses of Bau; they had been making their own alliances with some of the same outside peoples for generations. Still, the calculated giving of chiefly women in marriage, especially royal women, was institutionally and explicitly a matter of state interest.

Several tactical patterns were common in Bau. Much favored was the

33. So the inside face-of-the-land is sometimes designated 'priest-herald,' *bete matanivanua* (Rokowaqa 1926).

offer of a royal woman to one of the houses—in the craftiest case, to the junior one—competing for the rule of another land, or within Bau, competing for control of an important clan. As a promise of power, implying a future for the wife-receivers as *vasu* of Bau, the alliance could well secure the chiefship for them—and a client chief for the Bau king. Ratu Cakobau was notorious for this sort of marital politics, whether it involved taking greater purchase on an already subject place, "turning" the allies (*bati*) of Rewa or Verata to Bau, or subverting the allegiance of Bauan subjects from the Roko Tui Bau to himself. The chiefs of the inland fighting allies (*bati*) of the principal Fijian kingdoms were notable for an independence that reflected their usual status as the *vasu* to great nobility—and their willingness to change sides for a more advantageous offer of a chiefly woman from an enemy kingdom. The same sister that Ratu Cakobau gave the Lasakau chief Ratu Gavidi in the Ratu Raivalita affair had previously been offered to the chief of an important Rewan ally in the Delta, Tui Nakelo (as a wife for the latter's son), in a successful attempt to induce him to come over to the Bauan side. In the event, however, the Nakelo alliance was again reversed in favor of Rewa when the royal woman was accorded instead to Ratu Gavidi (Wallis 1851: 167–68, 211, 245). It is as if Ratu Cakobau did not have control of enough Bauan great women to cover all his political intrigues. Here is how those intrigues worked, as viewed from the other side by a well-informed notable from the land of Namata, a warrior-ally (*bati*) of Bau: "If our land is under Bau, and if there are senior noblemen here who are *vasu* to various other foreign lands, they will not be installed as Chiefs of the Land. Only those who are *vasu* to Bau are installed; although they may be juniors, still they will drink the sacred kava of installation" (Rabuku 1911: 155; cf. Hocart 1970a: 105–6).[34]

The reverse tactic of taking ranking women from other lands as wives for Bau chiefs was also highly recommended, not only because it would make the already powerful Bauan houses *vasu* to those lands, but because the polygynous habits of ruling chiefs allowed them to acquire this advantage in a number of different places. Not to suppose that Bau ruling chiefs, whom the missionaries and other *Papalagi* castigated with having wives by

34. An early twentieth-century account by a member of the Bau Vunivalu group, Ratu Etuate Wainiu, was meant to demonstrate the extent of Bau's dominion to the British colonial administration: "Chiefly women [*marama*] were regularly given from Bau to marry into Naitasiri and Suva. Its meaning was that Bau would take hold of the land and people, that they would be obedient to [i.e., 'listen to,' *vakarorogo*] us. Those whose mothers came from Bau are still living in both these lands today. They are the chiefs in both these lands today, on account of their *vasu* connection to Bau" (E. Wainiu CSO MP 259/1910).

the score, could expect to sire *vasu* in proportion. Only those women who were formally married (*vakabau*), with the appropriate proceedings and transactions, could bear legitimate sons and recognized uterine nephews. Sexual prowess was indeed a hallmark of Fijian chiefliness—a quality consistent not only with the chiefly gift of prosperity, but with the original transmission of the land's reproductive powers to the chiefly *vasu*. Yet most of the so-called wives of great men were women of lesser rank with something of the status of concubines and/or domestic servants. Even so, most Bauan traditions and genealogies credit Ratu Tānoa with nine authentic, chiefly wives who bore him sons. The women's homelands were widely distributed: two from Bau proper; two from Bauan subject lands in the Koro Sea islands (Koro and Sawaieke, Gau); two from Cakaudrove; one from the old noble kingdom of Vuna in Taveuni Island (latterly dominated by Cakaudrove); one from the Nakorotubu kingdom on the northeast coast of Viti Levu; and one from Rewa, Adi Qereitoga the mother of Ratu Raivalita. Besides, collateral lines of the war king's clan (Tui Kaba) repeatedly acquired wives from ranking houses of Lau, Nairai Island, and Cakaudrove, and formerly also from Verata. Such matrimonial cosmopolitanism contrasted radically with the endogamous practices of ordinary Fijians, who generally married within their own lands if not their own villages. But it would be particularly politic for the arriviste war kings of Bau to cast their marital net widely abroad as well as deeply at home: abroad, in order to recuperate the alliances made by their predecessors; at home, in order to recuperate their predecessors by marrying their daughters—as in the case of Ratu Cakobau, whose principal wife as well as whose mother came from the former greats of Bau.

Wife-taking and *vasu*-making were often one-way in Bau's favor when the women came from lesser countries. The flow itself could be taken as a sign of submission. W. T. Pritchard, British consul in Fiji in the late 1850s and early 1860s, relates an incident in which a Lau notable presumptuously declared, in Ratu Cakobau's presence, that he was not subject to Bau. But the Lauan had to back down when Ratu Cakobau asked, "Then how came so many of your Lakeba ladies [*marama*] to Bau? Were they not brought as tribute to our chiefs, and hence [the number of] our *vasu ki* Lakeba [*vasu* to Lakeba]?" (Pritchard 1968: 330). The implication of tribute to a superior, however, disappears in the largely reciprocal movements of royal women between Bau and the greatest of other Fijian kingdoms, Rewa and Cakaudrove. A dense network of alliances connected the houses of current and former dynasties of Bau, especially the war kings (Vunivalu), with the current and former kings of Rewa. The effect was that virtually any ruler or would-be ruler of either kingdom could claim to be the *vasu* of the other. Native *vasu* of Bau, Ratu Cakobau was exceptional in this regard, but his father was a *vasu* to Rewa, whose king, a *vasu* to Bau, was married to Ratu Tānoa's daughter, making his children *vasu* to Bau (fig. 3.3).

The intricate system of unions that brought women from near and far into Bau as the wives of its great men thus represented—and through their sons, played out—the larger political relations and forces of eastern Fiji. One could practically read the shifting fortunes of various countries by the provenances of in-marrying women in the genealogies of Bau and the local careers of their sons.

Yet what is an alliance by marriage between chiefly groups of different lands is also a division among chiefs of the same land. The noble women taken into Bau will, if they bear sons, differentiate the ruling houses by their respective matrilateral affiliations, the mothers' brothers upon whom their sons (as *vasu*) can draw support. Conversely, these in-marrying noble women, continuing to represent their natal groups—and as "sacred blood," forming new lines attached to that group—thus relay the fortunes of their brothers' lands to the chances of their sons in the hypercompetitive arena of Bauan politics. So would Rewa's fate in the war with Bau ride on the machinations of their *vasu* Ratu Raivalita. This insertion of greater political issues into the relations between brothers or kindred houses could only add to the ferocity of their conflicts. It also made certain women key players in the fate of countries. As daughters, they may have been sent away in marriage without their consent and for reasons of state that did not directly concern them or their happiness. But as wives and as mothers, they found themselves in the midst of a political fray in which they were contending parties, with their own interests and means of affecting the outcome.

Vasu and Fratricidal Strife

Death attended Fijian *vasu* relations in several forms. It might only be in the unsubstantiated reports that women sent from certain countries as wives to Bauan nobility were instructed to procure abortions so that their homelands would not have Bauan *vasu* to tyrannize them. The Macuata people took it as proof of that policy that "there never has been a great *vasu* to Mathuata in Bau" (Pritchard 1968: 330). The Lakeba people were indeed tyrannized by a great *vasu* from Bau in the mid-nineteenth century, Ratu Mara Kapaiwai, but that did not dim their contradictory memories of a Lau chief named "Hides Lakeba" (*Sa Vuni Lakeba*) after "the custom of Lakeban ladies married to Bau to procure abortions so as not to have sisters' sons; they hid Lakeba from the Bau people who could use the sister's son to plunder Lau" (Hocart *WI:* 281). Basil Thomson said it was a general rule in Fiji, and in Bau most particularly, to send professional abortionists with every chiefly woman who married out, along with instructions to produce miscarriages, so that they would not have uterine nephews making demands on them (1908: 221). It is clear from genealogies of Bau and other lands with which Bauans have intermarried that such reports were exaggerated, if ever they were true at all. Like many modern "urban myths," their truth value lies rather in stretching certain structural dispositions to the point of antisociality or criminality, and so revealing certain contradictions in the normal order. What is signified in these abortion stories is the transgressive side of the *vasu* relationship and its dangers to the mother's people.

However, the structurally inverse death, the killing of the widowed mother that legitimates the *vasu* prerogatives of her son, is amply witnessed, with horror, in the nineteenth-century texts of missionaries and other *Papalagi.* The suttee-like strangulation of the wives of a deceased chief by their natal kinsmen, preferably their own brothers, had several values, but preservation of the *vasu* relationships—which might otherwise be compromised by a widow's remarriage—was prominent among them (Williams and Calvert 1859: 158). The astute beachcomber John Jackson ("Cannibal Jack") thought that fixing the *vasu*'s rights could well be the main reason for strangling widows, as "it is taken for a certain proof that [their] children are legitimate, and claim their rights as *vasu* to the places their deceased mothers belonged" (1853: 448). Just so, at the untimely death of one of the sons of the Cakaudrove king, his brother had only the widows with children strangled, "because he knew that would be a means of his nephews' vasuing property, and supplying him with an inexhaustible store of goods" (ibid.).

Considered in this context, the fratricidal strife of Ratu Raivalita and Ratu Cakobau was not extraordinary—that is, given that *vasu* relations have always been, in a literal sense, deadly serious.[35] Deadly serious, again, because the fate of their respective mothers' countries was at stake in their contention. "These king's brothers," observed Cannibal Jack, "are generally at the head of all mischief which is so frequently happening at all the

35. "Not infrequently . . . jealousies and intrigues between the sons of one father, by different mothers of high rank, led to intervention by interested kingdoms and war. Many of the wars of historical times, and the bitterest of them, were civil wars, and nothing more than family feuds on a large scale" (Derrick 1950: 57).

islands, and at all parts of the islands, and often simultaneously, so that the whole of the country, or rather its inhabitants are stirred up into a perpetual turmoil, the complications of which are almost impossible to conceive" (Diapea 1928: 102). Jackson was speaking most immediately of Lau, but he probably knew of the similar fraternal battles royal in Rewa, Bau, Cakaudrove, and Macuata, among others. Conflicts between full brothers were the minority of such affairs, but they could be disruptive enough. One was going on for years in Rewa just before the great war with Bau, pitting the king Ro Kania against the flamboyant and charismatic Ratu Qaraniqio. Before they were finally reconciled, their quarrel was marked by incidents known also to the strife between half-brothers: adultery between the ambitious younger brother and one of the king's wives, and, partly in consequence, the banishment or self-imposed exile of the younger brother—in the case of Ratu Qaraniqio, to Bau, where he found refuge for a period with his mother's people.

A recurrent tactic in these fraternal conflicts, the adultery of a king's wife with a fraternal rival was *lèse-majesté* not only as an insult to the ruler's masculinity and reproductive powers, but as a usurpation of his marital alliances. However, everything suggests that the royal women involved took an active part in these subversive affairs. Whatever the personal attractions, some among the king's several wives could always better their interests—which is also to say, the interests of their brothers and sons—by forming a liaison with their royal husband's competitors. In the instance at hand, we do not know which of the Rewa king's wives had an affair with his younger brother. But it is known that his principal wife, Adi Qoliwasawasa, who "to speak in plain terms wears the breeches," served her husband with a wicked tongue and, by report, a string of her own lovers (Osborn *J:* 31 January–25 February 1834). Considered a great beauty by European visitors of the 1830s and 1840s, Adi Qoliwasawasa was said to have a certain taste also for "foreign luxury" (Jackson 1853: 467–68). Clearly, royal wives could play the critical role in the fraternal struggles for the kingship.[36]

Their role could be decisive in advancing the chances of their own sons for their husband's title. Quarrels among the co-wives of royal households— as, in recent times, among the wives of brothers in extended fam-

36. On Adi Qoliwasawasa, see also Eagleston (*UD,* 2:213–14) and Wallis (1851: 152). Cannibal Jack speaks of her sharp tongue: "'Kaisi mata vaka puaka' (you pig-faced slave), such expressions being quite common, and especially with her to her spouse, who, although king, was much inferior in birth and appearance to Qoliwasawasa, the queen. He was much older than she" (Jackson 1853: 467).

ilies—make up a recurrent theme of Fijian ethnography. The possibilities of dispute were only exacerbated by the indeterminacies of succession. True that one of the wives of a king was installed in the official title that went with his own. But it seems that even her title could be given to another; and in any case nothing guaranteed that her sons would take precedence in inheritance over the sons of other royal wives.[37] It is commonly remarked (in *Papalagi* sources) that rank among paternal half-brothers depended on the rank of their mothers. But often the relative status of these women would be difficult to determine, insofar as they came from different lands. In practice, much depended on the current power of the wife's natal land and its strategic value to her husband's. And then, something depended as well on favor in the king's eye, his personal preferences among his wives, which may or may not have reflected their political values. Here was a structural space for fateful contingencies.

Beginning around 1820 and lasting into the time of the Polynesian War, the ruling Roko Tui Dreketi title of Rewa was up for grabs among the sons of a famous king, Ro Tabaiwalu. Their mutual slaughter did not spare their father either, and their hostility carried on to the stasis of 1844–45 that saw one of the surviving brothers and his partisans defect to the oncoming Bauan enemy.[38] Because of its carnage, this conflict in the ruling house of Rewa got a lot of ink in the chronicles of European visitors, but it was not different in character from the royal fratricides and parricides that Fijian tradition relates of Lau and Bau of a generation or two earlier (Cross in Lyth *TFR,* 1:121–23; Hocart 1929; Reid 1990). The assassination plot of Ratu Raivalita may likewise be taken as an instance of this recurrent pattern. Hence the well-documented Rewa case is worth examining here for its implications for the analogous Bauan struggle.

37. In 1840 a Bau woman, a daughter of Ratu Tānoa, was for political reasons married to the old king (Tui Cakau) of Cakaudrove and given the royal consort title of Radi Cakau. Two months later, however, when relations with Bau worsened, the woman was dumped by the Cakaudrove king (Lyth *J:* 25 September, 30 November 1840).

38. The principal historical sources for the Rewan regicides are the following: Calvert (*J:* 28 June 1855); Cary (1972: 33–34); Eagleston (Log *Emerald:* 15 May 1834; *UD,* 2:14–15); Hudson (*J:* 22 May 1840); Pickering (*J:* 19, 21 May 1840); Reynolds (*Le:* 21 September 1840); Sinclair (*J:* 15 January 1840); Waterhouse (1866: 36–42); Wilkes (1845, 1:131–34); Williams (*MN:* 120–22); Williams and Calvert (1859: 103–4). The Wilkes expedition reports of 1840 are the most detailed, especially Hudson's, which was based on accounts supplied by the Rewan chief Ro Cokānauto and Paddy O'Connell, the longtime henchman of Rewan kings, as well as on information gathered by the ethnographer Horatio Hale, whose own Fijian notes unfortunately did not survive. Wilkes's people as well as the missionaries and others no doubt had additional local sources, but they are unnamed.

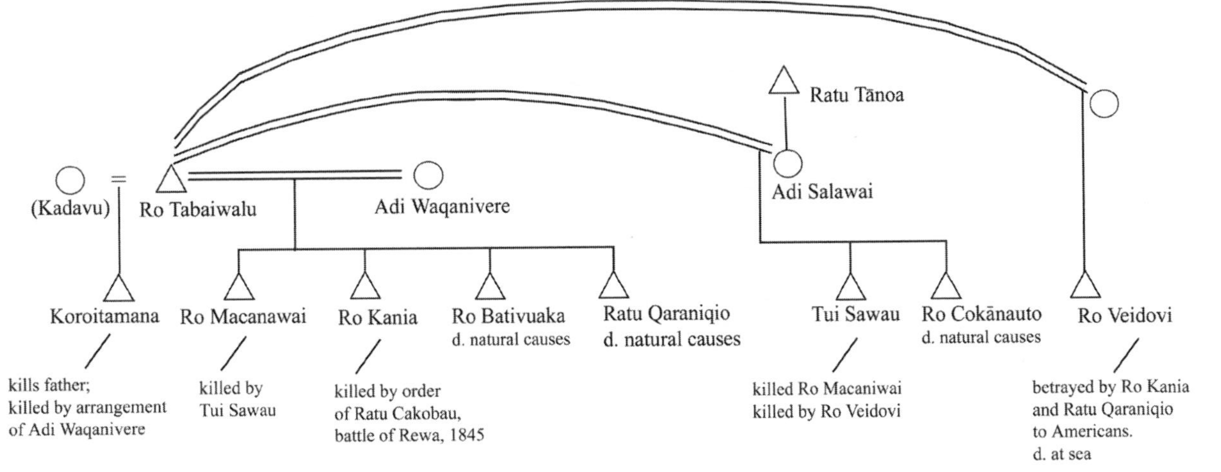

Ratu Tānoa
(Kadavu)
Ro Tabaiwalu
Adi Waqanivere
Adi Salawai
Koroitamana
Ro Macanawai
Ro Kania
Ro Bativuaka
d. natural causes
Ratu Qaraniqio
d. natural causes
Tui Sawau
Ro Cokānauto
d. natural causes
Ro Veidovi
kills father;
killed by arrangement
of Adi Waqanivere
killed by
Tui Sawau
killed by order
of Ratu Cakobau,
battle of Rewa, 1845
killed Ro Macaniwai
killed by Ro Veidovi
betrayed by Ro Kania
and Ratu Qaraniqio
to Americans.
d. at sea

3.5 Murder in high Rewan places

The relationships among the main Rewan royals are indicated in the accompanying genealogy (fig. 3.5).

In or about the year 1820 one Koroitamana, the oldest son of the Rewa king Ro Tabaiwalu by a Kadavu woman (name unknown), thus a *vasu* to that place, clubbed his father to death. By all indications, Koroitamana's diminishing chances of succeeding to the paramount kingship, the Roko Tui Dreketi title, was a motive of the parricide, perhaps *the* motive. Though his mother was apparently the first among the king's wives, she was now certainly second to another: Adi Waqanivere (a.k.a. Adi Waqaniveno), a daughter of the old royalty of Bau (Nabaubau/Batitobe). Adi Waqanivere was formally Rewa's queen (Radi Dreketi) and the mother of four of Ro Tabaivalu's sons.[39] In the interest of her own sons, Adi Waqanivere poisoned her husband's mind against Koroitamana, although as is common in such cases, the *vasu* to Kadavu is said to have given his father cause enough for anger by committing adultery with one of his other wives—for which she was killed. A version preserved in Fijian chant has Koroitamana driven from place to place because of the quarrel with his father—from Ra to Bau to Kadavu—until he was suffered to return to Rewa (Waterhouse 1866: 39). Here, however, he would be the lesser man to Ro Macanawai, the first son of Adi Waqanivere and now the heir-apparent. Yet killing his father did not reverse the situation. By a stratagem, Ro Macanawai's mother concealed the king's death for several days, meanwhile giving it out that he wanted Koroitamana's life. Some whale teeth presented to certain chiefly parties procured the deed.[40] Now Ro Macanawai was king: at least for a short while, until his skull was crushed by the club of another half-brother,

39. Ro Tabaivalu had many wives, as Captain Hudson learned, the chief of whom was from Bau, "from the family that reigned there before the father of Tānoa gained the kingdom" (Hudson *J:* 22 May 1840). That Adi Waqanivere's sons were *vasu* to the old nobility of Bau and positioned to succeed in Rewa helps explain the report (of years later) that Koroitamana's assassination of the Rewa king was done "under the sanction of Naulivou, the Vunivalu of Bau, Ratu Tānoa's older brother" (Calvert *J:* 28 June 1855). For the old Bauan nobility were the enemies of this Vunivalu. Presumably, if Koroitamana's coup had been pulled off, the Bau *vasu* would not have inherited the throne. Another fateful contingency that changed the course of Fijian history.

40. Alternative versions have Koroitamana killed in Rewa, or else fleeing north to the Rewan warrior land of Tokatoka, where his attempt to raise war against Rewa was denied and he was clubbed instead—but not yet dead. Wounded, he fled again to Nakelo, another Rewan ally (*bati*), where he was finally killed.

Another issue on which there are diverse traditions is whether Ro Tabaivalu died immediately and his wife successfully concealed the fact for eight days—which is the usual story—or whether he lingered for that period before dying.

Tui Sawau. Tui Sawau was also a *vasu* to Bau, but to the house of the current war king, not, as his fraternal victim was, to the old Bauan nobility. (The rivalry between these royal houses of Bau no doubt contributed to the antagonism between their respective uterine nephews in Rewa.) Following Ro Macanawai's death, his mother Adi Waqanivere and the surviving brothers fled to Bau, leaving Tui Sawau to rule Rewa. Which he did until 1828, when he was shot and killed by another half-brother, Ro Veidovi, whose mother was again from Kadavu. Ro Veidovi is said to have been put up to the deed by the Adi Waqanivere crowd in Bau by means of a large bribe. Certainly they profited from the occasion by returning to Rewa, where the oldest brother, Ro Kania, now became Roko Tui Dreketi. That was the end of outright fratricide, parricide, and regicide. Yet the head that wore the Rewa crown was still uneasy, as the brotherly hostilities continued in other ways.

In 1840 Capt. W. L. Hudson of the U.S. Exploring Expedition, using the friendly services of the Rewa king Ro Kania and his brother Ratu Qaraniqio, hunted down and captured their half-brother Ro Veidovi, the same who had shot their rival Tui Sawau twelve years earlier (plate 4). The Americans wanted Ro Veidovi for an attack on the crew of the Salem brig *Chas. Doggett* off Kadavu in 1834, killing ten men—although according to some, the plot had been concocted with Ratu Qaraniqio, and according to others, with Ro Kania himself.[41] Put in chains aboard the U.S. *Peacock,* Ro Veidovi was summarily judged guilty, and died on his way to America as a prisoner. It appears his royal brothers were quite content to be rid of Ro Veidovi. Some years earlier the American *bêche-de-mer* trader John Eagleston had evidence of such fraternal feeling when he tried to capture Ro Veidovi for his part in the *Chas. Doggett* killings. For it was Ro Kania who informed on Ro Veidovi and his alleged accomplice, a certain

41. Lieutenant Wilkes chose to believe the testimony, as of one James Magoon of the *Chas. Doggett,* that Ro Veidovi was exclusively to blame, but other members of the U.S. Exploring Expedition gathered embarrassing evidence that the Rewa royals, with whom Wilkes had good relations, were in on the massacre. Mr. Emmons, for example, explicitly countered Magoon's testimony that Ro Veidovi was the prime mover: "There is no doubt in my mind from the unvarnished statement of an artless & honest Wahoo [Oahu] man, who was at the time living with the king's brother at Rewa, & understood the Feegee language well, that the King of Rewa, Tu-in-drekete, originated the plan, & selected Bendova [Ro Veidovi] to carry out his designs" (*J:* 21 June 1840). Much closer to the time of the event, George Cheever of the *Emerald* (Capt. John Eagleston) came to the same conclusion about Ro Kania's involvement (*J:* 14 May 1834).

Manilla-man (cf. Clunie 1984).[42] The same two were betrayed by still another half-brother, Ro Cokānauto ("Phillips"), as plotting to take Captain Eagleston's own ship. From all this, Captain Eagleston judged that Ro Veidovi's brothers, "bearing him no good will, could I quietly trap the devil, would, for a fine whale's tooth, and gladly, let him pass to the other side" (*UD,* 2:14).

Ro Veidovi escaped from Captain Eagleston's trap in 1834, but not from Captain Hudson's in 1840—thanks to Ratu Qaraniqio's efforts on the Americans' behalf. First holding the Rewa king and Ratu Qaraniqio hostage on the *Peacock,* Captain Hudson then deputed the latter to bring Ro Veidovi to the ship. Ratu Qaraniqio soon delivered. The existing state of animosities and amities among the long-struggling Rewan brothers had given the Americans some confidence that Ratu Qaraniqio would be willing to turn in Ro Veidovi. The only problem, as Lieutenant Reynolds said, "was whether the victim would be living or dead" (*Le:* 21 September 1840). Ro Veidovi at this time was a partisan of Ro Cokānauto and an enemy of Ratu Qaraniqio, even though Ro Veidovi had shot Tui Sawau, Ro Cokānauto's full brother, in the latter's own house. As the Americans understood it, Ratu Qaraniqio's delivery of Ro Veidovi to captivity was a well-timed move, for "Veidovi had always been his rival" and the only brother who backed Ro Cokānauto (Wilkes 1845, 3:129, 136). Immediately thereafter, Ratu Qaraniqio seized Ro Veidovi's property, including his wives. "He is a fine-looking man," Charles Pickering commented of Ratu Qaraniqio, "but there is something in the expression of his countenance that would stamp him as a rascal anywhere, and it is said that we could not have done him a greater favor than to capture his brother" (*J:* 15 June 1840).

That left only Ro Cokānauto as the last of the paternal half-brothers, sons of Ro Tabaivalu, to challenge the power of Ro Kania and Ratu Qaraniqio. He was, moreover, the *vasu* to Ratu Tānoa and his people, whereas his fraternal rivals were *vasu* to the old Bauan nobility of Nabaubau, enemies to Ratu Tānoa. And Ro Cokānauto had his ambitions. "Oh yes . . . me would like to be King!" he told Mr. Pickering. "Me would like to walk

42. "Manilla men" were Spanish-speaking, Malay and mestizo denizens of the outskirts of Manilla recruited as crews of some vessels in the early *bêche-de-mer* trade—though they had an unsavory reputation as very rough customers among the Yankee traders. A mutiny of the Manilla brig *Laurice* in 1825, in which the officers were murdered, resulted in a number of Manilla men settling in Fiji among important chiefs. The Manilla man or men mentioned in the present account, notably one "Battan," were likely survivors of the *Laurice* (Clunie 1984).

about & direct this thing & that thing to be done" (*J:* 19 May 1840). In 1844 or 1845, he half got his wish. Ratu Tānoa had him installed as the Roko Tui Dreketi in the Rewan town of Nukui after he had defected to Bau's side—though Ro Kania was still reigning under that title in the capital.[43] Ro Cokānauto died in 1851—of dysentery and delirium tremens—by which time Ro Kania was also dead and Ratu Qaraniqio alone was carrying on the war with Bau.

THE PREHISTORY OF THE ASSASSINATION

The hostility between Ratu Raivalita and Ratu Cakobau was not just personal. Or rather, their personal animosity was driven by the dynamics of the larger political situation, the changing relations of Bau and Rewa, in which they had specific roles by virtue of their respective *vasu* relations to the two kingdoms. Briefly the story is this. The coup of 1832–37 that deposed Ratu Tānoa as Vunivalu in different ways strengthened the political position of the two young Bauan chiefs. Ratu Raivalita, the *vasu* to Rewa, benefited because Ratu Tānoa relied critically on Rewan support to restore him to power, a condition that also valorized the status of Ratu Raivalita's mother Adi Qereitoga, sister of the Rewa king. Meanwhile, as *vasu* to Bau, Ratu Cakobau was able to remain on the island and organize an uprising against the chiefs who had deposed Ratu Tānoa—which restored his father to the *de jure* status of war king while giving him the *de facto* power. These two politics of Ratu Tānoa's return to Bau were complementary, for not only did the Rewans afford him sanctuary in the last years of his exile, they also materially subsidized the overthrow of the rebels in Bau. In the years immediately following the restoration, Ratu Cakobau's political stock climbed dramatically, as he undertook the wars that allowed Bau to regain the ascendancy in Fiji that had been undermined during the coup. In the early 1840s, however, Bau's successes, together with continuing conflicts among the Rewan royalty, brought the two kingdoms into opposition and finally into all-out war. That did Ratu Raivalita no good with regard to his increasingly powerful brother, Ratu Cakobau, the *vasu* to Bau. The deteri-

43. Ro Cokānauto had accurately predicted his ascension to the kingship in 1840, as reported by Capt. Sir Edward Belcher on a visit to Fiji. Speaking of the Rewa royals: "The present king [Ro Kania], who is considered a very weak-minded man, and despised by his brothers, succeeded his father, who, according to custom was murdered to make room for him [*sic*]. It is not improbable that his death will shortly enable one of the remaining brothers to succeed him. Indeed Phillips [Ro Cokānauto] said in his presence, 'I shall be king in four years'" (Belcher 1843: 46; was Cokānauto speaking English?).

orating relations between Bau and Rewa also put the two brothers on a collision course.

Relations between Bau and Rewa were better at the beginning of Ratu Tānoa's reign. His ascension to the Vunivalu title in 1829 improved relations with Rewa—to an extent that irritated his enemies in Bau and played a part in the coup d'état of 1832. Ratu Tānoa was himself a *vasu* to Rewa: his mother, Roko Lewasau, was the daughter of a former Roko Tui Dreketi, apparently of a different house than Ro Kania et al. This connection was solidified by his marriage to Adi Qereitoga around 1820, and by the regard he thenceforth showed her. Adi Qereitoga was a full sister of the king Ro Kania by one account (Wallis 1851: 152), a half-sister by a different mother according to another (Eagleston *UD,* 1:380–81). She was, accordingly, a woman of very high standing in Rewa: second only to the king and queen, "and treated with as much respect," said the trader Warren Osborn, who in 1835 saw her living there "in great state," with numerous attendants and a large house of her own (*J:* 31 January–25 February 1835).[44] Contemporary documents variously refer to Adi Qereitoga's position in Bau as "the Queen," "the Head Queen," or again as the "chief wife," "principal wife" or "favorite wife" of Ratu Tānoa.[45] Technically, however, she was not the "Head Queen" (Radini Levuka). That title was held by another of Ratu Tānoa's wives, Adi Talātoka, a daughter of the Cakaudrove king (Tui Cakau), who was previously married to Ratu Tānoa's brother and predecessor, Ratu Naulivou.[46] Adi Qereitoga, however, may have held the sec-

44. Adi Qereitoga had fled to Rewa during the exile of Ratu Tānoa from Bau. This is when Osborn saw her there, along with Ratu Raivalita. In all probability, Adi Qereitoga also had her own house in Bau, that is, the house called "Tarakaibau" (or "Taranikaibau"), which was originally built for Ratu Tānoa's mother, Roko Lewasau, also from Rewa, and was by some accounts the house of Ratu Raivalita (TR/EB [Tailevu, Bau], testimony of Aisea Komaitai; Toganivalu *TkB:* i, 5). Others say Ratu Raivalita's house was "Naisogolaca," which I believe more likely.

45. Diverse characterizations of Adi Qereitoga's matrimonial status may be found in Eagleston (*UD,* 1:380–81, 2:[23 January 1835]; Log *Emerald:* 11 May 1834); Osborn (*J:* 31 January–25 February 1835); Wallis (1851: 53); Williams and Calvert (1859: 433); (*WMMS/L,* Hunt to Lyth: 7 January 1843). That Adi Qereitoga may have held the second, Radini Kaba title is suggested by the name by which she was known in later life, after her fall from grace in Bau: *Koya na malo,* usually an abbreviation of *Koya na malasivo,* 'She of the retired loin cloth,' referring to chiefs who have retired from titled offices. On the possibility of dividing the titles of the Vunivalu's consort among different ranking women, see Hocart (*HF:* 344).

46. Adi Talātoka was not the titular queen, Radini Levuka, in Ratu Naulivou's time. Adi Kawanawere was; she was strangled at Ratu Naulivou's death (Lyth *RC:* 26). It is likely that Adi Talātoka was installed in the title together with Ratu Tānoa's investiture c. 1833 as Tui Levuka by the Levuka people in Lakeba, Lau (Twyning 1996: 88–90). The original 'own-

ond of the Bau royal consort titles (Radini Kaba). And despite that she was in the Whitemen's eyes "without any show of nature's fine gifts," she was certainly highly regarded and preferentially treated by Ratu Tānoa. She could well be described as his "favorite wife"—so long as Rewa remained his favored ally.

Ratu Tānoa was exchanging favor with Rewa from well before the coup—as noted, that was one of the complaints against him in Bau. Most probably he was in (or led) the party of Bauans that William Cary accompanied to a feast in Rewa in May 1831. Even if the Rewans only gave their visitors half the thousand pigs that Cary said they laid on, the occasion would have been grand indeed by Fijian standards (Cary 1972: 70). Grand, too, was the double canoe given the next year by Ratu Tānoa to his wife's brother, the Rewa king. Captain Eagleston reckoned it was probably the largest canoe in the Pacific Ocean: some 105 feet in the larger hull with a mast of 63 feet, yards of 83 feet, and a 22-foot platform; it had taken seven years to build and could carry several hundred men, "the natives say 700" (Eagleston *UD,* 1:392). The resentment incited by such exchanges among certain factions in Bau—not so much, perhaps, because of the diversion of Bauan resources, but because of Rewa's support for what they really hated, Ratu Tānoa's rule—the resentment was aggravated by Ratu Tānoa's protection of *bêche-de-mer* traders whose ships his Bauan enemies were anxious to pillage (Clunie 1984; Eagleston *UD,* 1:383, 387, 438–40; Osborn *J:* 7 July 1835).[47] Led by the warrior chiefs Ratu Mara and Seru Tānoa, the same Bauan elements were also put out by Ratu Tānoa's refusal to sanction their raids on Rewan towns.[48] Indeed during these hostilities, Ratu Tānoa

ers' (*i taukei*) of Bau Island, then living in Lau, the Levuka people accorded Ratu Tānoa the title when he was visiting Lakeba. At the time, Ratu Tānoa was living in Cakaudrove, where he had been first taken refuge after the coup of 1832. The installation of his Cakaudrove wife as Radini Levuka in the ceremonies at Lakeba would have been most politic.

47. Regarding two schooners out of Hawaii, apparently about to be attacked by Bau and Viwa men until the would-be attackers were driven off by Ratu Tānoa, Captain Eagleston wrote, "The King's protection to these schooners caused a deep and bitter feeling towards him on the part of many of the leading Chiefs, who had for some time greatly disapproved of his friendship to the whites visiting them" (*UD,* 1:383). This was in July 1831, about fourteen months before the coup. Ratu Tānoa also informed Captain Archer of the ship *Glide* of a plot by the same Bauan and Viwa chiefs (Ratu Mara and Ratu Namosimulua) to take his vessel (ibid., 1:387).

48. One such raid, said to have resulted in more than a hundred deaths, was the upshot of a complicated scheme to take Captain Eagleston's ship *Emerald* in 1832 (Clunie 1984: 66–67; Eagleston *UD,* 1:296–97). The conspirators included the Bauan rebel-in-waiting Ratu Mara, a rogue Manilla-man named Battan, long in the service of the Rewa king Ro Kania, and several (unnamed) Rewa chiefs—one suspects the king among them (cf. Cheever *J:* 14,

was supplying "war material"—probably including guns—to the Rewa king, the brother of his wife Adi Qereitoga (Eagleston *UD,* 1:438). On one occasion Adi Qereitoga visited Rewa even as the Rewans were preparing the bodies of two downed Bauans for the ovens. Captain Eagleston, who was also there, remarked that she was well received; and for that matter, he considered that Ratu Tānoa himself, as *vasu* to Rewa, would be accorded the same good treatment, war or no war (ibid., 1:391).

While Ratu Tānoa's partiality toward Rewa and protection of the European shipping surely fueled the animosity toward him in Bau, the rebellion that deposed him in 1832 was inherited from older conflicts of the same nature, originating long before his own accession to the Vunivalu title. Ratu Tānoa's predecessor of the ruling (and usurping) Tui Kaba clan had likewise battled against the old Bauan nobility—the Nabaubau, the Dewala, and the Roko Tui Bau—together with their great warrior allies of Vusaradave and other henchmen within and outside of Bau. The most prominent rebel, Ratu Mara, was a leading member of this native aristocracy, as well as the *vasu* of the Vusaradave warriors.[49] Captain Eagleston described him as a very tall man "of fine form and high feeling, with an eye like an eagle, and a great warrior," but all the same, "a great scamp and no friend to the Whites or to the King [Ratu Tānoa] or his favorites" (*UD,* 1:386). Encountering Ratu Mara shortly after the 1832 coup, Captain Eagleston found him "very bitter in his expressions against the old king [Ratu Tānoa], and his greatest pleasure would be in making a feast off of him" (*UD,* 1:437). Seru Tānoa, the headman of the Vusaradave fighting men (*bati*)—thus "commander in chief of the Feejee forces" in Captain Eagleston's estimation—and Ratu Namosimalua, the paramount of Viwa Island, were two other significant figures in the 1832 uprising. They were characterized in much the same way as Ratu Mara by the American traders—except that the first of the two was an excessive kava drinker and hospitable to the *Papalagi,* while the other was a "treacherous daredevil" who was again no friend either to the foreigners or to Ratu Tānoa (ibid., 1:385–

15, and 21 May 1834). The caper failed when it was disclosed to Captain Eagleston, first by the young Rewa chief Ro Cokānauto, half-brother to the Rewa king, then by certain Whitemen, one of whom, David Whippy, was presumably acting on behalf of Ratu Tānoa. Blaming the Rewans for betraying the scheme, Ratu Mara mounted the aforementioned attack on a Rewan town, with unusual slaughter.

49. Warren Osborn (*J:* 7 July 1837) identifies Ratu Mara as a member of Vusaradave, but Bauan genealogies, whatever the other variations about his ancestry, regularly make him the descendant of a previous holder (or holders) of the Vunivalu title, and his mother a Vusaradave woman—for example, the "Dewala Genealogy" in NLC/TR (Tailevu North [Bau]) or the Bauan genealogy in the Evans Collection (MS).

87; Osborn *J:* passim). Also, Seru Tānoa was "hawk-eyed" where Ratu Mara was "eagle-eyed." Parenthetically, as many of our citations suggest, one should here take note and endorse Fergus Clunie's assessment of Capt. John H. Eagleston as "a flamboyantly acute observer, who understood Bauan political machinations as well as any outsider since" (1984: 58).

The "conspiracies à la Bau" that Captain Eagleston knew in his day had been preceded several years before by a dress rehearsal of the 1832 coup, as well as a full-blown stasis some decades earlier, both involving the same alignments of contending forces. In 1825 Ratu Tānoa's older brother, the reigning war king Ratu Naulivou, was threatened with rebellion by an adventitious shift in the balance of power in Bau, the result of a mutiny on board the Spanish brig *Laurice* by its crew of Manilla-men. When the *Laurice* was beached at Bau, its stores of ammunition fell into the hands of the Vusaradave warrior chief, the self-same Seru Tānoa. (It is also suggestive—of the Roko Tui Bau's complicity—that the *Laurice*'s masts were later used as houseposts for the principal temple of Bau, Navatanitawake, where the sacred king presided, and the ship's anchor remains in place up against the front of the temple platform to this day.) The trader William Driver of the *Clay* recounted the sequel to the beaching of the *Laurice* as he heard it in Bau (*J:* 6 October 1827). Quarrels broke out and deaths resulted among the mutineers, and the chiefs were also "agitated," until the king Ratu Naulivou, "finding his head in danger contrived to have the town burnt & so destroyed the seeds of faction, with the stores, arms and ammunition taken from the brig all burnt."

The contentious relations between Ratu Naulivou and his (typically) outrageous younger brother, Ratu Tānoa, whose "canibal [*sic*] disposition" had already brought him into disputes with the king, were worsened by the fire (Driver *J:* 6 October 1827). Ratu Tānoa went off to Lau with hundreds of Bauans—one-fourth of the population, according to Captain Driver—vowing never to return. As of Driver's writing, he still had not come back, although he did return by 1829, when he succeeded Ratu Naulivou as Vunivalu. Whether Ratu Tānoa was conspiring with the Vusaradave and Roko Tui Bau people to overthrow Ratu Naulivou is not known. Although these were the same people who were to depose Ratu Tānoa several years later, his alliance with them in this instance against his older brother would not be beyond the "black arts" of Bauan politics. On the contrary, it would be largely analogous to Ratu Raivalita's enlistment of the old Bauan nobility in his struggle against Ratu Cakobau. And we shall see the like again in the coup of 1832, when certain of Ratu Tānoa's paternal half-brothers made common cause against him with the same inveterate enemies of the Tui

Kaba war kings. The structure of rebellion in Bau is almost formulaic: a combination of convenience between a paternal half-brother of the ruling Vunivalu and native noble clans nursing the bitterness of ancient usurpations with the hopes of regaining their former glory.

Whether or not Ratu Tānoa conspired with the Bauan enemies of Ratu Naulivou in the 1820s, he had first established the fearsome reputation that disturbed his royal brother by the slaughter he inflicted some decades earlier on the same native aristocracy—the Nabaubau, Roko Tui Bau, and Vusaradave crowd. Sometime around the beginning of the nineteenth century, these people had tried to retake control of the Bau kingdom by driving out the Tui Kaba rulers. Instead, their plot discovered, the would-be rebels fled Bau, pursued by Ratu Tānoa. Tradition has it he caught up with them at Vanuabalavu in northeastern Fiji and killed many, including the sacred king (Roko Tui Bau) of the time. For that he earned the warrior name *Visawaqa,* literally "canoe-burner," but probably figuratively, as a combination of the titles of multiple man-slayers (*visa* + *waqa*), something like "excessive killer."

Considering the adversaries, then, the rebellion of 1832 was decades old before it began.[50] Fundamentally, it was the eruption of antagonisms long sedimented in the relations among Bauan chiefs. So far as these antagonisms were ancestral, bringing the former rulers and the parvenu war kings once more to the breach, there was no need to disinter ancient quarrels as though they had been long-buried and half-forgotten. In Fiji, as modern ethnographers know, the reproduction of historic relations works in other ways. The wounds inflicted in old quarrels or usurpations are kept alive in quotidian interactions or the lack thereof: in daily rounds of who visits with whom, who drinks kava informally with whom, which households exchange food regularly and which not. One house fails to appear in the life crisis rites celebrated by another. And then in public rituals, especially kava circles, the superiority of the old aristocracy to the nouveaux arrivistes is either recognized or it is ignored—thus raising the old battles in any case. So it is no surprise that the same chiefs who threw out Ratu Tānoa in 1832 were again conspiring with Ratu Raivalita to get rid of him and Ratu Cakobau in 1845.

50. Among the better and more extensive accounts of the rebellion of 1832 are Reverend Cross's "A Short Account of the Late War at Bow, Feejee" (*Ext:* September 1838) and the narratives of Waterhouse (1866: 56–66) and Anon. of *Na Mata* (1891 [2] and [3]). The on-the-ground observations of Warren Osborn (*J*) and Captain Eagleston (*UD*) during this period are of capital importance and will be cited in the course of the discussion.

Nor will we be surprised (by now) to learn that certain of Ratu Tānoa's paternal half-brothers joined in overthrowing him in 1832, one of whom, Ratu Ramudra, replaced him as the Vunivalu of Bau. Ratu Ramudra was a *vasu* to Nairai, a subject island of Bau, an undistinguished place in the nineteenth century although its paramount was descended from native Bau royalty (an even earlier dynasty of war kings than the Nabaubau).[51] But Ratu Ramudra was a figurehead king nonetheless, more convenient as a puppet of the powerful chiefs who made him the Vunivalu than he was the cause of their rebellion. In personal characteristics, he was indeed the opposite of the active king of the Bau diarchy—by a few hundred pounds. A "monster of fat," Captain Eagleston called him, weighing on the order of five hundred pounds, he thought: so fat he could not move without assistance (*UD,* 1:437). The captain offered the use of the ship's block and tackle to hoist him aboard when Ratu Ramudra visited the *Peru* in December 1832, but the king "not liking the arrangement, he concluded to let his men assist him, and it was some time before six accomplished the task" (ibid.). His immobile, brief, and otherwise unremarkable reign earned Ratu Ramudra the lasting sobriquet in Fijian tradition of "the Reclining War King" (*Na Vunivalu Davodavo*). So inoffensive was he that Ratu Tānoa pardoned him upon resuming power, instead of eating his liver raw—as was the fate of several other Bau chiefs. Yet if the obese rebel king came to nothing, the fortunes of Ratu Cakobau and Ratu Raivalita were enhanced, and also in significant ways counterposed, by the machinations that led to Ratu Tānoa's restoration. Ratu Raivalita benefited from the strategic position of his mother Adi Qereitoga, who was Ratu Tānoa's effective link to Rewa. Meanwhile, Ratu Cakobau was organizing the resistance in Bau.

Ratu Cakobau remained in Bau throughout the five years of Ratu Tānoa's exile—which is rather a mystery, considering his commitment to his father's cause. Bau traditions attribute his survival to something like luck and the dissembling air of callow youthfulness he used to cover his underground intrigues (Anon. of *Na Mata* 1891 [2]: 14–15). But there was more to it. The story of his opportune escape from rebel assassins at the begin-

51. This is the greater stock called Dewala or Rokodurucoko. A man of this ancestry was solicited from Bau by the Nairai people to become their chief (*kere turaga*), some generations back, according to Nairai tradition (NLC/TR [Lomaiviti (Nairai)]). This distinguished descent helps explain why Ratu Banuve, the father of Ratu Tānoa, was reputed to be *vasu* to Nairai and why Ratu Tānoa numbered a Nairai woman among his true wives—as well as why Ratu Ramudra and his younger brother Ratu Caucau figure among the rebels of 1832.

ning of the coup reveals, once more in the form of a *real-life myth,* the structural relationships that were safeguarding him. As the story goes, the rebels, before setting out after Ratu Tānoa—he was at Koro Island when the uprising began—decided to eliminate two of his sons, Ratu Tubuanakoro and Ratu Cakobau. A *vasu* of Sawaieke in Gau Island, Ratu Tubuanakoro was a man of parts—as we already know from the testimony of Dumont D'Urville (see above, chapter 1). To judge from such European reports, Ratu Tubuanakoro and Ratu Cakobau (or Ratu Seru as he was known then) were the most prominent and accomplished of Ratu Tānoa's sons. (Ratu Raivalita was a boy of about ten in 1832.) Intending their death, the rebels summoned the brothers to a certain house "Naduruvesi" where they were holding a meeting, or in another version, to an adjacent canoe slip (see fig. 3.1). But when passing the great temple of Bau (Navatanitawake), the habitual haunt of the Roko Tui Bau, Ratu Cakobau was summoned inside by the sacred king to prepare his kava. The young chief obeyed, while his brother continued on to the rendezvous. The Bauan legend has it that Ratu Cakobau could see his brother being clubbed from the temple doorway and made a move to join him, but he was restrained by the Roko Tui Bau and bade to resume serving the kava. By another, contemporary account, however, Ratu Tubuanakoro was not struck down in Bau itself. Moreover, according to Captain Eagleston, it was his open contempt for the rebels that doomed him:

> A meeting of the Chiefs and leading men was now held, to decide on their future proceedings, at which they got into a hot dispute, in which Tooboonoocooroo [Ratu Tubuanakoro], the King's son, declared if he lived he would revenge his father's wrongs, this sealed his fate and by treachery he was clubbed on board a canoe, receiving the first blow he quickly rose, spit in his murderer's face and called him a woman. The blow about to be repeated, it was stayed by a Chief, who said—Don't kill him like a pig—let him die as a Chief, and accordingly he was choked. (Eagleston *UD,* 1:440)

The legend of Ratu Cakobau's escape while serving the sacred kava seems as unconvincing referentially as it is revealing structurally. Unconvincing, because it leaves unexplained why Ratu Cakobau was not killed any time afterward, when he was not attending the Roko Tui Bau at the temple. Revealing, because his relationship to the Roko Tui Bau must have helped protect him. Ratu Cakobau, recall, was a native *vasu* to Bau, his mother a daughter of the former nobility, the Nabaubau people, who were closely associated also with the Roko Tui Bau title. Ratu Cakobau was thus a sacred sister's son to the leading rebels. So just as a *vasu* would have immunity in his mother's land when it was at war with his own, this native *vasu* could live out a rebellion against his father in which his mother's people figured prominently. (It could also be relevant that Ratu Cakobau's titled wife of later times, Adi Samanunu, was a daughter of the Roko Tui Bau, although whether he was married to her in 1832–37 is not certain.) "It seems," said the Fijian historian Setariki Koto, "that Ratu Cakobau secured protection from the Roko Tui Bau and his maternal uncles of Nabaubau" (MS, Bau chapter).

The parallel tradition, that Ratu Cakobau was able to deflect suspicion of his politics by acting the part of a feckless youth, may also be exaggerated. "Cakobau strolls about as though careless / His plot is deep under the ground," goes the historical chant (Waterhouse 1866: 64, 432). Yet the characterization does not fit Ratu Cakobau's bearing as Captain Eagleston described him a few months before the coup, in a discussion of "the leading and most prominent" of the high bloods of Bau. Under the name of Ratu Seru, Ratu Cakobau was listed fifth among nine such notables by the well-informed Salem trader, who said of him: "Saroo, son to the King, is a tall and noble looking man, very observing and inquisitive, but proud, with high royal feelings" (Eagleston *UD,* 1:385–86).[52] Nor does tradition suggest that during the coup Ratu Cakobau altogether escaped suspicion (Anon. of *Na Mata,* 1891 [2]; Koto MS). But evidently he was allaying it by outward collaboration with the usurpers. He went traveling with the rebel Ratu Mara (Osborn *J:* 2 August 1834). His wife gave birth and recuperated in the house of the usurper, the Reclining Vunivalu (ibid., 29 May–1 June 1834). He fought in at least some of the attacks gotten up by the Bau chiefs against Rewa, Ratu Tānoa's greatest ally (ibid., 26 May, 3 June 1834). Yet all the time he was secretly agitating on his father's behalf with certain loyal chiefs on the Viti Levu mainland and, what proved decisive, with the Lasakau fisher-warriors on Bau. It is said he plied the Lasakau people with food, whale teeth, and promises. A populous and dreaded group, the notorious "dangerous men," the Lasakau occupied their own section or *koro* of Bau, which sometime in early March 1837 they set about fortifying with a palisade as a challenge to the rebels. According to one account, the Lasakau agreed with their adversaries not to use muskets; in any case, a battle

52. Ratu Cakobau is followed in Captain Eagleston's list by the ill-fated Ratu Tubuanakoro, and preceded by the two leaders of the 1832 coup, hawk-eyed Seru Tānoa and eagle-eyed Ratu Mara.

began in which incendiary spears and arrows turned out to be the most effective weapon. Victory came when a wind-abated fire spread through the rebels' town and sent them flying for their lives to the Viti Levu coast. Some died trying to reach sanctuary. Others lived only to be sacrificed later by their clans as the price of reconciliation demanded by Ratu Tānoa.

Ratu Cakobau was largely credited with the restoration of Ratu Tānoa, and he came out of the affair as the evident strong man among the latter's sons and the obvious successor as Vunivalu of Bau (cf. Cargill *J:* 6 May 1839). The name *Cakobau,* meaning 'Bau wars' or 'Bau is bad,' was now accorded him for his part in the counter-coup.[53] Yet this part was never so singlehanded as it is typically alleged in Bauan narratives and historical chants. The Rewan king and his people had easily as much to do with it. And this means that the political standing of Ratu Tānoa's Rewan wife Adi Qereitoga, together with that of their son, Ratu Raivalita, the *vasu* to Rewa, was also boosted substantially by these events.

Adi Qereitoga was the liaison between Ratu Tānoa and Rewa throughout his exile—hence the European characterizations of her in this period as his "favorite wife," "Head Queen," and so forth. In the first two years, however, the relationship was long-distance. Ratu Tānoa initially took refuge in Cakaudrove, where the protection afforded him no doubt owed something to his *de jure* principal wife, Adi Talātoka, a daughter of the Cakaudrove ruling house.[54] Even so, in the years passed at Cakaudrove, he maintained an affectionate contact with Adi Qereitoga at Rewa. Adi Qereitoga had escaped the fate she at first shared with the other wives of Ratu Tānoa, who were commandeered along with his kingdom by the rotund rebel ruler Ratu Ramudra (Eagleston *UD,* 2:11; Eagleston, Log *Emerald:* 11 May 1834). But by the beginning of 1835, if not earlier, she was living in state at Rewa, with her son Ratu Raivalita (Osborn *J:* 31 January–25 February 1835). How much communication she maintained with Ratu Tānoa through Fijian intermediaries we do not know, but the journals of European traders indicate that certain *Papalagi* were being enlisted for that purpose. In February 1835, when Captain Eagleston was at the Cakaudrove capital Somosomo, he was entrusted by his old friend Ratu Tānoa with two large bales of tapa cloth for "his Queen" at Rewa (Log *Emerald:* 23 Febru-

53. The name Cakobau, however, was not invented for the occasion; there was an earlier Bauan of that name known to Captain Eagleston.

54. It is said that Ratu Tānoa's initial intention, when he left Koro Island, escaping from the coup, was to make Rewa, but contrary winds forced him to Cakaudrove (Anon. of *Na Mata* 1891 [2]: 14).

ary 1835). A month earlier, Warren Osborn, on encountering Adi Qereitoga at Rewa, testified in an indirect way to her reciprocal regard for "Old Snuff" (Ratu Tānoa). "The ex-Queen of Bowe [Bau] Old Snuffs head wife," Osborn wrote, considered Captain Eagleston "her particular friend & out of gratitude to the assistance he endeavoured to lend her husband, she brings him many presents of provisions &c when any of us visit her, she is very hospitable" (*J:* 31 January–25 February 1835). (Rather different is this from Captain Eagleston's pre-coup description of Adi Qereitoga: "She is a great beggar, but any little present satisfies her for the visit" [*UD,* 1:380–81].)

Sometime toward the end of 1835, Ratu Tānoa joined Adi Qereitoga at Rewa, where her brother the king not only gave him protection but actively campaigned to restore him to power in Bau. As Reverend Waterhouse described it, "Rewa supported Tanoa, their *vasu,* with all the men and means it possessed. Several important towns were conquered for the Bau king by its armies" (1866:62; cf. Wilkes 1845, 3:64–65). Mr. Waterhouse also indicates that Ratu Cakobau was a party to the military strategy, although when he disagreed with the Roto Tui Dreketi over the disposition of the conquered town of Kaba, the latter overruled his wish to destroy the lot of them.[55] There is some indication of other, critical outside support for Ratu Tānoa's restoration. Some Europeans of the small beachcomber-trader settlement at Ovalau, who had their own quarrels with the Bau usurpers, are said to have "privately presented a large quantity of ammunition to [Ratu] Seru, who went by night to beg their assistance" (ibid., 63). The report is hard to verify. But not so for the Rewan source of the material inducements that Ratu Cakobau offered the Lasakau warriors to join Ratu Tānoa's party. Indeed Reverend Cross's "Short account of the late war at Bow, Feejee" (*Ext:* 1 January 1839) credits the whole counter-coup to the intriguing of the Roko Tui Dreketi with the Lasakau people, without benefit of Ratu Cakobau's involvement. Mr. Cross had his information in September 1838 from a Rewan convert, "who had a better opportunity of knowing the particulars of the war [the Lasakau uprising of 1837] than any other, being frequently employed as the [Rewa] king's messenger."[56] The

55. As the immediate homeland of the Vunivalu people, the Tui Kaba clan, Kaba's affiliation with the rebels would be particularly galling to Ratu Tānoa's faction, thus in their view worthy of the fate advocated in the analogous case of Mytilene by Cleon: "Punish them as they deserve and teach your allies by a striking example that the penalty of rebellion is death" (Thuc. 3.40.7).

56. From this description, the "messenger" in question would be the constituted Envoy to Bau (*Mata ki Bau*), that is, of the Navolau people of Rewa.

messenger told Mr. Cross: "The king of Rewa promised them [the Lasakau fisher-warriors] he would have a number of canoes built for them if they would exert themselves in the destruction or dispersion of Tānoa's enemies. They agreed to the proposal and began to build a fence and dig a trench to separate themselves from the other part of Bow" (ibid.). Indeed, whatever else Ratu Cakobau was slipping the Lasakau people in the way of whale teeth and pledges of future powers and privileges, the Rewa king endowed these sea warriors with an extraordinary fleet of canoes. Built at the king's command by the expert carpenters of Kadavu, fifty sailing canoes arrived at Rewa for presentation to him, along with other valuables, in August 1838 (Cross *D:* 31 August 1838). Not two weeks later, the Roko Tui Dreketi went to Bau to present forty-nine canoes to the newly restored Vunivalu, Ratu Tānoa (ibid., 15 September 1838).

In the years immediately following Ratu Tānoa's return to power, he continued to exchange friendly visits and material respects with Ro Kania the Rewa ruler, while at the same time Bau was aggressively regaining its hegemony in eastern Fiji. His sons Ratu Raivalita and Ratu Cakobau profited accordingly: the first from the amicable relations with Rewa, he being the connection of "sacred blood"; the second from the hostile relations with other kingdoms, he being the effective commander of Bau's armies.

The older ruling kings Ratu Tānoa and Ro Kania, however, were the principals in the ongoing exchanges between Bau and Rewa. Five or six times in the period 1838–40 Ratu Tānoa personally visited Rewa, while Ro Kania returned the favor by three or four trips to Bau.[57] Some of these occasions were festivals (*sōlevu*) involving considerable visiting parties, stays of many days in the host community, lavish hospitality and feasting of the visitors, entertainments, and large gifts of wealth—thus "total prestations," as Marcel Mauss would have said. Other visits might be categorized as diplomatic: the attempts at pacific intervention in the other kingdom's internal quarrels, for example. Ro Kania attended the meeting of both rebel and loyalist chiefs called in Bau by Ratu Tānoa after his return, and was instrumental in effecting a reconciliation among them (Cross *Ext:* September 1838). He also interceded to resolve a violent dispute between two

57. Notices of these reciprocal visits are found in Cargill (*J:* 4 May 1839); Cross (*D:* 2 February, 4 September 1838, 9 November 1840); and Jaggar (*J:* 3 May, 19 October 1839, 31 January, 19 September, 24 September, 1 October, 6–9 November, 3 December, 28 December 1840). Ratu Cakobau also visited Rewa at least twice (Jaggar *J:* 26 July 1839, 19–20 April 1840).

Bauan towns (ibid., 4 September 1838). Conversely, Ratu Tānoa went to Rewa to persuade the chiefs to desist from their attacks on recalcitrant subject towns in Noco country (Jaggar *J:* 6 November 1840). At one point in Bau's deteriorating relations with Cakaudrove, Ratu Tānoa asked the Roko Tui Dreketi for military assistance. The campaign never came off, although Rewa mobilized forces and rebuilt temples for the war (Jaggar *J:* 15, 17, 25–26 November 1840). Ratu Cakobau also got involved in Rewa's affairs. He tried to intercede in a longstanding quarrel between Ro Kania and his younger brother Ratu Qaraniqio by presenting a ritual atonement (*i soro*) to the former on the latter's behalf (ibid., 14 April 1841). The atonement was refused, a slap in the Bauan chief's face that was exacerbated when the Rewa king and Ratu Qaraniqio were reconciled shortly afterwards—without help from Bau, thank you. This was a harbinger of worse things to come, but until the early 1840s the relations of the two kingdoms were overwhelmingly friendly. And of all the exchanges between them, the most estimable were the mutual gifts of cannibal victims.

"Great things," these bodies were. Especially did Bau favor Rewa with them, beginning with the part of one of the rebel chiefs sent to Ro Kania by Ratu Tānoa shortly after he regained power (Cross *D:* 14 January 1838; Jaggar in *WMMS/L:* 23 August 1839). Then there was the time a Verata man killed by the Bauans was salted down for an expected visit of Ro Kania, who was bringing a house post for the construction of a new temple (Jaggar *J:* 18, 22 October 1839). On two other occasions, twenty victims of Bauan massacres—first, twenty Verata people, then twenty from Namena—were sent along to the Rewa king.[58] The distribution of these bodies by Ro Kania among Rewans and their fighting allies (*bati*) would do some good for his own authority—at the same time that the one-sided flow of *bakola* ('cannibal victims') from Bau to Rewa would reinforce a certain deference to Ratu Tānoa.[59] At this time the Rewa king was taking orders from the Bau Vunivalu on how to deal with missionary entreaties to become Christian (negatively) and how to deal with the European shipping (hospitably).

58. The dispatch and reception (including distribution and consumption) of the two batches of twenty victims can be followed in Cargill (*J:* 31 October, 1 November 1839); M. Cargill (1855: 232); Cross (*D:* 30 October 1838); and Jaggar (*J:* 31 October, 1 and 2 November 1839, 29 and 30 May 1841).

59. The one exception in the direction of *bakola* gifts I can find is four bodies sent from Rewa to Bau following the massacre of a Kadavu town subject to Rewa (Jaggar *J:* 24 October 1841). Directed by Ratu Qaraniqio as a matter of personal vengeance, this Rewan attack on Kadavu, however, displeased Ratu Tānoa, according to the report heard by Mr. Jaggar (29 December 1841). By then relations between Bau and Rewa had soured, in any case.

Plate 1. Ratu Tānoa

Plate 2. Ratu Cakobau

Plate 3. Ratu Gavidi

Plate 4. Ro Veidovi

Plate 5. Rev. Richard B. Lyth

Plate 6. Rev. John Hunt

Plate 7. Rev. William Cross

Plate 8. Rev. Thomas Jaggar

Plate 9. Rev. and Mrs. James Calvert

Plate 10. Rev. Thomas Williams

Plate 11. Lt. Charles Wilkes, commander, U.S. Exploring Expedition (in Fiji, 1840)

But while the old kings were thus solidifying their accord, Ratu Cakobau and Ratu Raivalita were advancing their careers in different ways, Ratu Cakobau in a way that would soon undo the alliance with Rewa and set the brothers at deadly odds. This was the time of the reconquest. At Ratu Cakobau's instigation and under his leadership, Bau regained the ground it had lost during the coup years (see above, chapter 1). To briefly rehearse these events: for five years, from 1838 to 1843, Ratu Cakobau waged a brilliant campaign of repeated attacks on certain strategic enemies with the aim also of intimidating certain others. Verata, Namena, and Telau in Viti Levu were attacked, as were Macuata and other parts of northern Vanua Levu. Cakaudrove and Lau were intimidated. Verata made formal submission (*i soro*) to Bau in 1840, Cakaudrove in 1842. Lau in effect did the same by resuming its tributary status when Ratu Cakobau came on a prolonged visit in 1843. These were years when Lieutenant Wilkes and other passing Europeans spoke of Ratu Cakobau raising hell all over Fiji while displacing "Old Snuff," Ratu Tānoa, as the *de facto* king of Bau. It was also the time when the piratical raids of Ratu Raivalita and his entourage on subject towns of Bau were attracting unfavorable *Papalagi* attention. Besides these depredations, Ratu Raivalita was carrying out more official missions on the part of Ratu Tānoa, or else rendering him services that likewise suggested the *vasu* to Rewa was sharing in his father's regard for that kingdom. Lieutenant Wilkes met Ratu Raivalita while the young chief was en route to Macuata to fetch a daughter of the king who had been promised as wife to Ratu Tānoa (Wilkes 1845, 1:148–49). Ratu Raivalita led a party of Bauans to Cakaudrove on a ceremonial visit marking the recently concluded peace with that kingdom (Lyth *J:* 7 June 1842). Not long before he died, he likewise escorted the Cakaudrove king home from a state visit to Bau (ibid., 31 March 1845).[60] Yet on the whole, Ratu Cakobau's capture of the ruling power in Bau made the political situation of Ratu Raivalita increasingly ambiguous, for the chances of advancement and succession of the younger brother were slipping away.

Everything suggests that Ratu Cakobau's control of organized power was driving Ratu Raivalita into demonstrations of the opposed, transgressive mode of Fijian chiefship. Ratu Cakobau's military undertakings had far-reaching power-effects, even beyond those entailed in mobilizing arm-

60. Ratu Raivalita was also entrusted by Ratu Tānoa with the Hall's patent rifle that Lieutenant Wilkes had given him. This was to prevent Ratu Tānoa's own uterine nephew, Ro Cokānauto of Rewa, "from vasu-ing it," according to Wilkes (1845, 1:77). Ro Cokānauto's *vasu* prerogatives in Bau would thus be trumped by those of Ratu Raivalita in Rewa.

ies and directing campaigns. Consider also that "Fijian war is an expensive business," as Rev. Thomas Williams said, that it requires considerable accumulations of wealth to support and reward the armies and the gods. It follows that Ratu Cakobau's assumption of the war king role entailed a control that reached deeply into the life of the kingdom, its subject lands, and its allies. Ratu Cakobau was the master of the extensive Bauan imperial order. Any competition that Ratu Raivalita could offer would have to operate on the alternative claim to rule society based on a personal superiority to the established order. What was open to him was the *celeritas* way of the younger brother: the performative demonstration of his own *mana* by acts beyond the norms of sociality and the daring of ordinary men. He would have to be outrageous—"bad," thus "indeed a chief." His place in Bauan memory indicates that he made the point. Recall the historian Ratu Deve Toganivalu's take on Ratu Raivalita: "an even greater despot than Ratu Cakobau," he said, "a villain of the first order" whose "only delight was in tyranny and suffering" (*TkB,* Part 1).

It was a similar contention in the ruling house of Rewa that brought Ratu Cakobau and Ratu Raivalita into definitive rivalry in Bau. The competition between the Roko Tui Dreketi, Ro Kania, and his charismatic younger brother Ratu Qaraniqio eventuated in the deterioration of friendly relations between Rewa and Bau—and a corresponding decline in Ratu Raivalita's political stock. Bad blood between the Rewa king and his brother was already evident in 1838 and 1839, the first years of Wesleyan missionaries' residence. Indeed, it was partly expressed in Ratu Qaraniqio's tormenting of these missionary *Papalagi* whom the king, following Ratu Tānoa's advice if not also his own inclination, was disposed to tolerate. Otherwise the fraternal quarrel took the previously noted form of an adulterous liaison between Ratu Qaraniqio and one of the king's wives, followed by the younger brother's banishment to his kinsmen in Bau. Still, Ratu Qaraniqio rather overmatched Ro Kania in chiefly character. He clearly had the most imposing house and household in Rewa, and a demeanor to match. Estimated to be six feet or more in height, he was well built and well turned-out, "a dandy," but with a countenance and comportment that the *Papalagi* generally found troubling—the face of "a raskal," "a fierce and sanguinary disposition" (Reynolds *Le:* 21 September 1840; cf. Pickering *J:* 15 May 1840; Sinclair *J:* 15 June 1840). Ro Kania often drew even poorer reviews. A "great 6 footed ugly, bewiskered painted canibal" he was, in Warren Osborn's view, and "a big scoundrel, theif & beggar" as well, but for all that a good friend and protector of the White traders (*J:* 31 January–25 February 1835). Cannibal Jack described the Rewa king nearly ten years later as "fat, lazy and rendered effeminate by his luxurious life" (Jackson 1853: 467), and certainly none of the Whites saw him measuring up in style or substance to his younger brother.[61] Nor was he able to prevent Ratu Qaraniqio from demonstrating his bravado in a way that ruptured the peace between Rewa and Bau.

By Fijian and European opinion both, the massive Rewan attacks got up by Ratu Qaraniqio on the Bauan-affiliated town of Suva, culminating in 1843 in the destruction of the place and the slaughter of many of its inhabitants, was *the* cause of the great Polynesian War.[62] The notion is perhaps too simple, even if the question of cause were restricted to precipitating events, but it is manifest that the affair of Suva was a turning point in the relations of Bau and Rewa. This change from good to bad again involved the interaction between events at the interpersonal level—quarrels among the ruling chiefs, advancing and defending their honor and power—and the state of the collective forces. Moreover, the immediate hostilities at Suva evoked a much longer history, again like the Thucydidean "truest cause" of the Peloponnesian War, which could be appropriately transposed to Fiji as the growing power of the Bauans and the fear this inspired in the Rewans.

It was critical on all levels that the paramount of Suva, the Roko Tui Suva, was a *vasu* to the Vunivalu house of Bau, the son of one of Ratu Tānoa's daughters. If this was the instrumental (cum institutional) form of Suva's status as a Bauan town, it was also critical that previously—a matter of only two generations back, if the genealogy can be trusted—the chief of Suva was a *vasu* to Rewa, and by all indications allied rather with that kingdom (Hocart *FN:* 2090–91). Against this background comes Ratu Qaraniqio of Rewa into Suva in January 1841, where he proceeds to commandeer a large pig belonging to the current Suva ruler (the Roko Tui Suva). As uterine nephew to the Nabaubau royalty of Bau, Ratu Qaraniqio had the right to please himself in places subject to that kingdom—even as younger brother of the king of Rewa, he had the temerity. So when the Roko Tui Suva prevented the Rewa chief from *vasu*-ing the pig, the fracas that ensued brought into play the long contention in Bau between the old nobility and the ruling Tui Kaba, as well as the historic shift in the balance

61. Despite Osborn's characterization of Ro Kania as friendly to Whites, and Jackson's as "effeminate," in the early 1830s he was apparently the power behind at least two attempts on European ships (Clunie 1984).

62. The details of these events are described in M. Sahlins (1991) and will be only summarily discussed here. On the destruction of Suva as the cause of the Bau-Rewa war, see Calvert (*J:* 15 June 1855); Hocart (*FN:* 2596); Jaggar (*WMMS/L:* 5 July 1845); Koto (MS); NLC/TR (Tailevu North, Bau); Wall (1919).

of power between Bau and Rewa. The temporality of the event is precisely not momentary, confined to its own occurrence; it brings a long history to bear on its brief present. But besides its history, Suva's geographical situation was also pertinent. Suva was a Bauan town in Rewa's back yard and moreover strategically located near the mouth of the Wailevu River, the main access of Rewa to the sea and its principal island dependencies.[63] (The mosaic effect thus given to the Bau polity, with some of its confederated towns interspersed in areas dominated by other kingdoms, is not unusual in Fiji. The advantage for the outlying town such as Suva is that it is too far from Bau to be much troubled by it, while close enough to expect protection from it.) Hence, when Ratu Qaraniqio, insulted by the incident of the pig, organized a major attack on Suva, it had serious implications for the political relations between Bau and Rewa, for the personal relations between their rulers, Ratu Tānoa and Ro Kania, for the rivalry within Rewa between the Ratu Qaraniqio and the king—and, within Bau, for the fortunes of "the party of Rewa," Adi Qereitoga and Ratu Raivalita.

Already in February 1842, even before the Rewans' initial attack on Suva, Reverend Jaggar in Rewa was reporting rumors of an imminent war with Bau and the suspension of all sailing between the two kingdoms. Led by Ratu Qaraniqio, whose ostensible object was avenging his humiliation over the pig, this attack indicated that he was more than reconciled with his brother the king. Ratu Qaraniqio must have been dominating Rewan policy, since he could not have mustered the large attacking force of perhaps two thousand men, including contingents from allied and subject lands (*bati* and *qali*), without the acquiescence of both the Roko Tui Dreketi and the second, war king of Rewa, the Vunivalu, who in principle commanded the Rewan armies. Great as their numbers were, the Rewans were ignominiously driven off by the Suvans (Jaggar *J:* 23, 25 June 1842). But in April 1843 Ratu Qaraniqio gained satisfaction when another large and widely recruited Rewan army not only overran the town, but slaughtered the women and children who were evacuating the area under an agreement that was supposed to guarantee their safety.

The news of the Suva massacre was greeted with consternation and anger on Bau—but no immediate retaliation. In the weeks that followed, missionaries on both sides—Mr. Jaggar in Rewa, Mr. Hunt in Viwa—were reporting palpable tension and premonitions of imminent hostilities,

63. There is a somewhat uncanny resemblance between the Corinth-Corcyra dispute as a precipitating event of the Peloponnesian War and that between Rewa and Suva in setting off the Polynesian War, including the old affiliation of Corinth and Corcyra, and the strategic location of Corcyra as a western outlier of the Peloponnesus, looking overseas to Sicily.

but the war did not break out until the end of 1843, six months after Suva fell. One can deduce a plausible explanation for the delay from the actions of the main Bauan principals, Ratu Cakobau and Ratu Tānoa, on whom the decision for war would ultimately rest. Ratu Cakobau left Bau for a prolonged stay of nearly six months in Lau. Ostensibly, Ratu Cakobau, although outraged by the massacre at Suva, was taking a cautious tack, waiting to see what the Rewans' intentions were. The trip also had the virtue of confirming Bau's dominance over Lau—challenged by Cakaudrove during the 1830s coup—and its access to the wealth of that windward kingdom. Thus, the local missionary, Thomas Williams, recorded the arrival of the Bau fleet at Lakeba on 21 May, "to receive the homage and riches of the Tuinayau [the Lau king] and his people" (1931, 1:162–63). But Ratu Cakobau's motives for leaving Bau have to be judged also from his father's reaction to the Suva catastrophe. Ratu Tānoa was disturbed by it, according to Mr. Hunt, but not disturbed enough to go to war over it: "I remember having a conversation with Tānoa on the subject at this time, and he assured me that something further must be done by Rewa before hostilities would commence. He observed with his characteristic calmness: They have destroyed one town [Suva], but never mind, let them destroy another, then we will fight" (Hunt *J:* 19 October 1845).

Among the considerations inhibiting Ratu Tānoa, according to Reverend Calvert, was Ratu Raivalita. "Thakombau's rival brother," as the missionary characterized him, "was a high *vasu* to Rewa. . . . He would, therefore, as a matter of course, be favourable to his mother's relatives" (Williams and Calvert 1859: 348). This notice is significant, because by all accounts what turned Ratu Tānoa around, what found him burning for war when Ratu Cakobau returned from Lau, was his betrayal by Ratu Raivalita's mother. Adi Qereitoga had committed adultery and fled to Rewa along with several other women of the household, where they were all distributed as consorts to Rewan notables. As it took this insult to turn Ratu Tānoa against Rewa, one may reasonably conclude that it was his reluctance that had prevented the outbreak of war six months earlier. Ratu Cakobau's leaving the scene, moreover, implies that father and son were disagreeing about this war as they had disagreed about others before. Inhibited by his close relations to the Rewa king, not to mention his profound debt to him for decisive support during the 1830s coup, Ratu Tānoa would not be as quick as his bellicose son Ratu Cakobau to punish Rewa for the destruction of Suva.[64]

64. An analogous disagreement between Ratu Tānoa and Ratu Cakobau arose some years later—after Rewa had been destroyed twice over—when the old man objected to his

But Adi Qereitoga changed all that, ended the impasse. Here is Reverend Calvert's summary of how it happened:

> Another most grievous offence had been given to Mbau [Bau] in the case of Tanoa's principal wife [*sic*], the mother of Raivalita, who had been unfaithful to the King, and therefore went home to her brothers at Rewa, accompanied by several of the women of Tanoa's household. These women were given to different Chiefs at Rewa, whereby the grossest possible insult was offered to their late master, who, in his anger, forgot the help which the Rewa Chiefs had rendered him in his exile, and now burned with a desire for revenge. The breach was widened past healing, and, towards the close of the year, a formal declaration of war was made by messengers from both sides. (Williams and Calvert 1859: 348)

Mr. Calvert's résumé goes a way toward understanding Ratu Tānoa's reaction, but it ignores Adi Qereitoga's motivation. Clearly, she was an active agent in the affair, and no doubt aware of its consequences. The adultery in which she was involved in Bau began in late 1842 or early 1843 with a correspondent whom history does not record—though her infidelity was widely known, probably because she did not care to conceal it (Hunt to Lyth, *L:* 7 January 1843; Hunt *J:* 19 October 1845; Waterhouse 1866: 111). Adultery, flight, and the subsequent liaisons of Adi Qereitoga and her companions: any one of these would be *lèse-majesté* in itself—compounded by the known concern of "Old Snuff" for his declining virility. But then, the deteriorating relations between Bau and Rewa that began with Rewa's hostility toward Suva could only have had a similar effect on Adi Qereitoga's status as the so-called favorite wife of Ratu Tānoa. Her role as mediator between the two kingdoms was becoming a liability in Bau. And her son, Ratu Raivalita, as *vasu* to Rewa, would not only share the opprobrium, he was losing all possibility of ruling Bau to his brother Ratu Cakobau. The last political resource available to Ratu Raivalita, his last claim on Ratu Tānoa's favor, was dissolving along with Bau's amity with Rewa. So likewise did his mother's ties to Ratu Tānoa dissolve: probably she already

son's wish to attack Cakaudrove. The objection recalled Ratu Tānoa's strong political indebtedness to Rewa during the coup of the 1830s and his regret at what had happened since. The information came indirectly to Rev. Lyth (*DB:* 11 June 1849): "Simpson our ship carpenter informs me that Tui Viti [Ratu Cakobau] proposed to his father [Ratu Tānoa] to wage war agst Somosomo [Cakaudrove]. The old man said, 'I thought you were my son. Where is Rewa now that were our friends (during the rebellion [of the 1830s]) and Somosomo recd me when I must either have been killed or perished at sea. And you want to destroy it. But for them neither you nor I would have been here.' Tui Viti had no more to say."

hated him, as she clearly did in 1845, when Rewa was destroyed, and she was forcibly brought back to Bau: "The mother of Revelete [Ratu Raivalita] declares, that, though she is compelled to live in Bau, she will not be strangled [as would be appropriate] when the king (her husband) dies, for she hates him, and wishes she could stick sharp pointed stakes through his flesh" (Wallis 1851: 162).

But Adi Qereitoga's spectacular defiance of her husband two years earlier, her adultery and escape to Rewa, had already set off a political explosion, a war with Rewa, that counted her son's ambitions and his life among its casualties. Compared to the heroic status of the native *vasu* Ratu Cakobau, Ratu Raivalita was now something of an enemy alien. An incident recorded at the end of 1844 in Viwa by Mrs. Wallis indicates Ratu Raivalita's attachment to Rewa and, it seems, the embarrassment this had become. In broad daylight, the "handsome young man" abducted one of the young secondary wives of Ratu Nalila, the chief of the Lasakau fisher-warriors (Wallis 1851: 33).[65] Ratu Raivalita then took the stolen woman to a house in Bau "intended for the king of Rewa's daughter, to whom he is betrothed" (ibid., 55). When this marital arrangement occurred is not known. It may even have been decided when the intended were children, thus repeating the marriage of the Rewa royal daughter to the Bau chief that made Ratu Raivalita the privileged *vasu* to Rewa.[66] Now, at the end of 1844, the war with Rewa having begun, Ratu Raivalita as it were desecrates the house specially built for his Rewa future wife by installing a woman of lesser standing. Everything happened as if Ratu Raivalita were ostensibly denying the allegiance to Rewa that made him suspect in Bau, and thus dissembling the plot that aimed to make him ruler of that kingdom.[67]

65. More precisely, Ratu Nalila was the chief-in-exile, living in Viwa (where he was *vasu*) and in fear of Ratu Gavidi of Lasakau, whose half-brother he had killed and with whom he was contending for ascendancy among the Lasakau people. (Ratu Gavidi would soon have his revenge, killing Ratu Nalila and his father both while pretending to make peace with them around the kava bowl.) Now, as we know that Ratu Gavidi would be implicated in Ratu Raivalita's assassination plot, the latter's brazen abduction of a wife of the former's enemy may well have been a tactical move, designed to assure Ratu Gavidi's support against Ratu Cakobau.

66. Even so, a first cross-cousin (MBD) marriage of this kind is unusual. It was customary for the children of cross-cousins (thus second cross-cousins) to be betrothed in arranged marriages. I suspect that means Adi Qereitoga was a half-sister rather than full sister to the Rewa king, Ro Kania.

67. It only need be added to such "black arts" of Bauan politics that Ratu Raivalita had gained a reputation for excessive sexual conquests to go with the other outrages that establish chiefliness in the form of a personage above and beyond the social norms governing

The effect of the war with Rewa on the relative status of Ratu Raivalita and Ratu Cakobau in Bau can be judged from another of those living myths attached to this conflict. It is the story of a meeting of his sons convened by Ratu Tānoa in response to Adi Qereitoga's infidelity and flight to Rewa, the incident that finally set off hostilities. According to the version collected by Reverend Hunt, Ratu Tānoa angrily declared that he had been insulted by his Rewa kinsmen, and lamented that he had no son who would avenge him, no one to love him and punish his enemies. "The most bitter malignity had now evidently taken hold of the old man's heart," wrote Mr. Hunt, "and he determined on the utter destruction of Rewa, and of all those who should favour its interests." But although all his sons sympathized with their father, only Ratu Cakobau stepped forward, and with all his energy, to take up Ratu Tānoa's cause (Hunt *J:* 19 October 1845). Of course, the referential value of this text, its factuality, is dubious *a priori,* since Ratu Cakobau had long been in charge of Bau's forces, and apparently had an interest long before his father in leading them against Rewa—for which, as the sole native *vasu* to Bau, he was the best suited among the king's sons. Again, the text's truth value is rather in its indication of the relationships that events had brought into play. Its critical point is the invidious contrast between Ratu Cakobau and Ratu Raivalita, the former as the definitive successor to his father as ruler of Bau, the latter doomed to an early death. For if Ratu Cakobau stepped forward to take on Ratu Tānoa's war, Ratu Raivalita would have to be numbered among "all those who favoured [Rewa's] interest," and who were therefore destined to share in its destruction, "however dear they were to [Ratu Tānoa] himself." The myth ratifies Ratu Cakobau's ascension to power and portends Ratu Raivalita's demise.

In the same text, Mr. Hunt puts emphasis on the unusually malignant character of the war with Rewa. So furious were Ratu Tānoa and his sons that they immediately determined on a "war of chiefs." This was war "in its worst form, even in Fiji," according to Mr. Hunt, a conflict that could not end until "the leading chiefs" on one side or the other were killed (Hunt *J:* 19 October 1845). It seems, however, that like Ratu Tānoa's anger, a distinctively belligerent warfare took some time to develop. Certainly the Re-

---

ordinary people. A few months after Ratu Raivalita's death, the ruling chief of Cakaudrove was overheard by Rev. Thomas Williams comforting a young woman who was being sent to Bau as an attendant to the chief's daughter already residing there: "Do not think you are going to such a chief as the one just killed at Bou [Bau, a reference to Raivalita] who, if a child was taken to him went to bed with her at once. You will find a different one [meaning Ratu Cakobau?]" (Williams 1931, 2:330n).

wans did not get the message of a war to the death when the declaration of hostilities was sent to them. For their response was an offer to submit and humble themselves (*i soro*).[68] But it was too late. "Thakombau and his father had passed [*sic*] the Rubicon, and the malignant perseverence of the father, the ambitious perseverence of the son, to say nothing of the abilities and resources of each, rendered it quite unlikely that anything less than the blotting out of Rewa from the list of independent states in Fiji could satisfy them" (ibid.).

At least one modern historian has doubted whether this war was different from any other major Fijian conflict (Scarr 1975: 100). Nor did Mr. Hunt himself think the war was so unconditional when it first broke out, in November 1843. At that time, the missionary opined that the conflict would soon end with the submission of Rewa (Viwa Record: November 1843). A month later he observed that the two sides were evenly matched for war, and expressed the belief that they would soon tire of it (Hunt *J:* 25 December 1843). But it did not take much longer for Mr. Hunt to become convinced that the Bauans would not be satisfied by anything less than the death of the Rewa king. Likewise, Mr. Jaggar in Rewa was soon speaking in similar terms of Rewan war aims. Indeed, Mr. Jaggar had direct confirmation from the great herald of Bau (Tunitoga, the herald of the Vunivalu) that this was a unique war: "He said this was a bad war—a war for death, only end either in death of 2 chiefs of Rewa or 2 chiefs of Bau—that none like it before, a new thing this" (Jaggar *PJ:* 4 April 1844). In Rewa and Bau both, the missionaries were recording the venomous insults being voiced of the enemy rulers (cf. Lyth *R:* 84). "I know of nothing that would induce the Bau people to give up," Mr. Hunt wrote at one point, "except the death of Tanoa" (Hunt *L,* to Williams: 28 April 1845). As this was penned just a few months before Ratu Raivalita tried to strike just that fatal blow, it underscores the connection between his conspiracy and the course of the war.[69]

68. Mrs. Wallis, who apparently had access to Mr. Hunt's text about the beginning of hostilities and/or discussed the matter with him, reports in this connection: "The Rewa chiefs did not suppose that Bau ever intended its destruction. They were not aware of the enmity they had excited, and supposed that after a little skirmishing they could 'soro' [atone] to Bau, receive their pardon, and live on the same friendly terms as before. In this they were mistaken" (1851: 166). These differential reactions are a good illustration of the contrast between the transgressive Bauans and conventional Rewans discussed in chapter 1, above.

69. For other notices relevant to the issue of "a war of chiefs," see Hunt (*WMMS/L:* 17 October 1844, 28 November 1844; Lyth *L:* from Rev. J. Hunt, 28 March 1845; Williams

STRUCTURES AND CONTINGENCIES OF THE CONJUNCTURE

In the first six to eight months of war, Bau achieved a seemingly decisive advantage over Rewan forces that were fighting on their own territory and for the most part on the defensive. With the assistance of several different allied armies (*mataivalu*), the Bauans moved from north to south through the Rewa Delta in a series of attacks until they were within musket shot of the enemy capital. They also interdicted Rewa's southern access to the sea and its subject lands in the islands of Beqa and Kadavu. But in the latter half of 1844, the campaign stalled. The energy of the Bau advance slackened. The large-scale incursions into the Delta ceased. All for no apparent military reason.

The Bauans' early success had involved punctuated drives by their own forces and contingents conscripted from Viti Levu and the Koro Sea islands (Anon. of *Na Mata* 1891 [5]: 8–11). The first moves were coordinated sweeps by forces from Bau and Naitasiri, a powerful allied kingdom on the Wailevu River north of Rewa (fig. 3.6). The Bauans took the left bank of the Wailevu, beginning at Nadali, while the Naitasiri army attacked two towns on the opposite bank (Hunt *J:* 4 December 1843). By January 1844 there were reports of Naitasiri victories over certain towns of Toga, a land on the river allied to Rewa (ibid., 15 January 1844). About this time, Bau also recruited an army from Moturiki and Ovalau—a formally organized force known as the Pet Pigs (*Na Geti*)—and deployed it to some advantage against Tokatoka, an important border ally (*bati*) of Rewa, until it was driven off (ibid., 5 and 19 January 1844). Still other Bauan forces, like those of its own border ally Namata, joined the fray for a period—not always gloriously, as Rewa recorded some victories, but more or less relentlessly. Keeping up the pressure was the critical strategy. It was not always as important to defeat the enemy as it was to intimidate him. Intrigue and bribery could then complete what force alone had not accomplished.

Ratu Cakobau was waging a war as much by diplomacy and conspiracy as by main force. Powerful as the Bau armies were, they had their tactical limitations, especially when it came to subduing the stoutly palisaded and moated towns of the Rewa Delta. Not carrying large supplies but rather living off the land, the invading Bauan forces could not sustain prolonged campaigns or sieges. They usually withdrew from the field after a campaign

L: from Rev. J. Hunt, 28 April 1845); and Jaggar (*WMMS/L:* 9 July 1844, 4 October 1844, 25 November 1844, 5 July 1845; *J:* 3 March 1845). See also Calvert (Williams and Calvert 1859: 440–41).

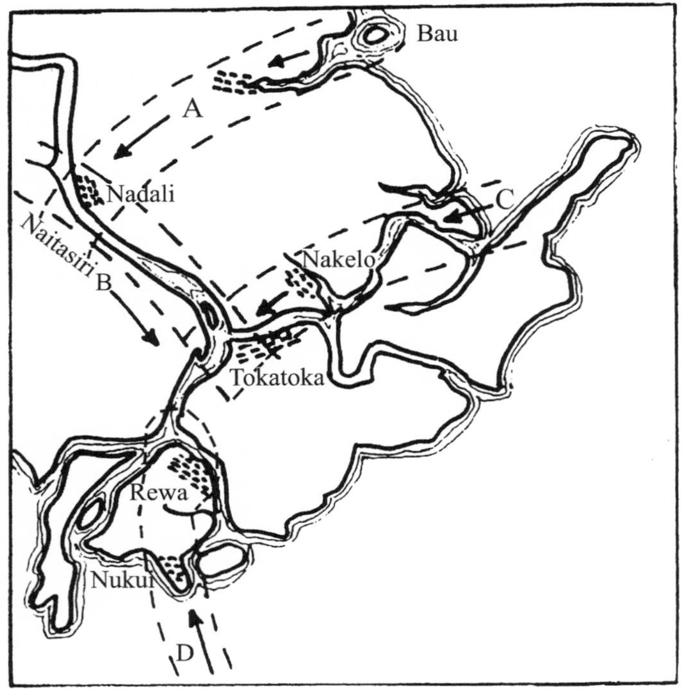

3.6 Bau campaigns in the Rewa Delta, 1843–45. A, B, C: Early campaigns; D: final campaign. (After Tippett 1973: 38)

of a few days. Employing a combination of terror and treachery, they had probably burned more deserted places than they stormed defended ones, and killed the most people when they managed to enter an enemy town by some devious stratagem. Nor would the Bauan armies take more than a few casualties themselves without breaking off the engagement—not to say, hastily retreating (cf. Derrick 1950: 48–49). For besides the logistical limitations, there were structural ones tending to the same disadvantages when it came to large-scale or prolonged battles—and to the same advantages to subverting the enemy resistance by other means.

Many of the Bauan armies and many of the Rewan towns consisted of independent fighting allies or 'borders' (*bati*) with their own rulers, their own gods, and a lively sense of their own interests. However customary or longstanding, their respective relationships to the kings of Bau and Rewa were considered contractual in origin and voluntary in practice. Indeed, the ruling line of the border warrior lands was characteristically descended from a royal woman of the dominant kingdom, and thus held a privileged *vasu* relationship to the ostensibly superior kingdom.[70] In short, the borders were 'lands in and for themselves' (*vanua vakaikoya*), with a considerable freedom of action. This was one of the reasons why war in Fiji was so expensive, as Reverend Williams observed. To mobilize its allies for incursions into the Delta, Bau would have to underwrite with food and treasure the control it did not possess by ascription or coercion. If the allied forces gained a victory, they repaired to Bau again for feasts and gifts. So besides the men lost, Bau's military successes were achieved at "great expense of food to the gods, of riches and provisions to the warriors, and of arms and ammunition, of which Thakombau had a large supply" (Hunt *J:* 19 October 1845). Thus the strategic value of the tributes Bau collected from Lau, Cakaudrove, Macuata, the Koro Sea islands, and elsewhere. And wealth was needed for undermining the alliances of Rewa as well as for upholding the forces of Bau. The Rewan border lands (*bati*) were no less independent and mindful of their own welfare, a corresponding fault of the Rewan hegemony, which made it vulnerable to subversion and defection. Just so, in 1844, things fell apart for Rewa. Ratu Cakobau used his military advantages, together with his famous talents and resources for conspiracy à la Bau (*vere vakaBau*), to dismantle the Rewan confederacy.

Already in January 1844, just two months into the war, Rewa had lost a strategic border ally to Bau, as well as one of its own ruling chiefs and his followers—and its troubles were only beginning (map 3.2). Nakelo, a large land of twelve towns, strategically situated athwart the Rewa Delta between Bau and Rewa, foreswore its customary allegiance to the Roko Tui Dreketi and joined the Bauan camp (Anon. of *Na Mata* 1891 [5]; Calvert *L:* 29 January 1844; Hunt *J:* 22 January 1844; Jaggar *J:* 22 January 1844).[71] It came out later that the Nakelo paramount, the Tui Nakelo, was promised a sister by Ratu Cakobau as the price of his changing sides (Waterhouse 1866: 124). (As we know, in 1845 the same woman, Adi Lolokubou, was accorded instead to the Lasakau chief Ratu Gavidi for revealing Ratu Raivalita's plot,

70. Hocart records an incident that indicates the close relationship between border warriors and wife-taking from the superior chief: "When I asked the people of Wailevu whether they had married ladies from Latu, they remarked 'He is seeking confirmation of the border relationship'" (*HF:* 437).

71. Although contemporary missionary reports and Fijian tradition speak of Nakelo as a whole defecting to Bau, this seems doubtful, given the usual divisive politics and contested chiefships of such lands. In this case, however, the paramount, Tui Nakelo, did switch allegiance—though he would go back to the Rewa side in 1845.

upon which the jilted Nakelo chief rejoined Rewa.)[72] At the same time Nakelo was going over to Bau on the north, Rewa was being hemmed in by other defections to the south. This was when Ro Cokānauto, the brother of the Rewa king, installed himself at Nukui, a fishing town in the southern reach of the Rewa Delta, taking "several large towns" with him to the Bau side (Jaggar *J:* 29 January, 8 February 1844; *WMMS/L:* 9 July 1844). Bau forces as well as the Rewan rebels now used Nukui as a staging area for attacks up the Delta, one of which, in mid-February, came close enough to Rewa to throw the town into a panic (Jaggar *WMMS/L:* 9 July 1844 [15 February 1844]). This was the time, too, when Bauan canoes, operating off Nukui, were attacking the traffic coming to Rewa from its tribute-paying lands in Kadavu (Jaggar *J:* 5 February, 23 March 1844; *WMMS/L:* 9 July 1844). Another subject people (*qali*) of Rewa, the land of Noco in the southeast part of the Delta, also went over to the Bauans—who promptly installed a contingent of fighting men there to make sure it stayed that way (Anon. of *Na Mata* [5]: 9). Lokia, a fishing town quite close to Rewa, when it likewise turned to Bau, provided the location from which musket fire would be directed into the enemy capital itself (Hunt *J:* 28 November 1844). Thus closing in from the south and the north, the Bauan pincer movement in the Delta deprived Rewa of many allied and subject towns, and in so doing left it also without the supplies of food, wealth, and manpower it needed for waging war.

By July 1845 Mr. Jaggar was reporting that Rewa was "surrounded by the enemy," that its own field of operation was "very circumscribed," that food was "very scarce" and was likely to remain so as long as there was war (*WMMS/L:* 9 July 1844). By August the scarcity of food and the threat to the town obliged Mr. Jaggar to abandon the mission at Rewa and join Mr. Hunt at Viwa. By November—not usually a time of plenty in any year, as the yam crop would be exhausted—both Mr. Hunt and Mr. Jaggar were speaking of "famine" in Rewa. "Famine is now making rapid and fearful progress in Rewa territories" (Hunt *WMMS/L:* 21 November 1844). "The horror of famine stares them in the face" (Jaggar *WMMS/L:* 15 November 1844). And by March 1845 the situation of Rewa was truly desper-

72. So the Fijian explanation went. Another reason given for Nakelo's flipflop was that the adjacent land of Tokatoka, likewise a traditional warrior ally of Rewa, went over to Bau (in 1845), and as Nakelo and Tokatoka were in an inherited relationship of rivalry—*veitabani,* 'opposite sides,' as descendants of cross-cousins—they could not both be allies of Bau (Anon. of *Na Mata* 1891 [5]: 10). Perhaps that was indeed brought into play, but it would not be a sufficient explanation of these maneuvers, since Nakelo and Tokatoka had both managed to be allies of Rewa for a long time before the war.

ate. The Rewans were still on the defensive; they had little food because of the loss of subject towns and the destruction of gardens by the enemy; they had little land left upon which they could plant and little seed to do so; they no longer had the wealth to collect an army or the provisions to sustain one (Jaggar *WMMS/L:* 3 March 1845).[73] You would think they were finished.

By all rights, Rewa should have been finished, opined Mr. Hunt in reflections on the first months of the war, except that Bau failed to follow up the decisive advantage it had achieved:

> Preparations for commencing the war were made at Bau with great spirit. The gods were supplicated, men and arms prepared, and the first towns that were attacked fell an easy prey to the Bau warriors. The Rewa people made but faint resistance, and such was the success of Thakombau [Ratu Cakobau] that had he known how to follow it up and used the advantages he gained the war might have terminated in six months. On one occasion the warriors approached very near Rewa, and threw the town into such panic that had it been attacked at once it would most likely have been evacuated and burned. Instead, however, of availing themselves of this easy success they must return to Bau to return thanks to the gods for their success and do honour to the men who had been successful in killing any of the enemy. (Hunt *J:* 19 October 1845)

By the end of 1844, even though Rewa was surrounded and impoverished, the war was practically at a standstill. It had been so for some months—and would remain so until Ratu Raivalita's death the next August. The large-scale forays of the Bauans and their allies into the Rewa Delta had ceased by July 1844 (Jaggar *WMMS/L:* 9 July 1844)—although this was not simply because they were too busy celebrating their earlier victories, as Mr. Hunt believed. The ensuing months saw an occasional attack on an outlying Rewan town, but most of the action now involved smaller Bauan raiding parties seeking their victims outside the enemy fortifications in ambushes by land or seaborne descents by canoe. "They are continually going out on such errands, and sometimes kill and bring home their prey,

73. Reverend Jaggar contradicts himself to some extent about the shortage of food in the Rewa capital. In the same letter of 3 March, he speculates that the yam harvest had come in, and though he speaks of it as "their little stock of yams," supposing the gardening area had been reduced, he notes that Fijians can go a long time on little food (Jaggar *WMMS/L:* 3 March 1845).

whilst at other times they return home unsuccessful" (ibid.).[74] It may well be that the Bauans were more interested in securing cannibal victims at this time than in destroying Rewan towns. They needed the *bakola* ('cannibal victims') for certain other purposes.

Human victims were needed for feasting the Cakaudrove people. Led by their old paramount king, the Tui Cakau, a large contingent of Cakaudrove came to Bau in March 1844, and stayed for nearly a year. Included in the visiting party were a group of Butoni sea warriors: fighting men who were Bauan in ancestry and dual in affiliation, as they retained their original identity and their loyalty to the Bau chiefs (see above, chapter 1). Relations between Bau and Cakaudrove had blown hot and cold for decades, but the Tui Cakau now came with two double canoes to present in submission (*i soro*) to Ratu Tānoa, and to ask for military assistance from Bau. Visits of this kind from Cakaudrove were highly ceremonious. They were marked by an initial several days of ritually obsequious conduct on the part of the visitors, followed by the provision of generous feasts with complements of cannibal victims on the part of their Bauan hosts.[75] Bau was strictly obligated to provide such *bakola,* and the Cakaudrove people were as strictly enjoined to eat them (cf. Calvert *J:* 2 July 1850). Such being the case, Bau's hostilities with Rewa took on another purpose. The hit-and-run raids that had replaced the campaigns by Bauan armies now served to furnish forth cannibal feasts for the Cakaudrove people. Reverend Jaggar described one such event for the edification of the Methodist officials in London:

> They have had a cannibal feast at Bau. Eleven of the Rawa [Rewa] people were killed in an ambushment and *cooked* and *eaten* by the Somosomo [i.e. Cakaudrove] people who were at Bau at the time. This was a *rich* repast for them, and usually considered a *delicacy.* They manufactured the poor creatures' leg-bones into *needles,* some of which I had one day in my hand. I also saw two human hands which had been hung over the fire and smoke dried! I also conversed with a gentleman [apparently,

74. Another customary stealth tactic of Fijian warfare, the lone feat of derring-do called *bati kadi,* where an individual warrior tries to make a name for himself by venturing into enemy territory, at night usually, and waylaying an unsuspecting man, woman or child, is not specifically mentioned by contemporary sources, but it may well have been practiced in this doldrum period of the war.

75. The rituals of Cakaudrove visits were supposed to recapitulate the original rescue of the half-drowned Cakaudrove god, in the form of a rat, by the Bauan people. The myth and the associated ritual behaviors of the Cakaudrove people at Bau are still well known in Fiji, as they also were in the mid-nineteenth century.

> Mr. Jaggar thus refers to a *Papalagi*] who had seen some part of the upper trunk of a man cooked; the pigs were likewise partaking of human entrails in the streets of Bau on that occasion! These, dear Sirs, are facts and realities. . . . Nothing but the Gospel can raise them fully from their degradation. (Jaggar *WMMS/L:* 4 October 1844)

Mr. Jaggar also tells of a stealth raid by Lasakau canoes that took twenty-eight prisoners back to Bau, where some were cast on red-hot stones while still alive (ibid., 3 March 1845). Indeed, the cannibal ovens were often lit during the stay of the Cakaudrove people. Mr. Hunt in late November estimated that "scarcely less than fifty persons have been eaten in Bau alone during the last three months, some of them Rawa [*sic*] chiefs of considerable rank" (Hunt *WMMS/L:* 28 November 1844). Yet despite that the bodies came mainly from Rewa or Rewan countries, the Cakaudrove visit was something of a diversion, involving a shift in Bau's military attention.

To believe Mr. Jaggar, "most of the attention of the Bauans has been directed to the Somosomo [Cakaudrove] people, who with their Chief have for more than a twelvemonth been visiting Bau" (*WMMS/L:* 3 March 1845). Their "Chief," the old Tui Cakau, was there to 'cry war' (*tagi valu*), to get Bau to help him punish the Natewa people of southeastern Vanua Levu. A traditional warrior ally (*bati*) of the Cakaudrove kings, this powerful and rebellious land had been giving the latter trouble for years (Lyth *J:* 4 March 1844; Williams 1931, 1:260). Even as the Tui Cakau was sojourning in Bau, his son Tui Kilakila, holding the official war king title (Vunivalu) in Cakaudrove, led several attacks on the Natewans, not all of them glorious. As for Bau's interest in the matter, it was widely believed that Ratu Cakobau was secretly inciting the Natewa revolt. Mr. Hunt presciently foresaw that if and when the Bau forces got involved, it would not only cost the Cakaudrove people dearly in treasure, but compel Cakaudrove "to bow its neck a little more willingly to the yoke of Bau" (Hunt *WMMS/L:* 26 February 1845). This is in fact what came to pass in 1846, when an army led by Ratu Cakobau effected the submission (*i soro*) of the Natewans to Bau rather than to their traditional Cakaudrove masters. Still, that was after Bau had apparently settled matters with Rewa by destroying the town in December 1845. And the question remains why Bau did not crush Rewa a year or eighteen months before, since the Cakaudrove situation seems more a convenient than necessary reason for the delay, and certainly not the only reason.

The greater necessity of the stalemate in the war with Rewa lay in the internal politics of Bau. It was the revival of the generations-old conflict between the ancient Bauan nobility led by the Nabaubau people (and including the Roko Tui Bau) and the parvenu Tui Kaba clan of war kings. The Nabaubau and their several *vasu* outside Bau were natural allies of Ratu Raivalita, who for his part was conspiring with the Rewan enemy to seize power—and thus end the war. Just a month before Ratu Raivalita's death, Mr. Jaggar, noting that there appeared to be "no prospect of a speedy termination" of the conflict with Rewa, alluded to a certain factionalism in Bau that he believed responsible for the military impasse: "The state of affairs in the Capital [Bau] seems to be doubtful, and we are sometimes led to think that an undercurrent is at work which would certainly stagnate their progress and damp the hopes and darken the prospect of success in war. It is true 'a kingdom divided against itself cannot stand.' I think the result of the long continued war between these two powerful Districts may be calculated on issuing in the death of the Rawa [*sic*] Chiefs should Bau hold with itself, but not otherwise" (Jaggar *WMMS/L:* 5 July 1845). Less elliptical and more precise, Mr. Hunt had identified the sources of dissension some months before. In January he wrote to Reverend Lyth: "I think Bau could easily crush Rewa now, but Tui ila ila [Tui Kilakila], Namosimalua, Tui Veikau, and the chief of Naitasiri, to say nothing of Raivalita, stand in the way of the death of the Rewa chiefs. Perhaps some of the obstacles will be removed. The Lord knoweth" (Lyth *L:* 4 January 1845).

By all evidence, what was impeding Bau's war with Rewa was a coalition of the old enemies of Ratu Tānoa, a coalition pivoting on the desperate ambitions of Ratu Raivalita, and joined through him to the equally desperate military situation of the Rewans. The conspiracies of Ratu Raivalita and his maternal uncles, the Rewa rulers, were thus fortified by Bauan grievances of the *longue durée.* Including the paramounts of Namara (Tui Veikau) and Viwa (Namosimalua), Mr. Hunt's list of the Bauan chiefs standing in the way of the death of the Rewa king overlaps with those who would soon be revealed as collaborators in Ratu Raivalita's plot to assassinate Ratu Cakobau and Ratu Tānoa (see above, pages 211–20). Even more striking is the correspondence between Mr. Hunt's list and another, compiled around a decade earlier by Reverend Cross, of important chiefs who were uterine nephews (*vasu*) to the deposed war kings of Bau, the Nabaubau or Batitobe. According to Mr. Cross's information, the aforementioned paramounts of Namara and Viwa, as well as the war king of Cakaudrove ("Tui ila ila" in Mr. Hunt's list) and the Rewa king (Ro Kania) were all daughters' sons of one "Savou," a bitter enemy of Ratu Banuve (the father of Ratu Tānoa). This was Ratu Banuve, the famous usurper, who bested Savou in their struggle for the Vunivalu title. Everything suggests that it was from the native aristocracy of Bau and their adherents, who had already demonstrated their willingness to be rid of Ratu Tānoa in the 1830s and would attempt to do away with Ratu Cakobau in the 1850s, that Ratu Raivalita was able to recruit "the strong party in his favour" in 1844–45. (Recall that one of Ratu Raivalita's boon companions, Ratu Nayagodamu, was of the house of the Reclining Vunivalu who had replaced Ratu Tānoa in the coup of 1832.) As for the other co-conspirators, the Rewa king and his brother Ratu Qaraniqio, they had motive aplenty: the assassination of Ratu Cakobau and his father could turn their imminent defeat in the war with Bau into a favorable peace.

It was this state of the collective forces that brought about the ultimate showdown between Ratu Raivalita and Ratu Cakobau. Accordingly, when Ratu Raivalita was killed at the command of Ratu Cakobau, the correlation of forces changed: the impasse in the war was broken. But it was Bau's swift advance in the first months of war that had set the stage for the death of kings. All but eliminated from succession to the rule of Bau by the onset of the conflict, Ratu Raivalita now saw his only hope in the removal of Ratu Cakobau and Ratu Tānoa. By the latter half of 1844, that stroke was also the only hope of the Rewa rulers for peace and their own survival. The plot of their Bauan *vasu* with the inherited enemies of the Tui Kaba clan helped significantly to slow the pace of Bau's campaign in the Rewa Delta. In the event, Ratu Raivalita became a double menace to Ratu Cakobau: an obstacle to his military success—which is also to say, his imperial ambitions—as well as a threat to his life. He had just as much necessity to remove Ratu Raivalita as Ratu Raivalita, him. The honor done to Ratu Raivalita in delegating him, along with an entourage of warriors, to escort the old Cakaudrove king home in March 1845 thus appears in another light, as a less violent expedient of the politics of elimination. But a few months after Ratu Raivalita's return to Bau, he became another victim of the fratricidal havoc that haunts Fijian dynastic histories.

The fall of Rewa in November 1845 was not only a sequel to Ratu Raivalita's death but something of a sequitur. Such was the opinion of Ratu Qaraniqio, to judge by the way he recounted the event a few years later. As he told the Catholic missionary, on the very night of the day Ratu Raivalita died, Ratu Cakobau marched on Rewa. The next day at dawn he attacked the town, and killed the king (Deniau, *HF2*). Months of skirmishing and intrigue were thus compressed by Ratu Qaraniqio into one eventful twenty-four hours, but was not this mythification a way of signifying causation? Reverend Calvert's account, though it followed a more reasonable temporality, explicitly involved the same explanation of Rewa's demise.

Ratu Raivalita's death, said Mr. Calvert, "was a heavy blow to the Rewan chiefs. . . . Their great hope and stay was gone, now that Raivalita was dead; and forced into submissive humility, they sued for peace" (Williams and Calvert 1859: 351). Even this, however, foreshortens the subsequent events. The death of Ratu Raivalita was surely a critical turn in the war, but what immediately followed was the end of the stalemate. Bau now undertook a further methodical encroachment into the Rewa Delta that soon enough left the enemy capital defenseless.

The final assault began early in November 1845, when the Bauans arrived on the south coast of the Delta near Nukui, the stronghold of their puppet Rewan king, Ro Cokānauto (map 3.2).[76] They had come to secure the defection of Dreketi, a land in a servile relation (*qali*) to the Rewa chiefs, a main provider of the chiefs' food. Beginning thus in Dreketi, the final Bauan advance had a certain mythical resonance. Rewan tradition has it that Dreketi was the original residence in the Delta of the immigrant chiefs who finally became the Rewa kings (thus, "Roko Tui Dreketi"), while their proximate stop, before assuming the kingship, was in the land of Burebasaga. Ratu Cakobau, of course, had good tactical reasons for moving now from Dreketi to Burebasaga, thus skirting and enclosing Rewa itself, but the route also retraced the mythical course of the Dreketi dynasty—on the mission of obliterating it. Burebasaga's capitulation to Bau effectively sealed Rewa's fate, since Burebasaga detained the office of mobilizing the fighting forces of Rewa's allies (*bati*) and subjects (*qali*). Perhaps, then, the fall of Burebasaga was the deciding reason for the defection to Bau of the important Rewan border land of Tokatoka, after what Mr. Hunt called its "noble resistance." Like other Rewan lands, Tokatoka was not taken by force, but was "wearied out with watching and hunger" (Hunt *J:* 19 October 1845). It was at this point, with Rewa virtually isolated, that the offer of surrender mentioned by Mr. Calvert was sent to Ratu Cakobau. However, the messenger, the designated Envoy to Bau (*Mata ki Bau*) was himself subverted by Ratu Cakobau, and entered into a plot to betray the capital to the enemy forces (see above, chapter 1). The "spirit of revenge" was too heavy on the Bau chiefs for them to accept surrender, fed as it was by the insults of the Rewans and their complicity in Ratu Raivalita's "treacherous plot" (Williams and Calvert 1859: 351).

76. I am principally following the accounts supplied to Reverend Lyth (*TFR* 2:201–7) by Reverend Jaggar, the most detailed for this period, as well as the reports of Ratu Deve Toganivalu (*TkB*); Hunt (*J:* 19 October 1845; cf. Waterhouse 1866: 125–27); and Anon. of *Na Mata* (1891 [5]).

In the destruction of Rewa that followed, Ratu Cakobau got his revenge on Ro Kania, the Roko Tui Dreketi—whose mother was his own mother's sister and whose wife was his close classificatory sister (FBD). Perhaps because the Rewa king was a great *vasu* to Bau, or perhaps because he never understood his enemy or the war in which he was engaged, he came off to Ratu Cakobau's canoe on the Wailevu River while his town was burning, evidently believing "that Thakombau would *not* kill him" (Lyth *TFR,* 1:206). Here was an ultimate expression, in the persons of the rulers, of the contrast between conventional Rewa and transgressive Bau. For the Rewa king's pleas of kinship were of no avail. By most accounts, Ratu Cakobau ordered Komainaua, the same who first clubbed Ratu Raivalita, to kill the Roko Tui Dreketi. There was a lot of irony in this. As we know, Komainaua, the *vasu* to Cakaudrove, had an ambiguous relation to Ratu Cakobau, as he had been a major instigator of Cakaudrove's attempt to undermine Bau's hegemony in 1839–41. So there may be at least as much logical motivation as there is factual for the stories that say that Komainaua refused to obey Ratu Cakobau's command or else fired at the Rewa king and missed him. According to Mr. Lyth's text, not only did he miss, but so did two other members of Ratu Cakobau's entourage—one being the son of Ratu Bativuaka, the Rewa king's deceased brother. Mr. Lyth's account goes on to underscore the contrast between the royal dispositions of the sacred ruler of Rewa and the war king of Bau. The former is said to have called out to Ratu Cakobau, "Why do you wish to kill me? Let me live. I am your relative." To which the Bauan terror replies, "No, I shall kill you; great have been your wicked speeches against me and my father" (Lyth *TFR,* 1:207).

At this point a foreigner enters the action, an otherwise unidentified Manilla-man, according to Mr. Hunt (*J:* 19 October 1845). The presence of such outsiders—including European beachcombers, Tahitians, and Hawaiians—in the coteries of Fijian ruling chiefs was observed earlier, notably in the analogous context of the attack on Ratu Raivalita. Besides the expertise these foreigners brought in fixing and firing muskets or distilling grog, they had a particular political value because of their immunity to, or indeed contempt for, the tabus on violating the persons of great chiefs. Such tabus fairly protected the likes of Ro Kania and Ratu Cakobau in purely Fijian warfare, but they could be without such effect where *Papalagi,* Tongans, or Manilla-men were concerned. By most accounts, then, it was the Manilla-man—described in Mr. Williams's text as "a foreigner residing at Bau"—who first shot and wounded the Rewa king when he came off to Ratu Cakobau's canoe (Williams *MN,* vol. 2). The Rewa king also suffered a flesh wound in the chest from the spear thrust of a Bauan, perhaps before, perhaps after he was wounded by musketball; the story varies with the telling. Most versions have it that Ratu Cakobau thereupon cleft the doubly injured king's skull with a battleaxe, still without killing him—which was only accomplished when Ratu Cakobau ordered him strangled. All this took place in the presence of the Rewa king's wife and children. They were brought off from the town at Ratu Cakobau's command, who at least in this instance knew how to honor kinship—and neutralize the Rewa heirs?—as she was his half-sister by Ratu Tānoa. So the conclusion of Mr. Williams's account: "On the canoe where [the king's] children were, there he fell, there he lay in blood, and thus the whole family were carried in savage triumph to the bloody city of Bau" (ibid.). But perhaps a more revelatory conclusion would be the expression attributed to Ratu Cakobau in the Fijian tradition of the event, supposed to have been uttered when he struck the Rewa king with his battleaxe: "Such is your custom, the *vasus* of Bau in every land. If another one of you raises such evil, he will be eaten by Uvinisiga [the name of Ratu Cakobau's club]" (Anon. of *Na Mata* 1891 [5]: 11).

CODA: STRUCTURE AND CONTINGENCY IN HISTORY

It could all have been otherwise. Given the availability of muskets and accomplices, the *vasu* to Rewa, Ratu Raivalita, might well have assassinated Ratu Cakobau. Peace would soon have been concluded, with Rewa spared destruction. To repeat Reverend Calvert's assessment, the Rewa rulers had engaged Ratu Raivalita "to kill his brother Thakombau, on condition that Rewa should become tributary to him on his assuming the government of Mbau" (Williams and Calvert 1859: 350). Beyond that turn of events, it would be difficult to imagine the counterfactual history of the Fiji Islands, absent Ratu Cakobau from August 1845 onward. But some sense of the significance of such a subtraction can be gained from what actually did happen: from the preeminence achieved by Ratu Cakobau and Bau in the subsequent course of Fijian history.

Decimated at the end of 1845 and its king killed, Rewa did not in fact capitulate. Ratu Qaraniqio escaped the slaughter and ably took up the Rewan cause from a sanctuary in the mountains, reviving certain connections to allied lands. Although Rewa was again destroyed by the Bauans in 1847, Ratu Qaraniqio once more survived and carried on the struggle until his sudden death in 1855 (see above, chapter 2). By then, Ratu Cakobau, under duress from Rewa and rebellious Bauans, had converted to Methodism, which gave him the decisive political and military assistance of the various Christian forces: the English missionaries whose scheming and bribery helped defuse the Bauan opposition, and the Tongans who delivered the *coup de grace* to Ratu Cakobau's remaining enemies in the decisive battle of Kaba in April 1855. Meanwhile, even as the war with Rewa was proceeding, Ratu Cakobau and the Bauans were busy in Vanua Levu, with mixed results. The large campaign in Vanua Levu in 1846, ostensibly to assist Cakaudrove against its fractious Natewan allies, substantially bolstered Bau's authority in eastern Fiji generally, but the gains were given back in the ill-fated *bêche-de-mer* campaign against Macuata in 1852 (see above, chapter 1). Still, at the end of the long Polynesian War, Bau was clearly the dominant power among Fijian lands, and Ratu Cakobau the strongest Fijian ruler. It is true that the war strengthened the various *Papalagi* forces operating in the islands: the Christian missionaries; the resident and visiting traders; and the governments, American and British principally, represented by naval vessels and diplomatic consuls. If, on the one hand, these foreigners progressively encroached on Fijian autonomy, on the other hand, it was largely by and through the Bauans—until his death in 1883, specifically through Ratu Cakobau—that they would have to assert their own power. It is arguable whether Bau did not attain a greater presence in Fiji, and effectively control a greater number of Fijians, with European backing and tutelage than it had on its own during the first half of the nineteenth century.

The title of Tui Viti, King of Fiji, that had come to Ratu Cakobau in the mail in 1844, in the letter so addressed by the British consul in Honolulu, became something more and something less of a political reality in the next forty years. We have noted that the missionaries were pleased to so designate Ratu Cakobau, especially after he was converted. In the cession of Fiji to Great Britain, which Ratu Cakobau negotiated with the British consul W. T. Pritchard in 1858, he was designated "Vunivalu of the armies of Fiji and Tui Viti, etc." That cession was refused by the British, but a series of ostensibly Fijian governments headed by Ratu Cakobau and promoted by *Papalagi* followed, the last of which, the so-called Cakobau government of 1871–74, saw him installed in the title of Tui Viti. Mr. Pritchard and the Whites were also critical in keeping at bay and finally neutralizing a Tongan threat to displace Bau as the hegemonic Fijian power. Under the leadership of their chief Ma'afu, a man of royal Tongan descent and a worthy adversary of Ratu Cakobau, the Tongans had gained control of Lau and much of Vanua Levu in the 1860s. But they failed to gain the decisive European backing for their larger ambitions. The Tui Viti was the principal Fijian agent of the cession of Fiji to Britain in 1874, and for decades after, the Bau chiefs dominated the colonial system of indirect rule.[77]

So while one cannot know what Fijian history would have been if Ratu Cakobau had died in 1845, it is safe to say it would have been quite different because of the different relations between the forces in play, let alone the persons instigating them. In all likelihood, there would not have been the same distribution of power among the kingdoms of Bau, Rewa, Cakaudrove, Lau, and Macuata. Nor, then, the same articulations of outside forces, European and Tongan, with Fijian politics. Absent Ratu Cakobau, the process of conversion to Christianity would have had another, probably more onerous, course. There would not have been the same political schisms between Protestantism and Catholicism, the latter gaining footholds in Rewa and Cakaudrove, as against the Protestant success in Bau and via Bau in most of Fiji. And would not the Tongans and Ma'afu—who was always selling himself as more friendly to Whites than Cakobau and more knowledgeable of their ways—have had a greater or even a dominant role in the late precolonial and colonial periods? The chances that Bau alone could have withstood the Tongans seem slim, when one considers its endemic factionalism and the less than likely possibility that Ratu Raivalita could have neutralized it, or even survived it for very long.

And yet either outcome, factual or counterfactual, however contingent, would have been culturally coherent and structurally motivated. The assassination was surely a contingency: Nothing in the relations of the conjuncture or the larger cultural system stipulated that Ratu Cakobau would eliminate Ratu Raivalita rather than vice versa. In relaying the larger order into the rivalry of those particular persons, authorizing them in their individuality to incarnate the destiny of social totalities, structure thus opens itself to contingency. Without doing away with structural order, as Raymond Aron recommends, we restore it to its limits. All sorts of biographical, psychological, and circumstantial conditions, quite beyond the respective *vasu* relations of Ratu Cakobau and Ratu Raivalita, their constituted enmity as half-brothers, or the strategic situation of the Bau-Rewa war, were involved in determining who succeeded in killing whom. In-

77. Bau remained powerful, one could say, until the death of Ratu Sir Lala Sukana in 1958. This high-ranking Bauan, *vasu* to Lau, head of the Native Lands Commission, secretary for Fijian affairs in the colonial government, was, next to Ratu Cakobau, the most famous leader in Fijian history.

deed, if the report be true that the pistol of a *Papalagi* on the scene misfired when he tried to retaliate against Ratu Cakobau after Ratu Raivalita was struck down, the affair could have ended with both of them dead. Yet whoever did succeed, the outcome would still be a logical dénouement of these same structural conditions that did not determine it. Without eliminating contingency, as Sartre says, we must restore to it its rationality. Ratu Raivalita's plot to kill Ratu Cakobau was clearly motivated in his *vasu* kinship to Rewa, the decline of some years in the relationship between Bau and Rewa that ruined his chances of succeeding to the kingship in Bau, and Rewa's beleaguered position of 1844–45 in the conflict with Bau. If Ratu Raivalita's fratricidal plan had worked, this structural context, these systemic conditions would have explained virtually everything about it—except why it worked.

Yet more interesting from the perspective of an anthropological historiography is that even if Ratu Raivalita had succeeded in killing and replacing Ratu Cakobau, the historic effects, although radically different from what actually happened, would also be consistent with the Fijian cultural order. Peace with Rewa? Ratu Raivalita was *vasu* to Rewa. Dissension again in Bau? The old chiefly enemies of Ratu Raivalita's people, the Tui Kaba, combine with a near kinsman to overthrow him. (The kinsman would probably be Ratu Mara Kapaiwai, who ten years later led a rebellion—which included the Vusaradave warriors—against his close classificatory brother Ratu Cakobau, almost toppling him.) The event was contingent, but it unfolded in the terms of a particular cultural field, from which the actors drew their reasons and the happening found its meanings. From the perspective of the cultural order, what happened was arbitrary, but what followed was reasonable. The culture did not make the contingency as such, only the difference it made.

Of course, the structural coherence of a contingent outcome gives the strong impression of cultural continuity, or even cultural determinism—as if the system were impervious to the event. But one need not be thus misled. The cultural continuity at issue was not the only one possible, and it was anything but prescribed. If the culture in this way reproduces itself, it reproduces itself in an altered state. It knows a different future, even as a system, than what might have been. That Fiji would have been the same had Ratu Cakobau died young—this statement should always make one laugh.

History's paradoxes reside in the dialogue of different registers, beginning with the motivated expression of collectives in individuals, categories in practices, structures in events. Thucydides, too, believed he was finding universals in particulars, in his case universals of human nature in the particulars of history. The argument here is that the problem is complicated, in a way doubled, when the universals are of culture rather than nature: the cultural schemes of the society (or societies) in which historical action unfolds. For cultural totalities are also historical particularities: so many distinctive schemes of values and relationships that variously empower certain subjects, individual or collective, as history-makers and give their acts specific motivation and effect. Who or what is a historical actor, what is a historical act and what will be its historical consequences: these are determinations of a cultural order, and differently determined in different orders. No history, then, without culture. And vice versa, insofar as in the event, the culture is neither what it was before nor what it could have been.

BIBLIOGRAPHY

* * *

An asterisk preceding an entry identifies unpublished sources. Abbreviations used in the notes are given in square brackets. A special section focusing on the Elián Gonzalez affair follows the main bibliography. The following abbreviations of archives and institutions are used in the bibliography:

CSO/MP	Colonial Secretary's Office, Minute Paper, National Archives of Fiji, Suva
ML	Mitchell Library, Library of New South Wales, Sydney
MOM	Methodist Overseas Mission Papers, Mitchell Library, Sydney
NAF	National Archives of Fiji, Suva
PMB	Pacific Manuscripts Bureau Microfilms, Australian National University, Sydney and subscription libraries
SOAS	Library of the School of Oriental and African Studies, University of London
WMMS	Wesleyan Methodist Missionary Society, London

Althusser, Louis. 1971. *Lenin and Philosophy and Other Essays.* New York: Monthly Review Press.

Andrewes, Antony. 1971. *Greek Society.* Harmondsworth, Middlesex, England: Penguin.

*Anonymous of *Gambia.* [*Log*] Log of the brig *Gambia* (Capt. Joseph Hartwell), voyage from Salem to New Zealand and Fiji, 1844–46. PMB 210. Original in Peabody Museum, Salem, Mass.

Anonymous of *Na Mata.* 1891. "Ai Tukutuku kei Ratu Radomo Ramatenikutu Na Vunivalu mai Bau." *Na Mata:* (1) 13–14 January; (2) 12–15 February; (3) 4–7 March; (4) 10–13 April; (5) 8–11 May; (6) 8–10 June; (7) 13–15 July; (8) 11–12 August; (9) 13–14 September.

Apollodorus. 1921. *The Library.* Trans. Sir James George Frazer. 2 vols. Loeb Classical Library. London: Heinemann.

Aristophanes. 1981. *Knights.* Ed. and trans. Alan H. Sommerstein. Warminster, U.K.: Aris & Phillips.

———. 1994. *Four Plays by Aristophanes.* Ed. and trans. William Arrowsmith, Richard Lattimore, and Douglass Parker. New York: Meridian.

———. 1998. *Aristophanes I: Clouds, Wasps, Birds.* Trans. Peter Meineck. Indianapolis: Hackett.

Aristotle. 1950. *Aristotle's Constitution of Athens and Related Texts.* Trans. Kurt von Fritz and Ernst Kapp. New York: Hafner.

Arnold, John H. 2000. *History: A Very Short Introduction.* Oxford: Oxford University Press.

Aron, Raymond. 1961. Thucydide et le récit des événements. *History and Theory* 1: 103–28.

Arrowsmith, William. 1994. Introduction to *The Birds,* by Aristophanes. In *Four Plays by Aristophanes,* ed. and trans. William Arrowsmith, Richard Lattimore, and Douglass Parker, 173–83. New York: Meridian.

Atheneus. 1928. *The Deinosophists.* Loeb Classical Library. London: Heinemann.

Austin, M. M., and P. Vidal-Naquet. 1977. *Economic and Social History of Ancient Greece: An Introduction.* Berkeley: University of California Press.

Bagby, Laurie M. Johnson. 1994. The use and abuse of Thucydides in international relations. *International Organization* 48: 131–53.

Barnes, Julian. 1984. *Flaubert's Parrot.* New York: Vintage International.

Barrett, Michèle. 1991. *The Politics of Truth: From Marx to Foucault.* Stanford: Stanford University Press.

Belcher, Capt. Sir Edward. 1843. *Narrative of a Voyage Round the World Performed in Her Majesty's Ship* Sulphur, *during the Years 1836–1842.* Vol. 2. London: Colburn.

Bloomfield, Rev. S. T., trans. and ed. 1829. *The History of Thucydides.* 3 vols. London: Longman, Rees, Orme, Brown, & Green.

Bourdieu, Pierre. 1996. *The Rules of Art: Genesis and Structure of the Literary Field.* Stanford: Stanford University Press.

Brewster, A. 1920. The chronicles of the Noemalu tribe or dwellers in Emalu. *Transactions of the Fiji Society* 1920: 6–15.

Brown, Clifford W. 1987. Thucydides, Hobbes, and the derivation of anarchy. *History of Political Thought* 8: 33–62.

Brunt, P. A. 1993. *Studies in Greek History and Thought.* Oxford: Clarendon Press.

Cahen, E. n.d. Panathenaia. In *Dictionnaire des antiquités grecques et romaines,* ed. Charles Daremberg, 4:303–31. Paris: Hachette.

Calame, Claude. 1990a. Du figuratif au thématique: aspects narratifs et interprétatifs de la description en anthropologie de la Grèce ancienne. In *Le discours anthropologique,* by Jean-Michel Adam, Marie-Jeanne Borel, Claude Calame, and Mondher Kilani, 111–34. Paris: Méridiens Klincksieck.

———. 1990b. *Thésée et l'imaginaire Athénien.* Lausanne: Editions Payot.

Calvert, Rev. James. 1856. *Events in Feejee: Narrated in Recent Letters from Several Wesleyan Missionaries,* by J. Calvert et al. 2d ed. London: John Mason.

*———. [*J*] Journals of Rev. James Calvert, 1838–86. WMMS (Box 1). SOAS.

*———. [*L*] Personal Papers and Correspondence of Rev. James Calvert. WMMS (Box 3). SOAS.

*———. [*Missions*] In Notebooks and Miscellaneous Papers of Rev. James Calvert. WMMS (Box 2). SOAS.

*———. [*WMMS/L*] *See under* Wesleyan Methodist Missionary Society, London.

Campbell, Ian. 1992. *Island Kingdom: Tonga Ancient and Modern.* Christchurch, N.Z.: Canterbury University Press.

Capell, A. 1973. *A New Fijian Dictionary.* 4th ed. Suva: Government Printer.

Carey, William S. 1972. *Wrecked on the Feejees.* Fairfield, Wash.: Ye Galleon Press.

Cargill, Rev. David. 1977. *The Diaries and Correspondence of David Cargill, 1832–1843.* Ed. Albert J. Schütz. Canberra: Australian National University Press.

*———. [*J*] Journal of Rev. David Cargill, 1832–38. ML (A 1817, 1818).

*———. [*WMMS/L*] *See under* Wesleyan Methodist Missionary Society, London.

Cargill, Margaret. 1855. *Memories of Mrs. Margaret Cargill.* 2d ed. London: Mason.

Cartledge, Paul. 1993. *The Greeks: A Portrait of Self and Others.* Rev. ed. Oxford: Oxford University Press.

———. 2001. *Spartan Reflections.* Berkeley: University of California Press.

———. 2002. *Sparta and Lakonia: A Regional History 1300–362 B.C.* 2d ed. London: Routledge.

Cartwright, David. 1997. *A Historical Commentary on Thucydides: A Companion to Rex Warner's Penguin Translation.* Ann Arbor: University of Michigan Press.

Casson, Lionel. 1991. *The Ancient Mariners: Seafarers and Sea Fighters of the Mediterranean in Ancient Times.* 2d ed. Princeton: Princeton University Press.

*Catholic Missionaries. [*CL*] Letters of the Catholic missionaries to Fiji. Marist Mission Archives, Rome.

Cawkwell, George. 1997. *Thucydides and the Peloponnesian War.* London: Routledge.

*Cheever, George N. [*J*] Journal of the ship *Emerald* from Salem to the islands of the South Pacific. Peabody Museum, Salem, Mass.

Clifford, James. 1983. On ethnographic authority. *Representations* 2 (Spring): 132–43.

Clunie, Fergus. 1977. *Fijian Weapons and Warfare.* Bulletin of the Fiji Museum, No. 2. Suva: Fiji Museum.

———. 1984. The Manila brig. *Domodomo: Fiji Museum Quarterly* 2 (2): 42–86.

———. 1986. *Yalo i Viti. Shades of Fiji: A Fiji Museum Catalogue.* Suva: Fiji Museum.

Cogan, Marc. 1981. *The Human Thing: The Speeches and Principles of Thucydides' History.* Chicago: University of Chicago Press.

Cohen, Edward. 2000. *The Athenian Nation.* Princeton: Princeton University Press.

*Colvocoresses, Lt. George M. [*J*] Journal of Lt. George M. Colvocoresses. Coe Collection, Yale University Library, New Haven, Conn.

*———. [*N*] Narrative, United States Exploring Expedition, miscellaneous

documents, 1838–42. PMB 539. Original in Yale University Library, New Haven, Conn.

Comaroff, Jean, and John Comaroff. 1991. *Of Revelation and Revolution: Christianity, Colonialism, and Consciousness in South Africa.* Vol. 1. Chicago: University of Chicago Press.

Connor, W. Robert. 1977. A post modernist Thucydides. *Classics Journal* 72: 289–98.

———. 1984. *Thucydides.* Princeton: Princeton University Press.

———. 1992. *The New Politicians of Fifth-Century Athens.* Indianapolis: Hackett.

Cook, Albert. 1985. Particular and general in Thucydides. *Illinois Classical Studies* 10: 23–51.

Cornford, Francis M. 1971. *Thucydides Mythistoricus.* Philadelphia: University of Pennsylvania Press.

*Council of Chiefs. [*Proceedings*] Notes of the Proceedings of a Native Council, 1875–1910. NAF.

Crane, Gregory. 1992a. The fear and pursuit of risk: Corinth on Athens, Sparta and the Peloponnesians (Thucydides 1.68–71, 120–21). *Transactions of the American Philological Association* 122: 227–56.

———. 1992b. Power, prestige, and the Corcyrean affair in Thucydides I. *Classical Antiquity* 11: 1–27.

———. 1998. *Thucydides and the Ancient Simplicity: The Limits of Political Realism.* Berkeley: University of California Press.

Crawley, R., trans. 1934. *The Complete Writings of Thucydides: The Peloponnesian War.* New York: Modern Library. [Originally published in 1876.]

*Cross, Rev. William. [*D*] Diary of Rev. William Cross, 28 December 1837–1 October 1842. ML (MOM 336).

*———. [*Ext*] Extracts from letters and diary, 1839–42. ML (B 686).

*———. [*WMMS/L*] *See under* Wesleyan Methodist Missionary Society, London.

*CSO. [MP 5947/17] Inquiry relating to chiefly privileges at Bau. CSO/MP 5947 of 1917.

*CSO. [MP 259/10] Petition to the Secretary of State for the Colonies . . . drafted by E. Wainiu. CSO/MP 259 of 1910.

Deane, Herbert A. 1963. *The Political and Social Ideas of St. Augustine.* New York: Columbia University Press.

DeLillo, Don. 1997. *Underworld.* New York: Scribner.

*Deniau, Alfred, S. M. [*HF2*] Histoire de Fidji: seconde partie. Photocopy. Marist Mission Archives, Rome.

Denicagilaba [Ilai Motonicocoka]. 1892–94. Ai Talanoa ni Gauna Makawa. *Na Mata,* series of 17 parts. Reprinted in *Na Mata* 1932–34, under another pseudonym, Ko Qase ni Viti Makawa.

Derrick, R. A. 1950. *A History of Fiji.* Suva: Government Press.

Detienne, Marcel. 2003. *Comment être autochtone.* Paris: Seuil.

Diapea, William [John Jackson, William Diaper]. 1928. *Cannibal Jack: The*

True Autobiography of a White Man in the South Seas. London: Faber & Gwyer.

Dillon, Matthew, and Lynda Garland. 2000. *Ancient Greece: Social and Historical Documents from Archaic Times to the Death of Socrates (c. 800–399 B.C.).* London: Routledge.

Diodorus Siculus. 1946. *Diodorus of Sicily.* 12 vols. Ed. T. E. Page et al. Loeb Classical Library. Cambridge, Mass.: Harvard University Press.

Dirlik, Arif. 1996. The past as legacy and project: Postcolonial criticism in the perspective of indigenous historicism. *American Indian Culture and Research Journal* 20 (2): 1–31.

*Driver, William R. [*J*] Journal of the ship *Clay,* voyage from Salem to Feejee Islands and Manilla, Capt. Wm. R. Driver, 1827–29. Peabody Museum, Salem, Mass.

Dumont, Louis. 1970. *Homo hierarchicus.* Chicago: University of Chicago Press.

———. 1977. *From Mandeville to Marx.* Chicago: University of Chicago Press.

D'Urville, Dumont M. J. 1832. *Voyage de la corvette* L'Astrolabe . . . *pendant les années 1826–1827–1828–1829: Histoire du voyage.* Vol. 4. Paris: J. Tastu.

*Eagleston, John H. [*J*] *Barque Peru* of Salem: Two voyages to the islands in the Pacific Ocean, 1830–33. PMB 205. Original in Essex Institute, Salem, Mass.

*———. [Log *Emerald*] Log of the ship *Emerald,* 1833–36. PMB 205. Original in Essex Institute, Salem, Mass.

*———. [*UD*] Ups and downs through life. 2 vols. Peabody Museum, Salem, Mass.

Ehrenberg, Victor. 1951. *The People of Aristophanes: A Sociology of Old Attic Comedy.* Oxford: Blackwell.

*Emmons, George Foster. [*J*] Journals of George Foster Emmons on U.S. Exploring Expedition, 1838–42, in the Pacific. Microfilm copy. Beinecke Library, Yale University, New Haven, Conn.

Erskine, John Elphinstone. 1853. *Journal of a Cruise among the Islands of the Western Pacific.* London: J. Murray.

Euripides. 1955. *The Heracleidae.* Trans. Ralph Gladstone, introduction by Richmond Lattimore, vol. 1: *Euripides,* 109–55. In *The Complete Greek Tragedies,* ed. David Grene and Richmond Lattimore. Chicago: University of Chicago Press.

———. 1958a. *Ion.* Trans. with introduction by Ronald Willetts, vol. 3: *Euripides,* 177–295. In *The Complete Greek Tragedies,* ed. David Grene and Richmond Lattimore. Chicago: University of Chicago Press.

———. 1958b. *The Suppliant Women.* Trans. with introduction by Frank Jones, vol. 4: *Euripides,* 51–104. In *The Complete Greek Tragedies,* ed. David Grene and Richmond Lattimore. Chicago: University of Chicago Press.

Evans collection. Documents mainly relating to Bau. NAF.

Figueira, Thomas. 1999. The evolution of Messenian identity. In *Sparta: New Perspectives,* ed. Stephen Hodkinson and Anton Powell, 211–45. London: Duckworth and Classical Press of Wales.

Finley, John H. 1963. *Thucydides.* Ann Arbor: University of Michigan Press.

Finley, M. I. 1964. *The Ancient Greeks.* New York: Viking Press.

———. 1972. Introduction to *Thucydides' History of the Peloponnesian War,* ed. Rex Warner, 9–32. Harmondsworth, U.K.: Penguin Books.

———. 1975. *The Use and Abuse of History.* New York: Viking Press.

———. 1981. *Economy and Society in Ancient Greece.* New York: Viking Press.

———. 1984. Politics. In *The Legacy of Greece: A New Appraisal,* ed. M. I. Finley, 22–36. Oxford: Oxford University Press.

———. 1986. *Ancient History: Evidence and Models.* New York: Viking Press.

———. 1999. *The Ancient Economy.* Rev. ed. Berkeley: University of California Press.

Fison, Lorimer. 1903. *Land Tenure in Fiji.* Suva: E. J. Marsh, Government Printer.

Fleiss, Peter J. 1966. *Thucydides and the Politics of Bipolarity.* Baton Rouge: Louisiana State University Press.

Forrest, W. G. 1968. *A History of Sparta.* New York: W. W. Norton.

Foucault, Michel. 1994. *Power.* Vol. 3. New York: New Press.

———. 2003. *"Society Must Be Defended": Lectures at the Collège de France, 1975–76.* New York: Picador.

Fougères, G. n.d. Hyacinthia. In *Dictionnaire des antiquités grecques et romaines,* ed. Charles Daremberg, 3:304–6. Paris: Hachette.

France, Peter. 1966. The Kaunitoni migration: Notes on the genesis of a Fijian tradition. *Journal of Pacific History* 1: 107–14.

Furet, François. 1982. *L'Atelier de l'histoire.* Paris: Flammarion.

Gabrielson, Vincent. 1994. *Financing the Athenian Fleet: Public Taxation and Social Relations.* Baltimore: Johns Hopkins University Press.

Gaimard, J. 1832. Extrait du journal de J. Gaimard. In *Voyage de la corvette* L'Astrolabe . . . *pendant les années 1826–1827–1828–1829: Histoire du voyage,* by Dumont d'Urville, 4:698–727. Paris: J. Tastu.

Gallie, W. B. 1963. The historical understanding. *History and Theory* 3: 149–202.

Geertz, Clifford. 1973. *The Interpretation of Cultures.* New York: Basic Books.

Gernet, Louis. 1981. *The Anthropology of Ancient Greece.* Baltimore: Johns Hopkins University Press.

Gildersleeve, Basil L. 1915. *The Creed of the Old South, 1865–1915.* Baltimore: Johns Hopkins University Press.

Girard, Jules. n.d. Dionysia. In *Dictionnaire des antiquités grecques et romaines,* ed. Charles Daremberg, 2:230–46. Paris: Hachette.

Goldenweiser, Alexander. 1917. The autonomy of the social. *American Anthropologist* 19: 447–49.

Gomme, A. W. 1937. *Essays in Greek History and Literature.* Oxford: Basil Blackwell.

———. 1945. *A Historical Commentary on Thucydides.* Vol. 1, *Introduction and Commentary on Book I.* Oxford: Clarendon Press.

———. 1956. *A Historical Commentary on Thucydides.* Vol. 3, *The Ten Years' War.* Oxford: Clarendon Press.

Goodman, M. D., and A. J. Holladay. 1986. Religious scruples in ancient warfare. *Classical Quarterly* 36: 151–71.

Grene, David. 1965. *Greek Political Theory: The Image of Man in Thucydides and Plato.* Chicago: University of Chicago Press.

———. 1989. Introduction to *The Peloponnesian War* [Thucydides]: *The Complete Hobbes Translation,* ed. David Grene. Chicago: University of Chicago Press.

Guthrie, W. K. C. 1971. *The Sophists.* Cambridge: Cambridge University Press.

Hale, Horatio. 1846. "Ethnography and Philology." *United States Exploring Expedition during the Years 1838, 1839, 1840, 1841, 1842, Under the Command of Charles Wilkes, U.S.N.* Vol. 6. Philadelphia: Lea & Blanchard.

Hall, Jonathan M. 1997. *Ethnic Identity in Greek Antiquity.* Cambridge: Cambridge University Press.

———. 2002. *Hellenicity: Between Ethnicity and Culture.* Chicago: University of Chicago Press.

Hall, Stuart. 1996. Introduction: Who needs society? In *Questions of Cultural Identity,* ed. Stuart Hall and Paul Du Gay. London: Sage.

Hanson, Victor Davis. 1996. Introduction to *The Landmark Thucydides,* ed. Robert B. Strassler, ix–xxiii. New York: Free Press.

———. 1998. *Warfare and Agriculture in Classical Greece.* Berkeley: University of California Press.

*Hazelwood, Rev. David. [*DB*] Day-book, 1844–46. ML (B 571).

*———. [*J*] Journals, 3 vols. ML (B 568–570).

*———. [*P*] Papers. ML (A 2494).

Herodotus. 1987. *The History.* Trans. David Grene. Chicago: University of Chicago Press.

Hexter, J. H. 1971. *Doing History.* Bloomington: Indiana University Press.

Hobbes, Thomas. 1962. *Leviathan.* New York: Collier Books.

Hobbes, Thomas, trans. 1989 [1629]. *The Peloponnesian War* [Thucydides]. Ed. David Grene. Chicago: University of Chicago Press.

Hocart, Arthur M. 1912. On the meaning of Kalou and the origin of Fijian temples. *Journal of the Royal Anthropological Institute* 42: 437–49.

———. 1913. Fijian heralds and envoys. *Journal of the Royal Anthropological Institute* 43: 109–18.

———. 1915. Chieftainship and the sister's son in the Pacific. *American Anthropologist* 17: 631–43.

———. 1923. The uterine nephew. *Man* 4: 11–13.

———. 1926. Limitations of the sister's son's right in Fiji. *Man* 134: 205–6.

———. 1929. *Lau Islands, Fiji.* Bernice P. Bishop Museum Bulletin, No. 69. Honolulu: Bishop Museum.

———. 1933. *The Progress of Man.* London: Methuen.

———. 1952. *The Northern States of Fiji.* Occasional Publications, No. 11. London: Royal Anthropological Institute.
———. 1968. *Caste: A Comparative Study.* New York: Russell & Russell.
———. 1969. *Kingship.* Oxford: Oxford University Press.
———. 1970a. *Kings and Councillors.* Chicago: University of Chicago Press.
———. 1970b. *The Life-Giving Myth and Other Essays.* London: Tavistock & Methuen.
*———. [*FN*] Field notes of A. M. Hocart. Turnbull Library, Wellington, New Zealand.
*———. [*HF*] Heart of Fiji. Manuscript. Turnbull Library, Wellington, New Zealand.
*———. [*WI*] The Windward Islands of Fiji. Microfilm, Cambridge University Library. Original typescript in Turnbull Library, Wellington, New Zealand.
Hodkinson, Stephen. 1983. Social order and the conflict of values in classical Sparta. *Chiron* 13: 239–81.
———. 2000. *Property and Wealth in Classical Sparta.* London: Duckworth and Classical Press of Wales.
*Holmes, Silas. [*J*] Journal of Silas Holmes, assistant surgeon of the *Peacock,* 20 August 1838–12 June 1842. Coe Collection, Yale University Library, New Haven, Conn.
Homer. 1990. *The Iliad.* Trans. Robert Fagles. New York: Viking Penguin.
Hornblower, Simon. 1987. *Thucydides.* Baltimore: Johns Hopkins University Press.
———. 1991a. *The Greek World, 479–323 B.C.* London: Routledge.
———. 1991b. *A Commentary on Thucydides.* Vol. 1. Oxford: Clarendon Press.
———. 1992. The religious dimension to the Peloponnesian War, or what Thucydides does not tell us. *Harvard Studies in Classical Philology* 94: 169–97.
———. 1996. *A Commentary on Thucydides.* Vol. 2. Oxford: Clarendon Press.
Hornell, James. 1926. The megalithic sea works and temple platforms at Mbau in Fiji. *Man* 26: 25–32.
Hoy, David Couzens. 1986. *Foucault: A Critical Reader.* Oxford: Blackwell.
*Hudson, William Leverath. [*J*] Journal of the U.S. Exploring Expedition. PMB 146. Original in American Museum of Natural History, New York.
Huizinga, J. 1954. *The Waning of the Middle Ages.* Garden City, N.Y.: Doubleday Anchor.
Hume, David. 1975. *Enquiries Concerning Human Understanding and Concerning the Principles of Morals.* Oxford: Clarendon Press.
———. 1985. *Essays: Moral, Political and Literary.* Ed. Eugene F. Miller. Indianapolis: Liberty Classics.
*Hunt, Rev. John. [*J*] Fiji Journals of John Hunt, 1 January 1839–20 July 1848. WMMS (Box 5b). SOAS.
*———. [*L*] Letters to and from Reverend John Hunt, 1841–47. WMMS (Box 5b). SOAS.

*———. [*WMMS/L*] *See under* Wesleyan Methodist Missionary Society, London.

Huxley, G. L. 1962. *Early Sparta.* Cambridge, Mass.: Harvard University Press.

Isocrates. 1991. *Isocrates.* Trans. George Norlin. 2 vols. Loeb Classical Library. Cambridge, Mass.: Harvard University Press.

Jackson, John [William Diapea, William Diaper]. 1853. Jackson's narrative. Appendix A in *Journal of a Cruise among the Islands of the Western Pacific,* by John Elphinstone Erskine, 411–77. London: Murray.

Jaggar, Thomas. 1988. *Unto the Perfect Day: The Journal of Thomas Jaggar, Feejee, 1838–1845.* Ed. Esther Keesing-Styles and William Keesing-Styles. Auckland, N.Z.: Solent Publishing.

*———. [*J*] Diaries of Thomas James Jaggar, 1837–43, including notes at the end of the diaries. Microfilm copy. Pacific Collection, Adelaide University Library. Original in NAF.

*———. [*Frag*] Fragmentary diary notes of Rev. Thomas Jaggar, 1844. ML (MOM 337).

*———. [*PJ*] Private journals of Rev. Thomas Jaggar. ML (MOM 579).

*———. [*SC/Y*] Yaqona drink of the king of Fiji. Jaggar Papers. Library, University of California, Santa Cruz.

*———. [*WMMS/L*] *See under* Wesleyan Methodist Missionary Society, London.

Jowett, Benjamin, trans. 1998. *History of the Peloponnesian War* [Thucydides]. Amherst, N.Y.: Prometheus.

Kagan, Donald. 1969. *The Outbreak of the Peloponnesian War.* Ithaca, N.Y.: Cornell University Press.

———. 1988. The first revisionist historian. *Commentary* 85 (5): 43–49.

Kallet, Lisa. 2001. *Money and the Corrosion of Power in Thucydides: The Sicilian Expedition and Its Aftermath.* Berkeley: University of California Press.

Kallet-Marx, Lisa. 1993. *Money, Expense and Naval Power in Thucydides' History 1–5.24.* Berkeley: University of California Press.

Kantorowicz, Ernst H. 1957. *The King's Two Bodies: A Study in Medieval Political Theology.* Princeton: Princeton University Press.

Kaplan, Robert D. 2002. *Warrior Politics: Why Leadership Demands a Pagan Ethos.* New York: Vintage Books.

*Koto, Setariki. [*MS*] Ko Viti. Typescript manuscript supplied by Dr. Deryck Scarr.

Ko Via Veivuke [pseud.]. 1897. O Viti e na Gauna Makawa. *Na Mata* (May): 79.

Kroeber, Alfred Louis. 1917. The superorganic. *American Anthropologist* 19: 163–213.

Kuhn, Thomas S. 1970. *The Structure of Scientific Revolutions.* International Encyclopedia of Unified Science. Vol. 2, No. 2. Chicago: University of Chicago Press.

———. 1977. *The Essential Tension: Selected Studies in Scientific Translation and Change.* Chicago: University of Chicago Press.

———. 2000. *The Road since Structure.* Chicago: University of Chicago Press.

Latour, Bruno. 2002. *War of the Worlds: What about Peace?* Chicago: Prickly Paradigm Press.

Lattimore, Owen. 1940. *Inner Asian Frontiers of China.* New York: American Geographical Society.

Lattimore, Steven, trans. 1998. *Thucydides: The Peloponnesian War.* Indianapolis: Hackett.

Lawry, Rev. Walter. 1850. *Friendly and Feejee Islands: A Missionary Visit to Various Stations in the South Seas, in the Year MDCCCXLVII.* 2d ed. London: Charles Gilpin.

Lester, R. H. 1941–42. Kava-drinking in Fiji. *Oceania* 12: 97–121, 226–54.

Lévêque, Pierre, and Pierre Vidal-Naquet. 1997. *Cleisthenes the Athenian: An Essay on the Representation of Space and Time in Greek Political Thought from the End of the Sixth Century to the Death of Plato.* Humanities Press.

Lévi-Strauss, Claude. 1952. *Race and History.* Paris: UNESCO.

Lockerby, William. 1925. *The Journal of William Lockerby Sandalwood Trader in the Fiji Islands during the Years 1808–1809.* Ed. Sir Everard Im Thurn. London: Hakluyt Society.

Loraux, Nicole. 2000. *Born of the Earth: Myth and Politics in Athens.* Ithaca: Cornell University Press.

Luginbill, Robert D. 1999. *Thucydides on War and National Character.* Boulder, Colo.: Westview Press.

*Lyth, Rev. Richard Birdsall. [*DB*] Daybooks of Rev. Richard Birdsall Lyth, 1842–55. 6 vols. ML (B 538, B 539, B 544, B 545, B 546, B 561).

*———. [*J*] Journals of Rev. Richard Birdsall Lyth, 1836–60. 7 vols. ML (B 533, B 534, B 535, B 536, B 540, B 541, B 542).

*———. [*L*] Letters to and from Rev. Dr. Lyth, 1836–54. ML (A 836).

*———. [*LF*] Letters of Rev. Richard Birdsall Lyth to his family, 1829–56. WMMS (Box 6b). SOAS.

*———. [*N*] Note-book. ML (B 552).

*———. [*NI*] Notes on Islands, attached to his day-book and journal, 1850–51. ML (B 539).

*———. [*R*] Reminiscences, 1851–53. ML (B 548).

*———. [*RC*] Reminiscences and customs. ML (B 551).

*———. [*TFR*] Tongan and Feejeean Reminiscences. 2 vols. ML (B 549).

*———. [*VJ*] Voyaging journals. 4 vols. ML (B 537).

*———. [*WMMS/L*] *See under* Wesleyan Methodist Missionary Society, London.

*MacGillvray, John. [*J*] Voyage of H.M.S. *Herald* under the command of Capt. Mangles Denham, R.N., being the private journal kept by John MacGillvray, naturalist. Papers of the Admiralty (Adm 7/852). Public Records Office, London.

*Madraiwiwi, Ratu Joni. [*FM/MS*] Ratu Joni Madraiwiwi on Bauan Affairs.

Copy of a letter to the Native Commissioner, 26 August 1913. Fiji Museum Manuscript Collection (629), Suva.

Manicas, Peter T. 1982. War, stasis, and Greek political thought. *Comparative Studies in Society and History* 29: 673–88.

*Marist Anonymous. [*HM*] Histoire de la mission de Fidji, Oceanie. Marist Mission Archives, Rome.

Martin, John, ed. 1827. *An Account of the Tongan Islands in the South Pacific Ocean.* 3 vols. 3d ed. Edinburgh: Constable.

Marx, Karl. 1964. *The Eighteenth Brumaire of Louis Bonaparte.* New York: International Publishers.

———. 1967. *Capital.* Vol. 1. New York: International Publishers.

———. 1973. *Grundrisse: Foundation of the Critique of Political Economy (Rough Draft).* Trans. Martin Nicolaus. Harmondsworth, U.K.: Penguin Books.

Marx, Karl, and Friedrich Engels. 1956. *The German Ideology.* London: Lawrence & Wishart.

McGregor, Malcolm F. 1987. *The Athenians and Their Empire.* Vancouver: University of British Columbia Press.

Meier, Christian. 1998. *Athens: A Portrait of the City in Its Golden Age.* Trans. Robert and Rita Kimber. New York: Henry Holt.

Meiggs, Russell. 1972. *The Athenian Empire.* Oxford: Clarendon Press.

Merquior, J. G. 1985. *Foucault.* Berkeley: University of California Press.

Momigliano, Arnaldo. 1944. Sea-power in Greek thought. *Classical Review* 58: 1–7.

———. 1993. *The Development of Greek Biography.* Rev. ed. Cambridge, Mass.: Harvard University Press.

*Moore, Rev. William. [*J*] Journal of Rev. William Moore, 1844–46. ML (MOM 567).

Nai Lalakai. 1980–81. Na i Tutu vaka-Gonesau. Series of articles in *Nai Lalakai* [Fiji language weekly], various authors. Suva.

Native Lands Commission. 1959. *Final Report . . . on the Provinces of Tailevu (North), Rewa, Naitasiri and Colo East.* Suva: Government Press.

*———. [NLC/EB (district)] Evidence books. By district. Native Lands Commission records. Suva: Native Lands Trust Board.

*———. [NLC/TR (district)] *Tukutuku Ravaba* [General Histories]. By district. Native Lands Commission records. Suva: Native Lands Trust Board.

Ollier, F. 1933–43. *Le mirage spartiate.* 2 vols. Paris: Boccard.

Orwin, Clifford. 1988. Stasis and plague: Thucydides and the dissolution of society. *Journal of Politics* 50: 831–47.

———. 1994. *The Humanity of Thucydides.* Princeton: Princeton University Press.

*Osborn, Joseph Warren. [*J*] Journal of a voyage in the ship *Emerald* owned by Stephen C. Phillips, Esq. and commanded by John H. Eagleston . . . during the years 1833, 1834, 1835, and 1836. PMB 223. Original in Peabody Museum, Salem, Mass.

Palmer, Michael. 1992. *Love of Glory and the Common Good: Aspects of the Political Thought of Thucydides.* Lanham, Md.: Rowman & Littlefield.

Parke, H. W. 1977. *Festivals of the Athenians.* Ithaca, N.Y.: Cornell University Press.

Parker, Robert. 1996. *Athenian Religion: A History.* Oxford: Clarendon Press.

Parry, John T. 1977. *Ring-ditch Fortifications in the Rewa Delta, Fiji: Air Photo Interpretation and Analysis.* Bulletin of the Fiji Museum, No. 3. Suva.

———. 1987. *The Sigatoka Valley: Pathway into Prehistory.* Suva: Bulletin of the Fiji Museum, No. 9.

Pausanias. 1979. *Guide to Greece.* Trans. Peter Levi. 3 vols. Harmondsworth, U.K.: Penguin Books.

Petterson, Michael. 1992. *Cults of Apollo at Sparta: The Hyakinthia, the Gymnopaidiai and the Karneia.* Skrifter Utgivna au Svonska Institutet I Athen, No. 12. Stockholm.

Picard, Olivier. 2000. *Guerre et économie dans l'alliance athénienne (490–322 av. J-C).* Liège: Sedes.

Pickering, Charles. 1849. *The Races of Man: And Their Geographical Distribution.* London: John Chapman.

*———. [*J*] Journal of Charles Pickering with the U.S. Exploring Expedition. Massachusetts Historical Society, Boston.

Plutarch. [*Mor*] 1931. *Plutarch's Moralia.* Vol. 3. Loeb Classical Library. Cambridge, Mass.: Harvard University Press.

———. [*Lives*] 1928. *Plutarch's Lives.* 11 vols. Loeb Classical Library. London: Heinemann.

Poesch, Jessie. 1961. *Titian Ramsey Peale and His Journals of the Wilkes Expedition.* Philadelphia: American Philosophical Society.

Polanyi, Karl. 1957. Aristotle discovers the economy. In *Trade and Market in the Early Empires,* ed. Karl Polanyi, Conrad M. Arensberg, and Henry W. Peterson, 64–94. Glencoe, Ill.: Free Press.

Powell, Anton. 1988. *Athens and Sparta: Constructing Greek Political and Social History from 478 B.C.* London: Routledge.

Préaux, Jean-G. 1962. La sacralité du pouvoir royal à Rome. In *Le pouvoir et le sacré,* by Luc de Heusch et al., 103–21. Annales du Centre d'Etude des Religions, No. 1. Brussels: Institut de Sociologie, Université Libre de Bruxelles.

Pritchard, W. T. 1968. *Polynesian Reminiscences.* [Facsimile of 1866 ed.] London: Dawsons of Pall Mall.

Quain, Buell. 1948. *Fijian Village.* Chicago: University of Chicago Press.

Rabuku, Niko. 1911. Ai Sau ni Taro me Kilai. *Na Mata:* 154–58, 172–76.

*Ravuvu, Asasela D. 1985. Fijian ethos as expressed in ceremonies. Ph.D. diss., University of Auckland, N.Z.

Rawson, Elizabeth. 1969. *The Spartan Tradition in European Thought.* Oxford: Clarendon Press.

Reid, A. C. 1990. *Tovata I and II.* Suva: Fiji Museum.

*Reynolds, William. [*Le*] Letter no. 15: to his father, *Peacock at Sea*, 21 September 1840. Photostat. Archives and Special Collections (MS 6 Box 2/11). Shadok-Fackenthal Library, Franklin and Marshall College, Lancaster, Pa.

Ricoeur, Paul. 1984. *Time and Narrative.* Vol. 1. Chicago: University of Chicago Press.

Rivers, W. H. R. 1914. *The History of Melanesian Society.* 2 vols. Cambridge: Cambridge University Press.

Rokowaqa, Epeli. 1926. *Ai Tukutuku kei Viti.* Suva: Wesleyan Missionary Society.

Romilly, Jacqueline de. 1963. *Thucydides and Athenian Imperialism.* Oxford: Blackwell.

———. 1967. *Histoire et raison chez Thucydides.* Paris: Societé d'Edition "Les Belles Lettres."

———. 1968. Guerre et paix entre cités. In *Problèmes de la guerre en Grèce ancienne*, ed. Jean-Pierre Vernant, 207–29. Paris: Mouton.

*Rosenthal, Mara. [*FN*] Field notes of Mara Rosenthal, mainly from Bau and Rewa areas, 1987–89. Photocopy.

Rosivach, Vincent J. 1987. Autochthony and the Athenians. *Classical Quarterly* 37: 294–306.

*Rougier, Père Emmanuel. [*FL*] Four lectures on the comparative work of the Catholic and Wesleyan missions in Fiji. In The history of Christianity in Fiji according to the Wesleyan mission. Typescript of translation by Rev. Joe Deyl. Archives of the Marist Mission, Rome.

Sahlins, Marshall. 1962. *Moala: Culture and nature on a Fijian Island.* Ann Arbor: University of Michigan Press.

———. 1983. Raw women, cooked men, and other "great things" of the Fiji Islands. In *The Ethnography of Cannibalism*, ed. Paula Brown and Donald Tuzin, 72–93. Special Publication. Washington, D.C.: Society for Psychological Anthropology.

———. 1985. *Islands of History.* Chicago: University of Chicago Press.

———. 1987. War in the Fiji Islands: The force of custom and the custom of force. In *International Ethics in a Nuclear Age*, ed. Robert J. Myers, 299–328. Ethics and Foreign Policy Series, No. 40. Lanham, Md.: University Press of America.

———. 1991. The return of the event, again: With reflections on the beginnings of the great Fijian war of 1843 to 1845 between the kingdoms of Bau and Rewa. In *Clio in Oceania*, ed. Aletta Biersack, 37–100. Washington, D.C.: Smithsonian Institution Press.

———. 1992. *Historical Ethnography.* Vol. 1 of *Anahulu: The Anthropology of History in the Kingdom of Hawaii*, by Patrick V. Kirch and Marshall Sahlins. Chicago: University of Chicago Press.

———. 1994. The discovery of the true savage. In *Dangerous Liaisons: Essays in Honour of Greg Dening*, ed. Donna Merwick, 41–94. Melbourne: Melbourne University Press.

———. 1996. The sadness of sweetness: The native anthropology of Western cosmology. *Current Anthropology* 37: 395–415, 421–28.

———. 2000. *Culture in Practice.* New York: Zone Books.

———. 2002. An empire of a certain kind. *Social Analysis* 46: 95–98.

Sahlins, Peter. 1989. *Boundaries: The Making of France and Spain in the Pyrenees.* Berkeley: University of California Press.

Sainte-Croix, G. E. M. de. 1972. *The Origins of the Peloponnesian War.* London: Duckworth.

Sartre, Jean-Paul. 1968. *Search for a Method.* New York: Vintage Books.

———. 1981–93. *The Family Idiot: Gustave Flaubert 1821–1857.* 5 vols. Chicago: University of Chicago Press.

Scarr, Deryck. 1975. Cakobau and Ma'afu. In *Pacific Island Portraits,* ed. J. W. Davidson and Deryck Scarr, 95–126. Auckland, N.Z.: A. H. & A. W. Reed.

Seeman, Berthold. 1973. *Viti: Account of a Government Mission to the Vitian or Fijian Islands, 1860–61.* Folkestone, U.K.: Dawson's of Pall Mall.

*Sinclair, George T. [*J*] Journals of George T. Sinclair, acting master aboard the *Relief,* the *Porpoise* and the *Flying Fish* [U.S. Exploring Expedition], 19 December 1838–26 June 1842. Records of the United States Exploring Expedition under the command of Lt. Charles Wilkes, 1838–42. Microfilm. Central Research Libraries, Chicago. Original in National Archives, Washington, D.C.

Smythe, Mrs. [S. M.]. 1864. *Ten Months in the Fiji Islands.* Oxford: John Henry & James Parker.

Starr, Chester G. 1978. Thucydides on sea power. *Mnemosyne* 31: 343–50.

Steegmuller, Francis, ed. 1953. *The Selected Letters of Gustave Flaubert.* New York: Farrar, Straus & Young.

Strassler, Robert B., ed. 1996. *The Landmark Thucydides.* New York: Free Press. [Crawley's translation.]

*Stuart, Frederic D. [*J*] Journal of Frederic D. Stuart, captain's clerk aboard the *Peacock,* 19 August 1838–18 July 1841. Records of the United States Exploring Expedition under the command of Lt. Charles Wilkes, 1838–42. Microfilm. Central Research Libraries, Chicago. Original in National Archives, Washington, D.C.

Taillardat, J. 1968. La trière athénienne et la guerre sur mer aux Ve et IVe siècles. In *Problèmes de guerre en Grèce ancienne,* ed. J.-P. Vernant, 183–205. Civilisations et Sociétés, No. 11. Paris: Mouton.

Tcherkézoff, Serge. In press. *First Contacts in Polynesia: The Samoan Case and Comparisons.* Christchurch, N.Z.: Macmillan Brown Center for Pacific Studies.

Thomson, Basil. 1908. *The Fijians: A Study in the Decay of Custom.* London: William Heinemann.

Thomson, Bobby, with Lee Heiman and Bill Gutman. 1991. *The Giants Win the Pennant! The Giants Win the Pennant! The Giants Win the Pennant!* New York: Zebra Books.

Thucydides. *History. See* Bloomfield 1829; Crawley 1934; Hobbes 1989; Jowett 1998; S. Lattimore 1998; Strassler 1996; Warner 1972.

Tippett, A. R. 1973. *Aspects of Pacific Ethnohistory.* Pasadena, Calif.: William Carey Library.

Todorov, Tzvetan. 1984. *Mikhail Bakhtin: The Dialogical Principle.* Theory and History of Literature, Vol. 13. Minneapolis: University of Minnesota Press.

Toganivalu, Ratu Deve. 1911. The customs of Bau before the advent of Christianity. *Transactions of the Fijian Society for 1911:* n.p.

———. 1912a. Ai Tovo mai Bau sa bera ni yaco mai na Lotu. *Na Mata* (January): 9–17. [Fijian version of Toganivalu 1911.]

———. 1912b. Ai Tukutuku kei Ratu Cakobau, Na Vunivalu mai Bau. *Na Mata:* (1) August; (2) September, 159–60; (3) October, 168–75.

———. 1912c. Ratu Cakobau. *Transactions of the Fijian Society for 1912:* 1–12.

*———. [*TkB*] Tukutuku kei Bau. NAF (F 62/247). English translation, "An island kingdom," NAF.

Tolstoy, Count Leo. 1962. *War and Peace.* New York: Modern Library.

Trotsky, Leon. 1980. *The History of the Russian Revolution.* New York: Path-Finder.

Turner, James West. 1997. Continuity and constraint: Reconstructing the concept of tradition from a Pacific perspective. *Contemporary Pacific* 9: 345–81.

Turner, Terence. 1995. Social body and embodied subject: Bodiliness, subjectivity and sociality among the Kayapo. *Cultural Anthropology* 10: 143–70.

*Turpin, Edwin J. [*DN*] Diary and narratives of Edwin J. Turpin. NAF.

Twyning, John P. 1996. *Wreck of the* Minerva. [Reprint of *Shipwreck and Adventures of John P. Twining among the South Sea Islands,* 1850.] Fairfield, Wash.: Ye Galleon Press.

Tygiel, Jules. 2000. *Past Time: Baseball as History.* New York: Oxford University Press.

Van Wees, Hans. 1999. Tyrtaeus' *Eunomia:* Nothing to do with the Great Rhetra. In *Sparta: New Perspectives,* ed. Stephen Hodkinson and Anton Powell, 1–41. London: Duckworth.

Vernant, Jean-Pierre. 1968. Introduction to *Problèmes de la guerre en Grèce ancienne,* ed. J.-P. Vernant, 9–30. Civilisations et Sociétés, No. 11. Paris: Mouton.

Veyne, Paul. 1984. *Writing History: Essay on Epistemology.* Middletown, Conn.: Wesleyan University Press.

———. 1988. *Did the Greeks Believe in Their Myths?* Chicago: University of Chicago Press.

Wagner, Roy. 1973. *The Invention of Culture.* Englewood Cliffs, N.J.: Prentice-Hall.

*Wainiu, Ratu Etuate. [*AY*] Ai Yalayala ni Vanua VakaBau, Na Yavusa Ko Kubuna. Tippett Collection, St. Mark's National Theological Centre Library, Canberra.

*———. [*BK*] Bure Kalou Vakaitokatoka ena Mataqali Tui Kaba kei na

Mataqali Bete. Filed with Wainiu, *AY*. Tippett Collection, St. Mark's National Theological Centre Library, Canberra.

Wall, Colman. 1919. Sketches in Fijian history. *Transactions of the Fijian Society for the Year 1919:* n.p.

Wallis, Mary ["A Lady"]. 1851. *Life in Feejee . . . or . . . Five Years among the Cannibals.* Boston: Heath.

———. 1994. *The Fiji and New Caledonia Journals of Mary Wallis 1851–1853.* Ed. David Routledge. Suva: Institute of Pacific Studies.

*———. Journal of Mary Wallace [*sic*], 1851–53. Peabody Museum, Salem, Mass.

Walzer, Michael. 1986. The politics of Michel Foucault. In *Foucault: A Critical Reader,* ed. David Conzens Hoy, 51–68. Oxford: Blackwell.

Warner, Rex, trans. 1972 [1954]. *History of the Peloponnesian War* [Thucydides]. Harmondsworth, U.K.: Penguin.

Waterhouse, Rev. Joseph. 1866. *The King and People of Fiji.* London: Wesleyan Conference Office.

*Wesleyan Methodist Missionary Society, London. Inward correspondence from Feejee, 1835–57. 8 vols. WMMS (Box 31). SOAS.

Westlake, H. D. 1968. *Individuals in Thucydides.* Cambridge: Cambridge University Press.

Whitby, Michael. 2002. *Sparta.* New York: Routledge.

White, Leslie A. 1949. *The Science of Culture: A Study of Man and Civilization.* New York: Farrar, Straus.

Wilkes, Charles. 1845. *Narrative of the United States Exploring Expedition during the Years 1838, 1839, 1840, 1841, 1842.* 5 vols. Philadelphia: Lea & Blanchard.

*Wilkinson, David. [*MS*] Personal notes. NAF, vol. 1.

Williams, Thomas. 1931. *The Journal of Thomas Williams, Missionary in Fiji, 184–1853.* Ed. G. W. Henderson. 2 vols. Sydney: Angus & Robertson.

*———. [*LW*] Letters to Thomas Williams, 1832. ML (A 852).

*———. [*MN*] Miscellaneous notes chiefly concerning Feejee and Feejeeans. 3 vols. ML (B 496–98).

*———. [*WMMS/L*] *See under* Wesleyan Methodist Missionary Society, London.

Williams, Thomas, and James Calvert. 1859. *Fiji and the Fijians.* New York: D. Appleton & Co. [2 vols. of British ed. in 1 vol.]

Wills, Garry. 2001. *Venice, Lion City: The Religion of Empire.* New York: Simon & Schuster.

Xenophon. [Pseudo-Xenophon, "Old Oligarch"]. *Constitution of the Athenians.* In *Scripta minora* [vol. 7 of Xenophon's writings], 135–90. Loeb Classical Library. London: William Heinemann.

Wycherley, R. E. 1978. *The Stones of Athens.* Princeton: Princeton University Press.

Yurchak, Alexei. 1997. The cynical reason of late socialism: Power, pretense and the *Anekdot. Public Culture* 22: 161–88.

THE ELIÁN GONZALEZ AFFAIR

ABCNews.com. [*ABC*] <http://www.ABCNews.com>

29 January 2000. Now, a pro-Cuban rally in Miami.

10 February 2000. Focus on Elian's Miami relatives.

27 March 2000. Cuban boy tells his story: Diane Sawyer's visit with Elian Gonzalez.

2 April 2000. Most Americans want Cuban boy returned to his father, by Gary Langer.

13 April 2000. Crowds grow in Miami.

17 April 2000. Waiting, waiting, by Alan Clendenning.

24 April 2000. Miami family continues fight.

28 June 2000. Good news, by Maria F. Durand.

Associated Press. [*AP*] <http://www.ap.org>

8 April 2000. Race called a key in Elián saga, by Paul Shepard.

6 June 2000. AP daily news.

Atlanta Constitution. <http://www.ajc.com> 23 January 2000. Elian grandmothers plead case with Reno, by Mike Williams.

BBC News. <http://news.bbc.co.uk> 29 January 2000. The Dalai Lama of Little Havana.

Capitalismmagazine.com. [*cm.c*]

14 January 2000. The Rights of Elián Gonzales, by Peter Schwartz.

26 January 2000. Interview: What Castro has in store for Elian, by Prodos Marinakis.

25 March 2000. A sin to deport Elian, by Leonard Peikoff.

25 March 2000. Interview with Edwin Locke. Elian Gonzalez: Why a father's rights can never supersede those of a child.

23 April 2000. Government assaults on cigarette companies, Microsoft and Elian Gonzalez violate individual rights, by Edwin Locke and Richard M. Salsman.

Chicago Tribune. [*CT*] <http://www.chicagotribune.com>

17 January 2000. For some exiled Cubans, Elian given role of modern-day Moses, by Laurie Goering.

19 January 2000. Cuban-American groups join cry to send Elian home.

19 January 2000. Parental authority: Elian belongs with his father, by Kathleen Parker.

22 January 2000. Back home with Grandma. [Editorial.]

22 January 2000. Grandmothers plead for Elian, by Mike Dorning.

24 June 2001. Elian fight revived Cubans on all sides, by Laurie Goering.

24 July 2001. Anti-Castro group's moderation makes waves, by Rafael Lorente.

Cleveland Plain Dealer. [*CPD*] <http://www.plaindealer.com> 22 December 1999. Morality compels U. S. to send young boy home, by Otis Moss, Jr.

CNN. <http://www.cnn.com>

4 January 2000. *Crossfire*. Transcript at <http://www.cnn.com>

28 March 2000. Image of Virgin Mary said to appear in Elian's Miami home.

Commondreams.org. <http://www.commondreams.org>

29 March 2000. Elián: Shipwrecked on dry land, by Gabriel García Márquez.

Denver Post. <http://www.denverpost.com>

11 January 2000. Plot over Elian thickens. [Editorial.]

13 January 2000. Reno halts Cuban farce, by Al Knight.

18 January 2000. Finding a home for Elian Gonzalez will be a tough job, by Ed Quillen.

Elovitz, Paul H., ed. 2000. The Elian Gonzalez obsession. Section in *Clio's Psyche* 7, no. 1 (June).

Geocities.com. <http://www.geocities.com> 2 April 2000. Madness in Miami, by Michael Lopez-Calderon.

George. May 2000, 64–69, 114–18. The untold Elian story, by Ann Louise Bardach.

Guardian. <http://www.guardian.co.uk> 12 April 2000. A small boy bails out the old dictator, by Isabel Hilton.

Libre. 2001. *Elián*. Libre supplement, Miami.

Los Angeles Times. <http://www.latimes.com> 25 January 2000. Commentary: There's no shortage of hypocrites; Cuba: The brouhaha over Elian Gonzalez provides a mirror for our across-the-board absurdity regarding the island, by Robert Scheer.

Miami Herald. [*MH*] <http://www.miamiherald.com>

13 December 1999. Elian gets to be a kid at Disney, by Phil Long.

13 December 1999. The deadly voyage: How it happened, by Elaine De Valle.

8 January 2000. Emotional bond compels protesters, by Paul Brinkley-Rogers.

10 January 2000. Mania over Elian rising, by Eunice Ponce and Elaine de Valle.

10 January 2000. Three Kings parade a spectacle for child, by Eunice Ponce and Ana Acle.

12 January 2000. Boy's cause in the hand of Miami image master, by Alfonso Chardy et al.

23 January 2000. Dolphins take the stuff of legend, by Ana Acle.

29 January 2000. Cubans pay homage to Marti, Elian. Associated Press.

30 January 2000. Planet Elian, by Carl Hiaasen.

1 February 2000. Exile group forges ironic alliances, by Karen Branch.

9 February 2000. Elian's great-uncles have had DUI convictions. Associated Press.

26 March 2000. Mary "appears" near Elian, by Sandra Marquez Garcia.

31 March 2000. Prayer vigil lifts Elian fervor to new high, by Meg Laughlin.

2 April 2000. Elian case puts Miami "republic" in spotlight, by Meg Laughlin.

10 April 2000. Elian a bridge linking rival fates, by D. Aileen Dodd.
14 April 2000. Throng outside house swells to thousands, by Sandra Marquez Garcia, Andrea Elliott, and Martin Merzer.
14 May 2000. Ceremony set to honor Elian's mom.
25 May 2000. Family members moving out of house where Elian stayed, by Ana Acle.
26 May 2000. Relaxed Marisleysis moving on, by Meg Laughlin.
28 June 2000. Supporters pray boy will remain, by Ana Acle.
30 June 2000. Miami relatives attend ceremony at Elian school, by Ana Acle.
23 November 2000. Elian's story waits for ending, by Andres Viglucci.

National Catholic Reporter. <http://www.natcath.com> 5 May 2000. The question in Miami is not the same asked elsewhere, by Tom Blackburn.

Newsday. <http://www.newsday.com> 9 April 2000. Devout see a "miracle" in Elian, by Ellen Yan.

Newsweek.
17 April 2000. The war over Elián, by Joseph Contreras and Evan Thomas.
24 April 2000. The Elián case, by Joseph Contreras and Evan Thomas.
24 April 2000. "Once more unto the breach," by Jonathan Alter.

New York Daily News. [*NYDN*] <http://www.nydailynews.com> 9 April 2000. Cult believes child is Cuban Messiah, by Roberto Santiago and Helen Kennedy.

New York Times. [*NYT*] <http://www.nytimes.com>
16 January 2000. Custody case is overshadowing shift among Cuban immigrants, by Peter T. Kilborn.
22 January 2000. Grandmothers make plea for Cuban boy's return, by Robert D. McFadden.
22 January 2000. Helping Cuban families is in America's interest, by Bernard W. Aronson and William D. Rogers.
24 January 2000. Grandmothers to fly to Miami. Associated Press.
26 January 2000. Elián Gonzalez and Congress. [Editorial.]
5 July 2000. Cuba sees fervor over Elián useful in other battles, by David Gonzalez.
2 September 2001. Heir to Cuban exile leader is finding his own voice, by Dana Canedy.
25 October 2001. Florida: Probation in kidnapping case.

New York Times International. <http://www.nytimes.com> 17 October 2002. Havana enshrines heroes of espionage, by David Gonzalez.

Ottawa Citizen. <http://www.ottawacitizen.com> 11 April 2000. Elian inspires mysticism in Miami, by Hillary Mackenzie.

PBS. [*pbs.org*] 26 April 2000. *NewsHour.* <http://www.pbs.org/newshour/bb/media/jan-june00/elian_4-26.html>
Frontline: Saving Elián. Published February 2001. <http://www.pbs.org/wgbh/pages/frontline/shows/elian/>

Religion in the News. [*RIN*] <http://www.trincoll.edu/depts/csrpl/RINVol3No2/elian.htm> Go down, Elian, by Thomas Hambrick-Stowe. Vol. 3, no. 2 (Summer 2000).

ReligiousTolerance.org. <http://www.religioustolerance.org/elian.htm> 13 April 2000. The Elián Gonzalez religious movement, by B. A. Robinson.

Rowe, John Carlos. 2002. Elián González, Cuban-American détente, and the rhetoric of family values. In *Transnational America: The Fading of Borders in the Western Hemisphere,* ed. Bundt Ostendorf, 139–48. Heidelberg: Universitätsverlag C. Winter.

St. Petersburg Times. <http://www.sptimes.com> 5 January 2000. Protesters rally for Cuban boy, by Sarah Schweitzer.

Salon.com. [*Salon*] <http://www.salon.com>

17 April 2000. Why can't they all just get along, by Myra MacPherson.

26 April 2000. Elián! Nature trumps politics, by Camille Paglia.

12 May 2000. "I never made myself famous," by Daryl Lindsay.

8 June 2000. Elián, politics, the Roman empire, by Camille Paglia.

29 June 2000. Adios Elián, by Myra MacPherson.

San Francisco Chronicle. <http://www.sfchronicle.com/chronicle> 9 April 2000. The mystical power of Elian, by Roberto Cespedes.

Seattle Post-Intelligencer. <http://www.seattlepi.nwsource.com> 8 April 2000. God will intervene, prevent Elian from leaving, Cubans say, by Mildrade Cherfils.

Seattle Times. <http://www.seattletimes.nwsource.com> 1 February 2000. Elian Gonzalez reaches divine status for some Cuban Americans.

Time Magazine. 17 April 2000. The second-class parent, by Lance Morrow.

USA Today. <http://www.usatoday.com> 7 January 2000. "Family values" exist in Cuba, too, by Jill Nelson.

Wall Street Journal. [*WSJ*] <http://www.wsj.com> 24 April 2000. Why did they do it? by Peggy Noonan.

Washington Post. [*WP*] <http://www.washingtonpost.com>

25 December 1999. For Cuban boy, 6, a Christmas outpouring.

1 January 2000. Council of churches seeks boy's return to Cuba.

16 January 2000. Rare act of Congress is planned for Elian; GOP leaders back citizenship bills, by Karen De Young.

22 January 2000. Little Havana's "El Milagro," by Hanna Rosin.

1 April 2000. Elian is something special for us, by Sue Anne Pressley.

1 April 2000. Little Havana's little prince, by Joel Achenbach.

5 April 2000. Rough draft: Battle for Elian is Armageddon, only bigger, by Joel Achenbach.

6 April 2000. A modern play of passions, by Gene Weingarten. 3-part series.

9 April 2000. Last-ditch efforts to keep Elian, by Karen De Young.

9 April 2000. Other Latinos more divided over fate of Cuban boy, by Philip P. Pan and Michael A. Fletcher.

14 April 2000. Elian's infantry, by Gene Weingarten.
14 April 2000. Fools for Elian, by Richard Cohen.
15 April 2000. Elian impasse widens Miami's ethnic divides, by April Witt.
17 April 2000. Viva Elian! Hero of the Revolution!, by John Ward Anderson.
20 April 2000. Seeing mystery and miracles in Miami, by April Witt.
23 April 2000. Raid reunites Elian and father, by Karen De Young.
26 April 2000. A fisherman and his 15 minutes, by Michael Leahy.
28 June 2001. Forever a poster child, by Gregory B. Craig.
25 November 2001. A shrine to Miami's angel who flew away, by Sue Anne Pressley.
25 November 2001. A year later, Elian's echoes linger, by Alex Veiga.

Washington Times. <http://www.washingtontimes.com>
4 April 2000. Santeria ceremony held to guard boy, by Tom Carter.
15 April 2000. Fear fueling Castro's fulminations, by Guillermo Cabrera Infante.

INDEX

* * *

In the text and in this index, all Fijian names of chiefly persons are prefixed by honorifics: "Adi" for women, "Ratu" or "Ro" for men.